ROGER D. HERRING

MULTICULTURAL COUNSELING IN SCHOOLS

A Synergetic Approach

AMERICAN COUNSELING ASSOCIATION
5999 Stevenson Avenue
Alexandria, VA 22304-3300

MULTICULTURAL COUNSELING IN SCHOOLS

10 9 8 7 6 5 4 3 2

American Counseling Association
5999 Stevenson Avenue
Alexandria, VA 22304

Acquisitions and Development Editor
Carolyn Baker

Managing Editor
Michael Comlish

Copyeditor
Elaine Dunne

Cover design by Jennifer Sterling, Spot Color

Library of Congress Cataloging-in-Publication Data
Herring, Roger D.
   Multicultural counseling in school environments : a synergetic
approach : manuscript submitted to the American Counseling
Association / by Roger D. Herring.
      p.   cm.
   Includes bibliographical references and index.
   ISBN 1-55620-160-5 (alk. paper)
   1. Educational counseling—United States.   2. Minority students—
Counseling of—United States.   3. Multiculturalism—United States.
I. American Counseling Association.   II. Title.
LB1027.5.H46   1997
371.4'04—dc20   96-7806
                                                            CIP

Contents

I

SYNERGETIC COUNSELING AND GUIDANCE

Chapter 3. The Synergetic Approach to School Counseling   27

Chapter 4. The Role of Culture   49

Chapter 5. The Inalienability of the School's Role in Culture   77

II

GENERAL ISSUES IN SCHOOL COUNSELING

III

THE SCHOOL COUNSELOR'S ROLE IN
MULTICULTURAL SCHOOLS

IV

MULTICULTURAL SCHOOL COUNSELING IN THE TWENTY-FIRST CENTURY

Chapter 12. Selected Case Vignettes for Study   253

Appendixes

Index   301

Preface

This book represents an alternative resource for counselor educators and school counselors who discover that available multicultural and cross-cultural texts do not meet their needs. Most current texts emphasize counseling with clinical and mental health populations and do not sufficiently address concerns and issues of school populations. In fact, neither formal academic course work nor internship experiences have yielded adequate improvement and advancement in the development of multicultural and cross-cultural counseling skills and expertise for school counselors (Herring, 1995). As a result, counseling ethnic minority youths from the perspective of the school counselor represents the focus of this text.

This resource does not aim to be a "recipe" or a "how-to" manual. Rather, the text is designed to enhance the school counselor's knowledge about cultural diversity and to provide appropriate interventions with ethnic and cultural minority students. The text provides school counselors-in-training and in-service school counselors with direction for synergetic and developmental interventions with students. These helping professionals may need to adjust their counseling goals, to create expanded guidance services, to develop or adapt new process skills, to acquire additional content knowledge, and to appropriately serve diverse students.

In this book, the term *school counseling* describes both the profession and the program of services established by school counselors. The term *counseling* is not limited to remedial relationships or interpersonal relationships, but rather refers to a wide selection of services and activities that are chosen to help students prevent disabling events, focus on their overall development, and remedy existing concerns (Schmidt, 1993). The term *youths* applies to both children and adolescents.

Currently, the society of the United States is in a state of tremendous social change, contributing complexities, turbulence, and uncertainty to lifestyles and value systems (Goldenberg & Goldenberg, 1994). This nation represents an increasingly diverse society. In fact, one in every four citizens in the United States today is a person of color (Homma-True, Greene, Lopez, & Trimble, 1993).

Demographic researchers project that European Americans will be an ethnic minority in every city with 50,000 or more people in the United States by the year 2000, and in the entire nation by the year 2010 ("Demographer," 1992). Indeed, Sue (1992) declared that society, in general, and the counseling profession, in particular, stand at the crossroads of choosing monoculturalism (i.e., ethnocentrism) or multiculturalism. Subsequently, an inherent purpose for this book exists as an assistance to those school counselors who will journey the "road less traveled."

Focus of the Book

This book combines the themes of (a) the relation of changing demographics to socioeconomic and psychoeducational imperatives in schools; (b) the balance between universalism (e.g., recognizing commonalities among humans) and cultural pluralism (e.g., recognizing that distinct ethnic, cultural, religious, gender, and class differences exist within this nation) within schools; (c) the resilience and adaptation of ethnic and cultural student groups; and (d) the ethnic and cultural status as stressors on the normal development of youths.

The author integrates theoretical, clinical, and empirical evidence relevant to the major ethnic and cultural youth populations in the United States to increase the understanding of these youths and the complex barriers they face in school settings and in society as a whole. This approach presents content material and synergetic counseling strategies, followed by experiential activities, integrating these variables in a practical manner for the school counselor.

Inherent Biases

Readers need to be aware of biases embedded in the following content. First, the author emphasizes within-group differences that exist among students from the same cultural and ethnic backgrounds. Professionals generally recognize that marked and significant intraethnic and intracultural group diversity exists, as well as considerable between-groups diversity. The existence of this variance is a fundamental principle of cross-cultural school counseling. The potential of stereotyping is considerable in any attempt to delineate and systemize knowledge about ethnic and cultural school youths into a principle of practice.

A second bias concerns the author's proclivity to synergetic counseling approaches as effective interventions for the school counselor. The purpose is not to present a thorough review of cross-cultural and multicultural training and theoretical precepts but rather to address the specific considerations that need to be confronted in incorporating multicultural and cross-cultural perspectives for school counselors to use with ethnically diverse students. The personal choice of the author is the cross-cultural specific model of synergetic counseling. As Dunn (1988) concluded:

> Our ignorance is in part a result of the way in which developmental psychology has grown and is practiced. Children have rarely been studied in the world in which these developments take place, or in a context in which we can be sensitive to the subtleties of their social understanding. (p. 5)

A third bias involves the use of the term *minority* without an appropriate adjective. Different terms and definitions have been applied to describe ethnic people and groups of the United States, including people of color, people from developing nations, racial minorities, linguistic minorities, the culturally different, the culturally diverse, oppressed minorities, and ethnic minorities.

The term *ethnic minority* is used as it encompasses three elements that are important in providing effective service to this specific population. *Ethnicity* denotes cultural uniqueness, which supplies meaning to the cross-cultural encounter between the school counselor and the student. *Minority* refers to a group of political and economic individuals who are relatively powerless, receive unequal treatment, and regard themselves as objects of discrimination. Finally, the *therapeutic encounter* requires that school counselors learn from students about their cultural values, signs, and behavioral styles. Hence, ethnic minority is more than a categorical description of race, culture, or color. It reflects the boundaries of separation and, in particular, how these boundaries are managed, protected, ritualized through stereotyping, and sometimes violated—these are the primary areas of interest and concern for school counseling (Ho, 1992).

A fourth bias concerns ambiguous terminology and labeling. For example, the use of the term "American" is used extensively, and in most instances exclusively, to refer to the citizens of the United States. Such usage, albeit acceptable to many, is insensitive to those other peoples of this hemisphere who also consider themselves to be Americans (e.g., Canadians, Mexicans, or Brazilians).

A final bias is the reluctance to use color for ethnic students. The error of presuming ethnicity by observing external physical characteristics is obvious. Labeling individuals simply by skin color is a gross misinterpretation of ethnicity. It is hoped that the reader will be convinced that all methods of stereotyping are archaic and insensitive to within-group differences.

Overview of Contents

This text is divided into four major parts. **Part I: Synergetic Counseling and Guidance** discusses the available theoretical options for school counselors who are seeking multicultural and cross-cultural counseling paradigms. The effect of the use of singular traditional counseling models and the need for a more appropriate model are stated. The Synergetic Model is offered as a viable choice for school counselors to consider. In addition, the role of culture and the inalienability of the school's role in culture are discussed. **Part II: General Issues in School Counseling** provides universal characteristics of school counseling with diverse student populations. General issues presented include content and process concerns within school counseling, socioeconomic and political issues, and psychoeducational issues and concerns. **Part III: The School Counselor's Role in Multicultural Schools** discusses how the school counselor can ensure a multicultural environment within school settings, especially in collaboration with teaching colleagues. Finally, **Part IV: Multicultural School Counseling in the Twenty-First Century** conveys implications for school counselor training programs and the projected status of multicultural counseling in schools for the twenty-first century. A final chapter describes areas of conflict, suggestions for intervention, and determination of counseling goals, as illustrated in selected vignettes.

Each chapter concludes with a section titled "Experiential Activities," which offers suggestions and ideas to incorporate within a school counseling setting and which may be adapted to various age and grade levels as well as learning styles. These activities are designed to integrate environmental and cultural factors into school counseling.

The future of school counseling rests on the efficacy of school counselors. As the twenty-first century rapidly approaches, school counselors must be ready to serve students from a range of socializations, including ethnic, cultural, religious, class, gender, lifestyle, and challenges of disability. These students must be prepared to meet the challenges of tomorrow. The author hopes that this text will become a facilitating experience in the development of effective multicultural and cross-cultural counselors for educational settings. To paraphrase an old adage, "Except for the skills of the school counselor, there go I."

References

Demographer sees a 2050 U.S. of 383 million, only 53% White. (1992, December 4). *Arkansas Democrat-Gazette*, p. 5-A.

Dunn, J. (1988). *The beginnings of social understanding.* Cambridge, MA: Harvard University Press.

Goldenberg, H., & Goldenberg, I. (1994). *Counseling today's families* (2nd ed.). Pacific Grove, CA: Brooks/Cole.

Herring, R. D. (1995, November 3). *Reflecting on multicultural training in counselor education.* Paper presented at the annual Southern Association for Counselor Educators and Supervisors Regional Convention, Knoxville, TN.

Ho, M. K. (1992). *Minority children and adolescents in therapy.* Newbury Park, CA: Sage.

Homma-True, R., Greene, B., Lopez, S. R., & Trimble, J. E. (1993). Ethnocultural diversity in clinical psychology. *The Clinical Psychologist, 46,* 50–63.

Schmidt, J. J. (1993). *Counseling in schools: Essential services and comprehensive programs.* Boston: Allyn & Bacon.

Sue, D. W. (1992). The challenge of multiculturalism: The road less traveled. *American Counselor, 1*(1), 6–14.

Acknowledgments

The author is indebted to a number of individuals for their contributions to, and assistance with, the development of this text. I gratefully acknowledge the dedicated support staff and faculty of the Department of Educational Leadership at the University of Arkansas at Little Rock: Ruba Musallam, for her invaluable computer, technical, and graphic arts contribution; David S. Spillers, Chair, and Keith Runion, Counseling Program Coordinator, for their continued support and encouragement. Sincere gratitude is also extended to the external reviewers for their invaluable suggestions for this text. And, of course, none of this would have come to fruition without the support and encouragement of my earth companion and soul mate C.A.M. A final salute to the assistance provided by the staff of the American Counseling Association, especially Carolyn C. Baker, Acquisitions and Development Editor.

About the Author

Roger D. Herring, Ed.D., NCC, NCSC, is currently Associate Professor of Counselor Education at the University of Arkansas at Little Rock. His background includes 20 years of experience in public school teaching, administration, and counseling. He has been the recipient of research awards on the state, regional, and national levels. Dr. Herring has published over 50 professional articles and chapters in edited works on cross-cultural counseling, emphasizing Native American Indian and genetically mixed youths and families. He is the author of *Counseling Diverse Ethnic Youth: Synergetic Strategies and Interventions for School Counselors* (Harcourt Brace).

Synergetic Counseling and Guidance

I

art I presents the most common theoretical options for the multicultural school counselor. The basic rationale is that the use of a singular theoretical orientation does not provide the most ethnically and culturally appropriate model for diverse student populations. To that end, the fundamental tenets of synergetic counseling are discussed from theoretical and practical perspectives, as related to school counseling with ethnic and cultural minority students.

The multiculturally aware school counselor should possess strategies and techniques that are congruent with current and historical experiences of students from diverse backgrounds. The synergetic school counselor should incorporate these culture- and ethnic-specific techniques into his or her repertoire of process skills. To ensure the appropriate delivery of services to diverse students, school counselors have to recognize their own limitations and biases, acquire multicultural awareness, and demonstrate their expertise and trustworthiness in their interactions with students. Fundamental to this initiative, school counselors must not be constrained by any one theoretical application. Rather, the school counselor should be competent enough to use the most appropriate strategy for the counselee in the context of session, with regards to the current and past influences of ethnicity, gender, socioeconomic class membership, and conditions of disabling challenges.

1 | Multicultural Counseling Options for School Counselors

In all of your . . . acts, self-interest shall be cast away. . . . Look and listen for the welfare of the whole people, and have always in view not only the present, but also the coming generations . . . the unborn of the future Nation.

—DEGANAWIDA, THE PEACE MAKER

The focus of multicultural counseling has shifted in its short history from an emphasis on the client (in the 1950s) to the counselor (in the 1960s) to the total counseling process itself (from the 1970s to the present; Gladding, 1996). During the late 1980s, multicultural counseling was described as "the hottest topic in the profession" (Lee, 1989, p. 165), and it remains so in the 1990s. Multicultural counseling is at a crossroads; despite the increased attention it has received, multicultural counseling is still considered to be in its infancy (Ponterotto & Sabnani, 1989). Significant scholarship has addressed the effect of culture and ethnicity on counseling. However, few mainstream textbooks have incorporated multicultural themes into their discussions of counseling and therapeutic theory (Capuzzi & Gross, 1995). For example, in a survey of experts in the field, Ponterotto and Sabnani (1989) found that "only 8.5% of the most frequently cited books in the field [were published] before 1970" (p. 35).

More recently, Heppner and O'Brien (1994) studied the perceptions of counselors-in-training during a multicultural counseling course. These researchers found that counseling students indicated a lack of importance in the assigned reading material, at least in contrast to the other course elements. In addition, Herring (1995) found that school counselors-in-training observed little conceptualization and implementation of multiculturalism during their internship experiences.

Wehrly (1991) stated, "In spite of the fact that the United States has been (and is) a nation of immigrants whose values differ, a major theme of Euro-American individualistic psychology seems to have been that of assimilation" (p. 4). This perspective has experienced, one hopes, a metamorphosis since Wehrly's observation.

Yes, the field of multicultural counseling is a young one, and most of the information generated thus far has been devoted to improving counseling services for non-European Americans. However, considering recent demographic projections for the twenty-first century, multicultural counseling will eventually include situations in which school counselors from all cultures and ethnicities are capable of providing appropriate counseling services to individuals from all cultures and ethnicities. This future interpretation is the "true ultimate goal of multicultural counseling" (Baker, 1996, p. 332).

Insights From the Literature

Gleaning pertinent information from the body of multicultural literature yields several themes relevant for school counselors, especially European American counselors. First, school counselors must accept and appreciate cultural and ethnic differences and familiarize themselves with between-groups and within-group characteristics of cultures and ethnicities different from their own (e.g., Herring, 1997; Locke & Parker, 1994). Romero (1985) considered the lack of bilingual school counselors to be one of the major barriers to achieving multicultural competence in school counseling. This perspective appears to be true given recent demographic data. For example, 3 million students in the United States speak little or no English, with Spanish being the native tongue of 70% of these students, followed by Asian languages (15%; see Hancock & Katel, 1995).

A second theme from the multicultural counseling literature challenges school counselors to view students from different cultures and ethnic groups as individuals (e.g., Locke & Parker, 1994; Pedersen, 1991). The recognition of within-group differences is inalienable to this concern. As Baker (1996) noted, some characteristics (e.g., language, customs, and values) are peculiar to specific groups, whereas other characteristics (e.g., intelligence, ambition, creativity, and ignorance) exist in all groups.

A third theme from multicultural literature is an advocacy of active counseling (e.g., Casas & Furlong, 1994; Kopala, Esquivel, & Baptiste, 1994). School counselors need to get out of offices and meet the students in their milieu, whether within the school environment or outside of the school. School counselors need to improve their efforts at informing students about the counseling process and relevant components, such as confidentiality.

A fourth theme reflects the need for school counselors and school counselors-in-training to become aware of their own biases and prejudices. Such self-awareness becomes even more salient in the differentiation between school counselor expectations and student expectations. School counseling training programs need to raise school counselors' consciousness about their beliefs and attitudes that may be unconsciously affecting their counseling behavior, thereby promoting the communication of deleterious expectations (Hamachek, 1995). For example, a high school counselor once remarked to his colleagues on the last school day of the year, "It was an uncomfortable revelation to realize at the end of the school year that practically every one of the counselees whom I personally favored did better academically and even socially than those about whom I felt less positive" (Hamachek, 1995, p. 70). **Something to Consider 1.1** suggests several strategies that school counselors can use to assist their teaching colleagues in recognizing how positive and negative expectations are conveyed to students.

A final theme from multicultural literature indicates that considerable differences exist in the perceptions of school counselors and counselors-in-training in relation to multicultural counseling. For example, school counselors in one sample believe their primary needs in cross-cultural and multicultural counseling are to have a practical counseling technology and to reduce dropout rates (Carey, Reinat, & Fontes, 1990). A more recent survey indicated, however, considerable ignorance among school counseling interns as to what multicultural counseling is and how to implement it (Herring, 1995).

In summary, multicultural counseling involves the preparation and practice that integrate culture-specific awareness, knowledge, and skills into counseling interactions (Arredondo & D'Andrea, 1995; Arredondo et al., 1996). For example, for some individuals, speaking openly of personal issues is not congruent with their cultural beliefs and ingrained appropriate behaviors (Corey, Corey, Callahan, & Russell, 1992). To pressure such individuals to participate can only intensify their discomfort and is likely to increase rather than decrease their withdrawal (Posthuma, 1996). In addition, the Association for Multicultural Counseling and Development distinguishes between the terms *multicultural* and *diversity*. The "term multicultural, in the context of

---

SOMETHING TO CONSIDER 1.1

Counselor and Teacher Self-Awareness

School counselors can play a major role in developing in-service workshops designed to revitalize faculty and staff awareness about how positive and negative expectations are transmitted. This participation is crucial because of the following reasons:

1. The school counselor's perspective of the dynamics of a school situation is generally more panoramic than that of any particular teacher.
2. The school counselor is able to see positive reasons why certain classrooms are functioning smoothly and at a high level of achievement, and why others may be sputtering along at a relatively low level.
3. The school counselor's perspective allows him or her to develop working hypotheses about why certain students' academic growth may be stunted or accelerated, along with some ideas about the part teachers may be playing in this process.

However, school counselors must not tell teachers how to do their jobs (a tactic doomed to fail), but rather provide opportunities in which both professionals can discuss their experiences and share refections that are designed to heighten awareness about the expectations they may be communicating.

SOURCE: Adapted from "Expectations Revisited: Implications for Teachers and Counselors and Questions for Self-Assessment," by D. Hamachek, 1995, *Journal of Humanistic Education and Development, 34*, pp. 65–74.

---

counseling preparation and application, refers to five major cultural groups in the United States and its territories: African/Black, Asian, Caucasian/European, Hispanic/Latino, and Native American or indigenous groups who have historically resided in the continental United States and its territories" (Arredondo et al., 1996, p. 43). The diversity refers to characteristics such as age, gender, sexual identity, religious or spiritual identification, socioeconomic class, and residence (i.e., rural, urban).

Multicultural, Cross-Cultural, and Minority Group Counseling

Currently, school counselors and school counselors-in-training have three general options in their selection of appropriate multicultural models: multicultural, cross-cultural, and minority group counseling. These generic models subsume specific examples of theoretical orientations, are defined variously, and are frequently interchanged. For the purposes of this chapter, some background information may be helpful to the reader. A *monocultural* perspective denies the differences of other cultures and captures the "common sense" of persons who have lived all their lives within a single culture, or who have accepted some creed that claims to be universal. Either way, the "margins" of their own culture function as boundaries rather than as limits. The distinctions between boundaries and limits are powerful, because individuals who believe that their own culture is the only one, or the "real" one, treat communication patterns appropriate to other cultures, but not to their own, as "mistakes" rather than "differences" (Pearce & Kang, 1988). Thus, proponents of monocultural thinking cannot, by definition, be effective or appropriate providers of *multicultural* perspectives in school counseling. In fact, the perpetuation of *monoculturalism* is counterproductive to the development of *multiculturalism* in school settings.

Culturally diverse school populations require the services of school counselors who are open-minded, knowledgeable, and accepting of diverse worldviews. The three options—multicultural counseling, cross-cultural counseling, and minority group counseling—support these qualities.

MULTICULTURAL COUNSELING

In reality, all counseling may be considered as multicultural counseling because all individuals are members of many cultures in which different values are required (Margolis & Rungta, 1986; Pedersen, 1988, 1994). For example, an ethnic minority female with a disabling condition holds membership in at least her ethnic culture, the culture of persons with disabilities, the culture of persons with similar disability, and the culture of female individuals. Additional cultures may be represented by religious and spiritual affiliations, being a housewife, being a mother, and so forth. However, for the purposes of this book, culture will be primarily interpreted more narrowly, except where otherwise noted.

Vontress (1988) defined multicultural counseling as "counseling in which the counselor and the client(s) are culturally different because of socialization acquired in distinct cultural, subcultural, racioethnic, or socioeconomic environments" (p. 74). Lee and Richardson (1991) defined multicultural counseling as "a relationship between a counselor and a client that takes both personal and cultural experiences into consideration in the helping process" (p. x). In addition, Axelson (1993) defined multicultural counseling as "the interface between counselor and client that takes the personal dynamics of the counselor and the client into consideration alongside the emerging, changing, and/or static configurations that might be identified in the cultures of counselor and client" (p. 13). Pedersen (1988) interpreted multicultural counseling as "a situation in which two or more persons with different ways of perceiving their social environment are brought together in a helping relationship" (p. viii). **Something to Consider 1.2** offers five key points of multicultural counseling.

SOMETHING TO CONSIDER 1.2

Key Points of Multicultural Counseling

1. School counseling techniques must be modified when counseling culturally different students.

2. The culturally sensitive school counselor is prepared to deal with the differences and difficulties that are anticipated during the counseling process.

3. Conceptions of the helping process are cultural.

4. Presenting complaints and symptoms, as well as the diagnosis, differ in their frequency of occurrence in diverse cultural groups and subgroups.

5. Cultural norms and expectations of the school counselor and student most likely will vary.

SOURCE: Adapted from "Dilemmas and Choices in Cross-Cultural Counseling: The Universal Versus the Culturally Distinctive," by J. G. Draguns, 1989. In P. B. Pedersen, J. G. Draguns, W. J. Lonner, and J. E. Trimble (Eds.), *Counseling Across Cultures* (3rd. ed., pp. 6–7).

CROSS-CULTURAL COUNSELING

Cross-cultural counseling generally emphasizes differences in the nature of the relationship between the majority cultural group and ethnic minority groups (Axelson, 1993). This relationship refers to "any counseling relationship in which two or more of the participants differ with respect to cultural background, values, and life style" (Sue et al., 1982, p. 47). This definition includes situations in which both the school counselor and the student are ethnic minority individuals but represent different ethnicities or different within-group subgroups (e.g., Asian American student, African American counselor) and situations in which the school counselor is an ethnic minority person and the student is European American (Atkinson, Morten, & Sue, 1993). Multicultural counseling is often used interchangeably with cross-cultural counseling. Review **Something to Consider 1.3** for additional insight into cross-cultural communication.

SOMETHING TO CONSIDER 1.3

Cross-Cultural Communication

Pearce and Kang (1988) discussed "travelers' tales" of differences between cultures. Travelers' tales of exotic customs, cultures, and peoples have been told since Herodotus, Marco Polo, Mark Twain, and Lowell Thomas. The authors present a "new paradigm" approach that allows for a sympathetic and rewarding "reading" of such tales. This approach focuses on the fact of cultural differences, the problem of describing them, and the "necessity" and significance of these differences. An isomorphism is noted between the experience of immigrants and modernity, indicating that the process of acculturation is a model for life in contemporary society.

MINORITY GROUP COUNSELING

Minority group counseling can be defined as any counseling relationship in which the student is a member of an ethnic or cultural minority group, regardless of the status of the school counselor (Atkinson et al., 1993). The school counselor may be a member of the same ethnic or cultural minority group, a different ethnic or cultural group, or the majority ethnic or cultural group. Historically, minority group counseling has emphasized the ethnic or cultural majority counselor and ethnic or cultural minority client relationship to the exclusion of other possibilities. This narrow view of minority group counseling ignores the uniqueness of a counseling relationship in which the counselor is also an ethnic or cultural minority person. In addition, the term minority group counseling suggests a minority pathology (e.g., "Black pathology"), an attempt to explain ethnic and cultural minority behaviors in terms of European American norms (Atkinson et al., 1993).

Regardless of the prefix *multi* or *cross*, this book focuses primarily on school counseling situations in which the students are members of an ethnic minority group and are culturally different from the school counselor. Accordingly, a major theme for this book reflects cross-cultural counseling precepts. This focus is also inclusive of the changing demographic status of the historical majority ethnic and cultural group, the European Americans.

Experiential Activities

1. Which multicultural option will you choose in future/present counseling?
2. If your interactions with students were videotaped for 1 week, what do

you suppose might be revealed about the way you interact with different students?

3. If a group of academically challenged students were to write a critique of you as their school counselor, what do you suppose they would say about your counseling behavior as it relates to factors such as the feedback you give them, the change of behavior you expect, the climate you create, and the input they receive from you? Would ethnic and cultural differences play a role?

References

Arredondo, P., & D'Andrea, M. (1995, September). AMCD approves multicultural counseling competency standards. *Counseling Today, 37,* 28–32.

Arredondo, P., Toporek, R., Brown, S. P., Jones, J., Locke, D. C., Sanchez, J., & Stadler, H. (1996). Operationalization of the multicultural counseling competencies. *Journal of Multicultural Counseling and Development, 24,* 42–78.

Atkinson, D. R., Morten, G., & Sue, D. W. (1993). *Counseling American minorities* (4th ed.). Dubuque, IA: William C. Brown.

Axelson, J. (1993). *Counseling and development in a multicultural society* (2nd ed.). Monterey, CA: Brooks/Cole.

Baker, S. B. (1996). *School counseling for the twenty-first century* (2nd ed.). Englewood Cliffs, NJ: Merrill.

Carey, J. C., Reinat, M., & Fontes, L. (1990). School counselors' perceptions of training needs in multicultural counseling. *Counselor Education and Supervision, 29,* 155–169.

Capuzzi, D., & Gross, D. R. (1995). *Counseling and psychotherapy: Theories and interventions.* Englewood Cliffs, NJ: Merrill.

Casas, J. M., & Furlong, M. J. (1994). School counselors as advocates for increased Hispanic parent participation in schools. In P. Pedersen & J. C. Carey (Eds.), *Multicultural counseling in schools: A practical handbook* (pp. 121–156). Boston: Allyn & Bacon.

Corey, G., Corey, M., Callahan, P., & Russell, J. M. (1992). *Group techniques* (3rd ed.). Pacific Grove, CA: Brooks/Cole.

Draguns, J. G. (1989). Dilemmas and choices in cross-cultural counseling: The universal versus the culturally distinctive. In P. B. Pedersen, J. G. Draguns, W. J. Lonner, & J. E. Trimble (Eds.), *Counseling across cultures* (3rd ed., pp. 3–21). Honolulu: University of Hawaii Press.

Gladding, S. T. (1996). *Counseling: A comprehensive profession* (3rd ed.). Englewood Cliffs, NJ: Merrill.

Hamachek, D. (1995). Expectations revisited: Implications for teachers and counselors and questions for self-assessment. *Journal of Humanistic Education and Development, 34,* 65–74.

Hancock, L., & Katel, P. (1995, October 23). The bilingual bog: Officials target programs that don't teach. *Newsweek,* 89.

Heppner, M. J., & O'Brien, K. M. (1994). Multicultural counselor training: Students' perceptions of helpful and hindering events. *Counselor Education and Supervision, 34,* 4–18.

Herring, R. D. (1995, November 3). *Reflecting on multicultural training in counselor education.* Paper presented at the annual Southern Association for Counselor Educators and Supervisors Regional Convention, Knoxville, TN.

Herring, R. D. (1997). Counseling Native American youth. In C. C. Lee (Ed.), *Multicultural issues in counseling: New approaches to diversity* (2nd ed.). Alexandria, VA: American Counseling Association.

Kopala, M., Esquivel, G., & Baptiste, L. (1994). Counseling approaches for immigrant children: Facilitating the acculturative process. *School Counselor, 41,* 352–359.

Lee, C. C. (1989). AMCD: The next generation. *Journal of Multicultural Counseling and Development, 17,* 165–170.

Lee, C. C., & Richardson, B. L. (Eds.). (1991). *Multicultural issues in counseling.* Alexandria, VA: American Counseling Association.

Locke, D. C., & Parker, L. D. (1994). Improving the multicultural competence of educators. In P. Pedersen & J. C. Carey (Eds.), *Multicultural counseling in schools: A practical handbook* (pp. 39–58). Boston: Allyn & Bacon.

Margolis, R. L., & Rungta, S. A. (1986). Training counselors for work with special groups: A second book. *Journal of Counseling & Development, 64,* 642–644.

Pearce, W. B., & Kang, K. (1988). Conceptual migrations: Understanding "travelers' tales" for cross-cultural adaptation. In Y. Y. Kim & W. B. Gudykunst (Eds.), *Cross-cultural adaptations: Current approaches* (pp. 20–41). Newbury Park, CA: Sage.

Pedersen, P. B. (1988). *A handbook for developing multicultural awareness.* Alexandria, VA: American Counseling Association.

Pedersen, P. B. (1991). Multiculturalism as a generic approach to counseling and development. *Journal of Counseling & Development, 70,* 6–12.

Pedersen, P. B. (1994). *A handbook for developing multicultural awareness* (2nd ed.). Alexandria, VA: American Counseling Association.

Ponterotto, J. G., & Sabnani, H. B. (1989). "Classics" in multicultural counseling: A systematic five-year content analysis. *Journal of Multicultural Counseling and Development, 17,* 23–37.

Posthuma, B. W. (1996). *Small groups in counseling and therapy: Process and leadership* (2nd ed.). Boston: Allyn & Bacon.

Romero, D. (1985). Cross-cultural counseling: Brief reactions for the practitioner. *The Counseling Psychologist, 13*(4), 665–672.

Sue, D. W., Bernier, J. E., Durran, A., Feinberg, L., Pedersen, P., Smith, C. J., & Vasquez-Nuttall, G. (1982). Cross-cultural counseling competencies. *The Counseling Psychologist, 10*(2), 45–52.

Vontress, C. E. (1988). An existential approach to cross-cultural counseling. *Journal of Multicultural Counseling and Development, 16,* 73–83.

Wehrly, B. (1991). Preparing multicultural counselors. *Counseling and Human Development, 24,* 1–23.

2 | The Synergetic Model

What treatment, by whom, is most effective for this individual, with that
specific problem, and under which set of circumstances?
—PAUL, 1967, p. 111

Counseling has been offered by family members, friends, and other untrained individuals throughout history. Professional counseling is relatively recent. It is oldest in the fields of law, accounting, and health and newest in the psychological areas dealing with cognition, affect, and behavior. Professional counseling requires study in a unique body of knowledge and is generally a full-time occupation. School counseling is designed to enhance the mentally healthy development of normal students by helping them complete the developmental tasks common to all, and by helping students resolve cognitive, affective, and behavioral concerns. This focus calls for counselors employed by educational institutions to organize programs to enhance the development of all members of the institution in addition to counseling individual members (Byrne, 1995).

Currently, few school counselors are strictly deterministic, antideterministic, directive, or nondirective. Rather, most prefer an eclectic, or integrative, approach toward working with students, especially on the secondary level. Such an approach requires school counselors to reflect on their own views of human nature, with the resulting outcome being a view of human nature that borrows from the varying viewpoints (Neukrug, 1994). The next section discusses the evolution of eclecticism and the accompanying criticisms of eclecticism as a counseling model. This section also sets the stage for the rise of the more structural synergetic model.

The Rise of Eclecticism as a Counseling Model

Eclecticism evolved from challenges of the more popular counseling models. Eclecticism, as this label is applied in counseling, simply means to integrate ideas from a diversity of sources (Young, 1992). Eclecticism is the practice of selecting and amalgamating what appear to be the best portions of various doctrines, methods, or styles (Byrne, 1995).

BASIC APPROACHES OF ECLECTICISM

Two basic approaches to eclecticism are currently being used: counselor- and process-centered. Counselor-centered eclecticism perceives that school counselors can be more effective with culturally diverse students if their counseling styles are congruent with their own personalities. The counselor's personal counseling style usually develops during the formal training of the counseling student. For example, Corey (1991) contended that

> Beginning students of counseling, by familiarizing themselves with the current major approaches to therapeutic practice, can acquire a basis for a counseling style tailored to their own personalities. Thus, I recommend a personal synthesis as a framework for the professional education of counselors. The danger in presenting one model that all students are expected to advocate to the exclusion of other fruitful approaches is that the beginning counselor will unduly limit his or her effectiveness with different clients. Valuable dimensions of human behavior can be overlooked if the counselor is restricted to a single theory. (p. 2)

Process-centered eclecticism contends that certain underlying factors are common to all counseling endeavors and focuses primarily on the behavioral skills of the counselor rather than the principles of the theories. The principal movement in process-centered eclecticism is found in the communication skills approaches. These approaches generally use the scientific method of goal identification and goal meeting but may borrow principles and techniques from whatever seems to work and is philosophically and conceptually compatible. Their most intensive borrowing has been from the person-centered approach, and their emphasis is on important counselor attitudes and actions (see **Chart 2.1**).

TYPES OF ECLECTICISM

Another method of differentiating eclecticism is by its three types: technical, synthetic, and theoretical (Norcross, 1986). Eclecticism provides both un-

°CHART 2.1

Comprehensive Developmental Counseling Program Goals and Approaches

Goals and Objectives	Approaches to Meet Overall Objectives
School counselors should strive to	
1. Understand the school environment	• Crisis intervention to gain control of a particular situation
2. Understand themselves	• Remedial approaches that focus on deficiencies
3. Understand attitudes and behavior	• Preventive approaches that anticipate problems to prevent their occurrence
4. Use decision-making and problem-solving skills	• Developmental approaches that help ethnic minorities acquire the necessary skills and experiences to be successful in school
5. Use interpersonal and communication skills	
6. Use school success skills	
7. Have career awareness and use educational planning	
8. Have community pride and involvement	

SOURCE: Adapted from *Developmental Guidance and Counseling: A Practical Approach*, by R. D. Myrick, 1987.

desirable and valuable outcomes when applied to counseling, depending on which type is used (Byrne, 1995). *Technical eclecticism,* coined by Lazarus (1967), uses one basic theory but may incorporate techniques originated in other schools of thought. Lazarus observed "that amalgamated theories only breed confusion worse confounded" (Lazarus & Beutler, 1993, p. 382). Lazarus and Beutler contended that effective counseling can be achieved if the "systematic process for selecting therapeutic procedures . . . are built upon empirical demonstrations of the conditions, problems, and clients with whom different procedures are effective" (p. 383). For example, if a school counselor states, "I use proven techniques from both Adlerian and reality theories when I find them useful," the school counselor is attesting to the wise practice of technical eclecticism.

Synthetic eclecticism attempts to integrate two or more theoretical orientations. The most common attempts of combining different models are behavioralism and psychoanalytic thought (Dollard & Miller, 1950), Freudian and learning theory, neo-Freudian and learning theory, and neo-Freudian and Rogerian theory (Garfield & Kurtz, 1977).

Theoretical eclecticism is defined as having no preferred theoretical orientation. The helping professional instead depends on personal and professional knowledge of many orientations, from both content and process perspectives, during the actual counseling process. "Eclecticism without epistemic criteria—i.e., choosing bits and pieces from the buffet of theoretical concepts without reference to an epistemology—is theoretical eclecticism, and is undesirable" (Byrne, 1995, p. 40).

The following statement epitomizes those made by school counselors frequently: "I am an Adlerian counselor, although with certain students I am a behaviorist." The fallacy within this statement is obvious. These theoretical orientations are incompatible, and thus the school counselor is demonstrating a lack of grounding in epistemology rather than the even-handedness or objectivity (or mastery of skills) the school counselor intends to demonstrate (Byrne, 1995).

PROFESSIONAL STATUS OF ECLECTICISM

Research endeavors have documented the popularity of eclecticism as a theoretical orientation. Surveys of clinical psychologists, counseling psychologists, and counselors revealed that 30% to 50% of the respondents considered themselves to be eclectic (Messer, 1986; Neukrug & Williams, 1993). A study of mental health counselors and counselor educators found that 75% of the respondents did not profess to one specific theoretical viewpoint (Young & Feiler, 1989). This study also indicated that the three theories of the future are eclecticism, family systems, and cognitive–behavioral. The emphasis on theoretical orientation appears to be currently, and for the immediate future, moving away from narrow viewpoints toward broader integrative approaches (see **Something to Consider 2.1**).

One criticism is that unless a school counselor knows the philosophy and assumptions of a primary theory and accepts a single orientation, then that school counselor is analogous to a "jack-of-all-trades and master of none" (Patterson, 1986; Young, 1992). This type of school counselor tends to "shoot from the hip" and uses a hodgepodge of techniques, which may end up being confusing to a student (Neukrug, 1994).

Quite naturally, the proponents of eclecticism have rebuttals for these and other criticisms of the orientation. The increasing number of practitioners

SOMETHING TO CONSIDER 2.1

Theoretical Orientations of Counselors and Counselor Educators and Predicted Theoretical Trend in the Field 5 Years From Now

Theoretical Orientation	Current	Predicted Trend in 5 Years
Eclectic	32	26
Person-centered	22	7
Family systems	10	23
Cognitive–behavioral	6	16
Reality therapy	6	2
Psychoanalytic	5	2
Psychoeducational	3	4
Behavior modification	3	4
Multimodal	3	5
Adlerian	2	1
Gestalt	2	1
Rational emotive	2	2
Eriksonian hypnosis	2	3
Existential	1	0.1
Other	3	4

NOTE: Data are in percentages and are based on $N = 125$.
SOURCE: Adapted from *Trends in Counseling: A National Survey*, by M. E. Young and F. Feiler, 1989, p. 5.

who affiliate with the eclectic movement speaks for itself. In addition, research studies have supported the counseling values of being able to draw from various models and the ability to incorporate appropriate techniques regardless of which generating theoretical orientation (Lambert, 1986; Young & Feiler, 1989).

One possible solution to the structural dilemma and other criticisms of eclectic approaches may be found in a more holistic synergetic counseling model. Such a theoretical orientation will be the focus of the remainder of this chapter.

Personal Rationale for a Synergetic Model

Baker (1996) directly claimed that "Eclecticism appears to be the appropriate approach for school counseling" (p. 44). In addition, Sue (1992) noted that an eclectic approach may also be the path to achieving multicultural competence in one's counseling interventions by becoming culturally flexible. Rather than take issue with these positions, this author aims to substantiate these views through extending the eclectic position.

This author's acceptance of synergistic school counseling reflects experiences from an often meandering and somewhat evolutionary path (Herring & Walker, 1993). The author has observed the application of various theoretical models in educational and noneducational settings, from the European American middle-class Protestant perspectives as manifested in the behavior modification practices of public education to the treat-the-symptom perspectives of community and private mental health agencies. Too frequently, these applications produced futile attempts to address mental health and developmental needs of culturally diverse students by means of insensitive or inappropriate techniques and perspectives. The school counselor's roles as a change agent and an advocate for the culturally different require a more integrated and more cultural- and ethnic-specific model for effective school counseling.

The author integrates three perspectives—personal, educational, and professional—in the quest for an appropriate counseling model. Experiences and observations within these three experiential perspectives have indicated that a more environmental and cultural theoretical orientation is needed. Thus, the choice of a synergetic counseling approach has evolved as a viable answer to the illusive question of what is the most appropriate orientation for school counselors in the providing of appropriate counseling for today's youths.

Conceptual Bases for Synergetic Counseling

Synergetic counseling contains features of eclecticism and the communication skills approaches but goes beyond the precepts of both. Synergetic approaches incorporate the concept of cooperation (i.e., working together to greater effect than would have been achieved by working independently) or "the synthesis of helping approaches with cultural and environmental factors" (Axelson, 1993, p. 376). Wachtel (1985) defined "synergistic effect" as "a situation in which each additional component not only adds to its own contribution, but increases or enhances the contribution of the other components" (p. 324). Thus, rather than being one distinctive approach, synergistic models are varied and are concerned with providing a more effective counseling model for culturally diverse students. Axelson (1993) continued:

> the major practical feature inherent or implied in the synergetic model is that of the counselor and client (i.e., student) working and cooperating together through the process that is most effective for them and toward the goals that are most important for or relevant to the client (i.e., student) in his or her cultural environment. (p. 378)

A synergetic perspective presumes that current theoretical models are incomplete and that the influence of environment and culture as determinative factors requires greater consideration. The interaction of ethnic minority students and their environments and cultures can be incorporated in the topic content, problems presented, and expectations for the helping relationship and helping process.

THEORY OF PERSONALITY

A survey of theories of personality reveals that no common philosophy unifies them. Most personality theories have different views of human nature and different concepts of therapy that are rooted in those views. Syntality is to a group what personality is to a person (Cattell, 1950). Synergism involves incorporating that cultural and environmental personality into the counseling process. In the development of a synergetic perspective, the school counselor's personal philosophical assumptions are important, because they specify how much reality the individual is able to perceive, and they direct the individual's attention to the variables that he or she is "set" to see (Corey, 1991). The school counselor does not subscribe exclusively to any one central view of human nature but remains open-minded and selectively incorporates a framework for counseling that is consistent with his or her own personality and belief system.

However, school counselors do need to be cautious in developing a personal synergetic model. As Byrne (1995) admonished:

> Among science's characteristics is its pragmatism, and thus a counselor will employ any technique no matter where it originated as long as its efficacy has been demonstrated and as long as it is in accord with the values of the counselor's life-views. This position about pragmatism does not favor an approach to counseling technology that is based solely on "what works," however; that stance would result only in pragmatists, in technicians, and mark those practitioners as theoretically sterile. (pp. 40–41)

The counselor should not attempt to integrate theories with incompatible assumptions. Determining and selecting the choice of theories and techniques primarily on the basis of subjective appeal can lead to irreconcilable differences among the systems that make integration impossible (Lazarus, 1981). The basic philosophies of classical psychoanalysis and radical behaviorism, for example, do not lend themselves to rapprochement.

NATURE OF HUMANS

Synergistic models emphasize counseling processes rather than how the individual is organized. Issues such as basic drives, motivations, and innate characteristics are not the primary focus of counseling either. Despite divergences in the numerous available counseling and personality theories, appropriate synthesis among some models can be achieved. For example, an existential component is imbedded in several models (e.g., Gestalt, person-centered, and cognitive). The fact that theories represent different perspectives from which to view human behavior does not mean that one is right and the others are wrong. Each viewpoint can offer the school counselor a perspective for helping ethnic and cultural students in their search for self.

Synergetic approaches provide a way to address today's culturally diverse society and the complex counseling problems of such a society. Synergetic counseling is based on two basic assumptions: (a) that the traditional counseling models are incomplete and (b) that the helping professions need a deeper understanding of the effect of environment and culture on the counseling process (Herring, 1997a). Most traditional theoretical models evolved from a European American, middle-class perspective and thus reflected the problems, concerns, and values of those particular ethnicities. Synergism involves the student and the school counselor interacting in a mutually chosen process toward goals that are applicable to the student in his or her cultural environment. Synergistic approaches aim to balance the student's psychological aspects with the environment (Herring, 1997a; Herring & Walker, 1993). Although psychodynamics are important, all problems, behaviors, and concerns of a person cannot be attributed solely to his or her inner self. Culture and environmental factors also play a viable role in the helping process.

ROLE OF THE ENVIRONMENT

Environment may be defined as those external sources and influences to which an individual or group is potentially sensitive. To examine a student's environment involves discerning those external forces that exert either a real or perceived influence on a student's behavior (Herring, 1997a). Environmental influences are derived from three basic elements: physical, social, and cultural.

Physical forces. The basic human physical need is personal security, which includes the need for food, clothing, and shelter. To exist and compete in today's technological society, an ethnic minority student will need well-developed coping skills and strategies to achieve personal security. However, many of the current physical environmental elements are beyond the control of the ethnic minority student. If these factors are to be appropriately considered in the helping process, school counselors have to be able to distinguish between what influences are external and what influences are internal, as the locus of the influencing factors will require differentiating interventions. For example, external factors may respond to environmental adjustment or coping strategies, whereas internal factors may require psychological or behavioral adjustment.

In addition, school counselors also need to examine environmental factors that are taken for granted in traditional counseling practice, such as the setting or time structure. The physical aspects of the counseling environment can have a great effect on an ethnic minority student's initial impression. In the time structure factor, "the basic question asked is whether effective counseling . . . needs to be equated with a lengthy or open-ended experience" (Axelson, 1993, p. 383). Time-limited therapy (therapy that has a specific number of sessions) appears as the most appropriate for students whose "general problems and issues of daily living constitute the major concern" (p. 384). For less immediate concerns, the option may be time-unlimited therapy, or open-ended therapy.

Societal forces. Social environmental forces are generally situational and student-specific. That is, these social forces include all of those other persons or groups to whom the ethnic minority student relates, or the external part of one's individual reality that has meaning. A danger exists in the ethnic minority student applying the principle of generalization to these societal forces. Generalization may represent an important element of the ethnic minority student's social situation in that it offers an opportunity for the ethnic minority student to carry parts of his or her personality across social situations. The appropriateness or inappropriateness of generalizations may, however, require counseling intervention and assistance.

Cultural forces. Cultural environmental factors consist primarily of the ethnic and cultural history of the group to which the ethnic minority student belongs, and they include that group's ideas or beliefs, values, and behavior. Axelson (1993) included *action preference*, which refers to the ethnic minority student's learned mode of action in moving toward a goal. The culture of the ethnic minority student normally provides him or her with certain problem-solving techniques. A creative and culturally sensitive school counselor can use the ethnic minority student's existing techniques to assist him or her in solving problems without a loss of cultural values. School counselors, however, do not need to become overzealous in the pursuit of a "group character." Ethnic and culturally ethnic minority students are not uniform in attitude and behavior, anymore than are members of the current majority culture (Atkin-

son, Morten, & Sue, 1989). In short, more variance exists within cultural
and ethnic groups than between those same groups.

Interaction of nature and environment. The Native American Indian
represents an excellent example of within-group variance and the differentiating interaction of nature and environment. This ethnic minority group currently reflects four distinct familial groups: traditional, nontraditional (bicultural), acculturated, and pantraditional (Herring, 1991, 1997b; Herring &
Erchul, 1988; Ho, 1992; Red Horse, 1980, 1988). The *traditional* family
overtly adheres to culturally defined lifestyles. Parents speak the native language and elders assume respected roles. This family type interprets life
events and activities in sacred terms. Relationships are expressed through
ritual ceremonies, and depending on tribal customs, this family articulates
with sacred bonds (e.g., ritual names, clans, and namesakes).

The *nontraditional* or *bicultural* family appears to have adopted many aspects of non-Native American Indian lifestyles. Typically, this family does not
transmit specific traditional knowledge across generations. Parents often may
understand their Native language but prefer to speak English at home. Parents
may be acquainted with ritual customs but have converted to non-Native
American Indian religions. Despite acquiring many characteristics of European American society, bicultural families are not integrated totally in non-
Native American society. They still prefer relationships with other Native
American Indians. To compensate for geographic isolation, the bicultural family attends powwows and other tribal functions in urban areas or on nearby
reservations (see **Something to Consider 2.2**).

The *acculturated* family is distinguished by its modal behavior similar to
the mainstream population (i.e., European American). Parents speak English
and use non-Native American child-rearing practices. They follow non-Native
American Indian religions, possess no linkages to land or kin, and maintain a
strictly nuclear family structure. In reality, this family has "bought into" the
European Protestant work ethic of the majority ethnic group.

The *pantraditional* family is characterized by its overt struggles to redefine
and reconfirm previously lost cultural lifestyles. This family speaks both
English and their Native language. A modified tribal belief system is practiced,
and involvement in tribal activities is required. This family struggles to maintain the historical extended family network.

From a synergetic perspective, the counseling focus for this ethnic minority
group must integrate multiple approaches (Herring, 1997a). Attneave's (1969,
1982) network therapy, drawn from her work with Native American Indians,
reminded us that multiple interventions are often necessary to produce and

SOMETHING TO CONSIDER 2.2

Native American Indian Families and Counseling Focus

Family Type	Basic Value Orientation	Counseling Focus
Traditional	Adhere to culturally defined lifestyles according to tradition and history; reside usually on reservations.	Prefer Native American Indian counselors but can adjust to others who demonstrate trustworthiness and acceptance; directive approaches integrated with traditional healing practices with nonintrusive strategies are most appropriate.
Nontraditional (bicultural)	Have adapted many aspects of the dominant European American value system but prefer close contact with tribal culture and peoples.	Prefer Native American Indian counselors but will accept traditional modes of counseling; eclectic and synergetic foci are appropriate.
Acculturated	Have completely adapted to or adopted the mainstream cultural value and belief system.	Culture- or ethnic-specific focus is not necessary; will accept styles and focus of mainstream counseling.
Pantraditional	Seek to return to historical lifestyles; militant attitude to non-Native American Indian values.	Will work only with traditional healing and sacred practices and tribal members; will not accept concept of "mental health needs" or intrusive interventions.

SOURCE: Adapted from "Native American Indian Identity," by R. Herring, 1994. In E. P. Salett and D. R. Koslow (Eds.), *Race, Ethnicity, and Self* (pp. 182–186). Washington, DC: National MultiCultural Institute.

maintain change. The physical, societal, and cultural dimensions are obviously different.

Counseling with traditional and pantraditional Native American Indians involves incorporating native healing and sacred practices, with nonintrusive strategies, and preferably by Native American Indian counselors. The nontraditional Native American Indian may respond to mainstream counseling interventions appropriate to biculturalism. Acculturated Native American Indians may be counseled with little ethnic-specific overtones. They have in essence surrendered their ethnic uniqueness to become members of mainstream society.

Concurrently, school counselors will need to remember that the Native American Indian ethnic group contains tremendous tribal variations as well (Herring, 1997a). The school counselor will be more successful if the ethnic minority student's tribal affiliation and degree of acculturation is understood initially. Then, specific Native and non-Native American Indian techniques may be chosen. In addition, the school counselor will need to recognize, address, and accept the influences of the divergent physical settings, societal adherences, and cultural diversities within this population.

Summary

The Synergetic Model emphasizes student and counselor collaboration toward mutual goals. Rather than trying to reconcile various theoretical orientations to the "presenting problem," synergetic school counselors select the most appropriate technique for that student at that time with regards for ethnicity, culture, environment, gender, and all the other characteristics of an individual student.

Experiential Activities

1. What is your preferred theoretical orientation? Why have you chosen that particular model? How does your "chosen" counseling model relate to ethnic and cultural differences? What specific techniques of practice can you list to support the multiculturalness of your preferred orientation?

2. What are your thoughts about the importance of synergetism in current and future counseling and therapeutic modalities? Do you have a handle on the differences between eclecticism and synergetic counseling?

3. Which synergetic model best fits your personality style? Why would you adapt that model or decline to use a particular model?

References

Atkinson, D. R., Morten, G., & Sue, D. W. (1989). *Counseling American minorities* (3rd ed.). Dubuque, IA: William C. Brown.

Attneave, C. (1969). Therapy in tribal settings and urban network interventions. *Family Process, 8,* 192–210.

Attneave, C. (1982). American Indian and Alaska native families: Emigrants in their own homeland. In M. McGoldrick, J. Pearce, & J. Giordano (Eds.), *Ethnicity and family therapy* (pp. 55–83). New York: Guilford Press.

Axelson, J. (1993). *Counseling and development in a multicultural society* (2nd ed.). Monterey, CA: Brooks/Cole.

Baker, S. B. (1996). *School counseling for the twenty-first century* (2nd ed.). Englewood Cliffs, NJ: Merrill.

Byrne, R. H. (1995). *Becoming a master counselor.* Pacific Grove, CA: Brooks/Cole.

Cattell, R. B. (1950). *Personality: A systematic, theoretical, and factual study.* New York: McGraw-Hill.

Corey, G. (1991). *Theory and practice of counseling and psychotherapy* (4th ed.). Pacific Grove, CA: Brooks/Cole.

Dollard, J., & Miller, N. (1950). *Personality and psychotherapy.* New York: McGraw-Hill.

Garfield, S. L., & Kurtz, R. (1977). A study of eclectic views. *Journal of Consulting and Clinical Psychology, 45,* 78–83.

Herring, R. D. (1991). Counseling Native American youth. In C. C. Lee & B. L. Richardson (Eds.), *Multicultural issues in counseling: New approaches to diversity* (pp. 37–47). Alexandria, VA: American Association for Counseling and Development.

Herring, R. D. (1994). Native American Indian identity. In E. P. Salett & D. R. Koslow (Eds.), *Race, ethnicity, and self* (pp. 182–186). Washington, DC: National Multi-Cultural Institute.

Herring, R. D. (1997a). *Counseling diverse ethnic youth: Synergetic strategies and interventions for school counselors.* Fort Worth, TX: Harcourt Brace.

Herring, R. D. (1997b). Counseling Native American youth. In C. C. Lee (Ed.), *Multicultural issues in counseling: New approaches to diversity* (2nd ed.). Alexandria, VA: American Counseling Association.

Herring, R. D., & Erchul, W. P. (1988). *The applicability of Olson's Circumplex Model to Native American families.* Charleston, WV: Resources in Education. (ERIC Document Reproduction Service No. 308 050)

Herring, R. D., & Walker, S. S. (1993). Synergetic counseling: Toward a more holistic approach. *Texas Counseling Association Journal, 22,* 38–53.

Ho, M. K. (1992). *Minority children and adolescents in therapy.* Newbury Park, CA: Sage.

Lambert, M. J. (1986). Implications of psychotherapy outcome research for eclectic psychotherapy. In J. C. Norcross (Ed.), *Handbook of eclectic psychotherapy* (pp. 436–462). New York: Brunner.

Lazarus, A. A. (1967). In support of technical eclecticism. *Psychological Reports, 21,* 415–416.

Lazarus, A. A. (1981). *The practice of multimodal psychotherapy.* New York: McGraw-Hill.

Lazarus, A. A., & Beutler, L. E. (1993). On technical eclecticism. *Journal of Counseling & Development, 71,* 381–385.

Messer, S. B. (1986). Eclectism in psychotherapy: Underlying assumptions, problems, and trade-offs. In J. C. Norcross (Ed.), *Handbook of eclectic psychotherapy* (pp. 379–397). New York: Brunner/Mazel.

Myrick, R. D. (1987). *Developmental guidance and counseling: A practical approach.* Minneapolis, MN: Educational Media.

Neukrug, E. (1994). *Theory, practice, and trends in human service: An overview of an emerging profession.* Pacific Grove, CA: Brooks/Cole.

Neukrug, E., & Williams, G. (1993). Counseling counselors: A survey of values. *Counseling and Values, 38,* 51–62.

Norcross, J. C. (1986). Eclectic psychotherapy: An introduction and overview. In J. C. Norcross (Ed.), *Handbook of eclectic psychotherapy* (pp. 3–24). New York: Brunner/Mazel.

Patterson, C. H. (1986, Summer). Counselor training or counselor education? *Association for Counselor Education and Supervision Newsletter,* pp. 10–12.

Paul, G. (1967). Strategy of outcome research in psychotherapy. *Journal of Consulting Psychology, 31,* 109–118.

Red Horse, J. (1980). Family structure and value orientation in American Indians. *Social Casework, 61,* 462–467.

Red Horse, J. (1988). Cultural evolution of American Indian families. In C. Jacobs & D. Bowles (Eds.), *Ethnicity and race: Critical concept in social work* (pp. 186–199). Silver Spring, MD: National Association of Social Workers.

Sue, D. W. (1992). The challenge to multiculturalism: The road less traveled. *American Counselor, 1,* 6–14.

Wachtel, P. (1985). Integrative psychodynamic therapy. In S. Lynn & J. Garske (Eds.), *Contemporary psychotherapies: Methods and models* (pp. 287–329). New York: Merrill.

Young, M. E. (1992). *Counseling methods and techniques: An eclectic approach.* New York: Merrill.

Young, M. E., & Feiler, F. (1989). *Trends in counseling: A national survey.* Unpublished manuscript.

3 | The Synergetic Approach to School Counseling

School counseling represents an important segment of the helping profession called the counseling profession. Specifically, school counselors are among the professionals who assist ethnic minority students with developmental tasks, particularly in elementary, middle, and high school settings. School counselors offer "services to ethnic minority students, parents, and teachers for the purpose of assuring that ethnic minority students have equal opportunity to reach their educational goals, choose appropriate career directions, and develop as fully functioning members of today's society."
—SCHMIDT, 1993, p. 1

A Comprehensive and Developmental Program

Recent research indicates that school counseling should be conceptualized in terms of a comprehensive developmental model (Gysbers & Henderson, 1988, 1994; Myrick, 1987). *Comprehensive* implies that school counseling programs should function as an integrated part of a K–12 program, not as separate grade or level entities. *Developmental* suggests that school counseling programs should be organized around a life span perspective. That is, mental health issues and counseling concerns differ for children, adolescents, adults, and the elderly.

PROGRAM GOALS AND OBJECTIVES

The goals and objectives of a school counseling program mirror the goals and objectives of the larger school purpose and mission. In the implementation of the comprehensive counseling program, school counselors serve three populations (i.e., ethnic minority students, parents, and teachers). The varied services provided include individual and group counseling, consulting, testing and assessment, group instruction, and referrals. School counselors design and implement programs and services that address the development of ethnic minority students in three basic areas: educational development, career development, and personal and social development. This chapter concerns mainly the linking and reinforcement of the basic components of a comprehensive school guidance and counseling program by means of synergetic precepts.

Educational development may involve assessing ethnic minority students' abilities, guiding teachers in the placement of these students, providing services for parents, counseling ethnic minority students about their goals in life, and emphasizing lifelong education. *Career development* may involve classroom and individual sessions involving the route to career success by planning, choosing, and following a satisfying career. School counselors assist in this process by providing accurate information about careers, assessing ethnic minority students' career interests and abilities, and encouraging ethnic minority students to keep their options open and to avoid career myths and stereotypes.

Personal and social development includes helping ethnic minority students to learn social skills and identify personal strengths and weaknesses. Ethnic minority students are assisted in understanding and accepting themselves individually and in using this information to successfully relate with others. Additional school counseling goals may include creating social interest, finding meaning in life, examining old decisions and making new ones, developing trust in oneself, reducing anxiety, attaining self-actualization, shedding maladaptive behaviors, and learning adaptive patterns.

GRADE AND AGE LEVEL DISTINCTIONS

The counseling processes used at elementary, middle, and high school levels to help ethnic minority students with their educational, career, and personal and social development are similar. The distinction between these levels rests in the varying developmental stages and needs reflected by age and gender differences (see **Table 3.1**).

From a multicultural perspective, however, the school counselor is always wary that many ethnic and cultural youths do not progress through developmental levels according to theory. Erikson's (1950/1963) life span developmental theory has been criticized for its lack of applicability for ethnic minority

TABLE 3.1

Developmental Tasks, Goals, and Counseling Strategies

School Level	Developmental Tasks	Counseling Goals	Counseling Strategy
Elementary	Industry and initiative	Foster independence and self-autonomy.	Individual and group counseling to promote self-concept development; encouragement strategies to help ethnic minority students believe in their capabilities and implement activities on their own; and self-control interventions for ethnic minority students whose impulse control interferes with their ability to complete tasks.
Middle school	Identity formation	Help ethnic minority students gain a clear understanding of who they are as individuals.	Individual and group counseling to promote self-awareness and value clarification.
High school	Intimacy	Promote social interest and interpersonal effectiveness.	Individual, group, and family counseling to promote social interest and compassion for others. Group counseling to foster interpersonal effectiveness. Career counseling to relate to the world of work.

SOURCE: Adapted from *The Art and Science of Counseling and Psychotherapy*, by M. S. Nystul, 1993, p. 305.

youths (Gilligan, 1982). The multicultural perspective contends that different ethnic groups progress through the life span differently. For example, Erikson defined a major task of puberty and adolescence as developing a sense of personal identity. For ethnic minority groups, this search for self-identity may be delayed (e.g., Japanese and other Asian groups are socialized to the identity of the family over the individual), compounded by a search for ethnic identity (e.g., any ethnic youth), or even nonexistent (e.g., African and South American societies in which individual identity is subsumed by the group identity). These ethnic and cultural variances will need to be identified and recognized to effect successful counseling.

The work of two Japanese scholars has been instrumental in the integration of multicultural concepts with developmental task completion. Tamase (1991) sought to learn how an individual's life history affected present functioning. Introspective–developmental counseling (IDC) is Tamese's integration of Japanese Naikan therapy (Reynolds, 1990), Erikson's life span theory (1950/1963), and developmental counseling (Ivey, Ivey, & Simek-Morgan, 1993). **Something to Consider 3.1** offers additional insight.

SOMETHING TO CONSIDER 3.1

Naikan Theory

Naikan therapy aims to assist ethnic minorities to discover the meaning in life and to improve interpersonal relationships with others. In addition, Naikan therapy assists ethnic minorities to move from self-centeredness to awareness of how the individual was and is formed by important relationships. A narrow focus on self only leads to neurotic distress.

The goals of therapy are to listen and assist the ethnic minority client to review the past. By listening carefully, the counselor recognizes repeated patterns and guides the client to his or her own interpretations to these patterns. The counselor incorporates specific sensorimotor, concrete, formal, and dialectic/systemic developmental questions to amplify these interpretations. Naikan therapy has been called an introspective–developmental counseling (IDC) because it seeks to learn how the ethnic minority client's life history affects present experiencing. As it is an integrative theory and incorporates environmental and cultural factors, Naikan or IDC meets the criteria of being synergetic models.

SOURCE: Adapted from "Development Over the Life Span," by A. E. Ivey & S. Rizazio-DiGilio, 1993. In A. E. Ivey (Ed.), *Developmental Strategies for Helpers: Individual, Family, and Network Interventions* (pp. 128–134).

Fukuhara (1984, 1990) has also contributed to the infusion of developmental counseling with multicultural counseling. Fukuhara contended that despite cultural differences, much of "counseling theory is basically applicable to individuals whatever their problems . . . or background" (1984, p. 6). Fukuhara insisted however that the script of the interview and the degree of attachment and separation of the "presenting" and "real" problem have to be adjusted to fit different ethnic and cultural minority students (see **Case Study 3.1**).

Diversity of counseling goals can be simplified by considering the degree of generality or specificity of goals. Goals can be seen as existing on a continuum from specific, concrete, and short term to general, global, and long term. For example, the cognitive theories stress the former, and the relationship-oriented theories tend to stress the latter. School counselors may need to make these distinctions depending on the grade-level population being served.

CASE STUDY 3.1

Ivey, Ivey, and Simek-Morgan (1993) described Fukuhara's (1984) use of developmental counseling and therapy assessment and treatment in a successful seven-interview series of sessions with a young female (age 18) student in Japan. Early in the initial interview (as translated from Japanese), the student introduced her problem as follows:

> This spring, I met this boy . . . and thought our love would last a long time. However, when I returned from summer vacation, he did not even seem to want to talk to me. This finally made me so angry that I became aggressive and we had a fight. Surprisingly, my boyfriend seemed to like being told off. Still, he doesn't ask me out and the only time I see him is at the activity club. . . . I project into the future and think that if I continue to love him, we would eventually get married. What would my life be then? Would I have to make sacrifices to his will? Would this eventually destroy my love for him? Should I give up on him now? (Ivey et al., 1993, p. 1)

This young woman's issue appeared to be one of intimacy, but this issue manifests itself differently in Japanese culture—that is, the level of involvement would not typically appear among European American ethnic minorities. Considerable sensorimotor emotion is expressed; yet, the female student's verbalizations are concrete and descriptive. What would you do?

In addition, ethnic minority students initially tend to have vague ideas of what to expect from counseling. Thus, school counselors might begin with explorations of the ethnic minority student's expectations and goals. The intake session can be used more productively by focusing on the ethnic minority student's goals or lack of them. The school counselor and the student initially decide whether they can work with each other and whether their goals are compatible. Such decisions are based on developmental needs of individual students, regardless of grade, age, status, ethnic, and other considerations. The school counselor may compare the communication skills approaches of Egan (1982), Carkhuff (1981), and Ivey and Authier (1978) to be more informed in their choices in relation to the counseling process (see **Chart 3.1**).

CHART 3.1

Communicative Skills Approaches

A. Egan's (1982) "The Skilled Helper Approach"

Stage 1: *Initial problem clarification*: primary-level accurate empathy and respect.

Stage 2: *Setting goals on the basis of dynamic understanding*: challenging skills, information sharing, advanced accurate empathy, confrontation, and self-disclosure sharing.

Stage 3: *Facilitating action*: program development—means to goals; facilitating action—preparation, challenging, and supporting evaluation.

B. Carkhuff's (1981) "The Human Resource Development Model"

Level 1: *Process goals*: exploration, understanding, and action.

Level 2: *Intermediate goals*: skills result from achieving process goals. Physical skills—exercise, diet, and other functional habits; interpersonal skills—attending, listening, responding, and initiating; and cognitive skills—analyzing, synthesizing, and interpreting.

Level 3: *Ultimate goals*: self-actualizing through high levels of responsiveness and initiative in the human experience.

C. Ivey and Authier's (1978) "The Microcounseling Skills Approach"

1. Basic attending and self-expression skills (verbal/nonverbal).
2. Microtraining skills.

   Attending skills (giving attention to the client): closed/open questions, minimal encouragement, paraphrase, and reflection of feeling.
   Influencing skills (leading the client): directives, expression of content, influencing summary, and interpretation.

3. *Focus dimensions* (who/what is the center/target of discussion content): client, others, topic, helper, direct mutual communication, and cultural–environmental context.
4. *Qualitative dimensions* (process facilitators that underlie the attending skill): concreteness, immediacy, respect, confrontation, genuineness, and positive regard.

ASSESSMENT STRATEGIES

School counselors coordinate the assessment or appraisal of ethnic minority students' characteristics and behaviors with a variety of assessments and appraisal resources. In assessing ethnic minority students, school counselors administer standardized tests, interest inventories, behavior rating scales, and nonstandardized procedures to individual students as well as in group situations.

A most important assessment coordinated by the school counselor involves the influence of environment on ethnic minority students' development and learning. The question is posed, "What therapy activities are most appropriate for what type of problem, by which therapist, for what kind of ethnic minority student?" (see Lazarus & Beutler, 1993). It is critical to be aware of how ethnic minority students' cultural backgrounds contribute to their perceptions of their problems. Although it is unwise to stereotype ethnic minority students because of their heritage, it is useful to assess how the cultural context interacts with the ethnic minority students' concerns. Some techniques are contraindicated because of ethnic minority students' unique socialization experiences. Thus, the ethnic minority student's responsiveness (or lack of it) to certain techniques is a critical barometer in judging the effectiveness of these methods.

Consequently, the school counselor's task becomes one of appraising the influences of environmental factors on the ethnic minority student. To obtain a complete and accurate description of ethnic minority students, the school counselor will assess factors such as the school atmosphere, classroom environment, peer groups, and family and home environments.

Value of Synergetic Assessment

The value of synergetic assessment is the integrating of multiple approaches into an organized paradigm of delivering appraisal services successfully to ethnic and cultural minority students, depending largely on the school counselor's primary theoretical orientation (Herring, 1997). Several models are available that illustrate synergetic school counseling. For example, Lazarus's (1981) multimodal therapy reflects a major effort to organize primarily behavioral tenets into his "BASIC-ID" paradigm (Behavior, Affective response, Sensations, Images, Cognition, Interpersonal relationships, and Drugs). His paradigm created a holistic approach and was one of the first to move eclecticism to an organized, or a synergetic, format. Additional examples of synergetic models will be presented in a subsequent section of this chapter.

Integrative theorizing is currently becoming more common and influential. Theoretical approaches involving cognitive–behavioral theory and developmental counseling have brought diverse theories together in a coherent fashion. For example, Attneave's (1969, 1982) network therapy involves extensive multiple interventions and assessments with individuals, families, and the community to produce and maintain change, especially with Native American Indian students.

According to Ivey et al. (1993), synergetic counseling does not

dismiss traditional methods but rather recognizes their value, as long as they are employed in a culturally meaningful and culturally sensitive fashion. . . . Rather than to impose a theory on the client, these approaches seek to find how the client constructs and makes meaning in the world and stress an egalitarian, non-hierarchical therapist/client relationship. They suggest that counselor and client together draw from other theories in an integrated fashion to meet individual, family, and cultural needs. . . . In effect, self-in-relation becomes the focus rather than individually oriented self-actualization. (p. 361)

The Synergetic Counseling Process

Fundamental processing concepts are inherent to synergetic models just as they are with most theoretical perspectives (Herring, 1997). Several concepts are presented briefly.

FUNDAMENTAL ASSUMPTIONS

First, synergetic counseling begins with the awareness that current theories of counseling and psychotherapies are incomplete and inappropriate for most ethnic and cultural youths in today's schools. In most instances, traditional theories are antiquated and resistant to today's socioeconomic and political societies, not to mention ethnic and cultural variances. An example of this reluctance to change is seen in a 1991 special issue of *Individual Psychology: The Journal of Adlerian Theory, Research, and Practice,* which focused on "beyond Adler." In this special issue, Nystul (1991) suggested that the Adlerian movement has become isolated and focused too much on well-developed concepts such as the four goals of misbehavior (i.e., attention getting, power, revenge, or assumed inadequacy) and logical consequences. In other words, a broader, more permeable boundary is needed for Adlerian psychology to become responsive to mainstream contemporary psychology.

This transformation is especially necessary for school counseling. Adlerian approaches need to be adapted to reach nontraditional students such as victims of family violence, AIDS-infected students, gay and lesbian students,

students from single or parentless homes, as well as ethnic and culturally diverse ethnic minority students. Mosak (1991) echoed this theme by noting that the Adlerian theory overemphasizes the psychology of abnormality rather than the psychology of normality. A recent research effort (Herring & Runion, 1994) emphasized Adlerian precepts that are effective with ethnic and cultural minority school populations.

Another cogent criticism of traditional theories exists in the tendency of these theories to remain stagnant—theories developed to fit the needs of the European American masculine middle-class value system. Society currently reflects, and future society will reflect even more, a more diverse middle class than the one when most traditional theories were developed.

The second basic assumption of synergetic counseling is the inalienable influence that environment and culture have on an ethnic minority student in the counseling process. *Environment* may be defined as consisting of all external and historical factors to which a person or group is actually or potentially responsive. Thus, school counselors need to take into consideration factors in the counseling environment itself, as well as cultural and ethnic environments. In doing so, the counselor will consider physical, social, and cultural elements. A counseling procedure is most effective when there is synergism with an ethnic minority student's background and situation (Tainsri & Axelson, 1990).

FRAMES OF REFERENCE

School counselors need to be cognizant of differences among ethnic minority students and the importance of the effects of family and cultural factors on the way ethnic minority students view the world. The viewing of self-in-relation to others and to social and cultural context is inalienable to a synergetic model. The school counselor and the ethnic minority student aim to work cooperatively in the community and society to alleviate and prevent future concerns and problems.

The school counselor needs to understand and accept ethnic minority students as being unique and reflective of their environment, culture, and heritages, particularly as manifested in their families of origin. Culture and cultural awareness are the emphases. Wrenn (1985) described the "culturally encapsulated counselor" as one who cannot escape his or her own worldview. Subsequently, such a school counselor would have difficulty in accepting other perspectives.

Awareness of an ethnic minority student's cultural frame of reference is important and necessary. However, the school counselor must extend beyond this knowledge and be competent to understand and appreciate the ethnic minority student's uniqueness as an individual. The understanding of both the school counselor's and the ethnic minority student's worldviews is essential to successful cross-cultural counseling. *Worldview* is a construct that can individualize the school counseling process (Ibrahim, 1991; Sue, 1978b; Sue & Sue, 1990). Worldview is a multifaceted construct that has been defined as the presuppositions and assumptions an individual holds about the makeup of his or her life (Sire, 1976) or how a person perceives his or her relationship to the world (Sue, 1978b). Ibrahim (1991, 1993) included a person's thoughts, feelings, and perceptions of social relations and the world in her perspective.

The multicultural or cross-cultural school counselor will view students in a family and cultural context (Ivey et al., 1993). The school counselor considers that student and family problems are often the products of environmental factors (e.g., racism, sexism, and socioeconomic status). In essence, school counseling will only be effective if environmental factors are addressed by incorporating them in the process.

One method of determining an ethnic minority student's worldview is *The Scale to Assess World Views* (Ibrahim & Kahn, 1984, 1987). This 45-item Likert-type instrument, based on Kluckhohn's (1951, 1956) five essential categories, has been used successfully to assess the student's view of human nature, social relations, relations with nature, time orientation, and activity orientation. The primary author (Ibrahim, 1991) suggested the use of this scale during the initial counseling session to differentiate between worldview and cultural view.

Another popular model of identifying differing worldviews and frames of references is the internal or external locus of control and responsibility model of Sue and his colleagues (Sue, 1978a; Sue & Sue, 1990). Rotter (1966, 1975) first presented the concept of internal–external control dimension. This dimension refers to students' beliefs either that reinforcements are contingent on their own actions and that they can control their own futures (internal control) or that reinforcements occur independently of their control (external control).

The second dimension in worldview formulation is derived from the attribution theory concept of locus of responsibility (Jones et al., 1972). This dimension accounts for the amount of responsibility or blame directed by a student to self or the system. As Sue and Sue (1990) described this dimension, the lower standard of living status of some ethnic minority individuals may be attributed to their personal inadequacies (internal responsibility) or to racial discrimination and lack of opportunities (external responsibility). The former blames the individual, whereas the latter blames the system.

Sue and his associates (Sue, 1978a; Sue & Sue, 1990) combined these two dimensions into a conceptual model for understanding worldviews and identity development among ethnic and cultural minority populations (see **Figure 4.2, page 67**). Each quadrant represents a different worldview. If the school counselor is aware of a student's degree of internality or externality on the two dimensions of loci, the school counselor could place the student in one of the four quadrants. For example, the quadrant representing the best portrayal of the U.S. society as a whole would be the internal locus of control–internal locus of responsibility (IC-IR) view of Quadrant I. This quadrant reflects the individualistic and competitiveness of the Protestant ethic. This model offers practical and research implications for multicultural and cross-cultural school counseling. (See Chapter 4, p. 66, for further discussion of locus of control and locus of responsibility.)

CURRENT TRENDS

Traditional counseling theories have historically been unaware of culture in their focus on values of individualism, rationalism, and self-determination. Counseling and therapy research indicates that the typical counselor education student is European American, educated, middle class, and female (even though theories were predominantly generated by European American men (Ivey et al., 1993). However, many ideas generated by women have been incorporated by men, especially in the psychoanalytic field (Grosskurth, 1991).

Parham (1990) reminded us that African American scholars generated many concepts of multicultural counseling that were ignored until European American men began presenting similar ideas, often without recognizing African American contributors. Such omissions of recognition are rapidly disappearing. More and more ethnic minority researchers and theorists are receiving their proper respect. Two distinct trends dominate the field of multicultural and environmental counseling today. The *universal trend* emphasizes that every session contains multicultural issues and is represented primarily by the work of Fukuyama (1990), who argued for a transcultural, universal approach to multicultural counseling and therapy, maintaining that certain factors are important regardless of culture.

The *focused trend* emphasizes the importance of culture-specific understanding (Locke, 1990, 1992). Locke stressed the specialness of critical cultural groups. School counselors need to gain cultural expertise on specific ethnic minority groups that are likely to be encountered in practice. He argued for what he termed a *focused approach* in which it is important "to see people both as individuals and members of a culturally different group" (Locke, 1990, p. 23).

Some of the prerequisite components for synergetic counseling are inherent to the approaches of these models. More specific and concrete examples of current synergetic models will be presented briefly in the following section.

Synergetic Approach Models for School Counseling

Several theoretical models are currently available that contain synergetic features. These models emphasize the counseling of culturally diverse ethnic minority individuals from integrated and multiple approaches, albeit from different perspectives. The reader will be advised to consult the cited resources for an indepth perspective on these representative models. The models are not presented in any order of preference, chronology, or efficacy.

NONRACIST COMMUNICATION APPROACH

The nonracist communication approach (Patterson, 1973) originally addressed the underlying school counselor attitude in counseling disadvantaged African American students. The basic premise is that a racist attitude works against the helping process, whereas a nonracist attitude facilitates the process. Biased attitudes vary in degree of communicating an overtly racist attitude of hopelessness to a covertly racist attitude of false hope. Unbiased facilitative communication involves the collaborative effort of the school counselor and the ethnic minority student to help the student clarify his or her internal reality and to learn more of the external reality in order to be better prepared to make a choice (Axelson, 1993). The efficacy of this model to other ethnic minorities has not been established.

ACCOUNTABLE ACTION APPROACH

The accountable action approach (S. J. Tucker, 1973) uses the school counselor's problem-solving skills to work with disadvantaged ethnic minority students. The goals are specific, and the school counselor works aggressively to ensure the emotional involvement of the ethnic minority student through raising hopes and expectations. To accomplish this, the school counselor builds a relationship of trust with the ethnic minority student, and then follows certain steps to facilitate growth. These steps include outreach, communicating trust, determining the problem, setting up long- and short-term objectives, assessing current conditions, determining priority of needs, and determining a strategy to achieve the goals.

SYSTEMIC APPROACH

The systemic approach (Gunnings, 1973; Gunnings & Simpkins, 1972) posits that the system (i.e., society) causes the problems of the ethnic minority student, and thus the system must be counseled. A faulty system may result in human problems such as feelings of frustration, aloneness, inferiority, and hostile, deviant behavior (R. N. Tucker & Gunnings, 1974). It is a problem-oriented, not an ethnic-minority-student-oriented approach and stresses cause rather than symptoms. The school counselor is an advocate of the ethnic minority student, and the goal of the counseling process is to establish effective relationships.

TRANSCENDENT APPROACH

Transcendent counseling first appeared as a theory for counseling African Americans. Transcendent counseling has since been modified into a transcultural or multicultural theory of counseling, with universal applications and value for a number of different cultural groups (Harper & Stone, 1986, 1993). This model also presents a paradigm (multiethnic phases of development) that explains the major identity phases that are deemed relevant and applicable to all ethnic minority groups (Harper & Stone, 1986, 1993; Stone, 1975, 1984).

The basic proposition of the transcendent approach (Harper & Stone, 1974; Stone, 1973) is that school counselors should focus their helping efforts with ethnic minority students to satisfying their basic needs, to developing new lifestyles, and to transcending the undesirable environmental conditions of U.S. society that work against positive growth and mental health (Harper & Stone, 1974; Stone, 1973). The approach stresses the responsibility of both school counselor and ethnic minority student, and it follows the sequential steps of assessment, prescription, counselor action, and student action. The goals of transcendent counseling are governed by the nature of the presenting problem of the ethnic minority student together with assessment and diagnostic information from the intake interview concerning the student's lifestyle (Harper & Stone, 1993).

The ultimate objectives are the satisfying of basic needs, changing or adjusting lifestyle and behavior, and rising above negative environmental influences. The process of transcendent counseling is presented by the acronym APART, and corresponds to (a) assessment, (b) prescription, (c) action, (d) review, and (e) transcendence. Also, this acronym symbolizes the term *apart*, as with apart from the old self or old lifestyle to a new self-identity and a new way of living (Harper & Stone, 1993).

CULTURALLY SPECIFIC APPROACH

The culturally specific approach (Stikes, 1972) requires school counselors to view counseling from the perspective of the host culture rather than from the traditional European American frame of reference (Nwachuka & Ivey, 1991). Stikes (1972) contended that "because of the hostility of the environment and because of their cultural heritages, these minorities have maintained behaviors and values different from those of the dominant society" (p. 15).

Axelson (1993) described this model as being "optimistic, positive, and oriented to the motivational pride that comes from cultural identity" (p. 393). Although the "melting-pot" idea has been prevalent in U.S. society, overlooking the diversity of cultures within this country has led to ineffective school counseling practices. Herr (1987) stated that such counseling practices are intracultural rather than intercultural and operate on the philosophy that all people are mostly alike. The culturally specific approach recognizes the diversity and influence of culture on the ethnic minority student and requires that the school counselor possesses knowledge and skill in all areas of cultural heritage. A basic aim of the school counselor is to facilitate movement of ethnic minority students toward a self-understanding and positive means of incorporating emotional content into their personal awareness of social reality.

CROSS-CULTURAL DIFFERENCES APPROACH

The cross-cultural differences approach (Marsella & Pedersen, 1981; Pedersen, Draguns, Lonner, & Trimble, 1981; Sue & Sue, 1990) represents the most widely accepted model of cross-cultural counseling today. In essence, the school counselor and the ethnic minority student view themselves as culturally different. These cultural differences are acquired through "socialization in distinct cultural, subcultural, racioethnic, or socioeconomic environments" (Vontress, 1988, p. 73). The model outlines four critical areas for school counselors: (a) barriers to effective counseling, (b) relationship factors, (c) cultural identity, and (d) conditions for the culturally skilled counselor (Sue & Sue, 1990).

Sue and Sue (1990) integrated Rotter's (1966, 1975) concept of internal and external locus of control and the attribution theory (i.e., locus of responsibility) into the interpretation of the ethnic minority student's worldview. Finally, Sue and Sue delineated skills that culturally skilled counselors should possess and stressed the importance of proficiency in a number of theoretical approaches to help the ethnic minority student achieve the desired outcomes.

PERSON–ENVIRONMENT METATHEORY APPROACH

The person–environment metatheory approach (Ivey & Matthews, 1984) describes other models and seeks greater understanding of the interplay among the school counselor, ethnic minority student, and environment. It is essentially an expansion of conceptual goals of the microcounseling skills approach and operates on several dimensions, especially the person and environment dimension (Ivey et al., 1993). Individual environment is viewed as transactions the ethnic minority student has with self, and environment is defined as the transactions the student has with others. In the counseling situation, the school counselor is the ethnic minority student's environment and the ethnic minority student is the school counselor's environment, and each has his or her own individual environment. Thus, in a literal sense, all counseling is cross-environmental or cross-cultural. The counseling process in this metamodel is seen as a coevolving process of interpersonal relationships in which new knowledge is being constructed by both the school counselor and the ethnic minority student, with the worldview of the ethnic minority student providing the framework from which the school counselor develops appropriate techniques (Ivey & Matthews, 1984). Incorporated into the theory are other dimensions of intentionality, assessment, decision-making process, and process skills.

STYLISTIC MODEL FOR TRANSCULTURAL COUNSELING

The stylistic model for transcultural counseling (McFadden, 1986) originally addressed the needs of African American people in the United States. This model has proved subsequently to be applicable to other oppressed and underrepresented groups as well. The design of this model is thematically constructed around the dimensions of cultural–historical, psychosocial, and scientific–ideological (McFadden, 1993). The cultural–historical dimension relates to the specific culture of a people and how the history of those people has evolved. The psychosocial dimension relates to the psychological framework of how an ethnic minority student's psyche influences his or her development. The scientific–ideological dimension is based primarily on an individual ethnic student's plan of action.

This model focuses on the learning process wherein the school counselor enjoys teaching, motivating, and setting examples to capture the ethnic minority student's perception to change his or her lifestyle. This approach emphasizes active and reciprocal processes in a mutually acceptable environment for those concerned (McFadden, 1993). The model not only encourages school counselors to work across diverse cultures but also empowers those involved to travel through and beyond all cultural barriers empathizing and experiencing cultural meshing through transference and countertransference processes (d'Ardenne & Mahatani, 1989). The stylistic transcultural approach uses self-examination as the means in which ethnic students can better view themselves and thus avoid self-righteousness.

The most important objective of this approach is to create an overall trusting relationship between the school counselor and ethnic minority student for successful interaction. The model strives to empathize with the social perspective and relate to human development nationally and across nations by constructing broader parameters for cross-cultural understanding and appreciation. To this end, transcultural school counselors find it beneficial to understand the family system technique (Nichols, 1984) and extrapolate and compare it in a diverse environment.

RAMIREZ'S MULTICULTURAL APPROACH

Ramirez (1983) concluded that European perspectives have influenced the psychology of the peoples of the Western hemisphere too excessively. Ramirez also contended that an emerging psychological perspective is compatible with peoples of the Western hemisphere. This maturing perspective reflects the current, popular multicultural emphasis. To address this need for a multicultural focus, Ramirez (1991) offered the following abbreviated objectives of his model: (a) to present a theoretical perspective for the concern and problems faced by students living in multicultural societies in the Western hemisphere; (b) to provide a culturally compatible counseling paradigm and eclectic strategies that will facilitate personal development of ethnic students toward a more culturally congruent status; and (c) to restore good student relations with significant others in their social environment.

The multicultural counseling approach is based on (a) the psychology of individual and cultural differences and (b) a cultural and cognitive dual theory of personality. Psychological adjustment and development are seen as functions of personality flexibility and a multicultural orientation toward life. To this end, psychological adjustment is a matter of the degrees of cultural and cognitive match and mismatch between a student and his or her environments. The purpose of school counseling then is to assist students who feel different and alienated to understand their own uniqueness and to develop cultural values and cognitive flexibility in the direction of a multicultural personality.

The theory and strategies of multicultural counseling are based on an eclecticism drawn from diverse approaches (i.e., synergetic approach). The school counselor seeks to develop his or her own multicultural personality and is alert to his or her own behaviors that might interfere with the student's development of flexibility. The final phase of multicultural counseling seeks to work against the fear that counseling is a tool of conformity. The societal ideal is cooperation, harmony, and sensitivity toward cultural and individual differences.

Summary

Sue (1992) contended that the counseling profession currently stands at the crossroads. One road is to monoculturalism or ethnocentrism, from which most traditional theories have been developed. "The other path, multiculturalism, is the road less traveled. It recognizes and values diversity, . . . values cultural pluralism, and acknowledges our nation as a cultural mosaic rather than a melting pot" (pp. 8–9). For counseling professionals, multiculturalism demands change.

The synergetic approach to school counseling is a road less traveled, but surely worth taking. To be effective with all ethnic minority students, regardless of race, culture, color, or national origin, school counselors and counselor education programs must broaden their base of cultural knowledge and be willing to develop new structures, policies, and strategies that are more responsive to all ethnic minority students. This enhancement is important not only because of humanistic reasons, but also because within the next 20 years, racial and ethnic minorities will become a numerical majority, and European Americans the minority (Sue, 1992). At its best, synergetic school counseling can be a creative synthesis and a selective blending of the unique contributions of diverse theories. This model presents a dynamic integration of those concepts and techniques that fit the school counselor's unique personality and style. In addition, the cultural and environmental worldview of the ethnic and cultural minority student is recognized and respected. Finally, synergetic school counseling perspectives represent an opportunity to assist counselor education programs to reflect a pluralistic society.

Experiential Activities

1. The concept of worldview may be described as the way an individual thinks about how the world "works." Individuals tend to "think" about the world differently and geocentrically. In addition, each individual possesses multiple "thoughts"—racial, cultural, contextual, and spiritual—about the workings of the world. Examine your own "thoughts" and

"views" of the world. Where would you place yourself on Sue's (1978) graphic quadrants, and what are your justifications?
2. What are your feelings about the future of multicultural and cross-cultural counseling and development in the school systems? How does synergetic precepts intersect with your feelings?
3. As a school counselor or school counselor-in-training, what can you do personally to further enhance counseling training programs? In-service workshops?

References

Attneave, C. (1969). Therapy in tribal settings and urban network interventions. *Family Process, 8,* 192–210.

Attneave, C. (1982). American Indian and Alaska native families: Emigrants in their own homeland. In M. McGoldrick, J. Pearce, & J. Giordano (Eds.), *Ethnicity and family therapy* (pp. 55–83). New York: Guilford Press.

Axelson, J. (1993). *Counseling and development in a multicultural society* (2nd ed.). Monterey, CA: Brooks/Cole.

Carkhuff, R. R. (1981). *Toward actualizing human potential.* Amherst, MA: Human Resource Development Press.

d'Ardenne, P., & Mahatani, A. (1989). *Transcultural counseling in action.* London: Sage.

Egan, G. (1982). *The skilled helper* (2nd ed.). Pacific Grove, CA: Brooks/Cole.

Erikson, E. (1963). *Childhood and society* (2nd ed.). New York: Norton. (Original work published 1950)

Fukuhara, M. (1984). *Is love universal? From the viewpoint of counseling adolescents.* Paper presented at the 42th Conference of the International Association of Psychologists, Mexico City, Mexico.

Fukuyama, M. (1990). Taking a universal approach to multicultural counseling. *Counselor Education and Supervision, 30,* 6–17.

Gilligan, C. (1982). *In a different voice.* Cambridge, MA: Harvard University Press.

Grosskurth, P. (1991, September 29). Mothers of psychoanalysis. *New York Times Book Review,* p. 12.

Gunnings, T. S. (1973). Systemic counseling: An effective approach to counseling ethnic minorities. In *Proceedings: First national conference on counseling minorities and disadvantaged youth* (pp. 18–19). East Lansing: Michigan State University, College of Urban Development.

Gunnings, T. S., & Simpkins, G. (1972). A systemic approach to counseling disadvantaged youth. *Journal of Non-White Concerns, 1,* 4–8.

Gysbers, N., & Henderson, P. (1988). *Developing and managing your school guidance program.* Alexandria, VA: American Association for Counseling and Development.

Gysbers, N., & Henderson, P. (1994). *Developing and managing your school guidance program* (2nd ed.). Alexandria, VA: American Counseling Association.

Harper, F. D., & Stone, W. O. (1974). Toward a theory of transcendent counseling with Blacks. *Journal of Non-White Concerns, 2,* 191–196.

Harper, F. D., & Stone, W. O. (1986). Transcendent counseling: Toward a multicultural approach. *International Journal for the Advancement of Counseling, 9,* 251–263.

Harper, F. D., & Stone, W. O. (1993). Transcendent counseling: A transcultural theory. In J. McFadden (Ed.), *Transcultural counseling: Bilateral and international perspectives* (pp. 83–108). Alexandria, VA: American Counseling Association.

Herr, E. (1987). Cultural diversity from an international perspective. *Journal of Multicultural Counseling and Development, 15,* 99–109.

Herring, R. D. (1997). *Counseling diverse ethnic youth: Synergetic strategies and interventions for school counselors.* Fort Worth, TX: Harcourt Brace.

Herring, R. D., & Runion, K. R. (1994). Counseling ethnic minority children and youth from an Adlerian perspective. *Journal of Multicultural Counseling and Development, 22,* 215–226.

Ibrahim, F. A. (1991). Contribution of cultural worldview to generic counseling and development. *Journal of Counseling & Development, 70,* 13–19.

Ibrahim, F. A. (1993). Existential world view theory: Transcultural counseling. In J. McFadden (Ed.), *Transcultural counseling: Bilateral and international perspectives* (pp. 23–57). Alexandria, VA: American Counseling Association.

Ibrahim, F. A., & Kahn, H. (1984). *Scale to Assess World Views.* Unpublished manuscript, University of Connecticut, Storrs.

Ibrahim, F. A., & Kahn, H. (1987). Assessment of world views. *Psychological Reports, 60,* 163–176.

Ivey, A. E., & Authier, J. (1978). *Microcounseling* (2nd ed.). Springfield, IL: Charles C Thomas.

Ivey, A. E., Ivey, M. B., & Simek-Morgan, L. (1993). *Counseling and psychotherapy: A multicultural perspective* (3rd ed.). Boston: Allyn & Bacon.

Ivey, A., & Matthews, W. (1984). A meta-model for structuring the clinical interview. *Journal of Counseling & Development, 63,* 237–243.

Ivey, A. E., & Rizazio-DiGilio, S. (1993). Development over the life span. In A. E. Ivey (Ed.), *Developmental strategies for helpers: Individual, family, and network interventions* (pp. 128–134). North Amherst, MA: Microtraining Associates.

Jones, E. E., Kanouse, D., Kelley, H. H., Nisbett, R. E., Valins, S., & Weiner, B. (Eds.). (1972). *Attribution: Perceiving the causes of behavior.* Morristown, NJ: General Learning Press.

Kluckhohn, C. (1951). Values and value orientation in a theory of action. In T. Parsons & E. A Shields (Eds.), *Toward a general theory of action* (pp. 338–433). Cambridge, MA: Harvard University Press.

Kluckhohn, C. (1956). Toward a comparison of value-emphases in different cultures. In L. D. White (Ed.), *The state of the social sciences* (pp. 116–132). Chicago: University of Chicago Press.

Lazarus, A. A. (1981). *The practice of multimodal psychotherapy.* New York: McGraw-Hill.

Lazarus, A. A., & Beutler, L. E. (1993). On technical eclecticism. *Journal of Counseling & Development, 71,* 381–385.

Locke, D. C. (1990). A not so provincial view of multicultural counseling. *Counselor Education and Supervision, 30,* 18–25.

Locke, D. C. (1992). *Increasing multicultural understanding: A comprehensive model.* Newbury Park, CA: Sage.

Marsella, A. J., & Pedersen, P. B. (Eds.). (1981). *Cross-cultural counseling and psychotherapy.* New York: Pergamon Press.

McFadden, J. (1986). Stylistic dimensions of counseling minorities. *International Journal for the Advancement of Counseling, 9,* 209.

McFadden, J. (Ed.). (1993). *Transcultural counseling: Bilateral and international perspecitves.* Alexandria, VA: American Counseling Association.

Mosak, H. (1991). Where have all the normal people gone? *Individual Psychology: The Journal of Adlerian Theory, Research, and Practice, 47,* 437–446.

Myrick, R. D. (1987). *Developmental guidance and counseling: A practical approach.* Minneapolis, MN: Educational Media.

Nichols, M. P. (1984). *Family therapy concepts and methods.* New York: Gardner Press.

Nwachuka, U., & Ivey, A. (1991). Culture-specific counseling: An alternative training model. *Journal of Counseling & Development, 70,* 106–111.

Nystul, M. S. (1991). An interview with Jon Carlson. *Individual Psychology: The Journal of Adlerian Theory, Research, and Practice, 47,* 498–503.

Nystul, M. S. (1993). *The art and science of counseling and psychotherapy.* New York: Merrill.

Parham, T. (1990). *Do the right thing: Racial discussion of counseling psychology.* Paper presented at the American Psychological Association Convention, Boston.

Patterson, L. E. (1973). The strange verbal world. *Journal of Non-White Concerns, 1,* 95–101.

Pedersen, P. B., Draguns, J. G., Lonner, W. J., & Trimble, J. E. (Eds.). (1981). *Counseling across cultures* (Rev. ed.). Honolulu: University of Hawaii Press.

Ramirez, M. (1983). *Psychology of the Americas: Mestizo perspectives on personality and mental health.* New York: Pergamon Press.

Ramirez, M. (1991). *Psychotherapy and counseling with minorities: A cognitive approach to individual and cultural differences.* New York: Pergamon Press.

Reynolds, D. (1990). Morita and Naikan therapies—similarities. *Journal of Morita Therapy, 1,* 159–163.

Rotter, J. (1966). Generalized expectancies for internal versus external control of reinforcement. *Psychological Monographs, 80,* 1–28.

Rotter, J. (1975). Some problems and misconceptions related to the construct of internal versus external control of reinforcement. *Journal of Consulting and Clinical Psychology, 43,* 56–67.

Schmidt, J. J. (1993). *Counseling in the schools.* Boston: Allyn & Bacon.

Sire, J. W. (1976). *The universe next door.* Downers, IL: Intervarsity.

Stikes, C. S. (1972). Culturally specific counseling: The Black client. *Journal of Non-White Concerns, 1,* 4–8.

Stone, W. O. (1973). *Transcendent counseling for Blacks: A modular-conceptual theory.* Paper presented at the second annual Region V, TRIO Conference, Fontana, WI.

Stone, W. O. (1975). Career development for ethnic minorities. In R. C. Reardon & H. D. Burck (Eds.), *Facilitating career development: Strategies for counselors.* Springfield, IL: Charles C Thomas.

Stone, W. O. (1984). Serving ethnic minorities. In H. D. Burck & R. C. Reardon (Eds.), *Career development interventions* (pp. 267–291). Springfield, IL: Charles C Thomas.

Sue, D. W. (1978a). Eliminating cultural oppression in counseling: Toward a general theory. *Journal of Counseling Psychology, 25,* 422.

Sue, D. W. (1978b). World views and counseling. *The Personnel and Guidance Journal, 56,* 458–462.

Sue, D. W. (1992). The challenge of multiculturalism: The road less traveled. *American Counselor, 1,* 6–14.

Sue, D. W., & Sue, D. (1990). *Counseling the culturally different: Theory and practice* (2nd ed.). New York: Wiley.

Tainsri, R., & Axelson, J. A. (1990). Group sensitivity training with Thai workers and managers as a process to promote inter- and intrapersonal relations, and work performance. *International Journal for the Advancement of Counseling, 13,* 219–226.

Tamase, K. (1991, April). *The effects of introspective-developmental-counseling.* Paper presented at the annual conference of the American Association of Counseling and Development, Reno, NV.

Tucker, R. N., & Gunnings, T. S. (1974). Counseling Black youth: A quest for legitimacy. *Journal of Non-White Concerns, 2,* 208–216.

Tucker, S. J. (1973). Action counseling: An accountability procedure for counseling the oppressed. *Journal of Non-White Concerns, 2,* 35–41.

Vontress, C. (1988). An existential approach to cross-cultural counseling. *Journal of Multicultural Counseling and Development, 16,* 73–83.

Wrenn, C. (1985). The culturally encapsulated counselor revisited. In P. Pedersen (Ed.), *Handbook of cross-cultural counseling and therapy* (pp. 323–329). Westport, CT: Greenwood.

4 | The Role of Culture

The fundamental premise of intercultural education says, in effect, no person knows his [her] own culture who knows only his [her] own culture.
—ALLPORT, 1958, p. 451

The United States has experienced an almost perpetual ethnical crisis since the Supreme Court ruled against de jure public school segregation in 1954. Whether or not this discord has been prompted by overt and subtle ethnocentrism or assumed ethnic and cultural differences in values and beliefs, the possible solution was phrased very pointedly a century ago by Frederick Douglass (1892/ 1962):

> I have found in my experience that the way to break down an unreason-able custom is to contradict it in practice. To be sure in pursuing this course I have had to contend not merely with the white race but with the black. The one has condemned me for my presumption in daring to associate with it and the other for pushing myself where it takes for granted I am not wanted. (pp. 366–367)

This "break down" of "an unreasonable custom" by contradicting "it in practice" reflects a central theme of this book.

History reveals that White separatists are correct when they con-tend that racial change creates conflict, and that if only the traditions of White supremacy were to go unchallenged, racial harmony might be restored (Pettigrew, 1974). On a deeper level, however, one of the quietest periods in racial history in the United States, 1885 to 1915, witnessed the subtle implementation of institutional racism that is currently being experienced by ethnic minorities—the "nadir of

Negro American history," as Logan (1957) stated. The price of those two decades of relative peace is still being paid by this nation. Even if it were possible now to gain racial calm by inaction, the United States could not afford the enormous cost, declared Pettigrew (1974). However, this nation is 20 years beyond these commentaries, and observable changes are not yet congruent with progress in other social and political domains.

Interactions between school counselors and students require different paths in different cultures. A common myth about ethnic groups is that they are all alike, which, of course, is not true. Ethnic cultures cannot be labeled homogeneously, even within group. Not only do they derive from a variety of ethnic and cultural backgrounds, but they are also reared in different environments with varied circumstances of their lives (Rice, 1993).

Numerous discussions in this text refer to the presence of between- and within-group differences. Differences between low socioeconomic status and middle-class ethnic minority youths are frequently highlighted, as are differences between ethnic minority and European American youths. Unfortunately, however, much of the available research has been conducted with European American middle-class youths. Although European Americans are currently the majority ethnic group, they certainly are not representative of all ethnic groups. In reality, this ethnic group is rapidly becoming a minority group.

What Is Culture?

A major challenge confronting school counselors is understanding the complex role of culture in the lives of their students. A knowledge of cultural realities has become a professional imperative as school counselors encounter increasingly diverse student groups. When culture is considered as a variable in the school counseling process, however, it has the potential of becoming a source of conflict and misunderstanding that may create barriers between school counselors and students who differ in terms of cultural background (Lee, 1991). Thus, a primary purpose of this chapter is to provide a conceptual framework for understanding the context of culture in school counseling endeavors. A secondary purpose is to review the more important dynamics in synergetic cross-cultural counseling.

A demographic review will, perhaps, encourage a more dedicated effort to address the current and future socioeconomic, cultural, and psychoeducational conditions in this pluralistic nation.

Current and Future Demographics

The United States is not the same nation as it was in the days of White (i.e., European American) domination, even though European Americans remain the dominant ethnic and cultural group in this nation. Baruth and Manning (1991) described that period in this manner:

> The United States has had its doors open to people of diverse cultural, ethnic, and racial origins for many years. Some . . . entered . . . with hopes of realizing the American dream; others . . . to escape oppressive conditions in their home countries. Still others were actually brought against their will and expected to conform culturally to the Anglo population. And there were those who first inhabited the land on which the American nation now exists and who were expected to adopt the "white man's ways." (p. 4)

A covert, and in many instances overt, aim of the national government existed in the acculturation and assimilation of these peoples into a *melting pot* of values, ideologies, and customs (e.g., Herring, 1989). Many immigrants and indigenous peoples rejected these coercive attempts and instead adopted a *salad bowl* ideology (McCormick, 1984). Savickas (1992) distinguished between these analogies for multiculturalism in the United States in the 1990s. In the melting pot, each distinct group loses its characteristics and "melts" together into one homogeneous amalgam. The salad bowl describes the mixing together of diverse groups into a heterogeneous cornucopia of interests, beliefs, traditions, and rituals, but in which each still retains their own specific character. The "salad dressing" performs the cohesion of this analogy. A similar analogy is the *mosaic*, in which the cement becomes the cohesive agent for the individual groups. In subsequent years, *cultural pluralism* became the more popular and appropriate ideology.

Table 4.1 depicts current ethnic ancestry groups in the United States, as reported by citizens on their 1990 census forms ("German-Americans," 1992). A long version of the 1990 census form was sent to one household in six. These forms asked individuals about their ancestry, and the Census Bureau used these responses to estimate national totals for each group. As the question was fill-in-the-blank format, many individuals responded with racial designations, such as "White," or continents, such as North American.

One U.S. citizen in 4 is of German ancestry and they constitute the nation's largest ethnic ancestry, as reported on the census forms. Irish ancestry is next, 1 citizen in 6; followed by the English, 1 in 8; African American, 1 in 10; and Italian, 1 in 17. It is interesting to note that more than 12 million people consider themselves to be just plain Americans—1 in 20.

From a regional and geographical perspective, California has the largest number of the northern and western European groups (e.g., German, Irish, and French). New York ranks first in eastern and southern European groups

---

TABLE 4.1

Ethnic Ancestries of U.S. Citizens (in Millions, for 1 Million or More), 1990 Census

German	57.9	Welsh	2.0
Irish	38.7	Spanish	2.0
English	32.7	Puerto Rican	2.0
African American	23.8	Slovak	1.9
Italian	14.7	White	1.8
American	12.4	Danish	1.6
Mexican	11.6	Hungarian	1.6
French	10.3	Chinese	1.5
Polish	9.4	Filipino	1.5
American Indian	8.7	Czech	1.3
Dutch	6.2	Portuguese	1.2
Scotch-Irish	5.6	British	1.1
Scottish	5.4	Hispanic	1.1
Swedish	4.7	Greek	1.1
Norwegian	3.9	Swiss	1.0
Russian	3.0	Japanese	1.0
French Canadian	2.2		

SOURCE: Adapted from "German-Americans Are Largest U.S. Ethnic Group, Census Says," by *Fayetteville Observer-Times*, 1992, December 20, p. 26-A.

(e.g., Italian, Polish, and Russian). Minnesota ranks first for Norwegians, Massachusetts first for French Canadians, Pennsylvania first for Slovaks, and Ohio first for Hungarians. Another interesting insight is depicted in the number of citizens who listed Native American Indian as their ancestry.

The 1990 census report revealed that nearly 2 million citizens identified themselves as Native American Indians. Yet, 8.7 million citizens claim Native American Indian ancestry. Perhaps, the fact that Native American Indian is the only ethnic group that requires documentation of its ethnicity influenced these incongruent figures.

The 1992 census projects a population of 383 million by the year 2050, with only 53% being European Americans ("Demographer sees," 1992). The gains and losses of selected ethnic groups are presented in **Something to Consider 4.1**. The 1992 census report foresees the pattern of negative gain only in the European American (White) population. Rationales for this loss can be found in differences in age, fertility rates, and levels of immigration.

SOMETHING TO CONSIDER 4.1

Demographics of the Years 1992 and 2050 (in Millions)

Ethnic Group	1992	% of Population	2050	% of Population	% Gain
Hispanics (all groups)	24	9	81	21	+12
African Americans	32	12	62	16	+4
Asian/Pacific Islanders	8	3	41	11	+8
Native American Indians	2	1	5	+1	<1
Non-Hispanics Whites	192	75	202	53	−22

SOURCE: Adapted from "Demographer Sees a 2050 U.S. of 383 Million, Only 53% White," by *Arkansas Democrat-Gazette*, 1992, December 4, p. 5-A.

These demographic figures and projections also illustrate the dramatic shift in ethnic populations that the United States is currently experiencing. Concurrently, the historical dichotomy of "Black versus White" is lessening as increases in non-African ancestral groups continue to increase.

Avoiding Ambiguous Cultural Terminology

This text does not focus on any single group or specific groups but rather on all the peoples who currently comprise the diverse society of the United States. The emerging trend of viewing "within-group" differences that exist among persons from the same ethnic and cultural background (e.g., Chinese Americans) is a central emphasis rather than viewing a generic group (e.g., Asian Americans; Casas, 1992; Sue, 1992).

To fully appreciate differences within cultures, terminology distinctions are warranted. It is hoped that the following discussion will clarify misconceptions and establish terminological uniqueness. School counselors are warned of the erroneous assumptions of these interchanges and are urged to use them in the proper context (S. D. Johnson, 1990).

CULTURE

The term *culture* has been defined in many ways and by many professionals. Webster's dictionary (1989) defined culture as "the customary beliefs, social forms and material traits of a racial, religious, or social group" (p. 314). The lack of specificity of this definition implies that culture is a multidimensional concept that encompasses the collective reality of a group of people (Lee, 1991). As Axelson (1993) indicated, this collective reality shapes and reinforces the attitudes and behaviors among a group of people.

A cultural group may be conceptualized as "any group of people who identify or associate with one another on the basis of some common purpose, need, or similarity of background" (Axelson, 1993, p. 3). On the other hand, Fairchild (1970) viewed culture as "all behavior patterns socially acquired and socially transmitted by means of symbols" (p. 80). Then again, Bruner (1990) believed that "culture is not a set of variables to be run off in chi-square tables" but "an integrated system, a coherent way of living and looking at the world" (p. 348); and Geertz (1973) advised individuals to embrace culture as a "text." Steward's (1972) definition included five activities: definition of social relations, motivation, perception of the world, perception of self, and the individual.

All counseling interventions, to some extent, are multicultural or cross-cultural in nature (Pedersen, 1988, 1994). Both school counselors and students bring to the counseling session a set of attitudes, behaviors, and values that have been reinforced through long-term association with a specific ethnic or cultural group. School counselors and students can be members of the same ethnic group; however, in most cases, their individual differences presume the presence of subtle cultural differences (Lee, 1991).

Then too, within the broader culture, *subcultures* have distinguishing patterns of behaviors and values that may differ from the larger culture. Examples include the subcultures of gay men and lesbian women, various religious groups, and regional cultures (e.g., the South; Porter & Samovar, 1985). These examples of subcultures illustrate the confusion and difficulty in ascertaining an inclusive definition of culture. The myriad of concepts embedded within subgroups can be synthesized to include institutions, values, language, religion, ideals, habits of thinking, symbols, artistic expressions, patterns of behavior, and patterns of social and interpersonal relationships (Banks, 1987; Lum, 1992).

Whitfield, McGrath, and Coleman (1992) identified 11 elements that can be used in understanding specific patterns. Each element can be defined for any culture and can include how members in each culture tend to:

- Define their sense of self
- Communicate and use language
- Dress and value appearances

- Embrace certain values and mores
- Embrace specific beliefs and attitudes
- Use time and space
- Relate to family and significant others
- Eat and use food in their customs
- Play and make use of leisure time
- Work and apply themselves
- Learn and use knowledge

Dominant cultural influences. Yet another factor influences the definition of culture when it is applied to the entire United States. That is, what influences have the culture of the historically dominant ethnic group of the United States (i.e., European American) had on ethnic minority groups in this nation? Locke (1992) stated, "We need to know how that culture defines a psychologically healthy individual, reinforces the family for its acculturation function, and defines the concept of community in terms of size and who is included in it" (p. 5). In short, we need to know what characteristics of European American culture have been subsumed by ethnic minority cultures in this nation.

Williams (1970) identified 15 cultural orientations that generally reflect the predominant European influences on the culture of the United States (see **Table 4.2**). The dominant culture must be understood from the perspectives of the individual, the family, and the community. In that light, perhaps a more succinct and practical definition is that culture is "the configuration of learned behavior and results of behaviors whose components and elements are shared and transmitted by the members of a particular society" (Linton, 1968, p. 32). Such a definition of culture meets the purposes of this text.

Emic, etic, and idioemic. Another way of viewing culture exists in the differentiation of the viewer's perspective. The terms *emic* and *etic* are often used to describe phenomena that have culture-specific (culturally localized) or universal (culturally generalized) application (Atkinson, Morten, & Sue, 1993; S. D. Johnson, 1990).

These terms reflect contrasting perspectives in the analyzing and describing of cultural phenomena. The emic–etic dichotomy describes a way of viewing a culture either from the outside or from the inside. Whereas etic focuses on similarities and dissimilarities of the cultures being examined, emic examines a given culture, rather than making an external comparison of cultures (Draguns, 1989). Viewing a culture as represented by individuals could be

---

TABLE 4.2

European American Influences on the Cultures of the United States

1. **Achievement and success:**	Rags-to-riches success stories
2. **Activity and work:**	Discipline and productivity
3. **Humanitarian mores:**	Spontaneous aid to others, especially the "underdog"
4. **Moral orientation:**	Life events and situations are judged in terms of right and wrong
5. **Efficiency and practicality:**	An emphasis placed on practical values of achievements
6. **Progress:**	An optimistic view is held that things will improve
7. **Material comfort:**	"The good life"
8. **Equality:**	Commitment to concept of equality
9. **Freedom:**	Individual right to individual freedoms
10. **External conformity:**	Uniformity in matters external to self (houses, etc.)
11. **Science and secular rationality:**	Esteem for the sciences as means of mastery over the environment
12. **Nationalism/patriotism:**	Strong sense of loyalty to the nation
13. **Democracy:**	Every person has a voice in political matters
14. **Individual personality:**	The group should not take precedent over the individual
15. **Racism:**	Emphasizes differential evaluation of racial, religious, and ethnic and cultural groups

SOURCE: Adapted from *American Society: A Sociological Interpretation*, by R. M. Williams, Jr., 1970.

---

described as taking an *idioemic* perspective (i.e., examining a particular manifestation of the emic). Thus, emic, etic, and idioemic are categorically related, as they are all classes of context, and none replicates the other exactly (S. D. Johnson, 1990).

Culturally deprived versus culturally disadvantaged. The term *culturally deprived* implies the lack or absence of culture. The racial and ethnic groups discussed in this book clearly possess and transmit their own cultures, as well as parts of the larger society's culture. The term *culturally disadvantaged* suggests that the group to which it is applied is at a disadvantage because that group lacks the cultural background formed by the controlling social structure. The use of *disadvantaged* rather than *deprived* is intended not only to recognize that the individual possesses a cultural heritage but also to suggest it is not the "right" culture.

The more acceptable terms *culturally different* and *culturally distinct* can also convey negative connotations when they imply that a person's culture is not equal to or incongruent with the dominant or accepted culture. The inappropriateness of these terms occurs when their reference is restricted to ethnically diverse students (Atkinson et al., 1993).

STEREOTYPING, PREJUDICE, RACISM, AND DISCRIMINATION

The concepts of stereotypes, prejudice, racism, and discrimination are often misinterpreted as referents to the same behaviors or values. In reality, these terms are not synonymous; rather, they denote distinct characteristics.

Stereotypes. Stereotyping individuals or groups is often the leading cause of prejudice, racism, and discrimination. A *stereotype* is an overgeneralization about an individual or group. Some authors conclude that stereotypes are inevitable and necessary coping mechanisms for avoiding cognitive overload (e.g., Schaefer, 1988). Stereotypes are often negative generalizations about a group that results in prejudiced individuals placing blame on the out-group, not admitting uncomfortable feelings about themselves, and structuring their own world according to their rationale (Brislin, 1981). In addition, stereotypes have been criticized for being incorrect generalizations, generalizations of unspecified validity, products of faulty thought processes characterized by rigidity, and conditioned beliefs based on limited experience.

The Native American Indian is an excellent example of an ethnic minority group that has been subject to historical and contemporary stereotyping. Stereotypical and negative images of these peoples have permeated textbooks, films, research literature, and the news media. These distortions have ranged from portrayals of Native American Indians as being naive and passive to being brutal and savage (Herring, 1991, 1997a, 1997b).

Prejudice. Morris (1980) defined *prejudice* as "an adverse judgment or opinion formed beforehand or without knowledge or examination of the facts" or "irrational suspicion or hatred of a particular group, race, or religion"

(Morris, 1980, p. 1033). In some instances, the development and perpetuation of stereotypes are necessary functions of prejudice (Schaefer, 1988), such as in the Klu Klux Klan.

Prejudices are operationalized in negative and positive ways, but for the present discussion, racial and ethnic prejudices are paramount. These prejudices continue to pervade both social and political realms in the United States (e.g., Ponterotto & Pedersen, 1993). Ethnic prejudice is a negative belief about an individual or group that is justified on the basis of skin color or other physical characteristics, or on behaviors or beliefs common to a group that set it apart (Bryant, 1994). Similarly, in the educational realm, prejudicial attitudes among college students have been clearly demonstrated (e.g., Ancis, Choney, & Sedlacek, 1996). Another example exists in the creation of the gay and lesbian minority by the psychological community out of the prejudices of the majority culture (Pope, 1995).

Racism. Morris (1980) defined *racism* as "the notion that one's own ethnic stock is superior" (p. 1075). Some authors take the position that racism is a disease, noting that, like other mental disorders, racism is based on a distortion of reality (Skillings & Dobbins, 1991). For those readers who are still reluctant to accept the continued presence of racism in the United States, the Anti-Defamation League (1992) found that, in surveying U.S. households, many citizens believe that a wide variety of subcultures in this nation experience prejudice and discrimination, as summarized in **Table 4.3**.

Whereas the concept of culture has been based on such characteristics as shared personality traits, values, belief systems, and life patterns, *race* has been defined in two ways: a biological classification and a biological social classification.

1. *Biological basis.* "To the biologist, a race, or subspecies, is an inbreeding, geographically isolated population that differs in distinguishable physical traits from other members of the species" (Zuckerman, 1990, p. 1297). Basic to a biological definition of race is the view that humans can be divided into a number of genetic groups on the basis of genetically transmitted physical characteristics and differences therein.

However, the biological definition of race becomes vague if the extent of intermarriage and the variance in physical characteristics of individuals who are of similar racial heritage are considered. Excluding superficial physical characteristics, more similarities between groups than differences are found and more differences exist within racial groups than between them (Littlefield,

TABLE 4.3

Percentage of Discrimination and Prejudice U.S. Citizens Think
Various Groups Face Today

Group	Tremendous Amount	A Lot	Some	A Little	None	Not Sure
African Americans	16	50	22	8	3	2
Jews	4	22	39	22	11	2
Italians	1	7	29	32	27	4
Homosexuals	21	53	14	6	4	3
Catholics	1	8	24	29	36	2
Whites in general	2	11	25	26	35	1
Women	5	29	37	20	8	1
Asians	3	26	38	21	9	4
Hispanics	6	32	37	16	6	3

SOURCE: Adapted from *Anti-Defamation League Survey on Anti-Semitism and Prejudice in America*, by the Anti-Defamation League, 1992, p. 4.

Lieberman, & Reynolds, 1982). Also, no biological explanation can be found explaining why some physical features have been selected to determine race whereas others have not.

The concept of different races evolving from a common genetic pool also can be questioned. Kuper (1956/1975) conceptualized that "the human species shares a pool of genes and may be defined as a community of genes" and the "vast majority of genes are the same for all human beings; only a relatively small proportion differentiates the races" (p. 15). Tobias (1972) estimated that 90% to 95% of genes "are common to all men [i.e., men and women]" and that only 5% to 10% of all human genes "are concerned with the little superficial frill of variation which makes for the differences among races" (p. 23). Schaefer (1988) emphasized that "given frequent migration, exploration, and invasions, pure gene frequencies have not existed for some time, if they ever did" (p. 12). Furthermore, scientists cannot agree on how many races exist, with estimates ranging from 3 to 200. L. C. Dunn (1975) suggested that "races are themselves changeable, which is to say that 'race' is not fixed or static but a dynamic one" (p. 41).

These disagreements suggest little agreement about the definition of race. However, although race in the biological sense has no biological consequences, what people believe about race has very profound social consequences (Mack, 1968). One major consequence is often manifested through ideological racism, an ideology that links physical characteristics of groups of people to psychological and intellectual characteristics (Feagin, 1989).

2. *Biological social basis.* A second definition of race combines biological and social components. Morris (1980) defined race as "any group of people united or classified together on the basis of common history, nationality, or geographical distribution" (p. 1075). This definition reinforces Cox's (1948) social perspective definition of race as "any people who are distinguished or consider themselves distinguished, in social relations with other peoples, by their physical characteristics" (p. 402). The social component is dependent on group identity, either evolving within the group or assigned by those outside the group. Regardless of its biological validity, the concept of race has taken on important social meaning in how outsiders view members of a "racial" group and how individuals within the "racial" group view themselves, members of their group, and members of other "racial" groups (Atkinson et al., 1993, p. 7).

Ascribed and self-reported racial designations have not been demonstrated to be useful in making meaningful distinctions between groups or adequate in amplifying within-group comparisons (Parham & Helms, 1982). In short, racial classifications draw attention to group characteristics, ignore or submerge the individual, and contribute to the perpetuation and maintenance of destructive racial stereotypes (S. D. Johnson, 1990).

Van den Berghe (1967) defined social racism as

> any set of beliefs that organic, genetically transmitted differences (whether real or imagined) between human groups are intrinsically associated with the presence or the absence of certain socially relevant abilities or characteristics, hence that such differences are a legitimate basis of invidious distinctions between groups socially defined as races. (p. 9)

If this definition of racism is accepted, three conditions must be present simultaneously to constitute an act of racism: the physical criteria; the belief that cultural, moral, or intellectual differences correspond to the physical differences; and social actions (e.g., discrimination) based on those beliefs.

Discrimination. Whereas prejudice and stereotyping represent attitudes and beliefs held by individuals, *discrimination* is an active behavior. The individual intentionally transforms irrational prejudices into physical acts of violence, hostility, or exclusion. Such acts negatively affect individuals within ethnic or cultural groups (Lum, 1992). For example, the incarceration of Japanese Americans into internment camps during World War II illustrates discrimination. Past and current unfair hiring practices also constitute discrimination.

ETHNICITY

Ethnicity is another term that contributes to confusion in multi- and cross-cultural counseling. Members of an ethnic group share a common ancestry that may include specific cultural and social patterns (Davis, 1978). Ethnicity is based on long-term patterns of behavior that have some historical significance and include similar religious, ancestral, language, and cultural characteristics (Neukrug, 1994).

Glazer (1971) defined ethnicity in much broader terms:

Thus one possible position on ethnicity and race, and the one I hold, is that they form part of a single family of social identities—a family which, in addition to races and ethnic groups, includes religions . . . language groups . . . and all which can be included in the most general term, ethnic groups, groups defined by descent, real or mythical, and sharing a common history and experience. (p. 447)

A more narrow definition of ethnicity distinguishes groups on the basis of nationality or cultural characteristics, with physical characteristics not necessarily a part of ethnic differences. Thus, an ethnic group may be defined as a group in which the members share a unique social and cultural heritage passed from one generation to the next or as a group "set apart from others because of their national origin or distinctive cultural patterns" (Schaefer, 1988, p. 9).

In short, various *ethnic* groups within *racial* categories have their own unique *cultures* (S. D. Johnson, 1990). Therefore, Jews, who share religious and perhaps similar ancestral characteristics, may be considered an ethnic group but may not share the same culture; similarly, Asian people may be considered a race by some but may not share the same culture or the same ethnic group (Neukrug, 1994).

DEGREE OF CULTURATION

School counselors need to be knowledgeable about their ethnic students' degree of culturation. Inherent to understanding cultural and ethnical differences and similarities, the school counselor must determine the degree of acculturation, enculturation, or assimilation of a student. The following distinctions serve as an encouragement for school counselors and counseling students to research further into the complexities of these concepts.

Acculturation. *Acculturation* is another term with various definitions, depending largely on the academic discipline. For example, anthropologists use the term to refer to "those phenomena which result when groups of individuals have different cultures and come into first-hand contact with subsequent changes in the original pattern of either or both groups" (Redfield, Linton, & Herskovits, 1936, p. 149). Gordon (1964) identified acculturation simply as one of seven different types of assimilation. Acculturation can refer to cultural assimilation or the acquisition of the cultural patterns of the dominant society. In addition, it requires that structural assimilation be achieved, or as suggested by McLemore (1983), that "members of the two groups interact with one another as friends and equals and that they select marriage partners without regard to ethnic or racial identities" (p. 35).

Although originally proposed as a group-level phenomenon, acculturation is also recognized as an individual-level phenomenon—*psychological acculturation*. At the individual level, psychological acculturation describes changes in an individual whose cultural group is experiencing acculturation collectively (Graves, 1967). Such changes may be manifested in both overt behaviors and covert traits.

Individuals who experience acculturation (by migration, displacement, or colonization) must deal with their new circumstances in some way (Berry, Kim, & Boski, 1988). Berry's (1976) study identified three strategies that individuals use in adapting to new cultural environments: adjustment, reaction, and withdrawal. In the adjustment strategy, the individual's behavioral changes reduce the conflict and increase the congruence between the environment and the individual. This strategy is often referred to as *adaptation*. In the reaction strategy, the individual's behavioral changes retaliate against the environment. In the case of withdrawal, the individual's behavior reduces

These three strategies of adaption are similar to the distinctions in the psychological literature made among "moving with or toward," "moving against," and "moving away" from a stimulus (Lewin, 1936; Munroe, 1955). **Figure 4.1** depicts a workable framework for the comparative study of acculturation. Within this framework, societies and individuals can be studied from the variables of voluntariness of contact and mobility factors. In addition, this matrix includes the variables of the five basic types of acculturating groups (i.e., immigrants, refugees, Native Peoples, ethnic groups, and sojourners).

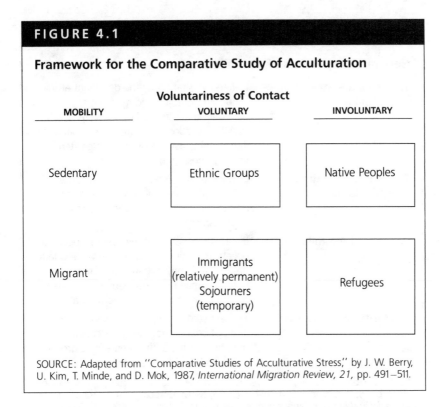

FIGURE 4.1

Framework for the Comparative Study of Acculturation

MOBILITY	Voluntariness of Contact	
	VOLUNTARY	INVOLUNTARY
Sedentary	Ethnic Groups	Native Peoples
Migrant	Immigrants (relatively permanent) Sojourners (temporary)	Refugees

SOURCE: Adapted from "Comparative Studies of Acculturative Stress," by J. W. Berry, U. Kim, T. Minde, and D. Mok, 1987, *International Migration Review, 21*, pp. 491–511.

Most current professionals who deal with cultural concepts accept Mc-Lemore's (1983) description of Gordon's (1964) model. **Table 4.4** presents a brief description of this model. As Axelson (1993) noted, "assuming that the preceding theoretical propositions are valid, individuals in a group may be at different stages of the inclusion process. Past a certain point, assimilation becomes inevitable" (pp. 78–79).

A dominant purpose of these categories of individuals is the desire to live in the way that they believe is the best or most natural for them. Whether a culturally pluralistic mode of existence can accommodate diverse groups and also sustain a national entity, of course, remains to be seen (Schlesinger, 1991). Currently, more popular concepts, such as multiculturalism and cultural diversity, are used when referring to this culturally pluralistic nation.

Implications of degree of culturation. Culturation (whether enculturation or acculturation) is a major and complex construct (Domino & Acosta, 1987). The concept describes "the changes in behaviors and values made by members of one culture as a result of contact with another culture" (Burnam,

TABLE 4.4

General Components of Assimilation

1. Secondary Structural Assimilation:	Defined as sharing by the dominant ethnic group and ethnic minority groups; generally characterized by formality and social interactions that are impersonal, cold, and distant; psychosocial climate often found in desegregated schools.
2. Primary Structural Assimilation:	Defined as the entry of ethnic minority groups into social functions such as clubs and cliques; less formal and personal, warm "friendships."
3. Cultural Assimilation:	Involves the loss of ethnic identity, personal beliefs and values, religion, native language, traditional family patterns, and interest in heritage; may be permanent, or resurgence of ethnic pride may occur occasionally.
4. Marital Assimilation:	The last step in the process toward cultural and national homogeneity; occurs between members of the assimilated ethnic group and members of the ethnic majority group.

SOURCE: From *Counseling and Development in a Multicultural Society*, by J. A. Axelson, 1993, p. 78; *Assimilation in American Life*, by M. M. Gordon, 1964, p. 24; as adapted by *Racial and Ethnic Relations in America*, by S. D. McLemore, 1983, pp. 38–39.

Telles, Hough, & Escobar, 1987, p. 106). The *ac* or *en* prefixes denote the voluntariness (*acculturation*) or coerciveness (*enculturation*) of that action.

Culturation can be understood as a one-way process in which an individual is assimilated into the host culture, or as a bicultural or multicultural process in which the individual selects or integrates different components from different cultures (Burnam et al., 1987; Domino & Acosta, 1987; Garza & Gallegos, 1985). A bicultural orientation implies that cultural change does not necessarily or exclusively entail movement toward the dominant culture. In fact, multicultural persons frequently demonstrate many adaptive strengths and flexibility.

Several studies have provided consistent evidence that the degree of culturation is related to how ethnic students perceive and respond to school counseling services: Hispanic American students (Kunkel, 1990; Pomales & Williams, 1989; Sanchez & Atkinson, 1983); Asian American students (Atkinson & Gim, 1989; Atkinson et al., 1993; Gim, Atkinson, & Kim, 1991; Gim, Atkinson, & Whiteley, 1990); and Native American Indian students (Herring, 1994, 1997b; M. E. Johnson & Lashley, 1989). These studies suggest that less-culturated ethnic minorities are more likely to trust and express a preference for, and a willingness to see, an ethnically similar school counselor than are their more culturated counterparts.

Worldview variances. Extremely cogent to a student's degree of culturation is that student's worldview, that is, from what perspective does that student look at his or her current status and future plans within society? Determining a student's worldview is essential for counseling success. The following three popular models have been developed to assist multicultural counselors in assessing ethnic minority students' world perspective.

1. *Fixed-role model.* The *fixed-role model* of Kelly (1955) attempts to change an individual's personal constructs that may be invalid, faulty, too narrow, or too broad. If a *personal construct* is defined as the way an individual consistently perceives likenesses and differences over time (Powell-Hopson & Hopson, 1990), then the goal of counseling would be to identify an individual's dichotomous personal constructs. This identification can be obtained through the use of the Cultural Attitudes Repertory Technique (Kelly, 1955; Neimeyer & Fukuyama, 1984).

2. *Existential world view theory.* A second model exists in the *existential world view theory* of Ibrahim and her associates (Ibrahim, 1991, 1993; Ibrahim & Kahn, 1984, 1987). This model attempts to reduce chances of racial and cultural oppression by considering pancultural issues related to human existence (Ibrahim, 1993). School counselors must consider their personal worldview and cultural identity before they attempt to analyze dissimilar students' reactions. The tendency to focus on the student, without understanding the person of the counselor, violates the student in many ways, and in a cross-cultural encounter qualifies as "cultural oppression." Ibrahim (1991) contended that knowledge of students' worldviews individualizes the counseling process. Ibrahim also acknowledged the influence of one's worldview on thoughts, feelings, perceptions, decision making, and problem solving. Worldviews should be determined during the initial session and a recommended instrument is *The Scale to Assess World Views* (Ibrahim & Kahn, 1984, 1987). This instrument assesses worldviews of human nature, social relations, relations with nature, and time orientation. In addition, this tool can differentiate between a student's worldview and cultural view (Ibrahim, 1991).

3. *Locus of control/locus of responsibility model.* Sue and his colleagues (Sue, 1978; Sue & Sue, 1977) defined a worldview as the way individuals perceive their relationship to the world, including people, institutions, nature, and things. One dimension of this worldview is based on Rotter's (1966, 1975) distinction between *internal locus of control* (IC), in which reinforcement is contingent on a person's own actions, and *external locus of control* (EC), in which consequences are perceived to result from luck, chance, fate, or powerful others. Sue added the dimension of an *internal locus of responsibility* (IR), in which success is attributed to a person's skills, resulting in "person blame," and an *external locus of responsibility* (ER), in which the sociocultural environment is more potent than the individual, resulting in "system blame." In Sue's classification, the following worldview mindsets result: IC-IR exemplifies European American middle-class cultural values; EC-IR describes ethnic minority persons likely to have little control over how others define them; EC-ER is typical among ethnic minorities who blame their problems on an oppressive social system in which they are powerless; and IC-ER assumes the belief in one's ability to achieve personal goals if given a chance (see **Figure 4.2**; see also Sue & Sue, 1990, for an in-depth discussion).

SOCIAL CLASS

An individual's *social class* may cut across an individual's common ethnic, cultural, or racial heritage. Therefore, even though individuals may share similar heritages, they may have little in common with one another because of differences in social class (Neukrug, 1994). For example, a poor, reservation Native American Indian may find little in common with a wealthy, urban Native American Indian. In essence, social class may be a "missing dimension" in understanding diversity (Hannon, Ritchie, & Rye, 1992).

POWER DIFFERENTIALS

Neukrug (1994) cautioned school counselors that, in the rapidly changing culture of the United States, power differentials may represent greater disparities between people than culture, ethnicity, race, or social class. The Japanese American businessman who holds an upper-level management position may be disliked because of the power he holds over his employees rather than his ethnicity. Or the Puerto Rican female gang leader may be disliked by a male African American gang member because of her position in the gang hierarchy.

FIGURE 4.2

Graphic Representation of Worldviews

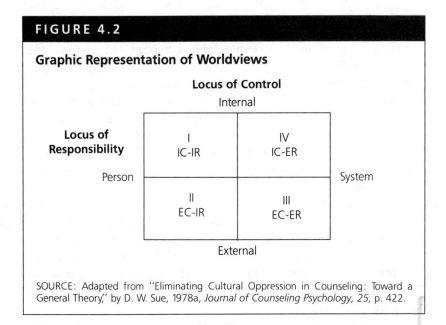

Locus of Control

Internal

Locus of Responsibility	I IC-IR	IV IC-ER

Person   System

	II EC-IR	III EC-ER

External

SOURCE: Adapted from "Eliminating Cultural Oppression in Counseling: Toward a General Theory," by D. W. Sue, 1978a, *Journal of Counseling Psychology, 25,* p. 422.

MINORITY

The term *minority* has been widely used in this country since the 1950s with reference to racial and ethnic groups and more recently with respect to nonethnic groups (Atkinson & Hackett, 1993). Its use is based on Wirth's (1945) definition that minorities are groups who "because of physical or cultural characteristics, are singled out from the others in society in which they live for differential and unequal treatment" (p. 347). In recent years, the term has been generalized to any group oppressed by those in power. This definition operationally includes racial and ethnic minorities, cultural groups, women, gay men and lesbian women, the elderly, and persons who are challenged medically, physically, or mentally. In addition, minority groups are generally considered to constitute less than 50% of the population.

In common usage, however, numerical size alone does not determine minority status. For example, from a regional perspective, Hispanics are the numerical majority in many cities such as East Los Angeles (94.7%) and San Antonio (55.6%); African Americans compose 62% of the population of New Orleans and 76% of the population of Detroit (*Rand McNally,* 1995). For the purposes of this discussion, racial and ethnic minority refers specifically to groups of people who are singled out for discrimination.

TERMS ASSOCIATED WITH SPECIFIC ETHNIC AND RACIAL GROUPS

A lack of unanimity exists about the most appropriate terms to use when referring to specific racial and ethnic groups, including the European Americans. Some terms may be acceptable regionally or generationally but not nationally. In addition, terms associated with specific racial or ethnic groups are problematic because they fail to recognize within-group ethnic differences in the larger group.

Terms such as African American, Asian American, Native American Indian, Hispanic American, and European American have become commonly accepted as appropriate, but by no means universally accepted, referents for the major ethnic groups in the United States. This author uses these terms for organizational purposes and acknowledges that such groupings are in reality an oversimplification, and apologizes to readers who may find the terms insensitive. This author also prefers noncolor designations of racial groups. This preference is congruent with the emerging trend of identifying the region (or more specifically, country) of ancestral origin (e.g., Chinese American rather than Asian American).

The school counselor must be sensitive to the ethnic minority student's preferred term for self-identification. If the issue of racial or ethnic identity appears ambiguous or if the topic is broached, the school counselor may want to simply ask the student how he or she self-identifies.

AMERICA/AMERICAN

These terms are continuously misused and inappropriately applied by professionals and lay persons. The basic error in the usage of these terms rests in the presumption of citizens of the United States that they are the only people with claim to the terminology. Other citizens of North America (i.e., Canadians and Mexicans), Central Americans, and South Americans are entitled to these designations just as legitimately as citizens of the United States are. The use of "America" and "American" may not be intentional arrogance or ethnic bigotry; however, citizens in this nation need to more sensitive to the potential impropriety of exclusive usage of them.

Having reviewed briefly the various interpretations of culture and the ambiguous terminology used in relevant discussions, the focus will now be on the role of culture and the family.

Culture and the Family

The importance of ethnicity to family dynamics and structure has too frequently been overlooked by school counselors. When not ignored or overlooked by school counselors, ethnic minority families more often are measured against the dominant culture's acceptance of what constitutes a "normal" family. J. Dunn (1988) stated that the school counselor's "ignorance is in part a result of the way in which developmental psychology has grown and is practiced. Children have rarely been studied in the world in which these developments take place, or in a context in which we can be sensitive to the subtleties of their social understanding" (p. 5).

The philosophical orientations and ideologies of the historically dominant culture are diametrically opposed to the indigenous cultural values and structures of ethnic minority families. In addition, the interactive patterns of the ethnic minority family have undergone structural changes over the years. As a result, ethnic minority families are often faced with adopting new roles, such as those of the single-parent and stepparent, that conflict with traditional cultural norms.

Considerable interethnic group diversity, as well as significant intragroup heterogeneity, exists within ethnic minority families. Consequently, attempts to delineate and systematize knowledge about ethnic minority family structures and principles risk potential stereotyping.

A culturally sensitive framework for counseling with ethnic families must incorporate six major factors that distinguish ethnic minorities from mainstream middle-class European American families. These factors are (a) ethnic minority reality, (b) impact of external systems on ethnic minority cultures, (c) biculturalism, (d) ethnic difference in minority status, (e) language, and (f) social class (Ho, 1987).

The development of a healthy ethnic identity originates in the individual's personal group identity. Ethnic identity begins with the individual's family network. Children begin to understand that they are members of a particular group as early as 5 years of age, and by the age of 10, they are able to distinguish specific differences between groups (Allport, 1958). The importance of a family and the rewards of being a part of the family reinforce the group values of that family. These values are interrelated and associated with the family's religion, ethics, culture, ethnic affiliations, as well as occupational and social status.

Ethnic socialization refers to the developmental processes by which children acquire the values, perceptions, attitudes, and behaviors of a specific ethnic group and evolve to view themselves and others as members of such groups (Rotheram & Phinney, 1987). At early elementary age, ethnicity and culture influence children primarily through the family, peers, and school. The initial phase of children's ethnic identity development involves learning about the ethnicity of their parents. As children reach middle childhood, their understanding of society expands. During this phase, ethnic minority children learn about discrimination, political power, and the socioeconomic resources of their ethnic group. As they approach and enter the adolescent phase, teenagers begin to develop a personal self-identity and an ethnic identity. An entirely different process occurs in genetically mixed children.

Ethnic minority youths are often faced with a conflict between the values of their own group and those of the majority culture. Rather than the degree of culturation, the lack of bicultural involvement and flexibility appears to be a major source of stress for ethnic minority children (Szapocznik & Kurtines, 1980).

For illustrative purposes, Valencia, Henderson, and Rankin (1985) studied the relationship between family variables and cognitive performance. These authors examined the relative contribution of several family status variables (child and parental language, parental schooling attainment, and socioeconomic status) and a family constellation variable (family size) to predict cognitive performance among 140 Mexican American preschool children from low-income backgrounds. Within the limitations of generalization, the research suggested that home environmental processes show a strong association with intellectual development, independent of parental schooling, language, socioeconomic status, and family constellation.

A more recent study (Manaster, Chan, & Safady, 1992) attempted to compare academically successful and academically unsuccessful high-risk Mexican American migrant high school students. The results indicated that the unsuccessful student group came from families that were larger, poorer, more rural, and more foreign (i.e., more parents and children were born in Mexico) than the successful students' families. Regarding the psychological indicators of culturation, the successful group was found to score higher on modernism, to be more stably culturated, to have a clearer sense of self, to have higher occupational aspirations, and to tend to desire jobs with greater responsibility and stability than did the unsuccessful group.

In summary, Ho (1987) contended that "the ethnic minority families' retention of their traditional heritage and persistent adherence to their own ethnicity should have important implications in the conceptualization of a practice theory that addresses their needs and problems" (p. 19). In addition, as has already been emphasized, the degree of culturation and assimilation will have an important impact on the specifics of the counseling process.

Summary

This chapter has attempted to survey the role of culture in the development of ethnic minority youths. A primary emphasis is placed on the importance of school counselors' understanding of the importance in distinguishing terminology and assessing the degree of culturation among their ethnic minority students. Inherent to these emphases, school counselors are held accountable for ensuring that their counseling and guidance program planning and implementation are culturally and ethnically appropriate. In the words of Lee (1996),

> Although there may be questions raised and frustration expressed by school counselors attempting to address the educational, career, and personal/social concerns of students from diverse cultural backgrounds, the major demographic changes impacting the nation's schools present these professionals with a great opportunity. (p. 14)

School counselors will meet this challenge. They will provide the most appropriate counseling services for their students. They will ensure that each student is afforded the opportunity to become the best that they can. School counselors will succeed in this endeavor—they can do no less.

Experiential Activities

1. In your particular situation, how have you observed the changing ethnic demographics?
2. What examples of prejudice and stereotyping have you observed? Instances of racism and discrimination?
3. What are your thoughts about the issue of race, given that less than 1% of the population of the world can document pure racial ancestry? Is ethnicity a more accurate term? Why or why not?
4. How have you "bought" into the European influences on the culture of this country? Respond even if you are of European American heritage.
5. Give some examples of how you, as a school counselor, can incorporate the information presented in this chapter into a school counseling program. In school counseling practice.

References

Allport, G. W. (1958). *The nature of prejudice*. New York: Addison-Wesley.

Ancis, J. R., Choney, S. K., & Sedlacek, W. E. (1996). University student attitudes toward American Indians. *Journal of Multicultural Counseling and Development, 24*, 26–27.

Anti-Defamation League. (1992). *Anti-Defamation League survey on anti-semitism and prejudice in America*. New York: Author.

Atkinson, D. R., & Gim, R. H. (1989). Asian-American cultural identity and attitudes toward mental health services. *Journal of Counseling Psychology, 36*, 209–212.

Atkinson, D. R., & Hackett, G. (1993). *Counseling diverse populations*. Dubuque, IA: Brown & Benchmark.

Atkinson, D. R., Morten, G., & Sue, D. W. (1993). *Counseling American minorities: A cross-cultural perspective* (4th ed.). Dubuque, IA: Brown & Benchmark.

Axelson, J. A. (1993). *Counseling and development in a multicultural society* (2nd ed.). Monterey, CA: Brooks/Cole.

Banks, J. A. (1987). *Teaching strategies for ethnic students* (4th ed.). Boston: Allyn & Bacon.

Baruth, L. G., & Manning, M. L. (1991). *Multicultural counseling and psychotherapy: A lifestyle perspective.* New York: Merrill.

Berry, J. W. (1976). *Human ecology and cognitive style: Comparative studies in cultural and psychological adaptation.* New York: Sage/Halsted.

Berry, J. W., Kim, U., & Boski, P. (1988). Psychological acculturation of immigrants. In Y. Y. Kim & B. Gudykunst (Eds.), *Cross-cultural adaptations: Current approaches* (pp. 62–89). Newbury Park, CA: Sage.

Berry, J. W., Kim, U., Minde, T., & Mok, D. (1987). Comparative studies of acculturative stress. *International Migration Review, 21,* 491–511.

Brislin, R. W. (1981). *Cross-cultural encounters: Face-to-face interaction.* New York: Pergamon.

Bruner, J. (1990). Culture and human development: A new look. *Human Development, 33,* 344–355.

Bryant, B. K. (Compiler). (1994). *Counseling for racial understanding.* Alexandria, VA: American Counseling Association.

Burnam, M. A., Telles, C. A., Hough, R. L., & Escobar, J. I. (1987). Measurement of acculturation in community population of Mexican Americans. *Hispanic Journal of Behavioral Science, 9,* 105–130.

Casas, E. (1992, August). *Multicultural counseling research: Proposing an agenda for the 90s.* Paper presented at the annual convention of the American Psychological Association, Washington, DC.

Cox, O. C. (1948). *Caste, class, and race.* Garden City, NY: Doubleday.

Davis, F. J. (1978). *Minority–dominant relations: A sociological analysis.* Arlington Heights, IL: AHM.

Demographer sees a 2050 U.S. of 383 million, only 53% White. (1992, December 4). *Arkansas Democrat-Gazette,* p. 5-A.

Domino, G., & Acosta, A. (1987). The relation of acculturation and values in Mexican Americans. *Hispanic Journal of Behavior Science, 9,* 191–250.

Douglass, F. (1962). *Life and times of Frederick Douglass: The complete autobiography.* New York: Collier Books. (Original work published 1892)

Draguns, J. G. (1989). Dilemmas and choices in cross-cultural counseling: The universal versus the culturally distinctive. In P. Pedersen, J. G. Draguns, J. Lonner, & J. E. Trimble (Eds.), *Counseling across cultures* (3rd ed., pp. 3–21). Honolulu: University of Hawaii Press.

Dunn, J. (1988). *The beginnings of social understanding.* Cambridge, MA: Harvard University Press.

Dunn, L. C. (1975). Race and biology. In L. Kuper (Ed.), *Race, science and society* (pp. 31–67). New York: Columbia University Press.

Fairchild, H. P. (Ed.). (1970). *Dictionary of sociology and related sciences.* Totowa, NJ: Rowan & Allanheld.

Feagin, J. R. (1989). *Racial and ethnic relations.* Englewood Cliffs, NJ: Prentice Hall.

Garza, R. T., & Gallegos, P. I. (1985). Environmental influences and personal choice: A humanistic perspective on acculturation. *Hispanic Journal of Behavioral Science, 7,* 365–379.

Geertz, C. (1973). *The interpretation of cultures.* New York: Basic Books.

German-Americans are largest U.S. ethnic group, Census says. (1992, December 20). *Fayetteville Observer-Times,* p. 26-A.

Gim, R. H., Atkinson, D. R., & Kim, S. J. (1991). Asian American acculturation, counselor ethnicity and cultural sensitivity, and ratings of counselors. *Journal of Counseling Psychology, 38,* 57–62.

Gim, R. H., Atkinson, D. R., & Whiteley, S. (1990). Asian-American acculturation, severity of concerns, and willingness to see a counselor. *Journal of Counseling Psychology, 37,* 281–285.

Glazer, N. (1971). Blacks and ethnic groups: The difference, and the political difference it makes. *Social Problems, 18,* 447.

Gordon, M. M. (1964). *Assimilation in American life.* New York: Oxford University Press.

Graves, T. (1967). Psychological acculturation in a tri-ethnic community. *Southwestern Journal of Anthropology, 23,* 337–350.

Hannon, J. W., Ritchie, M. R., & Rye, D. A. (1992, September). *Class: The missing dimension in multicultural counseling and counselor education.* Paper presented at the Association for Counselor Education and Supervision National Conference, San Antonio, TX.

Herring, R. D. (1989). The American Native family: Dissolution by coercion. *Journal of Multicultural Counseling and Development, 17,* 4–13.

Herring, R. D. (1991). Counseling Native American youth. In C. C. Lee & B. L. Richardson (Eds.), *Multicultural issues in counseling: New approaches to diversity* (pp. 37–47). Alexandria, VA: American Association for Counseling and Development.

Herring, R. D. (1994). Native American Indian identity: A people of many peoples. In E. P. Salett & D. R. Koslow (Eds.), *Race, ethnicity, and self: Identity in multicultural perspective* (pp. 170–197). Washington, DC: National MultiCultural Institute.

Herring, R. D. (1997a). *Counseling diverse ethnic youth: Strategies and interventions for school counselors.* Fort Worth, TX: Harcourt Brace.

Herring, R. D. (1997b). Counseling Native American youth. In C. C. Lee (Ed.), *Multicultural issues in counseling: New approaches to diversity* (2nd ed.). Alexandria, VA: American Counseling Association.

Ho, M. K. (1987). *Family therapy with ethnic minorities.* Newbury Park, CA: Sage.

Ibrahim, F. A. (1991). Contribution of cultural worldview to generic counseling and development. *Journal of Counseling & Development, 70,* 13–19.

Ibrahim, F. A. (1993). Existential world view theory: Transcultural counseling. In J. McFadden (Ed.), *Transcultural counseling: Bilateral and international perspectives* (pp. 23–57). Alexandria, VA: American Counseling Association.

Ibrahim, F. A., & Kahn, H. (1984). *Scale to Assess World Views.* Unpublished manuscript, University of Connecticut, Storrs.

Ibrahim, F. A., & Kahn, H. (1987). Assessment of world views. *Psychological Reports, 60,* 163–176.

Johnson, M. E., & Lashley, K. H. (1989). Influence of Native-Americans' cultural commitment on preference for counselor ethnicity and expectations about counseling. *Journal of Multicultural Counseling and Development, 17,* 115–122.

Johnson, S. D. (1990). Toward clarifying culture, race, and ethnicity in the context of multicultural counseling. *Journal of Multicultural Counseling and Development, 18,* 41–50.

Kelly, G. A. (1955). *The psychology of personal constructs: Vol. 1. A theory of personality. Vol. 2. Clinical diagnosis and psychotherapy.* New York: Norton.

Kunkel, M. A. (1990). Expectations about counseling in relation to acculturation in Mexican-American and Anglo-American student samples. *Journal of Counseling Psychology, 37,* 286–292.

Kuper, L. (Ed.). (1975). *Race, science and society.* New York: Columbia University Press. (Original work published as *The race question in modern science,* 1956)

Lee, C. C. (1991). Cultural dynamics: Their importance in multicultural counseling. In C. C. Lee & B. L. Richardson (Eds.), *Multicultural issues in counseling: New approaches to diversity* (pp. 11–17). Alexandria, VA: American Association for Counseling and Development.

Lee, C. C. (1996). *Counseling for diversity: A guide for school counselors and related professionals.* Boston: Allyn & Bacon.

Lewin, K. (1936). *Principles of topological psychology.* New Haven, CT: McGraw-Hill.

Linton, R. W. (1968). *The cultural background of personality.* New York: Appleton-Century.

Littlefield, A., Lieberman, L., & Reynolds, L. T. (1982). Redefining race: The potential demise of a concept in anthropology. *Current Anthropology, 23,* 641–647.

Locke, D. C. (1992). *Increasing multicultural understanding: A comprehensive model.* Newbury Park, CA: Sage.

Logan, R. W. (1957). *The Negro in the United States: A brief history.* Princeton, NJ: Van Nostrand.

Lum, D. (1992). *Social work practice and people of color: A process-stage approach* (2nd ed.). Monterey, CA: Brooks/Cole.

Mack, R. W. (1968). *Race, class and power.* New York: American Book.

Manaster, G. J., Chan, J. C., & Safady, R. (1992). Mexican-American migrant students' academic success: Sociological and psychological acculturation. *Adolescence, 27,* 124–136.

McCormick, T. E. (1984). Multiculturalism: Some principles and issues. *Theory Into Practice, 23,* 93–97.

McLemore, S. D. (1983). *Racial and ethnic relations in America* (2nd ed.). Boston: Allyn & Bacon.

Morris, W. (Ed.). (1980). *The American Heritage dictionary of the English language.* Boston: Houghton Mifflin.

Munroe, R. (1955). Schools of psychoanalytic thought. New York: Holt, Rinehart & Winston.

Neimeyer, G. J., & Fukuyama, M. (1984). Exploring the content and structure of cross-cultural attitudes. *Counselor Education and Supervision, 23,* 214–224.

Neukrug, E. (1994). *Theory, practice, and trends in human services.* Pacific Grove, CA: Brooks/Cole.

Parham, T. A., & Helms, J. E. (1982). The influence of Black students' racial identity attitudes on preference for counselor's race. *Journal of Counseling Psychology, 28,* 250–357.

Pedersen, P. B. (1988). *A handbook for developing multicultural awareness.* Alexandria, VA: American Association for Counseling and Development.

Pedersen, P. B. (1994). *A handbook for developing multicultural awareness* (2nd ed.). Alexandria, VA: American Counseling Association.

Pettigrew, T. F. (1974). Racially separate or together? In E. G. Epps (Ed.), *Cultural pluralism* (pp. 1–33). Berkeley, CA: McCutchan.

Pomales, J., & Williams, V. (1989). Effects of level of acculturation and counseling style on Hispanic students' perceptions of counselor. *Journal of Counseling Psychology, 36,* 79–83.

Ponterotto, J. G., & Pedersen, P. B. (1993). *Preventing prejudice: A guide for counselors and educators: Vol. 2. Multicultural aspects of counseling series.* Newbury Park, CA: Sage.

Pope, M. (1995). The "salad bowl" is big enough for us all: An argument for the inclusion of lesbians and gay men in any definition of multiculturalism. *Journal of Counseling & Development, 73,* 301–304.

Porter, R. E., & Samovar, L. A. (1985). Approaching intercultural communication. In L. A. Samovar & E. E. Porter (Eds.), *Intercultural communication: A reader* (pp. 15–30). Belmont, CA: Wadsworth.

Powell-Hopson, D., & Hopson, D. (1990). *Different and wonderful: Raising Black children in a race conscious society.* Englewood Cliffs, NJ: Prentice Hall.

Redfield, R., Linton, R., & Herskovits, M. J. (1936). Outline for the study of acculturation. *American Anthropologist, 38,* 149–152.

Rice, F. P. (1993). *The adolescent: Development, relationship, and culture* (7th ed.). Boston: Allyn & Bacon.

Rand McNally almanac of world facts. (1995). New York: Rand McNally.

Rotheram, M., & Phinney, J. (Eds.). (1987). *Children's ethnic socialization: Pluralism and development.* Newbury Park, CA: Sage.

Rotter, J. (1966). Generalized expectancies for internal versus external control of reinforcement. *Psychological Monographs, 80*(1, Whole No. 609).

Rotter, J. (1975). Some problems and misconceptions related to the construct of internal versus external control of reinforcement. *Journal of Consulting and Clinical Psychology, 43,* 56–67.

Sanchez, A. R., & Atkinson, D. R. (1983). Mexican-American cultural commitment, preference for counselor ethnicity, and willingness to use counseling. *Journal of Counseling Psychology, 30,* 215–220.

Savickas, M. (1992, August). Innovations in counseling for career development. In L. J. Richmond (Chair), *New perspectives on counseling for the 21st century.* Symposium conducted at the annual convention of the American Psychological Association, Washington, DC.

Schaefer, R. T. (1988). *Racial and ethnic groups* (3rd ed.). Glenview, IL: Scott, Foresman.

Schlesinger, A. M., Jr. (1991). *The disuniting of America: Reflections on a multicultural society.* Knoxville, TN: Whittle Direct Books.

Skillings, J. H., & Dobbins, J. E. (1991). Racism as a disease: Etiology and treatment implications. *Journal of Counseling & Development, 70,* 206–215.

Steward, E. C. (1972). *American cultural patterns.* La Grange Park, IL: Intercultural Network.

Sue, D. W. (1978). World views and counseling. *Personnel and Guidance Journal, 56,* 458–463.

Sue, D. W. (1992, August). *Multicultural counseling research: Proposing an agenda for the 90s.* Paper presented at the annual convention of the American Psychological Association, Washington, DC.

Sue, D. W., & Sue, D. (1977). Barriers to effective cross-cultural counseling. *Journal of Counseling Psychology, 24,* 420–29.

Sue, D. W., & Sue, D. (1990). *Counseling the culturally different: Theory and practice* (2nd ed.). New York: Wiley.

Szapocznik, J., & Kurtines, W. (1980). Bicultural involvement and adjustment in Hispanic American youths. *International Journal of Intercultural Relations, 4,* 353–365.

Tobias, P. V. (1972). The meaning of race. In P. Baxter & B. Sansom (Eds.), *Race and social difference* (pp. 19–48). Harmondsworth, Middlesex, England: Penguin Books.

Valencia, R. R., Henderson, R. W., & Rankin, R. J. (1985). Family status, family constellation, and home environmental variables as predictors of cognitive performance of Mexican American children. *Journal of Educational Psychology, 77,* 323–331.

Van den Berghe, P. L. (1967). *Race and racism.* New York: Wiley.

Webster's ninth new collegiate dictionary. (1989). Springfield, MA: Merriam-Webster.

Whitfield, W., McGrath, P., & Coleman, V. (1992, October). *Increasing multicultural sensitivity and awareness.* Paper presented at the annual conference of the National Organization for Human Services Education, Alexandria, VA.

Williams, R. M., Jr. (1970). *American society: A sociological interpretation.* New York: Knopf.

Wirth, L. (1945). The problem of minority groups. In R. Linton (Ed.), *The science of man in the world crisis* (pp. 123–151). New York: Columbia University Press.

Zuckerman, M. (1990). Some dubious premises in research and theory on racial differences. *American Psychologist, 45,* 1297–1303.

5 | The Inalienability of the School's Role in Culture

The bonds of culture are often invisible, and its walls are glass. We may think we are free. We cannot leave the trap until we know we are in it.
—FERGUSON, 1985, p. 105

E ducation shares with families and other reference groups the responsibility of providing ethnic and cultural minority students with an appropriate multicultural and cultural-specific education. Other reference groups are groups to which students relate themselves as a part of, or to which they aspire to relate themselves psychologically, such as religious-based affiliations and social or recreational groups (Allport, 1958). Positive and negative connotations of these groups are both situational and individually determined.

Allport's (1958) contention is further amplified by the U.S. Commission on Civil Rights (1967), in which the following belief is recorded:

> We believe that white children are deprived of something of value when they grow up in isolation from children of other races, when the self-esteem and assurance may rest in part upon false notions of racial superiority, when they are not prepared by their school experience to participate fully in a world rich in human diversity. (p. 14)

Intergroup relationships represent one of the most difficult and complex sources of problems that school counselors confront (Deaux &Wrightsman, 1988). One significant characteristic of strained group relations is racial or (as this author prefers) ethnic and cultural prejudice. Verbal assaults, verbal ridicule, and physical forms of ethnic intimidation continue to occur in today's schools, especially secondary schools (e.g., Mendoza, 1994; Smart & Smart, 1995; Spenser, 1990; Welsh, 1989). School counselors are most interested in the individual and must be able to distinguish the context of the group (i.e., culture or ethnicity) from the context of the individual by understanding that the individual shares the group in a unique way, but the individual context is never the same as the group context (Johnson, 1990).

Referents deserve to be specified when either culture or ethnicity is used. Although both culture and ethnicity have the capacity for multiple referents, school counselors are expected to have solid positions and theoretically grounded referents for their use of terms such as race, culture, and ethnicity. School counselors must hold each other accountable for being as unambiguous as possible (Johnson, 1990).

The degree of culturation is a measure of within-group diversity that has been found to be related to a number of counseling process variables. School counselors who work with ethnic minority students should be aware not only of the students' background but also of the extent to which students identify with and practice the culture of their ancestors (Atkinson, Morten, & Sue, 1993). Such knowledge will assist the school counselor in developing strategies for presenting problems such as identity formation, both adolescent identity and ethnic identity.

Specific Roles of the School

Specific areas in which the school has a major role in effecting ethnic and cultural awareness and acceptance are the school's mission statement and commitment, the faculty and staff, curriculum organization and objectives, and the students. These areas of educational policies can be proactive in their support and advocacy for multicultural education in the following ways.

MISSION STATEMENT

Multiculturalism is an important part of any school's philosophical base and mission. Printed descriptions of the school's mission with its multicultural components are needed for students, faculty, and the community. This mission can be easily incorporated into normal school publications such as the student and faculty handbooks. With a multicultural mission statement already implemented, the prerequisites are accomplished for the accreditation agency.

In addition, the school must be committed to multicultural education and not just render "lip service." Easily identifiable checks on the school's commitment may be seen in disparate standardized test scores, examples of multicultural activities, incidences of ethnic prejudicial statements, the general atmosphere of the school, and the attitude of the ethnic community.

FACULTY AND STAFF

Faculty and staff must also make a strong commitment to infusing multiculturalism throughout the educational services rendered. However, a general faculty commitment is not singularly sufficient. A core of each school's faculty must be experienced in dealing with diverse students. In most situations, this core group includes the counseling staff in leadership roles.

School counselors can serve a major role within the school. If individual school counselors are not multiculturally aware, workshops and academic courses become necessary. One role of school counselors can be in the development of teacher–counselor partnerships and collaborations to facilitate multicultural infusion (Herring, 1995; Herring & White, 1995). Faculty and staff must also be willing to examine and challenge their own personal attitudes, values, and beliefs about other ethnic people.

CURRICULUM DEVELOPMENT AND OBJECTIVES

The overall school program and mission statement must reflect multicultural perspectives. However, to ensure that multicultural perspectives become more than idealized rhetoric, schools must operationalize program goals into specific objectives for every course in the curriculum. For example, textbook consideration must be undertaken with multicultural issues in mind and with multicultural selection committees. Textbooks that continue to perpetuate stereotypes and misinformation should be eliminated.

STUDENTS

Students need to be aware of their school's mission and program objectives. The dissemination of such information can be achieved easily and efficiently through course syllabi, handbooks, and other printed materials. Students also need to be aware of where they can go and with whom they can discuss problems, discomforts, and developmental crises. The school's organizational structure should provide avenues for students to express their ethnic pride in positive and educational forums. Both curricula and extracurricular activities can be infused with representative ethnic perspectives.

Conflict/Conflict Intervention and Mediation: The School's Multicultural Commitment

Conflict intervention and mediation is frequently interpreted as *crisis intervention* or *crisis counseling*. That blending of terminology is not the intention of this discussion. A *crisis* may be defined as "a perception of an event or situation as an intolerable difficulty that exceeds the resources and coping mechanisms of the individual" (Gilliland & James, 1993, p. 3). As stress (the key element in crisis development) increases to unusual proportions and the student's coping skills become increasingly ineffective, the potential for crisis occurs, resulting in a downward spiral of ineffective behavior (Greenstone & Leviton, 1993). Thus, crisis conflict intervention becomes an "act of interrupting the downward spiral as skillfully and as quickly as possible and, in so doing, of returning the victim to a pre-crisis level of coping" (p. 1). School counselors must be alert to signals sent by students who are experiencing or foreseeing a crisis. **Something to Consider 5.1** presents a profile of how students may be indicating potential or real stress.

SOMETHING TO CONSIDER 5.1

Profile of a Student in Crisis

1. **Bewilderment:** "I never felt this way before."
2. **Danger:** "I am so nervous and scared."
3. **Confusion:** "I can't think clearly."
4. **Impasse:** "I feel stuck; nothing I do helps."
5. **Desperation:** "I've got to do something."
6. **Apathy:** "Nothing can help me."
7. **Helplessness:** "I can't take care of myself."
8. **Urgency:** "I need help now!!!!!!!"
9. **Discomfort:** "I feel miserable, restless, and unsettled."

SOURCE: Adapted from *Elements of Crisis Intervention*, by J. L. Greenstone and S. C. Leviton, 1993, pp. 4–5.

Conflict intervention and counseling must be separated in terms of function and application. Conflict intervention attempts to deal quickly with an immediate problem. Crisis counseling or other forms of therapy are appropriate after the conflict intervention. Naturally, school counselors will benefit from developing conflict/crisis intervention skills; however, to presume that conflict or crisis intervention and counseling are the same is courting disaster (Corsini, 1981).

MODELS OF CONFLICT MEDIATION

Several models of conflict mediation are available for the school counselor or other school officials to consider for adoption. These models are differentiated by the component of violence.

Conflicts without a violent component. Conflict situations that are not characterized by a component of violence may adapt Gilliland's (1982) simple but efficient model of intervention. The six steps described within this model are (a) defining the problem, (b) ensuring student safety, (c) providing support, (d) examining alternatives, (e) making plans, and (f) obtaining commitment. This model "emphasizes actively, assertively, intentionally, and continuously assessing, listening, and acting to systematically help the client regain as much of the precise equilibrium, mobility, and autonomy as possible" (Gilliland & James, 1993, p. 33).

Conflicts with a violent component. Management of potentially violent situations should also proceed in a sequential manner. The most efficacious model for achieving this goal is the nine-stage model developed by Piercy (1984). The stages are education, avoidance of conflict, appeasement, deflection, time out, show of force, seclusion, restraints, and sedation. **Table 5.1** presents a brief description of these stages. For each stage, personal responsibility is paramount (Gilliland & James, 1993), because the first person who comes in contact with the problem is the most likely to be the student's focus of attention (Moran, 1984).

Stages 1 through 5 rely heavily on talking rather than acting, reflecting one of the primary goals of conflict intervention with violence-prone students—getting them to "talk it out" rather than to "act it out." This approach may seem obvious, but it is difficult to achieve. The agitated student clearly has a "limited ability to talk and think through problems, as opposed to acting on them and giving little thought to the consequences" (Tardiff, 1984, p. 52).

MULTICULTURAL PERSPECTIVES

D. W. Sue (1992) contended that multicultural helping is enhanced when the school counselor "uses methods and strategies and defines goals consistent with the life experiences and [cultural] values" of the student (p. 13). Similarly,

TABLE 5.1

Stages of Intervention for Potentially Violent Situations

STAGE 1: EDUCATION
Students need to be educated about what is happening to them and why and how it is happening. Assume the role of a student advocate. Open-ended questions and reflection of feelings are crucial.

STAGE 2: AVOIDANCE OF CONFLICT
Matching threats will usually work in the opposite manner desired. Allow the student to cool down.

STAGE 3: APPEASEMENT
Attempted if the student's demands are simple and reasonable. May not be applicable in all situations. Probably more appropriate in emergency settings in which immediate assistance is not available.

STAGE 4: DEFLECTION
Shifting to other less-threatening topics. Using problem-solving techniques allows the "bigger" problem to be broken into smaller, more manageable segments.

STAGE 5: TIME OUT
When students cannot contend with the emotion of the moment, ask them to go into a reduced-stimulus environment, to be alone and think things out.

STAGE 6: SHOW OF FORCE
If the student is unable to proceed to time out or is otherwise noncompliant or acting out, a show of force is needed. This action demonstrates that any threat of or act of violence will not be tolerated.

STAGE 7: SECLUSION
Differentiated from time out by its length, its setting, and its involuntary nature. Once placed in seclusion, the student is oriented to what is going to occur, and an adult is assigned to monitor the student.

STAGE 8: RESTRAINTS
If the student is acting out and will not go to seclusion, restraints will have to be used to avoid harm to self or others. Adequate staff (normally five persons) should be available for this procedure.

STAGE 9: SEDATION
If all else fails, the student may require some form of sedation. Depending on the type of sedation, the problem becomes clearly a medical one. Recent technology has developed means of stunning that may be appropriate for severe educational settings.

SOURCE: Adapted from "Violence: The Drug and Alcohol Patient," by D. Piercy, 1984. In J. T. Turner (Ed.), *Violence in the Medical Care Setting: A Survival Guide* (pp. 123–152).

Belkin (1984) stated that the principal cross-cultural impediments to cross-cultural counseling are language differences and class- and culture-bound values. Identified barriers to effective ethnic counseling have also been identified. Barriers identified include unjustified assumption of shared feelings, student transference, counselor countertransference, inability to adjust to worldview differences, failure to recognize different value and belief systems, counseling process and content concerns, and reluctance to integrate culture-specific theoretical perspectives (e.g., Belkin, 1984; Herring, 1990; Pedersen, 1987; D. W. Sue, 1992; D. W. Sue & Sue, 1990).

Benefits of cross-cultural counseling include empathic sharing, student willingness to self-disclose, a common mode of communication, and the reduction of stereotypes relating to individuals, behaviors, or groups. As D. W. Sue (1992) concluded, without multicultural "awareness and understanding, we may inadvertently assume that everyone shares our world view. When this happens, we may become guilty of cultural oppression, imposing values on the culturally different student" (p. 10).

GENERAL PREVENTIVE MEASURES

From the counselor's perspective, assessing and encouraging multicultural curriculum development that attempts to deal openly with the issues of prejudice and group conflict are recommended. Instruction must be directed toward eliminating the negative stereotypes that nourish prejudice and developing an understanding of the dynamics of within- and between-groups differences. Addressing group differences is especially needed in secondary schools where the potential for in-group and out-group rivalry is greatest. A determined effort to involve the ethnic communities greatly facilitates school–community interaction. In addition, curricula should promote positive relations among youths, including concepts from Allport's (1958) *The Nature of Prejudice*.

THE SYNERGETIC MODEL

The synergetic model for school counseling was presented in Chapters 2 and 3. For current discussion, an overview of its usefulness for conflict resolution will be presented. Synergetic methods involve the intentional, systematic selection and integration of culture- and ethnic-specific concepts and strategies from varied theoretical perspectives. The following are the three major objectives of this model (e.g., Gilliland, James, & Bowman, 1989, pp. 297–298; Herring, 1997; Herring & Walker, 1993; Thorne, 1973, p. 451):

1. To identify valid elements in all theories and to integrate them into an internally consistent model that does justice to the behavior to be explained.
2. To consider all pertinent theories, models, and standards for evaluating and manipulating clinical data according to the most recent knowledge of time.
3. To identify with no specific theory, keep an open mind, and continuously use those strategies that produce successful results.

The model presumes that all students and circumstance are unique and that cultural and environmental factors influence both the student and the circumstance.

In dealing with conflicts and conflict mediation and resolution with diverse youths, the synergetic school counselor is potentially the most appropriate and most capable professional at hand. The synergetic school counselor is frequently condemned as being a "jack-of-all-trades, master-of-none." However, synergetic school counselors bring multiple theoretical perspectives to the mediation table. Their selective content knowledge and process skills enable these professionals to be malleable and to offer the most appropriate ethnic-specific strategies.

School Counselor and Ethnic/Cultural Student Congruence

Sensitivity to and consideration of students' diverse backgrounds are crucial variables in the efficacy of the counseling relationship. School counselors are bound by ethical obligations to ensure that each student is given the respect and dignity of being a human being and is provided counseling services without prejudice as to person, character, belief, or practice (American School Counselor Association's [1984] *Ethical Standards for School Counselors* [revised in 1992]; hereinafter referred to as the *Standards)*.

Section A.4 of the *Standards* requires the school counselor to refrain "from consciously encouraging the counselee's acceptance of values, lifestyles, plans, decisions, and beliefs that represent only the counselor's personal orientation," and Section A.7 of the *Standards* requires the school counselor to make "appropriate referrals when professional assistance can no longer be adequately provided to the counselee."

Ethical standards do not preclude school counselors from possessing personal worldviews and biases. Rather, they exist to prevent encapsulated school counselors from projecting those personal values and biases on students. Ideally, counselors would examine their biases in order to be more aware of the potential of negative intrusions into students' cultural and ethnic realities.

Miscommunication and inappropriate counseling often result from the school counselor's failure or refusal to recognize belief systems and values that are outside a preconceived norm (Herring, 1990). **Something to Consider 5.2** provides additional insight regarding the communication process in developing school counselor and student congruence.

SOMETHING TO CONSIDER 5.2

Guidelines to Communication Processes in Multicultural Counseling

1. Encourage counselees to speak their own language (words and phrases) to best illustrate how they are feeling at the moment for ease of expression. This encouragement provides an opportunity for catharsis of feeling and voicing.
2. Check with counselees for the accuracy of interpretations when in doubt because nonverbal expressions are often culturally based.
3. Learn culturally meaningful expressions of the counselee to accurately describe the counselee's inner process. Ask for their help with pronunciation and proper usage in the context of counseling.
4. Make use of alternative modes of communicating other than a solely verbal exchange, such as art, music, story telling, and photography.
5. Pay attention to, or invite the discussion of, dreams and fantasies as sources of new explanations and understandings, not psychodynamic interpretations.
6. Plan a show-and-tell session to allow counselees to establish culturally significant markers as a way to enhance the counseling relationship.
7. Change the place and environment for counseling and break the monotony. Many counselees would prefer or enjoy counseling sessions out of the office.

SOURCE: Adapted from "The Communication Process as a Critical Intervention for Client Change in Cross-Cultural Counseling," by M. J. Westwood and F. I. Ishiyama, 1990, *Journal of Multicultural Counseling and Development, 18*, pp. 163–171.

Becoming knowledgeable about all ethnicities and cultures is not very feasible for school counselors. In addition, geographical and residential locations often dictate the diversity of student populations. Rather, the school counselor needs to be aware of the ethnic and cultural groups within the local school population. Nevertheless, all school counselors need to possess a base from which to appreciate and consider the unique cultural circumstances that influence the behaviors of ethnic minority students (Burn, 1992; Pedersen, 1988). As Ponterotto and Casas (1987) concluded, "One must consider how this [student's] cultural background (including values, expectations, perceptions, expression of symptoms, nature of stressors, and available resources) interacts with the power-dominant host society's cultural patterns" (p. 433). For example, what would you have done to help Tommy in Case Study 5.1?

CASE STUDY 5.1

Tommy Youngblood

Tommy Youngblood is a 12-year-old, single child of Oglala Sioux parents. His parents decided to leave the reservation in hopes of making more money. While attending the Bureau of Indian Affairs school on the reservation, Tommy was outgoing, involved in athletics, and an above-average academic student. After enrolling in a public urban school in the Midwest, Tommy's involvement in extracurricular activities dwindled, and his grades dropped. His school counselor, an African American female, claimed that she had tried everything she knew but Tommy was not responsive. In the home, the parents' main focus centered around supporting the family, and they viewed Tommy as not trying to "fit in." During the second grading period, Tommy ran away from home and managed to return to the reservation. He expressed a desire to remain there and live with his grandparents. However, his parents would not allow this separation.

Minority students from diverse groups are underrepresented in school counseling, and the inability of school counselors to provide appropriately responsive services suggests that these students may perceive conventional counseling as irrelevant to their needs. S. Sue and Zane (1987) believed that "the single most important explanation for the problems in service delivery (for ethnic minority students) involves the treatment" (p. 37).

Two major criticisms of school counseling are (a) that it is not directly applicable to ethnic minority students (Wilson & Stith, 1991) and (b) that traditionally trained school counselors are encapsulated in a culturally biased framework (Ponterotto & Casas, 1991; Ponterotto, Casas, Suzuki, & Alexander, 1995). The demonstration of cultural sensitivity by school counselors has been determined to be of highest value among Asian Americans (Gim, Atkinson, & Kim, 1991), African Americans (Pomales, Claiborn, & LaFromboise, 1986), Native American Indians (LaFromboise, Trimble, & Mohatt, 1990; Trimble & Fleming, 1989), Hispanic Americans (Casas & Pytluk, 1996; Zapata, 1996), and Filipino Americans (Atkinson, Jennings, & Liongson, 1990).

Does this imply that ethnic minority students prefer to see school counselors who are sensitive to and knowledgeable about their cultural background? Research appears to support this congruence. When given a choice between an ethnically similar and an ethnically dissimilar school counselor, numerous ethnic minority students prefer an ethnically similar school counselor. This preference has been found to be true for African Americans (Atkinson et al., 1993; Harrison, 1975; Sattler, 1977), Native American Indians (Haviland, Horswill, O'Connell, & Dynneson, 1983), Asian Americans (Atkinson, Maruyama, & Matsui, 1978; Gim et al., 1991; Wu & Windle, 1980), Hispanic Americans (Keefe, 1978; LeVine & Padilla, 1980; Padilla & Ruiz, 1973; Ponce & Atkinson, 1989), and West Indian Americans (McKenzie, 1986).

On the other hand, factors other than ethnicity are important. For example, perceived trustworthiness (e.g., sincerity and honesty) has been found to be a more highly valued trait for counselors than ethnicity for some students (LaFromboise, 1988; LaFromboise & Dixon, 1981). Self-disclosure is very influential to this attribute as counselors are often perceived by students to be "agents of the Establishment" and their trust is not inherent to the role (D. W. Sue & Sue, 1990). The school counselor has to demonstrate counseling attributes that are valued highly by ethnic minority students.

For example, Thomason (1991, 1996) suggested that a non-Native American Indian school counselor can effect positive change with Native American Indian students through the blending of traditional healing practices and tribal elders, with non-Native American Indian strategies. In addition, Vontress's (1991) study of Africans indicated the importance of traditional healing for that population as well. The incorporation of such practices would of course depend on the degree of culturation of the student.

The multicultural and cross-cultural school counselor must be knowledgeable in a multitude of areas. Axelson (1993, p. 18) synthesized these areas into four categories of awareness for ideal school counselor and student congruence.

1. *Culture-total awareness*: What movements are taking place in the general society and in specific cultural environments?
2. *Self-awareness*: What are your own personal and professional strengths and points for improvement in multicultural counseling? Where are you now?
3. *Client awareness*: What is the external/internal frame of reference through which your student counselee views his or her world?

4. *Counseling procedure awareness*: What goal and which process are most appropriate for your student counselee in his or her situation at this time?

To Axelson's (1993) four categories of awareness, this author would add a fifth:

5. *Within-group variances*: Why are there more variances within ethnic groups than between ethnic groups?

Summary

This chapter emphasized the inalienability of the school's role in culture. To that end, curriculum exists as the driving force in the school's cultural existence. It encompasses everything that students experience under the aegis of the school (Ladson-Billings, 1995). This infers that schools may have identical advertised curricula and course guides, but the school climate, extracurricular activities, staffing patterns, tracking, parent support and involvement, student population, and so on may render the curriculum in School A different from that of School B. It is hoped that such a difference reflects the infusion of appropriate multicultural components.

Culture is discussed in relation to its multiple roles in the developmental process of diverse students. Demographic trends are identified and terminology distinctions are explored further, particularly the identification of student worldviews.

The interactions between culture and family are noted, and specific roles of the school in culture are identified. Conflict intervention is presented as being a check on the efficacy of the school's multicultural efforts. In addition, the use of the synergetic model of school counseling in conflict mediation is suggested. Finally, although optimal counseling is inherent with counselor–student similarity, certain characteristics can override this incongruence.

Experiential Activities

1. Observe the conditions under which parents react to their infant's involvement with objects in your culture. How is parental responsiveness linked to cultural values? How does it compare with the findings in **Special Emphasis 5.1**?

2. To clarify your understanding, respond to the following sentence stems:
   a. I believe race is . . .
   b. I believe culture includes . . .
   c. I believe ethnicity consists of . . .

SPECIAL EMPHASIS 5.1

!Kung Infancy: Acquiring Culture

Researchers have examined how parents respond to their infants' play with objects among the !Kung, a hunting and gathering society living in the deserts of Botswana, Africa. Daily foraging takes small numbers of adults several miles from the camp, but most obtain enough food to contribute to group survival by working only 3 days a week. A mobile life also prevents the !Kung from collecting possessions that require extensive care and maintenance. Adults have hours to relax, which is spent in intense social contact with one another and with children.

In this culture, objects are valued as things to be shared, not as personal possessions. This message is conveyed to !Kung infants between 6 and 12 months when grandmothers begin to train the infants in the importance of exchanging objects by guiding them in handing beads to relatives. First words generally include *i* (here, take this) and *na* (give it to me).

In !Kung society, no toys are made. Rather, natural objects (e.g., twigs, stones, and nutshells) are always available, as are cooking implements. However, adults do not encourage babies to play with these objects. In fact, adults are unlikely to interact with infants while they are exploring objects independently. But when a baby offers an object to another person, adults become highly responsive, encouraging and vocalizing much more than at other times. Thus, !Kung cultural emphasis on the interpersonal rather than physical aspects of existence is reflected in how adults interact with the youngest members of their community.

SOURCE: Adapted from *The Adolescent: Development, Relationships, and Culture*, by F. P. Rice, 1993, p. 213; "!Kung Infancy: The Social Context of Object Exploration," by R. Bakeman, L. B. Adamson, M. Konner, and R. G. Barr, 1990, *Child Development, 61*, pp. 794–809; and "Technological Change and Child Behavior Among the !Kung," by P. Draper and E. Cashdan, 1988, *Ethnology, 27*, 339–365.

3. Review Allport's (1958) five degrees of prejudice (i.e., antilocution, avoidance, discrimination, physical attacks, and extermination). Using these five degrees as referents, describe the evolution of prejudice against an ethnic or cultural group of your choice.

4. The role of communication in intercultural exchanges has been studied from various perspectives. Respond to the following questions from your personal perspective.

   a. Are there actually differences among cultures in forms of communication?

   b. If so, how should the differences be described?

c. Do these differences have to occur? Why are they necessary? and
d. What differences do these differences make? What are the implications of these forms of communication?

5. The Alligator River*

In class, do the following values clarification exercise. But, first, read the following story.

> Heather is very much in love with James, who lives on the other side of Alligator River. She wants to see James but the bridge is out. She would swim across the river, but she is afraid of the alligators. Therefore, she goes to Kenny, who is the only person with a boat on the river, and asks him to take her across.
>
> Kenny has always been secretly in love with Heather. He has a severe hearing impediment, has low self-esteem, and is naive about dating. He makes only a subsistence living ferrying people across the river. When Heather asks him to take her across he states, "Heather, I've always been in love with you, and I'll take you across the river if you'll make love with me." Heather is initially disgusted, and asks her friend Jamie for advice. Jamie states, "This is your problem and you're going to need to work it out on your own." Heather ponders quite a while and then decides that because she's slept with many men, why not just do it, and then she'll be able to see James. She agrees to make love with Kenny (she insists that he use a condom).
>
> Because Heather has a very honest relationship with James, she tells him the whole story. He becomes enraged and states, "Get out of my life, I never want to see you again." She becomes distraught, goes to her friend Howard, and tells him the whole story. He becomes infuriated with James and punches him out.

Now, rate each of the five characters in the story on the following scale:

1. The person you liked most.
2. The person you liked second best.
3. The person you liked third best.
4. The person you liked next to least.
5. The person you liked least.

Have the instructor gather all the ratings and place them on a grid on the board with each name going across the top and ratings 1 through 5, on the side (y-axis). Count the number of 1s, 2s, and so forth for each person in the story and compare the distribution for each character.

Then, as a class, respond to the following questions:

a. What does the distribution tell about how students view individuals with differing values?
b. Did you assume the characters were male and female based on their names or roles?
c. If Heather were a male, would you have rated the characters differently?

*Source: Adapted from Values Clarification: A Handbook of Practical Strategies for Teacher and Students, by S. B. Simon, L. W. Howe, and H. W. Kirschenbaum, 1991, p. 104.

d. If Heather were a male and James a female, would you have rated the characters differently?

e. If the characters in the story were of differing ethnic, cultural, or religious backgrounds, would you have responded differently to them? and

f. If you were in a helping relationship with any of the characters in the story, how would your positive or negative stereotypes affect your work with them?

6. Imagine that you are invited to a very swank cocktail party in which the other guests were doctors, lawyers, accountants, computer specialists, and other high-powered and highly paid professionals. Imagine that you arrive late and when queried why you were late you replied, "Oh, I had to finish my project for my curriculum class." The questioner stands perplexed for a second and then asks, "What is curriculum?" Frame an answer to this question that is coherent to this audience. How would that answer be modified if the question was, "What is multicultural curriculum?" (adapted from Ladson-Billings, 1995).

References

Allport, G. W. (1958). *The nature of prejudice*. New York: Addison-Wesley.

American School Counselor Association. (1984). *Ethical standards for school counselors*. Alexandria, VA: American Association for Counseling and Development.

Atkinson, D. R., Jennings, R. G., & Liongson, L. (1990). Minority students' reasons for not seeking counseling and suggestions for improving services. *Journal of College Student Development, 31*, 342–350.

Atkinson, D. R., Maruyama, M., & Matsui, S. (1978). The effects of counselor race and counseling approach on Asian Americans' perceptions of counselor credibility and utility. *Journal of Counseling Psychology, 25*, 76–83.

Atkinson, D. R., Morten, G., & Sue, D. W. (1993). *Counseling American minorities: A cross-cultural perspective* (4th ed.). Dubuque, IA: Brown & Benchmark.

Axelson, J. A. (1993). *Counseling and development in a multicultural society* (2nd ed.). Monterey, CA: Brooks/Cole.

Bakeman, R., Adamson, L. B., Konner, M., & Barr, R. G. (1990). !Kung infancy: The social context of object exploration. *Child Development, 61*, 794–809.

Belkin, G. S. (1984). *Introduction to counseling* (2nd ed.). Dubuque, IA: William C. Brown.

Burn, D. (1992). Ethical implications in cross-cultural counseling and training. *Journal of Counseling & Development, 70*, 578–583.

Casas, J. M., & Pytluk, S. D. (1996). Hispanic identity development: Implications for research and practice. In J. G. Ponterotto, J. M. Casas, L. A. Suzuki, & C. M. Alexander (Eds.), *Handbook of multicultural counseling* (pp. 155–180). Thousand Oaks, CA: Sage.

Corsini, R. J. (1981). *Innovative psychotherapies*. New York: Wiley Interscience.

Deaux, K., & Wrightsman, L. (1988). *Social psychology* (5th ed.). Monterey, CA: Brooks/Cole.

Draper, P., & Cashdan, E. (1988). Technological change and child behavior among the !Kung. *Ethnology, 27,* 339–365.

Ferguson, M. (1985). *The Aquarian conspiracy.* Los Angeles: Tarcher.

Gilliland, B. E. (1982). *Steps in crisis counseling.* Memphis, TN: Memphis State University, Department of Counseling and Personnel Services.

Gilliland, B. E., & James, R. K. (1993). *Crisis intervention strategies.* Pacific Grove, CA: Brooks/Cole.

Gilliland, B. E., James, R. K., & Bowman, J. T. (1989). *Theories and strategies in counseling and psychotherapy* (2nd ed.). Englewood Cliffs, NJ: Prentice Hall.

Gim, R. H., Atkinson, D. R., & Kim, S. J. (1991). Asian American acculturation, counselor ethnicity and cultural sensitivity, and ratings of counselors. *Journal of Counseling Psychology, 38,* 57–62.

Greenstone, J. L., & Leviton, S. C. (1993). *Elements of crisis intervention.* Pacific Grove, CA: Brooks/Cole.

Harrison, D. K. (1975). Race as a counselor–client variable in counseling and psychotherapy: A review of the research. *The Counseling Psychologist, 5,* 124–133.

Haviland, M. G., Horswill, R. K., O'Connell, J. J., & Dynneson, V. V. (1983). Native American college students preference for counselor race and sex and the likelihood of their use of a counseling center. *Journal of Counseling Psychology, 30,* 267–270.

Herring, R. D. (1990). Understanding Native American values: Process and content concerns for counselors. *Counseling and Values, 34,* 134–137.

Herring, R. D. (1995). Creating culturally compatible classrooms: Roles of the school counselor. *The North Dakota Journal of Counseling & Development, 1*(1), 28–33.

Herring, R. D. (1997). *Counseling diverse ethnic youth: Strategies and interventions for school counselors.* Fort Worth, TX: Harcourt Brace.

Herring, R. D., & Walker, S. S. (1993). Synergetic counseling: Toward a more holistic approach. *Texas Counseling Association Journal, 22,* 38–53.

Herring, R. D., & White, L. (1995). School counselors, teachers, and the culturally compatible classroom: Partnerships in multicultural education. *Journal for the Professional Counselor, 34,* 52–64.

Johnson, S. D. (1990). Toward clarifying culture, race, and ethnicity in the context of multicultural counseling. *Journal of Multicultural Counseling and Development, 18,* 41–50.

Keefe, S. E. (1978). Why Mexican Americans underutilize mental health clinics: Fact and fallacy. In J. M. Casas & S. E. Keefe (Eds.), *Family and mental health in the Mexican American community* (Monograph No. 7, pp. 91–108). Los Angeles: University of California, Spanish Speaking Mental Health Research Center.

Ladson-Billings, G. (1995). Challenging customs, canons, and content: Developing relevant curriculum for diversity. In C. A. Grant (Ed.), *Educating for diversity: An anthology of multicultural voices* (pp. 327–340). Boston: Allyn & Bacon.

LaFromboise, T. D. (1988). American Indian mental health policy. *American Psychologist, 43,* 388–397.

LaFromboise, T. D., & Dixon, D. N. (1981). American Indian perception of trustworthiness in a counseling interview. *Journal of Counseling Psychology, 28,* 135–139.

LaFromboise, T. D., Trimble, J. E., & Mohatt, G. V. (1990). Counseling intervention and American Indian tradition: An integrative approach. *The Counseling Psychologist, 18,* 628–654.

LeVine, E. S., & Padilla, A. M. (1980). *Crossing cultures in therapy: Pluralistic counseling for the Hispanic.* Monterey, CA: Brooks/Cole.

McKenzie, V. M. (1986). Ethnographic findings on West Indian-American clients. *Journal of Counseling & Development, 65,* 40–44.

Mendoza, J. I. (1994). On being Mexican American. *Phi Delta Kappan, 76*(4), 293–295.

Moran, J. F. (1984). Teaching the management of violent behavior to nursing staff: A health care model. In J. T. Turner (Ed.), *Violence in the medical care setting: A survival guide* (pp. 231–250). Rockville, MD: Aspen Systems Corporation.

Padilla, A. M., & Ruiz, R. A. (1973). *Latino mental health: A review of literature.* Washington, DC: Government Printing Office.

Pedersen, P. B. (1987). Ten frequent assumptions of cultural bias in counseling. *Journal of Multicultural Counseling and Development, 15,* 16–24.

Pedersen, P. B. (1988). *A handbook for developing multicultural awareness.* Alexandria, VA: American Association for Counseling and Development.

Piercy, D. (1984). Violence: The drug and alcohol patient. In J. T. Turner (Ed.), *Violence in the medical care setting: A survival guide* (pp. 123–152). Rockville, MD: Aspen Systems Corporation.

Pomales, J., Claiborn, C. D., & LaFromboise, T. D. (1986). Effects of Black students' racial identity on perceptions of White counselors varying in cultural sensitivity. *Journal of Counseling Psychology, 33,* 57–61.

Ponce, D. Q., & Atkinson, D. R. (1989). Mexican-American acculturation, counselor ethnicity, counseling style, and perceived counselor credibility. *Journal of Counseling Psychology, 36,* 203–208.

Ponterotto, J. G., & Casas, J. M. (1987). In search of multicultural competence within counselor education programs. *Journal of Counseling & Development, 65,* 430–434.

Ponterotto, J. G., & Casas, J. M. (1991). *Handbook of racial/ethnic minority counseling research.* Springfield, IL: Charles C Thomas.

Ponterotto, J. G., Casas, J. M., Suzuki, L. A., & Alexander, C. M. (1995). *Handbook of multicultural counseling.* Thousand Oaks, CA: Sage.

Rice, F. P. (1993). *The adolescent: Development, relationships, and cultures* (7th ed.). Boston: Allyn & Bacon.

Sattler, J. M. (1977). The effects of therapist–client racial similarity. In A. S. Gurman & S. M. Razin (Eds.), *Effective psychotherapy: A handbook of research* (pp. 252–290). New York: Pergamon.

Simon, S. B., Howe, L. W., & Kirschenbaum, H. W. (1991). *Values clarification: A handbook of practical strategies for teacher and students* (Rev. ed.). Hudley, MA: Values Press.

Smart, J. F., & Smart, D. W. (1995). Acculturative stress of Hispanics: Loss and challenge. *Journal of Counseling & Development, 73,* 390–396.

Spenser, R. L. (1990). Intergroup conflict on high school campuses. *Journal of Multicultural Counseling and Development, 18,* 11–18.

Sue, D. W. (1992). The challenge of multiculturalism: The road less traveled. *American Counselor, 1,* 6–14.

Sue, D. W., & Sue, D. (1990). *Counseling the culturally different: Theory and practice* (2nd ed.). New York: Wiley.

Sue, S., & Zane, N. (1987). The role of culture and cultural techniques in psychotherapy: A critique and reformulation. *American Psychologist, 42,* 37–45.

Tardiff, K. (1984). Violence: The psychiatric patient. In J. T. Turner (Ed.), *Violence in the medical care setting: A survival guide* (pp. 35–55). Rockville, MD: Aspen Systems Corporation.

Thomason, T. C. (1991). Counseling Native Americans: An introduction for non-Native American counselors. *Journal of Counseling & Development, 69,* 321–327.

Thomason, T. C. (1996). Counseling Native American students. In C. C. Lee (Ed.), *Counseling for diversity: A guide for school counselors and related professionals* (pp. 109–126). Boston: Allyn & Bacon.

Thorne, F. C. (1973). Eclectic psychotherapy. In R. Corsini (Ed.), *Current psychotherapies* (pp. 445–486). Itasca, IL: Peacock.

Trimble, J. E., & Fleming, C. (1989). Providing counseling services for Native American Indians: Client, counselor and community characteristics. In P. Pedersen, J. Draguns, W. Lonner, & J. Trimble (Eds.), *Counseling across cultures* (3rd ed., pp. 145–168). Honolulu: University of Hawaii Press.

U.S. Commission on Civil Rights. (1967). *Racial isolation in the public schools* (CCR Clearinghouse Publication No. 7). Washington, DC: Author.

Vontress, C. E. (1991). Traditional healing in Africa: Implications for cross-cultural counseling. *Journal of Counseling & Development, 70,* 242–249.

Welsh, P. (1989, March 5). A lesson in racism. *Washington Post,* p. C-1.

Westwood, M. J., & Ishiyama, F. I. (1990). The communication process as a critical intervention for client change in cross-cultural counseling. *Journal of Multicultural Counseling and Development, 18,* 163–171.

Wilson, L. L., & Stith, S. M. (1991). Culturally sensitive therapy with Black clients. *Journal of Multicultural Counseling and Development, 19,* 32–43.

Wu, I. H., & Windle, C. (1980). Ethic specificity in the relationship of minority use and staffing of community mental health centers. *Community Mental Health Journal, 16,* 156–168.

Zapata, J. T. (1996). Counseling Hispanic children and youth. In C. C. Lee (Ed.), *In counseling for diversity: A guide for school counselors and related professionals* (pp. 85–108). Boston: Allyn & Bacon.

General Issues in School Counseling II

The school counseling profession is being attacked from many sources. The thrust of these initiatives stems from parents' desire for their children to be afforded the best possible education for future success, from administrators' demand for accountability and credibility, and from confusion about the proper role for the school counselor. More important, school counselors encounter the wrath of ethnic and cultural minority students who complain of inadequate, inappropriate, and insensitive delivery of counseling and guidance services.

Part II attempts to address the most important issues that generate these concerns. The efficacy of school counseling rests on its members being able to translate these concerns into strategies and interventions that are sensitive to the needs of diverse students and their families. Socioeconomic, psychoeducational, and political issues require integration into content and process components of school counseling. School counselors and counselors-in-training must demonstrate competency in these areas of current and past environmental influences. Information and suggestions are included in Part II that will assist the school counselor in becoming more proficient in these issues.

6 | School Counseling: Content and Process Concerns

People pay for what they do, and still more, for what they have allowed themselves to become. And they pay for it simply: by the lives they lead.

—JAMES BALDWIN

E thnic and cultural minority youths continue to be misunderstood by the school counseling community (Abudabbeh, 1992; Herring, 1997b). Consequently, this population has not received the most appropriate consideration or the most effective benefit from counseling efforts. Dropout rates, alcoholism, unemployment and underemployment, drug abuse, suicide rates, violence, and other negative aspects have increased dramatically. Genetically mixed students are still being forced to choose one ethnic category or suffer the label of "other." The central dilemma of today's ethnic and cultural minority youths is a direct result of a history of sociopolitical attempts to either assimilate or isolate this population. School counseling efforts are extremely vital to the improvement of this population (Abu-Eita & Sherif, 1990; Herring, 1997b; Lee, 1996). School counselors have the responsibility to consider cultural and ethnic values within content and process emphases. In addition, the effective counseling with ethnic and cultural minority students involves infusing appropriate developmental issues in designing and implementing interventions.

The most effective method to integrate the various content knowledge and differentiated process strategies extends beyond functional eclecticism, which negates environmental and cultural influences. The most positive method also precludes allegiance to a single orientation. Thus, a more culturally appropriate alternative exists in the utilization of synergetic counseling precepts.

Developmental Issues

Ethnic and culturally diverse youths continue to experience stress in their growth and development. Current societal experiences have added influences such as changing familial patterns, AIDS, fetal alcohol syndrome, violence, and cultural diversity to inherent difficulties of normal development. The multiple problems facing current and future ethnic and cultural students require school counselors to be extremely knowledgeable of, and sensitive to, this population.

Developmental tasks are skills, attitudes, knowledge, and functions that one must master to become well-adjusted, functioning individuals. These tasks and their attainment are central to developmental theories such as Erikson's (1963) conflict stage model, Maslow's (1968) progression of human needs model, Freud's (1950) psychosexual stage model, Loevinger's (1976) ego development model, Piaget's (1977) cognitive development stage model, and Kohlberg's (1969) moral reasoning models.

The focus of this chapter is to incorporate content and process concerns into an ethnic and developmentally appropriate paradigm. To this end, a synergetic approach will be emphasized. Emphasis is placed on selecting the *most appropriate technique*, regardless of theoretical orientation, for *this* student at *this* time in *this* place, considering environmental and historical influences.

Vernon (1993) suggested that school counselors consider the following, with considerations of age and ability:

1. Students, especially young ones, may not be as verbal as adults, or able to identify or express feelings as readily.
2. Primary and elementary students' sense of time is more immediate. A problem today may not be a problem tomorrow, and these students may be more impatient about getting the problem solved.
3. Children and adolescents are less likely to refer themselves for counseling and may resist it because they do not think they have a problem.
4. Because of their inability to understand that having a problem does not mean they are deficient or inept, younger students do not want to admit that something is wrong.
5. Adolescents in particular may resent being the "identified patient" when they do not see themselves as being the source of the problem.

Modification of traditional school counseling approaches is necessary if effective developmental and ethnic-appropriate counseling is the goal. School counselors need to adopt strategies integrating techniques such as play, art, music, bibliotherapy, simulations, role playing, and natural healing practices. To be effective, school counselors must consider the context as they conceptualize the problem. Without that consideration, the interventions will likely fail.

Content Emphases

Content refers to the actual knowledge base of the school counselor. This knowledge includes not only developmental theories but also information about various ethnic and cultural groups' history and traditions. A sincere school counselor can enhance the counseling process through self-directed efforts. The counselor quite naturally cannot be an expert in all knowledge areas, but the counselor can become knowledgeable about the school and community population served. Such knowledge of local demographics can facilitate a more effective preparation and a more successful interaction with school youths.

Six basic content factors influence school counseling with ethnic and cultural minority students: potential worldview variances, special needs, the extent of value and belief systems, the importance of familial structures, the historical method of study and research about ethnic and cultural societies, and the miscommunication between school counselors and students.

A synthesis of content knowledge criteria (Brandell, 1988; Kazdin, 1989; Vernon, 1993) suggests that school counselors should:

1. Thoroughly understand the behaviors connected with each developmental stage.
2. Recognize which behaviors should normally ameliorate over the course of development and which will require treatment.
3. Comprehend how a multitude of interacting variables can influence all developmental levels of functioning.
4. Be aware of the individual's personal and developmental history.
5. Understand the individual's unique capacity for development.
6. Be knowledgeable about the probability of future developmental events.
7. Thoroughly appreciate the effect cultural background may have on all aspects of assessment and counseling.
8. Ensure that appropriate dialogue and nonverbal communication is evidenced during the counseling process, especially the initial session.

These criteria must be integrated into a school counseling content paradigm that emphasizes ethnic and cultural diversity, as well as developmental characteristics. Ivey, Ivey, and Simek-Morgan (1993) defined the term *culturally intentional counselor* as one who reflects these integrated qualities. According to those authors, the following key concepts are important in helping school counselors to generate their own counseling model.

1. *Worldview.* How do you and your student perceive meaning in the world? Are you and your student operating from the same locus of control and locus of responsibility? The cross-cultural counselor accepts ethnic students within a familial and cultural context. Each individual views the world through multiple frames, including cultural, contextual, religious, and ethnic. However, these same individuals share at least one worldview—that of being a citizen of the world.

2. *Cultural intentionality.* Ivey et al. (1993) concluded that the culturally intentional counselor would possess the abilities to generate

   a. A maximum number of thoughts and behaviors to communicate with self and others within a given culture.

   b. Thoughts and behaviors necessary to communicate with diverse groups and individuals.

   c. Actions on the many possibilities existing in a culture, and reflect on these actions.

3. *The scientist–practitioner.* This term implies that helping professionals rely on empirical research, in addition to practical experience, to base clinical and counseling decisions. The very fact that the reader is using this resource reflects an interest in discovering new ideas and approaches, current research findings, and different theoretical models. The profession of school counseling is not static, and school counselors must accept the responsibility to keep abreast of developments.

4. *Ethics.* Ethical counseling requires a multicultural and cross-cultural perspective. Korman (1973) declared over two decades ago that

   The provision of professional services to persons of culturally diverse backgrounds by persons not competent in understanding and providing professional services to such group shall be considered unethical; it shall be equally unethical to deny such persons professional services because the present staff is inadequately prepared; it shall be the obligation of all service agencies to employ competent persons or to provide continuing education for the present staff to meet the service needs of the culturally diverse population it serves. (p. 105)

Thus, school counselors have an ethical responsibility to ensure that no harm will come to their students. One means of ensuring this responsibility is by keeping informed of the changing ethics of counseling. The ethical guidelines found in Appendixes C and D will expand the following abridged guidelines for the school counselor's ethical journey.

1. *Ensure confidentiality.* The counselor must inform students of their right to confidentiality regarding disclosures during the session, excluding information that may endanger the life of student or others, damage to school property, and matters of child abuse. School counselors must also be able to distinguish between counselor confidentiality and the legal privileged communication rights of medical doctors, lawyers, and certain religious officials. The school counselor must be wary of the often insistent querying of teachers and administrators for information regarding what a certain student said or did not say. The counselor must also be knowledgeable about computer and interactive technological confidentiality.

2. *Know and accept your limitations.* School counselors, despite the public's and school's perceptions, cannot be the solution to all problems. School counselors must be aware of their personal limitations. Self-knowledge of liabilities would preclude counseling endeavors that could potentially be more harmful to the student than helpful. For example, school counselors are not trained to be pastoral or religious counselors. Even if school counselors possess additional training in these areas, public school counseling is not the area to practice that training.

3. *Refer and consult.* School counselors have the responsibility to seek more information about concerns not under their normal purview. Consulting with other professionals may render invaluable assistance. The other option is referral. School counselors are obligated to refer students to other professionals or resources for concerns outside their training as school counselors. For example, many school counselor training programs do not require courses in human sexuality for initial certification as a school counselor. The school counselor may need to refer students who are displaying symptoms beyond developmental issues of sexuality. Referral of such students does not imply, for example, that an elementary school counselor cannot counsel a child who frequently fondles himself or herself at school. If counseling the student (and perhaps family) of the inappropriateness of the behavior does not cease the behavior, then referral to a specialist is the recourse.

4. *Treat the student as you would like to be treated.* Most students will respond to fair and just treatment. Such treatment must be consistent and applicable to all students. Respect, dignity, kindness, and honestly

are always rewarded by similar behaviors. The students' perceived trustworthiness of the school counselor is more important than ethnic or cultural similarity between student and school counselor (LaFromboise & Dixon, 1981).

5. *Be constantly alert to individual differences.* One of the most important rules for the school counselor to remember is that more variance exists within groups than between groups. The emphasis on cross-cultural differences often usurps the importance of within-cultural group differences. For example, more compatibility exists between low socioeconomic status European American tenant farmers and Mexican American field workers than exists between that farmer and a European American lawyer. Developmental theoretical orientations need to be interpreted with respect to ethnic and cultural historical and contemporary overtones.

6. *Be alert to nonverbal behaviors.* The numerous ethnicities and cultures and the variability within each prevent a universal interpretation of nonverbal behaviors. The school counselor must remember that individual students may not behave in ways consistent with counselor expectations. For example, most research advise non-Native American Indian counselors to avoid intense direct eye contact with traditional Native American Indian students, because it can be considered disrespectful, and not to expect direct eye contact from traditional Native American Indian students (Attneave, 1985; Herring, 1990a, 1997a; Lewis & Ho, 1989).

7. *Keep informed of ethical standards.* School counselors are responsible for knowing the ethical standards of their profession. In 1991, for example, the Association for Multicultural Counseling and Development (AMCD) approved a document outlining the need and rationale for a multicultural perspective in counseling. The work of AMCD's Professional Standards committee went further in proposing multicultural and cross-cultural counseling competencies and strongly encouraged the American Counseling Association (ACA) in 1995 and the counseling profession to adopt these competencies in accreditation criteria (Sue, Arrendondo, & McDavis, 1992). In April 1995 in Denver, the Executive Board of AMCD adopted these competencies (Arredondo et al., 1996). In addition, ACA revised its Ethical Standards in 1995. The reader is advised to read these competencies in Appendix C carefully and to review the operationalization of these competencies in Arredondo et al. (1996).

8. *Keep informed.* School counselors must constantly be alert to changes in the counseling profession. Innovative counseling tools and interventions are constantly being disseminated in the literature and other resources, especially in the field of technology. School counselors need to keep abreast and be alert to these types of development.

Process Emphases

The method by which school counselors process content knowledge is vital in counseling with ethnic and cultural school youths. From a synergetic perspective, the school counselor selects the most appropriate techniques for the ethnic and cultural student, following the counseling direction warranted by environmental and historical influences. This section discusses selected variables in ensuring ethnic- and culture-specific school counseling.

PHYSICAL SETTING

The physical setting of school counseling sessions should be comfortable and appealing to students. School counselors should be aware of students' preferences in personal space because seating arrangement and physical distance between the school counselor and the student can affect the therapeutic relationship (Gladding, 1992; Herring, 1990b, 1991b, 1997b). The comfort level is influenced by many variables, including age, gender, cultural and ethnic background, and personal experiences (Herring, 1991b, 1997b). School counselors should allow students to determine their own comfort zone and should provide a variety of options.

BASIC HELPING SKILLS

The "core conditions" of the school counseling process include empathy, respect, and genuineness (Carkhuff & Berenson, 1967; Cormier & Cormier, 1991; Rogers, 1951).

Empathy. School counselors demonstrate empathic understanding when they perceive the world (or situation) the way their students do and accurately communicate this perceptual comprehension back to their students (Schmidt, 1993; Truax & Carkhuff, 1967). Two levels of empathy—primary and advanced—illustrate the varied behaviors and skills school counselors use to demonstrate their understanding to their students (Carkhuff, 1969; Gladding, 1992). *Primary empathy* is the process of understanding and communicating the essential feelings and behaviors expressed by the student and acknowledges the "experiences and behaviors underlying these feelings" (Gladding, 1992, p. 205). *Advanced empathy* requires responses that move the relationship beyond initial understanding toward increased "self-exploration by adding deeper feeling and meaning to the client's [student's] expression" (George & Cristiani, 1990, p. 158).

School counselors should remember that empathy is conveyed primarily by verbal and nonverbal messages (Cormier & Cormier, 1991). The school counselor will need to elicit information from the student that relates to relevant experiences, thoughts, and feelings. Some ethnic and cultural groups are not comfortable disclosing personal information and find rapid-fire questioning techniques of many European American counselors offensive (Ivey, 1988). For example, Hispanic American students tend to self-disclosure slowly and may need encouragement through storytelling, anecdotes, humor, and proverbs (Thompson & Rudolph, 1988). In addition, Asian American students may be reluctant to disclose in response to probing because of their reliance on the family to resolve problems (Sue & Sue, 1990).

Ethnic and cultural minority students may be more adept at interpreting nonverbal behaviors compared with European American students. Counselors who send conflicting verbal and nonverbal messages may be dismissed as untrustworthy. For example, a school counselor may appear to be listening intently to a student's concern while concurrently busily completing some form of paperwork. This dimension of the school counseling relationship has the potential for overcoming any initial problems between a majority group counselor and a minority group student, depending on compatibility of communication styles (Henderson, 1979).

Respect. School counselors demonstrate respect by valuing the student as an individual with worth and dignity. Sometimes referred to as *unconditional positive regard*, respect includes the ingredients of equality, equity, and shared responsibility. School counselors must suspend value judgments and convey warmth. Although warmth is communicated through verbal and nonverbal behaviors that have specific meaning within the European American culture, culturally different students may perceive these same nonverbal behaviors quite differently. For example, European Americans value direct eye contact and attribute avoidance of eye contact to negative traits; however, some cultures consider avoidance of eye contact or indirect gazing as respectful nonverbal behavior and consider direct eye contact rude and intrusive (Herring, 1990a; 1991a; Ivey, 1988; Sue & Sue, 1990).

Genuineness. Genuineness, sometimes called *congruence*, is a characteristic that allows school counselors to be who they are without playing a role or hiding behind a facade (Schmidt, 1993). Genuineness is best conveyed by being willing to work with the ethnic or cultural minority student and extended family members. Genuineness is evidenced through supporting nonverbal and role behavior, congruence, spontaneity, openness, and self-disclosure (Trotter, 1993).

The following considerations are important (Trotter, 1993):

1. Eye contact, facial expressions such as smiling, and forward-leaning posture may have a negative impact on culturally diverse students, who may interpret these nonverbals as aggressive and intrusive. The counselor needs to acknowledge such differences in the counseling process as exemplifying how cultures differ. The counselor might also help the student to recognize that mainstream culture views these attributes as positive, and they might need to be exhibited in mainstream settings (e.g., job interviews).

2. Role and position in the United States is much less an obstacle than in many non-Western cultures. School counselors might emphasize, at least initially, that all human beings are equal and have dignity as human beings, but that does not mean that all human beings have equal abilities.

3. Even though self-disclosure often generates an open and facilitative relationship between a majority counselor and student, culturally different students do not necessarily value sharing intimate details and may feel uncomfortable and embarrassed.

BASIC ATTENDING SKILLS

Basic attending behaviors (e.g., eye contact, body language, vocal tone, and facial expression) encourage communication by transmitting the message to students that the counselor respects them and is interested in what they have to say. Attending behaviors vary culturally and individually. Individual differences among ethnic students may be as important as cultural patterns. The counselor should be alert to within-group variances and not generalize patterns of attending behaviors.

Sue and Sue (1990) documented that many ethnic and cultural minority students terminate school counseling early and suggested that more sensitive approaches are needed. These researchers summarized research linking the vital importance of including spatial, nonverbal, and related dimensions to effective counseling. For example, a saying common among African Americans, "If you really want to know what White folks are thinking or feeling, don't listen to what they say, but how they say it" illustrates this point (Sue & Sue, 1990, p. 427).

Active listening skills. The ability to listen accurately to a student's problem is an essential component to effective school counseling. Students need to know if the school counselor has heard them correctly (Terry, Burden, & Pedersen, 1991). The four most common kinds of listening responses are clarification, paraphrase, reflection, and summarization.

> *Clarification*: A question, often used after an unclear student comment and usually starts with "Do you mean that . . ." or "Are you saying that . . ." along with a rephrasing of all or part of the student's previous comment.
> *Paraphrasing*: Rephrasing of the content part of the student's message.
> *Reflection*: Rephrasing of the student's feelings, or the affective message. For example, an Asian American high school student may feel very depressed (affect) about not excelling academically (content).
> *Summarization*: An extension of the paraphrase and reflection responses that involves tying together and rephrasing two or more different parts of a message.

To illustrate these responses, note the following examples of responses:

> *Student, a female high school senior*: My whole life fell apart when my parents were killed. I keep feeling so unsure about my ability to make it on my own. I am the only child and my parents made all my decisions for me. Now I haven't slept well since the funeral, and I've started drinking. I can't even think straight. Besides, I've put on 15 pounds and look like a witch. Who would even want to hire me after graduation?
> *Counselor clarification*: Are you saying that one of the hardest things facing you now is to have enough confidence in your ability to make the decisions alone?
> *Counselor paraphrase*: Since your parents' deaths, you have all the responsibilities and decisions on your shoulders.
> *Counselor reflection*: You feel concerned about your ability to shoulder all your responsibilities.
> *Counselor summarization*: Now that your parents are no longer here, you're facing a few things that are very difficult for you right now . . . handling your responsibilities, making decisions, graduating, thinking of a job, and trying to take care of yourself.

Observation skills. School counselors should constantly be aware of students' body language and understand the implications of nonverbal communication. In addition, they should reflect their observations to their students (Gilliland & James, 1988) but not attempt to interpret their meanings (Gladding, 1992). After trust is established in the counseling relationship, inconsistencies between verbal and nonverbal communications may be addressed (Meier, 1989).

Communication skills. School counselors need strategies and interventions that enable them to collect information without affecting the counseling process. In this endeavor, school counselors should generally talk less than their ethnic and cultural minority students. The following are some of the most common school counseling communication techniques (Gilliland & James, 1988; Gladding, 1992; Meier, 1989; Terry et al., 1991; Vernon, 1993):

1. *Initial contact*: School counselors should acknowledge the student's opening depth of interaction, expand it, and build on it.
2. *Minimal encouragers*: Minimum encouragers (e.g., nonverbal actions) are active, yet nonintrusive ways to encourage increased verbalization.
3. *Accentuation*: School counselors can encourage further disclosure by emphasizing words, metaphors, and key words.
4. *Open-ended questions*: School counselors may use open-ended questions and invite the student to complete them. They should not ask "why" to obtain information as this word can be associated with disapproval or challenge.
5. *Closed questions*: Closed questions are used generally to elicit limited information and tend to discourage open discussions.
6. *Requests for clarification*: Clarification requests are used for confusion about the student's message, to slow down a fast-paced disclosure, to focus on key points, or to reintroduce a topic that students mention, then quickly avoid (See **Chart 6.1**).
7. *Silence*: School counselors can use silence to give students the opportunity to digest and internalize new knowledge. In addition, the use of silence while nonverbally attending to ethnic and cultural minority students demonstrates a deep sense of empathy.
8. *Paraphrasing*: Paraphrasing conveys school counselor understanding, facilitates students' insights into their own experiences, and enables counselors to verify their interpretation of what the students said.
9. *Summarization*: School counselors can use this technique to organize ethnic and cultural minority students' thoughts and feelings, recap and connect themes, outline progress, give direction, and plan future strategies.

DIFFERENCES IN PRIORITY SETTING

Many students will participate in school counseling with variances in their perceptions of priority setting. For example, the traditional Native American Indian student would not be receptive to long-term goal setting or problem solving (Herring, in 1997a). On the other hand, an acculturated Native American Indian student would be responsive because that strategy would reflect that student's adopted worldview. Similarly, an ethnically ambiguous student's

CHART 6.1

Five Steps of Communication

1. Message	Sender has to understand the message to be sent
2. Message Sent	To the Receiver(s)
3. Message Received	By the intended Receiver(s)
4. Message Understood	All aspects (content, affect, etc.) understood by Receiver(s)
5. Feedback to Sender	Receiver(s) convey to the Sender through verbal or nonverbal means or writing that the Message was received and understood

priority may be ethnic identity rather than the counselor's priority of scholastic demonstration.

VARIED LEVELS OF CULTURATION

A few research studies have proved consistently that culturation relates to how students perceive counseling (Atkinson & Gim, 1989; Atkinson, Whiteley, & Gim, 1990; Gim, Atkinson, & Kim, 1991; Gim, Atkinson, & Whiteley, 1990). These studies suggest that less-culturated ethnic students are more than likely to trust and express a preference for and a willingness to see an ethnically similar school counselor than are their more culturated ethnic peers. School counselors should be aware not only of students' ethnic background but also of the extent to which students identify with and practice the culture of their ancestors (Atkinson, Morten, & Sue, 1993).

For example, Herring (1991a, 1997b) discussed two critical considerations for building trust between Native American Indians, and school counselors can play a lead role in achieving this goal. First, counselors must demonstrate awareness of the tribal identity and familial pattern of Native American Indian students to gain their respect and trust. Second, counselors must be knowledgeable of the distinct family patterns among Native American Indians: traditional, transitional, bicultural, and assimilated. School counselors need to be able to match their counseling strategies with the appropriate family and acculturation pattern.

SOCIOECONOMIC STATUS

The student characteristic having the most significant impact on the school counseling process is socioeconomic status (SES), or social class (Hannon,

Ritchie, & Rye, 1992). Government statistics regarding socioeconomic conditions in the United States indicate that racial and ethnic minority families are overrepresented among the poor. For example, citing U.S. census data for 1987, Ponterotto and Casas (1991) reported that whereas only 11% of European American families live in poverty, approximately 31% of African Americans, 28% of Mexican Americans, and 39% of Puerto Ricans are poor. Other government statistics summarized by Locke (1992) document that Native American Indians have the highest unemployment and the lowest average income of any ethnic minority group in this country.

Socioeconomic status affects the school counseling process, the quality of the relationship that is established, and the value placed on the counseling process itself by the ethnic minority student. For example, a knowledgeable school counselor would not destroy positive accomplishments by displaying signs of one-upmanship to a low-SES ethnic minority student (Herring, 1990a).

VALUE OF FAMILY COUNSELING

Successful school counseling with diverse students will have to involve their families. In all ethnic and cultural groups, the individual member develops in a familial system operating within a cultural setting. From this family of origin, the individuals learn the indigenous culture. The development and selection of a culturally sensitive orientation for school counseling with ethnic minority students must take into consideration factors that distinguish ethnic minority families from the mainstream middle-class European American families (Ho, 1987). These factors are discussed briefly below.

Ethnic minority reality. Racism, social and political discrimination, lack of education, unemployment and underemployment, and poverty dominate the existence of many ethnic and cultural minority families. These factors have a negative effect on the lives of students socialized within these families. These factors also affect these students' help-seeking behaviors, including underutilization of school counselors who generally are monolinguistic, middle class, and ethnocentric in problem diagnosis and counseling process (Acosta, Yamamoto, & Evans, 1982).

Impact of external system on minority cultures. Ethnic minority families may experience stress resulting from conflicting values of the European American mainstream society. European American middle-class values include an emphasis on control of nature, orientation on the future, fixation with youthful appearance, individual autonomy, competitiveness, vertical mobility, and the concept of the nuclear family. Most ethnic minority groups value the past and enjoy the past, emphasize harmony with nature, stress respect of elders, enjoy the status quo, prefer collectivity, and derive from extended family systems. The basic shared experiences of ethnic minority groups with the mainstream system are social injustice (e.g., overrepresentation of ethnic minorities in prisons), social inconsistency (e.g., personal rejection), and personal impotence (e.g., inadequate support systems; Chestang, 1976).

Biculturalism. Ethnic and cultural minority students are inevitably part of at least two cultures. They participate in several cultural systems that often require several sets of behaviors. These students also experience multiple ways of coping with tasks, expectations, and behaviors (Chestang, 1976). For example, a Japanese American man may behave cooperatively with his extended family, as his culture demands, but he may behave competitively at work as the European American culture requires. School counselors will need to consider age and gender, as well as educational, socioeconomic, political, familial, and linguistic factors in their assessment of an ethnic minority student's biculturalism.

Consequently, the school counselor must consider the level of culturation within both cultures, the degree to which the student is able to choose between two cultures, and the level of participation in each culture that is desirable and obtainable by each student or family (Ho, 1987, 1992).

Ethnic differences in minority status. Several factors influence the differentiated status of ethnic minorities in this nation. Historical and current governmental policies are two important influences. For example, a history of slavery and discrimination has rendered African Americans very demoralized. Similarly, Native American Indians have experienced attempts of annihilation, assimilation, disfranchisement, reservational placement, and self-determination to the point of being considered as "emigrants" in their own homeland. Also, to be eligible for federal programs, persons must be able to *prove* at least one-eighth "Indian blood" or one-quarter "Indian blood," depending on the agency.

Skin color is also an important factor in differentiating experiences of ethnic minority students, albeit that skin color does not itself determine ethnicity. Many ethnic minority students attempt to "pass" as European American because skin color is perhaps the most pervasive reason for discrimination. Students from a mixed heritage also can be easily traumatized by pressure to define themselves as "White" or "Black," complicated further when other family members are labeled differently (Gross, 1996; Ho, 1987, 1992).

Ethnicity and language. Ethnicity is experienced and is perpetuated through one's language (or languages). A common language acts as a unique common bond that signifies membership in a specific ethnic group. School counselors should provide bilingual service to students and families to ensure effective delivery of services. School counseling with students requires close examination of the language used by each ethnic minority student and as many variations of a language—whether from ethnic group to ethnic group, intergenerational, or even regional—that may impede effective communication (Ho, 1987, 1992). The counselor must not presume, for example, that a Mexican American student and a Puerto Rican student speak the same Spanish dialect, or that they may understand one another because of their language.

Ethnicity and social class. Gordon (1978) used the term *ethclass* to describe the point at which social class and ethnic group membership intersect. Although economically and materially successful, some ethnic minority members experience difficulty in being accepted by European American middle-class society and may concurrently feel alienated from their own ethnic group. In addition, the ethclass among ethnic minorities is positively correlated to a member's English language efficiency, level of education, and degree of culturation. The counselor must understand the student's level of retention of traditional heritage and degree of adherence to family ethnicity in addressing that particular student's needs (see **Case Study 6.1**).

The problems associated with the poverty experienced by ethnic minority parents can have a significant effect on their participation in the educational system (Kiselica, Changizi, Cureton, & Gridley, 1995). For example, Williams (1991) described the difficulties that poor, inner-city African American parents have in monitoring and participating in their children's education. These families were concerned about their children's academic performance. However, they were plagued by concerns such as caring for preschool children; one or both parents working in low-paying jobs located far from home; problems with health, housing, and crime; and dealing with governmental agencies. These concerns prevented most of the parents from performing an active role in their children's education or providing older children with parental supervision after school hours.

Many school districts have failed to implement programs that recognize and assist with poverty-related problems targeted to increase the involvement of low-income families in schools (McLaughlin & Shields, 1987). School coun-

CASE STUDY 6.1

Ethnic Identity Issues

Phinney and Rosenthal (1992, pp. 163–165) conducted interviews with Asian American, African American, and Hispanic American high school students. These interviews were conducted with two groups, those scoring relatively high or relatively low on ethnic identity. The issues and conflicts about their ethnicity faced by these adolescents were similar in both groups; for example:

> I am not ashamed of being Hispanic but . . . I am disappointed because I compare the Hispanic race to other races. . . . We have not done much.
> I am very proud of my ethnicity, I am proud of some of the good things my culture has done, and then again, there are certain things like in every culture, there are always some people who have to ruin it for everybody.

Significantly more high ethnic identity adolescents, when asked how they dealt with incidents of stereotyping and discrimination, stated that they responded actively, by explaining why stereotyping is inaccurate or why discrimination is wrong; for example:

> I'm going to let them know, just because you see that on TV, that's not reality.
> You talk about it and you try to change things. You try to make people see you not as White, Black, Asian, just see you for who you are and what you can do.
> The people I can help, the people I can reach, I try to talk to them.

Furthermore, a high ethnic identity was associated with an understanding that the prejudice was not personally directed at oneself:

> A lot of times we have been put down. Before, it used to hurt me a lot emotionally, because I did kind of feel that I was not as good as [the White students] were. . . . I think I matured. . . . What I saw is how ignorant people could be to think another person who is of a different color or of a different ethnic group is not as smart.

Adolescents who have achieved a secure, comfortable ethnic identity have dealt with their ambivalence, rejected negative stereotypes, and resolved conflicts associated with their ethnicity. They feel good about themselves.

> I am what I am, and I don't know if that is Asian or if that is American. . . . I usually think of myself as totally Americanized, [but] I know I don't want to be American [i.e., White], like brown hair and blue eyes. I am proud to be Japanese American.
> I am proud of my heritage and I am also proud that I know how to speak English and that I was born and raised here. I am happy the way I am.

SOURCE: Adapted from "Ethnic Identity in Adolescence: Process, Context, and Outcome," by J. S. Phinney and D. A. Rosenthal, 1992. In G. R. Adams, T. P. Gullotta, and R. Montemayor (Eds.), *Adolescent Identity Formation* (pp. 163–165).

selors are in a position to serve as a resource for ethnic minority parents (Lee, 1989, 1996). School counselors can work toward preventing and mediating value conflicts and misunderstandings, taking measures to reduce feelings of alienation, and assisting parents in overcoming socioeconomic hardships. School counselors must help ethnic minority parents to manage their multiple stressors if parental involvement with the schools is to increase (see **Something to Consider 6.1**).

Natural healing strategies. Traditional healing practices of ethnic minority cultures have both relevance and validity for the school counselor working with students from those cultures (Lee & Armstrong, 1996). Attitudes and beliefs about mental health vary among the subcultures of ethnic minority groups. The school counselor should be knowledgeable about such strategies and acknowledge their power with students. Incorporation of traditional healing methods may facilitate the wholesome development of the student and expedite closure of the presenting problem. However, the ethnic-dissimilar school counselor might consider allowing indigenous healers to facilitate such integration. Two examples follow.

1. *Native American Indian.* For example, one ancient Native American Indian idea about health is that health results from having a harmonious relationship with nature (Thomason, 1991, 1996). Harmony with nature is incorporated into the key Native American Indian philosophical concept of holism, and one of the most important symbols is the circle, or hoop of life (Heinrich, Corbine, & Thomas, 1990). The famous Lakota Oglala Sioux medicine man Black Elk described it in this manner:

> You have noticed that everything an Indian does is in a circle, and that is because the Power of the World always works in circles, and everything tries to be round. In the old days when we were strong and happy people, all our power came to us from the sacred hoop of the nation, and so long as the hoop was unbroken, the people flourished. (Brown, 1964, pp. 13–14)

Manson (1986) reported that "many traditional Indian and Native healing practices are gradually being incorporated into contemporary approaches to mental health treatment" (p. 64). He described three particular practices: (a) *four circles*, concentric circles of relationship between the individual and Creator, spouse, nuclear family, and extended family as a culturally based structural concept for self-understanding; (b) *talking circle*, a forum for expressing thoughts and feelings in an environment of total acceptance without time constraints, using sacred objects, the pipe, and prayer; and (c) *sweat lodge*, a physical and spiritual self-purification bathing ritual that is used before

SOMETHING TO CONSIDER 6.1

Strategies for Involving Ethnic Minority Parent Involvement

School counselors can serve as a resource for ethnic minority parents. Research findings suggest the following effective strategies for school counselors to consider.

1. To prevent cultural misunderstandings, educate school personnel about the value systems and cultural experiences of ethnic minority families (Atkinson & Juntunen, 1994; Lee, 1989; Nicolau & Ramos, 1990).
2. To reduce parental hesitation about being involved in schools, educate ethnic minority parents about the U.S. educational system, for example, community awareness workshops, parent training programs, print and media, interpreters, and letters (Atkinson & Juntunen, 1994; First, 1988; Liontos, 1992; Nicolau & Ramos, 1990; Nieto, 1992; Yao, 1988).
3. To reduce alienation from the school system, include genuinely showing an interest in how parents feel about the educational system and working to empower parents, for example, encourage parents to become leaders in their school communities, empathize with the perception that the school has taken away their control over their children's destiny in school (Casas & Furlong, 1994; Liontos, 1992).
4. To develop trust and confidence, match counseling styles with family types and degree of acculturation (Herring, 1991a, Herring & Erchul, 1988).
5. To enhance involvement of Hispanic parents, be committed to outreach, to communicate honestly, and to be respectful of cultural values and concerns, and use a personal approach such as home visits by the school counselor (Nicolau & Ramos, 1990).
6. To promote involvement of Asian parents, understand the cultural values of Asian peoples and genuinely care about the concerns of the parents, and look at each family on an individual basis in order to refrain from responding to Asian Americans in a stereotypic manner (Morrow, 1991).
7. To bridge the gap between home and school, develop a comprehensive family consultation model that includes school curriculum, standardized testing and placement, parental participation and involvement, and the educational and administrative structure of the school; within the home, provide academic counseling, personal–social counseling, parent skills training, and information on community resources (Cole, Thomas, & Lee, 1988).
8. To broaden the mission of schools and make them more relevant to their communities, develop partnerships with social and health agencies, remain open 7 days a week 12 months a year, and provide parents and children struggling to overcome the untold hardships of poverty a safe haven for health care, socializing, and recreation (Dryfoos, 1994; Murphy, 1993).

important ceremonies as well as for therapy for a variety of ailments and sometimes just to relax and to meditate. Hall (1986) concluded, "The possibility exists that, fostered by but not controlled by or restricted to alcohol treatment programs, the sweat lodge may have a major role in the prevention of alcohol abuse and in the creation of a new Indian identity" (p. 176).

2. *African.* Vontress (1991) described many different techniques used by African healers to help patients. He suggested that school counselors in the United States working with students from Africa "should take full responsibility for curing them, that they should use whatever methods necessary to do so, and that the strategies should recognize the significance of the spiritual in the lives of those who consult them" (pp. 248–249). For example, in Africa, healing often takes place in settings that may appear inappropriate to Western counselors. The environment may include loud music, chanting, and dancing. In some instances and for some students, the display of African artifacts and the presence of African music in the background alleviate their initial anxiety of being left alone in a quiet office.

As Heinrich et al. (1990) concluded:

> Counselors must affirm that ethnic minority students and cultures are not inherently inferior and that they possess values and meanings that are, at least in some dimensions, superior to those of the dominant culture. Counselors must be invested in learning, intellectually and affectively, a new language of culturally relevant metaphors that will, at least temporarily, alter their perceptions of what is real and what is possible. (p. 132)

Individuals experience stress and mental discomfort that interfere with daily functioning, regardless of the ethnicity or culture. Counseling professionals and traditional healers provide similar services despite perceived differences by the uninformed. Lee and Armstrong (1996) concluded,

> Although on the surface these two types of helpers appear to be very different, they have much in common. In fact, in many ways, traditional healers can be considered "psychologists" or "counselors," but instead of calling on Freud or Rogers, they call on spirits or deities from a cultural past. (p. 454)

Thus, to be effective, school counselors must be able to identify these crucial aspects of their ethnic minority student's culture: (a) ways in which health and illness is explained, (b) specific categories of illness and dysfunction, and (c) the meaning attributed to various symptoms and feelings (Good & Good, 1986).

Multicultural and Cross-Cultural Counseling Issues in School Counseling

The previous sections of this chapter have discussed developmental concerns with content and process issues when counseling with ethnic and cultural minority youths. In essence, the discussions sought to encourage school counselors to be synergetic in their counseling efforts with ethnic and cultural minority youths.

BARRIERS TO SCHOOL COUNSELING EFFECTIVENESS

Any approach to school counseling that claims to be multicultural or cross-cultural in nature must address the barriers to cross-cultural and multicultural counseling effectiveness facing school counselors. A synthesis of these barriers (D'Andrea & Daniels, 1991; Herring, 1997b; Lee, 1996; Pedersen, 1987; Sue & Sue, 1990; Trotter, 1993; Vernon, 1993) is reflected as follows:

1. Many school counselors, being neither skilled nor motivated to serve the interests of culturally different students, are unable or unwilling to consider their lack of cultural sensitivity in counseling and, furthermore, fail to refer students elsewhere.
2. Counselors experience varying degrees of cognitive dissonance, which comes from the discrepancy between the counselor's personal expectations of how culturally different students ought to think, feel, and react to life events and their own thoughts, feelings, and reactions.
3. Counselors fail to recognize the negative perceptions of self and the messages of hopelessness that permeate ethnic and cultural minority group terms, and this may mean compromising important elements of sociocultural identity.
4. Counselors underestimate the importance of student culture, holding that "they are just like us" or, conversely, they overemphasize cultural differences to the extent that culturally diverse students are considered deviant or are treated like rare and fragile specimens.
5. Counselors fail to see the overlapping contexts in which diverse students find themselves—that which is dominated by a culture of origin and that which is dominated by a majority culture.
6. Counselors assume that students have a common understanding of what constitutes "normal" behavior and that this understanding transcends socioeconomic and sociopolitical situations.
7. Counselors assume that school counseling should be directed primarily toward development of students and, in so doing, fail to take advantage

of the potential effectiveness of natural support systems: the family, peer group, or community.

8. Counselors define issues of a multicultural nature from a framework constricted by boundaries drawn by academic disciplines and not exchanging questions/insights with other professionals.

9. Counselors hold to the ideal that independence is valuable and dependence is undesirable.

10. Counselors try to change students to fit the system rather than intervene constructively to influence the system so it becomes more responsive to students.

11. Counselors focus on immediate events as more salient than personal history and deny the role of historical events as antecedents in determining ongoing behavior.

12. Counselors emphasize individual-centered forms of counseling and competition for status, recognition, and achievement.

13. Counselors stress the important of verbal expression of emotion and self-disclosure as essential goals in counseling through "talking therapy."

14. Counselors assume that obtaining insights or understanding into a student's deep, underlying dynamics is mentally beneficial.

15. Counselors conduct counseling as an ambiguous and unstructured activity.

The "in-tuned" school counselor will realize that these barriers have certain embedded stereotypes. The counselor's knowledge of within-group variances will spurn the effective use of within-group specifics in selecting the counseling process.

WHAT THE SCHOOL COUNSELOR NEEDS TO DO

If school counselors fail to understand the uniqueness of the ethnic minority students before them and their cultural influences, particularly as manifested in their families of origin, even the most well-intentioned school counseling effort is likely to fail (Ivey et al., 1993). Pedersen (1985) concluded:

> To some extent, all mental health counseling is multicultural. If we consider age, lifestyle, socioeconomic status, and gender differences, it quickly becomes apparent that there is a multicultural dimension in every counseling relationship. (p. 94)

And, for more emphasis, Sue (1992) noted:

> Counseling has been used as an instrument of oppression as it has been designed to transmit a certain set of individualistic cultural values. Traditional counseling

has *harmed* minorities and women. Counseling and therapy have been the hand-maiden of the status quo and as such, represent a political statement. (p. 6)

Wrenn (1962, 1985) described "culturally encapsulated counselors" as those who cannot, or will not, try to escape from their personal cultural self when working with dissimilar students. Multicultural and cross-cultural counseling begin with cultural awareness—*conscientizaçao*. Freire (1972) used conscientizaçao to mean a consciousness of self in relation to contextual and cultural issues. In other words, when students learn to discuss their issues in cultural context, they learn to balance what was previously seen as "their problem" with what may indeed be "society's problem" (p. 117). Conscientizaçao is the process of learning a balance of individual and societal responsibility and acting on that knowledge (Ivey et al., 1993). **Case Study 6.2** presents student situations that deserve appropriate timing of school counselor responses.

PRECONDITIONS FOR COUNSELING

In preparing to work with diverse ethnic and cultural students, school counselors should consider the following synopsis of suggestions (Henderson, 1979; Peterson & Nisenholtz, 1991; Sue, 1981; Sue, Ito, & Bradshaw, 1982; Vernon, 1993):

1. Have faith in the students' ability to grow and to fully realize their potential, given responsive, supportive, and developmental intervention across both cultural contexts in which the students are immersed. Native American Indian students (Herring, 1989a, 1989b) and students from Africa (Vontress, 1991), for example, might benefit from an approach that incorporates legends, rituals, and cultural traditions toward healing.

2. Examine their own personal attitudes and personality style and how these characteristics influence how they behave with culturally diverse students. Culturally skilled counselors should appreciate their own cultural heritage, values, and biases and be comfortable with incongruences between them and their students. They should recognize their limitations and be sensitive to conditions warranting referral.

3. Understand that sociopolitical forces influence how culturally diverse students act. Be prepared to exercise institutional intervention on behalf of multicultural students when warranted.

4. Become familiar with the differences in worldviews that characterize ethnic minority students and the implications for counseling. Differences in worldviews are particularly noteworthy in Native American Indian

---

CASE STUDY 6.2

Selecting Helping Strategies

Instructions: Listed in the left column are six student situations. Listed in the right column are the five guidelines for appropriate timing of strategy introduction and selection. Decide which of these five guidelines is represented in each of the situations. More than one guideline may "fit" any situation. Afterward, discuss how different ethnic and cultural minority students would interpret their situations.

_____ 1. The student has been late the last few weeks and on one occasion "forgot" the appointment.

a. Quality of the relationship

_____ 2. You asked the student to complete a self-report inventory during the week. The student started it but says he (she) needs another week to finish it.

b. Assessment of the problem

_____ 3. The student shifts the focus during the third readiness session from not being able to decide on a college major to the concern that he (she) is "going crazy."

c. Development of counseling goals and commitment

_____ 4. The student keeps changing his (her) mind about wanting his (her) relationship to be different.

d. Student and commitment

_____ 5. The student repeatedly asks you to solve issues for him (her).

e. Collection of baseline data

_____ 6. The student has left the session early the last two times.

SOURCE: Adapted from *Interviewing Strategies for Helpers*, by W. Cormier and S. L. Cormier, 1991, p. 304.

---

students, who tend to value cooperation and harmony, generosity and sharing, living in the present rather than planning for the future, and respect for older people (Herring, 1989a, 1991a; Sue & Sue, 1990) (see **Case Study 6.3**).

5. Have a clear working knowledge of many approaches to counseling and be able to use the techniques that best accommodate cultural and ethnic differences without aggravating the presenting problems.

CASE STUDY 6.3

Native American Indian Counseling Process

Sue and Sue (1990) concluded that the best processes for a school counselor to monitor in counseling with Native American Indian students are those of silence, acceptance, and restatement. Gibbs (1980) suggested that counseling with Native American Indian students may necessitate developing the process through specific stages. Gibbs identified these stages as appraisal, investigation, involvement, and engagement. Gibbs also postulated the following three propositions a counselor must be willing to accept: (a) Ethnic differences will exist in the initial orientation session; (b) interpersonal versus instrumental competence will permeate the entire counseling process; and (c) the ethnic differences will have significant importance for the implementation of the counseling process and its outcome.

The value of involving the family (Herring, 1989b; Herring & Erchul, 1988; Thomason, 1991) depends primarily on the degree of traditionalism of an individual versus the degree of acculturation to mainstream U.S. society (Thomason, 1991). Dillard (1983) described the continuum as stretching from "the very traditional individual born and reared on a reservation, who speaks the tribal language, to the Native American [Indian] reared in a city who speaks only English and may feel little identification with a tribe" (p. 110). Riner (1979) distinguished four types of Native American Indian families as being the isolated, the traditional, the bicultural, and the acculturated.

A final comment regarding a counseling process involving Native American Indian concerns counseling styles. Many Native American Indians do not respond sincerely or voluntarily to nondirective leadership. Native American Indian students may assign expert power status to non-Natives who are attempting to counsel them. School counselors should be flexible in the counseling process and should use leads to effect any positive result. Given the diversity of the Native American Indian population, school counselors need to be extremely careful to avoid stereotyping Native American Indian students on the basis of generic assumptions. The school counselor especially needs to be alert to diverse tribal values and to varied levels of acculturation.

ESTABLISHING AN EFFECTIVE HELPING RELATIONSHIP

School counselors might consider the following characteristics of effective helpers that can be applied to ethnic and culturally diverse youths, as adapted from Cormier and Cormier (1991) and others (also see **Table 6.1**).

1. Be competent with cultural diversity and be curious enough to know what is happening in the daily life of the student. Henderson (1979)

TABLE 6.1

Barriers and Benefits in Cross-Cultural Counseling

Barriers	Positives
Between-groups counseling	
Student resistance	• Willingness to self-disclose information
Student transference	• Less likely to see counselor as omniscient
Cultural restraints on self-disclosure	• Expectation for success may be enhanced
Student expectations	• Potential for considerable cultural learning by both student and counselor
Counselor countertransference	• Increased need for counselor and student to focus on their own processing
Counselor maladjustment to relationship	• Potential for dealing with culturally dissonant component student problem
Counselor misdirected diagnosis	
Counselor patronization of student's culture	
Counselor denial of culturally dissonant component of student problem	
Counselor "missionary zeal"	
Language differences and value conflicts	
Within-group counseling	
Unjustified assumption of shared feelings	• Shared experience may enhance rapport
Student transference	• Student willingness to self-disclose
Counselor countertransference	

SOURCE: Adapted from *Counseling American Minorities*, by D. R. Atkinson, G. Morten, and D. W. Sue, 1993, p. 61.

---

indicated that what separates effective and ineffective school counselors is more a function of understanding culture and language than the cultural match between student and counselor. Poyatos (1988) supported this perspective in stating that difference is not what makes for divisiveness; rather, lack of appreciation for diversity is what interferes with successful cross-cultural communication.

2. Be cognizant of motivational theory and be able to inspire hope and confidence in students to apply themselves in counseling and follow-through.

3. Be flexible rather than force-fitting the student to any one favored approach.

4. Work to reduce anxiety and promote the emotional security the student needs to take risks.

5. Be aware of any personal attitudes, thoughts, and feelings that might influence the ways in which the counseling relationship develops.

6. Have goodwill, work on behalf of students, and resist becoming dependent on the counseling relationship as a source of personal gratification and professional advancement.

WHAT THE SCHOOL COUNSELOR SHOULD NOT DO

Ineffective school counselor behaviors include lecturing and excessive questioning (Abudabbeh, 1992). These techniques block effective school counselor and student communication and thwart the essential counseling goal of empowering students to grow in self-chosen directions (Vernon, 1993). Gladding (1992) suggested that school counselors do not ask more than two consecutive questions and instead rely on a solid repertoire of attending, listening, and communication skills to encourage student disclosures. In addition, many school counselors tend to offer unilateral advice to students. They should note that advice in itself is not negative. However, the type of advice may be. School counselors need to offer options and alternatives rather than personal projections and value judgments. When school counselors solve problems for their students, they are teaching students to depend on other people's wishes rather than come to grips with their own (see **Something to Consider 6.2**).

PREVENTIVE GUIDANCE

School counselors need to consider, if not reconsider, developmental school counseling as the program of choice in determining how they carry out their professional responsibilities. Through this approach, school counselors are challenged to conduct classroom activities designed to address needs-driven student competencies. Increased awareness of culturally diverse populations is certainly a student competency deserving of concerted attention in the

---

SOMETHING TO CONSIDER 6.2

Eight Questions to Ask Yourself About the Counseling Process

1. What is your overall worldview, and how does it relate to multicultural issues? Have you carefully elaborated your worldview and its implications for your future practice?
2. What are the central dimensions of your definition of ethical practice?
3. As you think about empathic concepts, what is your personal construction of their meaning?
4. With which microskills and concepts do you feel particularly comfortable?
5. What is to be your position on research and keeping abreast of new ideas?
6. What is your understanding and integration of the challenge of multicultural counseling?
7. What theories of counseling appeal to you? What type of integration of these theories are you evolving toward? From what approach do you personally plan to start practice?
8. Have you examined how your personal developmental history in family and culture affects your answers to the above questions?

SOURCE: Adapted from *Counseling and Psychotherapy: A Multicultural Perspective,* by A. E. Ivey, M. B. Ivey, and L. Simek-Morgan, 1993, p. 372.

---

schools. Other strategies advocated by the American School Counselor Association (1988) are as follows:

1. Involve culturally diverse parents on curriculum planning boards and other school projects.
2. Develop workshops for culturally diverse parents to orient them to the school system's philosophy of education.
3. Provide awareness workshops for faculty and staff on the dynamics of cultural diversity.
4. Incorporate culturally diverse human and material resources into the educational process.
5. Promote schoolwide activities focusing on differences and contributions of culturally different people.
6. Provide liaison services to facilitate communication among diverse populations in the school and community.
7. Use materials that are free of culturally biased information.

Preventive counseling is often referred to as *guidance* or *guidance activities*. As opposed to counseling, guidance activities generally have as their purpose the education of the students in an effort to prevent inappropriate behaviors. School counselors will usually offer a didactic presentation, and although little in-depth self-disclosure occurs, an opportunity for some sharing of personal information may result (Neukrug, 1994). With the purpose being more educational than therapeutic, the end result is to increase the knowledge of the student. Guidance activities may be ongoing or can occur on a one-time basis. They may be conducted in small groups, intact classes, or individually. In today's schools, HIV/AIDS and other sexuality issues are viable candidates for guidance-type programs.

Summary

This chapter has identified the key process and content issues inherent to ethnic and cultural counseling in the schools. The need for school counselors to become more aware of and attuned to the unique characteristics and concerns of ethnic and cultural minority children and youths was stressed. School counselors can become more viable facilitators in alleviating the negatives presented by current counseling efforts.

Most counseling approaches used with children and adolescents have been geared toward the adult population. Interventions with students must take into account their developmental levels, which may be idiosyncratic to age, gender, ethnic background, SES, and other potential influencers. In working with culturally diverse students, school counselors must be flexible and able to adapt techniques to students. Understanding nonverbal communication is a central component to successful counseling, as are empathy, respect, and genuineness.

Experiential Activities

1. What is your basic counseling worldview?
   a. How do you view the goals of counseling? Write a statement of your values and belief structures in relation to the goals you have for counseling process.
   b. Where did your values and beliefs originate? How does your family, gender, and cultural background affect your value system?
   c. In what ways might your worldview be limited with some of your students? Which specific values and behaviors might give you difficulty?

    d. What are some additional questions you might ask of yourself and others?

2. In a role-play interaction or counseling session in which you function as the counselor, watch for some significant nonverbal behavior of the student (e.g., shifts in eye contact, voice tone, kinesics). (Do not focus on small nonverbal behaviors out of context with the verbal content.) Focus on this behavior by asking the student whether she or he is aware of what is happening to her or his voice, body posture, eyes, or whatever. Do not interpret or assign meaning to the behavior for the student. Notice where your focus takes the student.

3. Respond to the following. Share your comments with others in your group.

    a. Some of the descriptors of my ethnic/cultural group are . . .

    b. I first learned of my racial/ethnic/cultural group when . . .

    c. Some expected behaviors of my ethnic/cultural group are . . .

    d. Others should know these things about my ethnic/cultural group.

    e. Some similarities between/among my group and _____ are . . .

    f. What I like about _____ is that they . . .

4. Select a member of a different ethnic or cultural group. Have an intercultural dyadic encounter. Try to get to know each other ethnically and culturally. Ask questions of one another and attempt to attain a level of self-disclosure beyond a superficial one. Was it difficult? Why? On what level of self-disclosure was most of the encounter? What seemed to be the obstacles to a deeper level?

References

Abudabbeh, N. (1992). Treatment of post-traumatic stress disorders in the Arab American community. In M. B. Williams & J. F. Sommer (Eds.), *Handbook of post-traumatic therapy: A practical guide to intervention, treatment, and research* (pp. 141–201). Westport, CT: Greenwood Press.

Abu-Eita, S., & Sherif, N. (1990). Counselor competencies and personality traits at secondary schools in Kuwait. *International Journal for the Advancement of Counseling, 13,* 27–38.

Acosta, F., Yamamoto, J., & Evans, L. (1982). *Effective psychotherapy for low-income and minority patients.* New York: Plenum.

American School Counselor Association. (1988). *Position statement on cross/multicultural counseling.* Alexandria, VA: Author.

Arredondo, P., Toporek, R., Brown, S. P., Jones, J., Locke, D. C., Sanchez, J., & Stadler, H. (1996). Operationalization of the multicultural counseling competencies. *Journal of Multicultural Counseling and Development, 24,* 42–78.

Atkinson, D. R., & Gim, R. H. (1989). Asian-American cultural identity and attitudes toward mental health services. *Journal of Counseling Psychology, 36,* 209–212.

Atkinson, D. R., & Juntunen, C. L. (1994). School counselors and school psychologists as school-home-community liaisons in ethnically diverse schools. In P. Pedersen & J. C. Carey (Eds.), *Multicultural counseling in schools: A practical handbook* (pp. 103–120). Boston: Allyn & Bacon.

Atkinson, D. R., Morten, G., & Sue, D. W. (1993). *Counseling American minorities* (4th ed.). Dubuque, IA: Brown & Benchmark.

Atkinson, D. R., Whiteley, S., & Gim, R. H. (1990). Asian-American acculturation and preferences for help providers. *Journal of College Student Development, 31,* 155–161.

Attneave, C. L. (1985). Practical counseling with American Indian and Alaska Native clients. In P. Pedersen (Ed.), *Handbook of cross-cultural counseling and therapy* (pp. 135–140). Westport CT: Greenwood Press.

Brandell, J. (1988). Narrative and historical truth in child psychotherapy. *Psychoanalytic Psychology, 5,* 241–257.

Brown, J. E. (1964). *The spiritual legacy of the American Indian* (Pamphlet No. 135). Wallingford, PA: Pendle Hill.

Carkhuff, R. R. (1969). *Helping and human relations: Selection and training* (Vol. 1). New York: Holt, Rinehart & Winston.

Carkhuff, R. R., & Berenson, B. G. (1967). *Beyond counseling and psychotherapy.* New York: Holt, Rinehart & Winston.

Casas, I. M., & Furlong, M. J. (1994). School counselor as advocates for increased Hispanic parent participation in schools. In P. Pedersen & J. C. Carey (Eds.), *Multicultural counseling in schools: A practical handbook* (pp. 121–156). Boston: Allyn & Bacon.

Chestang, L. (1976). The Black family and Black culture: A study of coping. In M. Satomayor (Ed.), *Cross-cultural perspectives in social work practice and education* (pp. 113–142). Houston, TX: University of Houston, Graduate School of Social Work.

Cole, S. M., Thomas, A. R., & Lee, C. C. (1988). School counselor and school psychologist: Partners in minority family outreach. *Journal of Multicultural Counseling and Development, 16,* 110–116.

Cormier, W., & Cormier, S. L. (1991). *Interviewing strategies for helpers* (3rd ed.). Pacific Grove, CA: Brooks/Cole.

D'Andrea, M., & Daniels, J. (1991). Exploring the different levels of multicultural counseling training in counselor education. *Journal of Counseling & Development, 70,* 78–85.

Dillard, J. M. (1983). *Multicultural counseling: Toward ethnic and cultural relevance in human encounters.* Chicago: Nelson-Hall.

Dryfoos, J. G. (1994). *Full-service schools: A revolution in health and social services for children, youth, and families.* San Francisco: Jossey-Bass.

Erikson, E. (1963). *Identity: Youth and crisis.* New York: Norton.

First, J. M. (1988). Immigrant students in U.S. public schools: Challenges with solutions. *Phi Delta Kappan, 70*(3), 205–209.

Freire, P. (1972). *Pedagogy of the oppressed.* New York: Herder & Herder.

Freud, S. (1950). *Beyond the pleasure principle.* New York: Liveright.

George, R. L., & Cristiani, T. S. (1990). *Counseling theory and practice* (3rd ed.). Englewood Cliffs, NJ: Prentice Hall.

Gibbs, J. T. (1980). The interpersonal orientation in mental health consultation: Toward a model of ethnic variations in consultation. *Journal of Community Psychology, 8,* 175–207.

Gilliland, B., & James, R. (1988). *Crisis intervention strategies.* Pacific Grove, CA: Brooks/Cole.

Gim, R. H., Atkinson, D. R., & Kim, S. J. (1991). Asian American acculturation, counselor ethnicity, and cultural sensitivity, and ratings of counselors. *Journal of Counseling Psychology, 38,* 57–62.

Gim, R. H., Atkinson, D. R., & Whiteley, S. (1990). Asian-American acculturation, severity of concerns, and willingness to see a counselor. *Journal of Counseling Psychology, 37,* 281–285.

Gladding, S. (1992). *Counseling: A comprehensive profession* (2nd ed.). New York: MacMillan.

Good, B. J., & Good, M. J. D. V. (1986). The cultural context of diagnosis and therapy: A view from medical anthropology. In M. R. Miranda & H. H. L. Kitano (Eds.), *Mental health research and practice in minority communities: Development of culturally sensitive training programs* (pp. 1–27). Rockville, MD: National Institute of Mental Health. (ERIC Document Reproductive Service No. ED 278 754)

Gordon, M. M. (1978). *Human nature, class, and ethnicity.* New York: Oxford University Press.

Gross, J. (1996, January 14). Groups encourage redefining America's view of race. *Arkansas Democrat-Gazette,* p. 12-A.

Hall, R. L. (1986). Alcohol treatment in American Indian populations: An indigenous treatment modality compared with traditional approaches. In T. F. Babor (Ed.), *Alcohol and culture: Comparative perspectives from Europe and America* (pp. 221–243). New York: New York Academy of Sciences.

Hannon, J. E., Ritchie, M. R., & Rye, D. A. (1992, September). *Class: The missing dimension in multicultural counseling and counselor education.* Paper presented at the Association for Counselor Education and Supervision National Conference, San Antonio, TX.

Heinrich, R. K., Corbine, J. L., & Thomas, K. R. (1990). Counseling Native Americans. *Journal of Counseling & Development, 69,* 128–133.

Henderson, G. (Ed.). (1979). *Understanding and counseling ethnic minorities.* Springfield, IL: Charles C Thomas.

Herring, R. D. (1989a). The American Native family: Dissolution by coercion. *Journal of Multicultural Counseling and Development, 17,* 4–13.

Herring, R. D. (1989b). Counseling Native American children: Implications for elementary guidance. *Elementary School Guidance & Counseling: Special Issue on Cross-Cultural Counseling, 23,* 272–281.

Herring, R. D. (1990a). Nonverbal communication: A necessary component of cross-cultural counseling. *Journal of Multicultural Counseling and Development, 18,* 172–179.

Herring, R. D. (1990b). Understanding Native American values: Process and content concerns for counselors. *Counseling and Values, 34,* 134–137.

Herring, R. D. (1991a). Counseling Native American youth. In C. C. Lee & B. L.

Richardson (Eds.), *Multicultural issues in counseling: New approaches to diversity* (pp. 37–74). Alexandria, VA: American Association for Counseling and Development.

Herring, R. D. (1991b). *A cross-cultural review of nonverbal communication with an emphasis on the Native American.* Bloomington, IN: ERIC Clearinghouse on Reading and Communication Skills. (ERIC Document Reproduction Series No. 4941807)

Herring, R. D. (1997a). *Counseling diverse ethnic youth: Strategies and interventions for school counselors.* Fort Worth, TX: Harcourt Brace.

Herring, R. D. (1997b). Counseling Native American youth. In C. C. Lee (Ed.), *Multicultural issues in counseling: New approaches to diversity* (2nd ed.). Alexandria, VA: American Counseling Association.

Herring, R. D., & Erchul, W. P. (1988, August). *The applicability of Olson's circumplex model to Native American families.* Paper presented at the annual convention of the American Psychological Association, Atlanta, GA.

Ho, M. K. (1987). *Family therapy with ethnic minorities.* Newbury Park, CA: Sage.

Ho, M. K. (1992). *Minority children and adolescents in therapy.* Newbury Park, CA: Sage.

Ivey, A. (1988). *Intentional interviewing and counseling.* Pacific Grove, CA: Brooks/Cole.

Ivey, A. E., Ivey, M. B., & Simek-Morgan, L. (1993). *Counseling and psychotherapy: A multicultural perspective* (3rd ed.). Boston: Allyn & Bacon.

Kazdin, A. (1989). Developmental psychopathology: Current research, issues and directions. *American Psychologist, 44,* 180–187.

Kiselica, M. S., Changizi, J. C., Cureton, V. L., & Gridley, B. E. (1995). Counseling children and adolescents in schools: Salient multicultural issues. In J. G. Ponterotto, J. M. Casas, L. A. Suzuki, & C. M. Alexander (Eds.), *Handbook of multicultural counseling* (pp. 516–533). Thousand Oaks, CA: Sage.

Kohlberg, L. (1969). Stage and sequence: The cognitive-development approach to socialization. In D. Gosling (Ed.), *Handbook of socialization theory and research* (pp. 347–480). Chicago: Rand McNally.

Korman, M. (1973). *Levels and patterns of professional training in psychology.* Washington, DC: American Psychological Association.

LaFromboise, T. D., & Dixon, D. N. (1981). American Indian perception of trustworthiness in a counseling interview. *Journal of Counseling Psychology, 28,* 135–139.

Lee, C. C. (1989). Counseling the Black adolescent: Critical roles and functions for counseling professionals. In R. L. Jones (Ed.), *Black adolescents* (pp. 293–308). Berkeley, CA: Cobb & Henry.

Lee, C. C. (1996). *Counseling for diversity: A guide for school counselors and related professionals.* Boston: Allyn & Bacon.

Lee, C. C., & Armstrong, K. L. (1996). Indigenous models of mental health intervention: Lessons from traditional healers. In J. G. Ponterotto, J. M. Casas, L. A. Suzuki, & C. M. Alexander (Eds.), *Handbook of multicultural counseling* (pp. 441–456). Thousand Oaks, CA: Sage.

Lewis, R., & Ho, M. (1989). Social work with Native Americans. In D. Atkinson, G. Morten, & D. Sue (Eds.), *Counseling American minorities* (pp. 51–58). Dubuque, IA: William C. Brown.

Liontos, L. B. (1992). *At-risk families and schools: Becoming partners.* Eugene, OR: ERIC Clearinghouse on Educational Management.

Locke, D. C. (1992). *Increasing multicultural understanding.* Newbury Park, CA: Sage.

Loevinger, J. (1976). *Ego development: Conceptions and theories.* San Francisco: Jossey-Bass.

Manson, S. M. (1986). Recent advances in American Indian mental health research: Implications for clinical research and training. In M. R. Miranda & H. H. L. Kitano (Eds.), *Mental health research and practice in minority communities: Development of culturally sensitive training programs* (pp. 51–89). Rockville, MD: National Institute of Mental Health. (ERIC Document Reproductive Service No. ED 278 754)

Maslow, A. (1968). *Toward a psychology of being.* New York: Van Nostrand Reinhold.

McLaughlin, M., & Shields, P. (1987). Involving low-income parents in the schools: A role for policy? *Phi Delta Kappan, 69*(1), 159–160.

Meier, S. (1989). *The elements of counseling.* Pacific Grove, CA: Brooks/Cole.

Morrow, R. D. (1991). The challenge of Southeast Asian parental involvement. *Principal, 70,* 20–22.

Murphy, J. (1993). What's in? What's out? American education in the nineties. *Phi Delta Kappan, 74*(10), 641–646.

Neukrug, E. (1994). *Theory, practice, and trends in human services.* Pacific Grove, CA: Brooks/Cole.

Nicolau, S., & Ramos, C. L. (1990). *Together is better: Building strong partnerships between schools and Hispanic parents* (Report No. UD 027 472). New York: Hispanic Policy Development Project. (ERIC Document Reproduction Service No. ED 325 543)

Nieto, S. (1992). *Affirming diversity: The sociopolitical context of multicultural education.* White Plains, NY: Longman.

Pedersen, P. B. (Ed.). (1985). *Handbook of cross-cultural counseling and therapy.* Westport, CT: Greenwood Press.

Pedersen, P. B. (1987). Ten frequent assumptions of cultural bias in counseling. *Journal of Multicultural Counseling and Development, 15,* 16–23.

Peterson, J. V., & Nisenholtz, B. (1991). *Orientation to counseling* (2nd ed.). Boston: Allyn & Bacon.

Phinney, J. S., & Rosenthal, D. A. (1992). Ethnic identity in adolescence: Process, context, and outcome. In G. R. Adams, T. P. Gullotta, & R. Montemayor (Eds.), *Adolescent identity formation* (pp. 145–172). Newbury Park, CA: Sage.

Piaget, J. (1977). *The development of thought: Equilibrium of cognitive structures.* New York: Viking.

Ponterotto, J. G., & Casas, J. M. (1991). *Handbook of racial/ethnic minority counseling research.* Springfield, IL: Charles C Thomas.

Poyatos, F. (1988). *Cross-cultural perspectives in nonverbal communication.* Lewiston, NY: Hogrefe.

Riner, R. D. (1979). American Indian education: A rite that fails. *Anthropology and Education Quarterly, 10,* 236–253.

Rogers, C. R. (1951). *Client-centered therapy: Its current practice, implications, and theory.* Boston: Houghton Mifflin.

Schmidt, J. J. (1993). *Counseling in the schools: Essential services and comprehensive programs.* Boston: Allyn & Bacon.

Sue, D. W. (1981). Evaluating process variables in cross-cultural counseling and psychotherapy. In A. J. Marsell & P. B. Pedersen (Eds.), *Cross-cultural counseling and psychotherapy* (pp. 102–125). New York: Pergamon.

Sue, D. W. (1992). Derald Wing Sue on multicultural issues: An interview. *Microtraining Newsletter* (North Amherst, MA), p. 6.

Sue, D. W., Arredondo, P. A., & McDavis, R. J. (1992). Multicultural counseling competencies and standards: A call to the profession. *Journal of Multicultural Counseling and Development, 20,* 64–88.

Sue, D. W., Ito, J., & Bradshaw, C. (1982). Ethnic minority research: Trends and directions. In E. E. Jones & S. J. Korchin (Eds.), *Minority mental health* (pp. 37–58). New York: Praeger.

Sue, D. W., & Sue, D. (1990). *Counseling the culturally different: Theory and practice* (2nd ed.). New York: Wiley.

Terry, A., Burden, C., & Pedersen, M. (1991). The helping relationship. In D. Capuzzi & D. Gross (Eds.), *Introduction to counseling: Perspectives for the 1990s.* Boston: Allyn & Bacon.

Thompson, C., & Rudolph, L. (1988). *Counseling children* (2nd ed.). Pacific Grove, CA: Brooks/Cole.

Thomason, T. C. (1991). Counseling Native Americans: An introduction for non-Native American counselors. *Journal of Counseling & Development, 69,* 321–327.

Thomason, T. C. (1996). Counseling Native American students. In C. C. Lee (Ed.), *Counseling for diversity: A guide for school counselors and related professionals* (pp. 109–126). Boston: Allyn & Bacon.

Trotter, T. V. (1993). Counseling with young multicultural clients. In A. Vernon (Ed.), *Counseling children and adolescents* (pp. 138–155). Denver, CO: Love.

Truax, C. B., & Carkhuff, R. R. (1967). *Towards effective counseling and psychotherapy.* Chicago: Aldine.

Vernon, A. (Ed.). (1993). *Counseling children and adolescents.* Denver, CO: Love.

Vontress, C. E. (1991). Traditional healing in Africa: Implications for cross-cultural counseling. *Journal of Counseling & Development, 70,* 242–249.

Williams, C. W. (1991). *Black teenage mothers: Pregnancy and child rearing from their perspective.* Lexington, MA: Lexington Books.

Wrenn, C. (1962). The culturally encapsulated counselor. *Harvard Educational Review, 32,* 444–449.

Wrenn, C. (1985). The culturally encapsulated counselor revisited. In P. Pedersen (Ed.), *Handbook of cross-cultural counseling and therapy* (pp. 323–329). Westport, CT: Greenwood Press.

Yao, E. L. (1988). Working effectively with Asian immigrant parents. *Phi Delta Kappan, 70*(3), 223–225.

7 | Socioeconomic and Political Issues and Concepts in School Counseling

Prejudices, it is well known, are most difficult to eradicate from the heart whose soil has never been loosened or fertilized by education; they grow there, firm as weeds among stones.

—CHARLOTTE BRONTE

Socioeconomic and political issues and concerns have been mentioned superficially in previous chapters. This chapter strives to expand the school counselor's content awareness of the tremendous influences that these issues have on students, especially ethnic and cultural minority students. Many youths in this nation are socialized within the context of alcoholic, drug-dominated, and abusive familial environments. Socioeconomic limitations tend to reduce the ability to provide adequate financial resources for appropriate child-rearing practices, especially among ethnic minority groups.

Cogently, enhancing cross-cultural counseling processing skills will be stressed through synergetic precepts. As Ivey, Ivey, and Simek-Morgan (1993) concluded:

> Children are perhaps the most oppressed of all cultural groups. They are treated as property and have limited legal rights. In addition, they frequently suffer emotional and physical abuse and neglect. (p. 107)

A major criticism of traditional school counseling orientations is reflected in their perspective of mainstream culture. This monocultural and ethnocentric view is not directly applicable to the concerns of ethnic minority students (Wilson & Stith, 1991). Ponterotto and his associates (Ponterotto & Casas, 1991; Ponterotto, Casas, Suzuki,

| 131

& Alexander, 1995) noted that traditionally trained counselors are encapsulated in culturally conflicting and oppressive counseling approaches. The tendency by ethnic minority students to not use counseling services, therefore, is not surprising. The rate of terminating counseling after attending one session is far greater for ethnic minorities than for European Americans (see **Chart 7.1**). Ethnic minority groups generally consider the family as their primary source of support. Reliance on these natural support systems produces less feelings of defeat, humiliation to self and to the family, and powerlessness (Ho, 1992).

CHART 7.1

Reasons for Underutilization of Health and Mental Services

1. Distrust of counselors, especially European American counselors.
2. Cultural and social class differences between counselors and students.
3. An insufficient number of mental health facilities and bicultural professionals.
4. Overuse or misuse of a physician for psychological problems.
5. Language barriers.
6. Reluctance to recognize the urgency for help.
7. Lack of awareness of the existence of mental health clinics.
8. Confusion about the relationship between mental health clinics and other agencies.

SOURCE: Adapted from *Minority Children and Adolescents in Therapy*, by M. K. Ho, 1992, p. 13.

Synergetic counseling stresses the importance of incorporating issues of oppression and environmental and cultural influences. One of the great cognitive shifts of this century has been the self-awareness movement of ethnic minority groups, women, gay men and lesbian women, persons with challenging disabilites, the elderly, and others. For example, the changes in consciousness brought about by ethnic identity movements have achieved more for the mental health of African Americans than all counseling theories combined (Ivey et al., 1993).

The emphases here are socioeconomic and political issues and concerns. Selected components of these emphases include career development and peer group relations. Within these areas of discussion, the influences of socioeconomic status (SES) and political factors are incorporated. In addition, implications for the school counselor are offered.

A caution to the reader is necessary at this point. The discussions in this chapter may appear to be overly negative toward ethnic minorities. The United States is still a European American majority country (75.6%), but minority groups are increasing far more rapidly (Herr & Cramer, 1996). Currently, 14.5% of the U.S. population is classified as poor (income for a family of four is about $14,400; for a single person, $7,200), with 40% of the poor under the age of 18. The intent is to present evidence of the limitations endured by ethnic families as a result of their meager financial and career opportunities. In this vein, the effects do reflect a negative tone.

Socioeconomic Status of the Culturally Diverse

Social class refers to "differences in wealth, income, occupation, status, community power, group identification, level of consumption, and family background" (Duberman, 1975, p. 34). Membership in a social class provides parameters within which the developing student will experience a restricted range of opportunities, choices, and challenges in particular social contexts. Social class differences may actually be more profound than cultural differences (Baruth & Manning, 1991), but by themselves, social class differences may not be adequate for a full appreciation of ethnic differences (Ho, 1992). For example, low-SES European Americans may have more in common with Hispanic Americans in the same social class than with European Americans in a middle class. In addition, ethnic minority youths may vacillate behaviorally between their perceived class status in some situations and their actual cultural or ethnic identity in others.

Diagnostic and treatment bias is one problem that has been associated with social class. In an early study, S. D. Lee (1968) found that lower SES students received a diagnosis of mental retardation at a higher rate than upper SES students. Some evidence also suggests that school counselors become more involved with students from the upper class than with students from the lower class (Garfield, Weiss, & Pollack, 1973). When these findings are considered, it is not surprising that students with a lower SES tend to terminate counseling after one or two sessions (Berrigan & Garfield, 1981; Weighill, Hodge, & Peck, 1983). Socioeconomic class is an important variable to consider when planning a counseling approach (Atkinson, Morten, & Sue, 1989; Herr & Cramer, 1996). Thus, even via direct or circuitous routes, SES plays a major role in the development of ethnic minority youths.

Some specific examples of how socioeconomics and politics dictate the socialization resources available to ethnic minority youths illustrate this dilemma.

HISPANIC AMERICANS

Hispanic Americans are among the poorest of all ethnic groups in the United States. For example, it has been estimated that from 10% to over 25% of all citizens with Hispanic backgrounds exist below the poverty level (Fields, 1988; Kavanaugh & Retish, 1991). Some 24% of Hispanic families fall below the poverty level, compared with 9% of non-Hispanic families (del Pinal & DeNavas, 1990). A total of 39% of Hispanic Americans under the age of 16 lived below the poverty level in 1989; of these, 53% resided in the Northeast and 44% resided in the South, and the Midwest and West averaged approximately one third each (U.S. Bureau of the Census, 1990).

Mexican Americans are the largest and most prominent group of Hispanics, composing 63% (12.5 million) of the Hispanic population in the United States (Zapata, 1995). Both the history and culture of Mexican Americans are closely associated with the Southwest. Puerto Ricans consistently are the least educated, more often unemployed, and more likely to be poor (Carrasquillo, 1991). Of the three largest Hispanic subgroups in the United States, Cubans probably possess the greatest economic power (Arredondo, 1991). However, they still experience problems such as immigration, acculturation, and social deprivation (Gonzalez, 1991).

NATIVE AMERICAN INDIANS

Native American Indians have the lowest living standards of any ethnic group in the United States. Approximately 24% live below the poverty level (Locke, 1992; U.S. Bureau of the Census, 1991). Unemployment on some reservations is reported to be as high as 90%. The pattern is one of bare subsistence, with some of the worst slums in the United States existing on federal reservations (Rice, 1993).

A direct result of these disturbing conditions is that Native American Indian youths, particularly adolescents, have more serious mental health problems compared with all other reported populations in the United States (U.S. Office of Technology Assessment, 1990). They also are afflicted with major diseases to a much greater degree than other youths. For example, on one hand, they suffer more from hunger and malnutrition than does any other ethnic group in the United States. On the other hand, they are at very high risk for obesity and diabetes, caused primarily by patterns of eating and food preparation (Snow & Harris, 1989). Effects of their SES are also found in the high rates of eating disorders (e.g., bulimia), cirrhosis of the liver (attributable to poor nutrition and excessive drinking), suicide, substance abuse, and fetal alcohol syndrome (Backover, 1991; Lafromboise & Bigfoot, 1988; McShane, 1988; Snow & Harris, 1989). In addition, Native American Indian adolescents may be extremely susceptible to high stress levels engendered by the developmental task of identity establishment, in that they may feel "particularly caught between two cultures" (U.S. Office of Technology Assessment, 1990, p. 1).

Although exact causation may remain unknown, Native American Indian adolescents often have lives filled with stressors not shared by non-Native adolescents (Choney, Berryhill-Paapke, & Robbins, 1996). The lack of ample financial resources preclude early detection and proper attention to most of these health concerns. However, many health problems can be prevented or lessened with sufficient availability of health and medical care delivery services.

AFRICAN AMERICANS

The continually rising income of both European Americans and African Americans has not lessened the gap between these two groups; rather, the gap has increased (U.S. Bureau of the Census, 1991). In every occupational category, African Americans are paid less than European Americans for the same work. The data indicate that the plight of African Americans, especially inner-city men, is horrific, with over 50% of young urban African American men in the 1980s working part-time jobs involuntarily or earning poverty-level wages (Herr & Cramer, 1996). Unequal income, unequal education, segregation, and workplace discrimination remain stark realities.

The differentiated employment rates of ethnic minority students and European American teenagers are striking (Billingsley, 1988). For example, African American teenagers have a far greater unemployment rate than their European American peers. About one third of African American teenagers were unemployed in 1989, with large numbers wandering the streets with nothing to do (Rice, 1993). Teenage pregnancy among African Americans is proportionately higher than among any other ethnic group in the United States (Pete & DeSantis, 1990). African American teenagers constitute only 15% of the adolescent population, yet they account for 31% of all births to adolescents and 44% of all births to unmarried adolescents (U.S. Bureau of the Census, 1991). Few of these teenagers consider adoption, and most become single parents living with their families of origin (Mayfield-Brown, 1989; Pete & DeSantis, 1990).

Many school experiences for African American students are negative as a result of errors of both commission and omission (Locke, 1995). The miseducation of African Americans can be found in tracking, low expectations from teachers, the absence of role models, ethnic disparity in special education programs, and a disregard for cultural diversity. Poor motivational factors such as faulty perceptions of control, low expectations for the future, and inadequate interpersonal evaluations result in chronic school failure for this population (Berry & Asamen, 1989).

The preceding descriptions illustrate the socioeconomic obstacles that many ethnic minority youths have to overcome in order to become successful citizens. School counselors should not negate the significance of ethnicity in determining the psychological well-being of their students (Thomas & Hughes, 1986). To that end, school counselors need to develop ethnic-specific strategies that address the unique needs and SES limitations of ethnic minority youths (see **Chart 7.2**). The improvement of basic academic skills will also enhance employability skills.

Work and Career Development

Socioeconomic concerns are probably the least discussed, and therefore the least addressed, multicultural issue. Economic deprivation and discrimination in the workplace are only two of the issues faced by those of less advantaged status. The effect of unemployment and underemployment of ethnic minority youths is tremendous (Herr & Cramer, 1996). A central issue has been a tendency for male counselors to dominate female and ethnic minority students and direct them into stereotypical career choices (Cayleff, 1986; Jones, Krupnick, & Kerig, 1987).

For example, the median income for Hispanic American families is $20,306, compared with $31,610 for all other ethnic families; and approximately 26% of Hispanic American families have income below the poverty line, compared with 11% for the total population (U.S. Bureau of the Census, 1991). In general, Hispanic Americans are clustered in blue-collar and semiskilled jobs (58%), and a significant proportion are unemployed (Marin & Marin, 1991).

However, two additional problems also complicate factors in studying race and ethnicity in relation to career development. One reflects the confounding of race and ethnicity (Herr & Cramer, 1996). As previously discussed in Chapter 4, considerable disagreement exists regarding what is meant by *race* and whether or not the concept is useful even if an agreed-on meaning can evolve (Yee, Fairchild, Weizmann, & Wyatt, 1993). The second problem is the "overlap between being economically disadvantaged and being culturally disadvantaged, because poverty tends to cross racial and ethnic boundaries" (Herr & Cramer, 1996, p. 272).

CHART 7.2

Limitations of Low Socioeconomic Status

Limited alternatives: These youths have not been exposed to a variety of social and cultural settings and vocational opportunities. Poverty limits their educational and career choices. Limited vision and experience restrict the possibilities and opportunities in their lives.

Helplessness, powerlessness: Their skills are limited, they have little autonomy or influence in improving their status, they have little opportunity to receive additional training, and they are the most replaced workers. They have little political or social influence in their communities and, often, inadequate legal protection of their rights as citizens.

Deprivation: They are aware of the affluence around them and the achievement of and benefits received by others, but their situation makes them constantly aware of their own abject status and "failure," resulting in bitterness, embarrassment, withdrawal–isolation, or social deviation–rebellion.

Insecurity: They are at the mercy of life's unpredictable events: sickness, loss of work, injury, legal problems, school difficulties, family difficulties, and others. The lower their socioeconomic status, the more vulnerable they are to the stresses of life. They strive for security because they never feel certain about their own lives. They strive just to provide themselves with the basic necessities of life.

ETHNIC CAREER MYTHS

Most ethnic minority students display less satisfaction with program choices and give lower ratings on receiving help with job choice and career decisions than do European American students (Richmond, Johnson, Downs, & Ellinghaus, 1983). These weaknesses contribute to lack of self-awareness when students contemplate career choices.

Research also indicates that ethnic minority students exhibit differences from European American students in background experience, values, and orientation. These differences occur even though ethnic minority students' aspirations may equal or surpass those of middle-class European American students (Hispanic Research Center, 1991; Williams, 1979). These differences also tend to restrict an ethnic minority student's awareness of available careers and of the skills required. As a result, disproportionate numbers of ethnic minority students enter traditional career areas or remain unemployed (Burris, 1983). For example, Hispanic men are more likely to be employed in operator, fabricator, and laborer occupations than in any other occupational group, whereas non-Hispanic men tend to be employed in managerial and professional occupations (del Pinal & DeNavas, 1990).

The irrational beliefs held by ethnic minority students have been referred to as *career myths* (Dorn, 1987; Herring, 1990). These irrational thoughts most often are generated from historical, familial patterns of career ignorance and negative career developmental experiences. An example of a career myth is the belief that a career choice must be made before senior high school.

Irrational career beliefs generally result in dysfunctional cognitive schema when ethnic minority students contemplate career decisions (Herring, 1990). For example, Drummond and Hansford (1992) examined the career aspirations of 94 ethnic minority, pregnant female teenagers enrolled in a dropout prevention program. The career aspirations of these teenagers reflected several trends:

1. Many of the participants had unrealistic assumptions and want to be in a profession even if they do not have the academic and economic resources necessary to be successful.
2. Occupational choice was not the immediate concern of the pregnant teens. They have other basic needs—physical, safety, and self-esteem—that they need to address first.
3. Schools do not address the career development and career maturity issues adequately.
4. Teens are not aware of the labor market and the types of available high-demand jobs.
5. Teens do not aspire to high technological jobs requiring advanced education but choose many types of jobs in which they will only be able to earn a marginal salary.
6. Pregnant teens are representative of at-risk youths who tend to wind up in occupations for which there is an oversupply of workers.

The link between career myths and irrational attitudes is supported in the literature (e.g., Alden & Safran, 1978; Dryden, 1979; Herring, 1990). Research has also substantiated the relationship between irrational cognitions and indecisiveness in an ethnic minority student's career development experiences (Haase, Reed, Winer, & Bodden, 1979). In addition, irrational thinking has been found to be the basic component of ethnic minority students' career mythology (Slaney, 1983). Finally, research has demonstrated that the traditional career theorists have neglected to emphasize ethnicity and culture in their concepts (June & Pringle, 1977).

Chronic poverty and inappropriate education contribute to the persistence of career myths and low career aspirations among ethnic youths (Herr & Cramer, 1996). Having few positive career role models also limits career choices of these youths. Such limitations continue the cycle of disproportionate employment and stifle the natural potential of ethnic minority youths and low-SES youths in general.

ETHNIC CAREER COUNSELING

Some interesting trends can be discerned from the available research on ethnic career counseling. One recurring theme is the tendency of African American students to prefer social occupations more than do European American students and for this tendency to begin to appear as early as junior high school (M. J. Miller, Springer, & Wells, 1988). In addition, to survive the effects of dual discrimination in the workplace, African American women have developed a unique coping system (Evans & Herr, 1991). One component of that system is the avoidance of potentially discriminatory harmful working environments because of their ethnicity or gender (see **Special Emphasis 7.1**).

The degree of acculturation also affects ethnic minority students' career plans. Ethnic minority students displaying higher degrees of acculturation tend to have higher occupational aspirations and expectations than do less acculturated ethnic minority students (Mahoney, 1992; Manaster, Chan, & Safady, 1992). In general, the academic plans of qualified ethnic minority students do not diverge greatly from the patterns of European American students (Kerr & Colangelo, 1988). Exceptions exist in the proportion of African American students (35.4%) interested in engineering and the preference of Asian American students (29.5%) for health science.

Kerr and Colangelo's (1988) research offered additional insights. Overall, high-scoring ethnic minority students express somewhat higher degrees of preference for various services and special programs compared with European American students. African American students express higher levels of desire for study skills, personal counseling, independent study, honors programs, financial aid, and employment compared with other ethnic groups. Hispanic American students exceed European American students mainly in their desire for financial aid, independent study and honors, and employment. Asian American students exceed European American students mainly in their desire for educational, career, and personal counseling.

"Coming out" as a lesbian or gay person also influences career decision. A lesbian woman may realize early that she will never depend on a male partner's

SPECIAL EMPHASIS 7.1

Gender Stereotypes and Career Development

Students absorb many rigid ideas about gender-stereotyped occupations. The following suggestions might provide incentives for school counselors and related professionals to generate additional ideas and strategies to reduce these ideas.

1. **Wise men**. Assess awareness of one common stereotype by asking students to draw a picture of a doctor. After they are finished, discuss the similarities and differences among the drawings. What conclusions can be reached about the image of a doctor? Discuss characteristics of ethnicity, gender, dress, age, and so on. Do their answers represent a generalized idea or a stereotype?

2. **Take-daughters-to-work day**. Contact businesses in the community and invite successful women to addresss the students. Survey parents for suggestions of women who have interesting careers. Feature photographs, articles, and biographies of diverse career women. Use students' stereotypes to generate discussion. Pose questions that connect careers with early education and training.

3. **Influential women**. Women have been omitted from most accounts of history. They are rarely seen as developers of ideas, initiators of events, or inventors of technology. Have students generate a list of women's achievements. Groups of students can research each woman's life and accomplishments. Offer students biographies of women's roles, from politics to science to sports.

4. **Women in folklore**. Positive models and stories of successful women can help overcome obstacles. Folktales often reflect stereotypical gender roles. Present tales of strong women to counteract folklore images of passive women who need a man to rescue them (e.g., Cinderella, Sleeping Beauty).

5. **Featuring women artists**. Show that art is not the sole product of dead European men.

6. **Countering gender stereotypes in children's literature**. Stereotyped thinking and behavior is found frequently in the books available in classrooms. Over 75% of the characters in children's books are male. In addition, male characters tend to take action, whereas female characters remain passive. Practice critical thinking skills by identifying stereotypes and evaluating sexism in textbooks. Could the characters' gender be reversed? An alternative is to retell the story from another perspective.

7. **Gender-typed play**. Children's toys and games perpetuate ideas of gender role stereotypes. Ask students to list examples of boys' toys and girls' toys. Discuss why certain toys and games are presumed to be gender specific. This discussion should result in increased options for gender-typed play and decreased negative response to gender role behaviors.

SOURCE: Adapted from *Multicultural Teaching: A Handbook of Activities, Information, and Resources*, by P. L. Tiedt and I. M. Tiedt, 1995, pp. 78–82.

salary (Hetherington & Orzek, 1989) and may, therefore, choose a male-dominated occupation to maximize her earning potential (Atkinson & Hackett, 1995). In addition, many gay and lesbian youths may remain "closeted" in order to enter careers such as teaching, child care, and child psychology because of the myth that they recruit children to the gay or lesbian lifestyle. School counselors can help these youths explore their career options and distinguish between realistic and unrealistic fears; they also can provide information and support (Atkinson & Hackett, 1995).

ETHNIC CAREER COUNSELORS

Insufficient numbers of ethnic minority school counselors often prevent students' contact with ethnic-similar counselors. A significant percentage of ethnic students, especially African American students, prefer ethnic-similar counselors (Gunnings & Gunnings, 1983). To significantly increase the number of ethnic minorities in the field of career planning and placement, however, requires multiple strategies. A short-term alternative can be found in a secondary school guideline developed by Campbell and Hadley (1992):

1. To design, implement, and evaluate a training program that allows ethnic minority staff to explore the field of career planning and placement as a career possibility.
2. To provide opportunities for selected staff to acquire a theoretical knowledge of career development concepts and issues and a core of career development skills.

Planning, implementing, and evaluating career development programs for diverse students is an important role for school counselors. A culturally responsive school counselor should orient students to the world of work within the context of values, interests, and abilities developed in diverse cultural contexts. Such orientation would include promoting interest in careers in which ethnic and culturally diverse groups have been underrepresented (C. C. Lee, 1995; see **Chart 7.3**).

Peer Group Relations

Peer group relations are fundamental to the developmental and socialization processes of children and adolescents. Socioeconomic factors strongly influence the choice of peer group identification among ethnic minority youths (U.S. Bureau of the Census, 1991). Peer group decisions also require careful monitoring as peers strongly influence development (Slavin, 1991). Peer relationships allow children to assert themselves and present their own views.

CHART 7.3

13 Better Ways to Pass Along Career Information

1. **Tailor the message**: Be sensitive to the student's exact informational needs.
2. **Resist the "loading down" syndrome**: Most students learn best with a single career placement task to accomplish.
3. **Don't leap over goal setting**: Thinking and speaking clearly about goals is significant.
4. **Promote career knowledge**: Differentiate job title, job function, work environment, and industry.
5. **Avoid jargon**: Discuss career planning in down-to-earth terms.
6. **Go easy on cliches**: Encouraging words/actions need to be combined with clear instructions.
7. **Get student feedback**: Ask if information was useful or whether the student can follow up.
8. **Use anecdotes for effect**: Stories about real students influence more than statistics or urgings.
9. **Help students visualize career messages and jobs**: Use functional language with the students.
10. **Explain both sides of the job**: Explain the challenges of a job as well as a "bad day."
11. **Start by destroying career myths**: It is always helpful to mention a few myths that students believe and ask for reactions. The student needs to relate to them as well as refute them.
12. **Enhance learning with visuals**: Pictures, diagrams, and charts, plus humor, can make career planning procedures and steps more understandable.
13. **Help students find positive connections**: We use the term *transferable skills*, but usually only to mean from job to job, not education to job, or college to career.

SOURCE: Adapted from "13 Ways to Pass Along Real Information to Students," by T. Bachhuber, 1992, *Journal of Career Counseling & Development, 52*, pp. 66–69.

Peer conflicts also permit children to see that others have thoughts, feelings, and viewpoints different from their own, and they heighten children's sensitivity to the effects of their behavior on others.

GENERIC PEER GROUP DEVELOPMENT

Certain aspects of peer group development may be generalized across cultures and ethnicities. For example, the family, which was the major force during the early childhood years, continues to be an influence during middle childhood. Parents provide role models in terms of attitudes and behaviors. Yet, the peer group increases in importance.

In the lower elementary grades, peer groups usually consist of children of similar gender and age. By the sixth grade, however, students often form mixed-gender groups. For both boys and girls, membership in groups tends to promote feelings of self-worth; *not* being accepted can bring serious emotional problems (Berk, 1993). Herein lies the major cause of the preadolescent's changing relationship with parents. Preadolescents do not care less about their parents, but their friends are *more* important than ever. The need for peer acceptance is illustrated by the popularity of fads in dress, music, magazines, TV shows, and so on.

The middle childhood years often bring changes in the relationship between children and their school counselors. In primary school, children easily accept and depend on their teachers and counselors. During the upper elementary years, this relationship becomes more complex. Children's behaviors range from revealing personal information they would not tell their parents to talking back in ways they would never have considered several years earlier.

Friendship popularity, conflicts with peers, conflicts with parents, dating, and sexual relationships dominate adolescence. The influence of peers increases as adolescents attempt to establish their own identity. Teenage gossip spreads quickly, and telephones become an essential possession. Adolescents with similar interests develop friendships that often endure for life—if not in reality, at least in memory.

ETHNIC PEER GROUP DEVELOPMENT

Many ethnic groups differ in their emphases during the highly volatile adolescent years. Cultural differences in values, attitudes, the self, and behaviors influence ethnic minority youths to believe that their value system is inferior to that of European Americans (Ho, 1992). For example, many ethnic youths are reared with an emphasis on "passive involvement," which is often misconstrued as laziness or lack of motivation by European American counselors and teachers with a strong middle-class "doing orientation" (Bellah, 1985).

In addition, the socioeconomic and political structure of mainstream society perpetuates the nuclear family myth, which conflicts with the extended and single-parent families common to many ethnic minority groups (Ho, 1992). Many ethnic minority youths find themselves personally rejected by such external patterns of mainstream society. Concurrently, they may be receiving inadequate support from their own family and group. The negative effect that the external system has on the ethnic minority culture tends to alienate the ethnic minority youths, potentially causing conflict within the family and at the same time leaving the ethnic minority youths without an adequate and appropriate model to emulate (Rice, 1993).

The following examples briefly illustrate some of the basic differences between ethnic minority adolescents and European American adolescents in terms of peer group relations.

Low SES. Adolescents from low-SES families tend to maintain weaker ties with parents than do those from middle-class families. Peer groups are stronger and more lasting than parental ones. The two dominant reasons for this difference are that (a) low-SES adolescents do not gain status through their familial identifications and (b) the need for security is inalienable (Rice, 1993).

Adolescence brings additional pressures of employment to supplement family income. Research documents that low SES correlates positively with early withdrawal from school (Manaster, 1977). For example, the dropout rate is higher among students from low-SES familial backgrounds. Numerous considerations are necessary to understand this trend appropriately (Rice, 1993; Svec, 1986).

1. Low SES students often lack positive parental role models and socialization processing.
2. Teachers are often prejudiced against youths from low-SES families.
3. Low-SES students receive fewer rewards for doing well and for staying in school.
4. Low-SES students often do not possess the verbal skills of their middle-class peers.
5. Peer influences on low-SES youths are often antisocial and delinquency prone, emphasizing early marriage for the girls and gang activities for the boys.

Several examples further illustrate the potential detriments of low SES. As previously presented, the intent of these examples is not to describe inherently negative images. Rather, they serve to inspire the reader to become a more active advocate in the elimination of the causative factors to the precipitating realities of current mainstream society.

Hispanic American adolescents. Hispanic American youths represent the second highest number of ethnic youths being reared below the poverty level—37% (U.S. Bureau of the Census, 1991). Mexican Americans and

Puerto Rican Americans, representing the two largest subgroups of Hispanic Americans, illustrate the results of an inadequate socioeconomic base.

1. *Mexican Americans.* Mexican Americans currently constitute the second largest ethnic group in the United States, and about 9% of this total reflects adolescents (U.S. Bureau of the Census, 1991). These youths are primarily urbanized (79%) and tend to segregate in residential ghettos called *colonias* or *barrios* ("neighborhoods").

Mexican American parents emphasize values that hinder the advancement of adolescents in an individualistic, highly competitive, materialistic society (Ho, 1992). Examples of these values include an emphasis on family ties, authority, present-time orientation, and politeness. In many ways, this excessive family dependence hinders the development of autonomy and independence (Codega, Pasley, & Kreutzer, 1990). For example, the Mexican American male adolescent is expected to take an interest in girls and demonstrate his virility (*machismo*). On the other hand, Mexican American female adolescents are not to learn about sexual relations by either conversation or experience. The result of these contrary gender values is seen in the boys experimenting with "bad" girls and prostitutes, thus increasing the chances of unwanted pregnancies and sexually transmitted diseases.

Migrant Mexican American adolescents frequently present conflicting views in their selection of positive role models (Mendelberg, 1986). Identification with members of outside groups appears blocked for them. At the same time, encounters with outside groups appear to undermine identification processes that develop within their families and community. These relationships interfere with the internalization of characteristics and attitudes of significant others.

In addition, many Mexican American adolescents have only recently immigrated to the United States. A study of 244 Mexican American immigrant adolescents in five Los Angeles schools revealed the adjustment stresses of these youths (Zambrana & Silva-Palacios, 1989). The highest ranking perceived stress items related to family: getting sick, family member arrested, leaving relatives and friends in Mexico, and insufficient finances. The second highest stress item related to language and ethnic differences, especially at school. A third source of stress related to social adjustments (e.g., living in a crime-ridden neighborhood).

2. *Puerto Rican Americans.* Puerto Rican Americans represent the third largest ethnic minority group in the country, with 20% being adolescents (U.S. Bureau of the Census, 1991). Puerto Rican families in the United States have the highest rate of divorce and female-headed households than any other

Hispanic group (Vega, 1990). In 1988, 52% of Puerto Rican families consisted of married couples, 44% were headed by female householders with no spouse present, and 4% were headed by male householders with no spouse present (U.S. Bureau of the Census, 1991). The problems confronting most Puerto Rican families are partly the result of their adverse socioeconomic living conditions (Rice, 1993). Puerto Ricans have the highest rate (9%) of unemployment of all Hispanic groups and exist on a median family income of $15,185 (U.S. Bureau of the Census, 1991).

Adolescents often lack appropriate parental role models and therefore lack adaptive behaviors and values to imitate during adolescence. Thus, they experience an identity crisis compounded by inter- and intracultural and generational conflicts (McLoyd, 1990). Traditional families from Puerto Rico emphasize highly segregated gender roles, whereas those born and reared in the United States emphasize more egalitarian roles (Rogler & Procidano, 1989). These experiences contribute to high rates of delinquency compared with populations of African Americans and European Americans (Costantino, Malgady, & Rogler, 1988).

African American adolescents. For generations, African American families, especially those of low SES, battled the attempts of the dominant European American society to force them into an inferior role. Today, the image of African Americans is changing. Increasingly, African American adolescents are accepting the fact that they are human beings of worth, with a positive identity, united with each other in proclaiming their admission into the human race and into middle-class culture (Mboya, 1986).

Nonetheless, differences between unemployment rates of African American teenagers and European American teenagers are striking (Billingsley, 1988). African American teenagers have a far greater unemployment rate than their European American peers: for European Americans, boys = 13.7%, girls = 11.5%, for African Americans, boys = 20.2%, girls = 18.2% (U.S. Bureau of the Census, 1991). About one third of African American teenagers worked in 1989, which leaves large numbers wandering the streets with nothing to do.

One of the prime purposes of desegregation was to integrate diverse students together in school settings. These efforts have proved to be only mildly successful, and the process does not automatically ensure high levels of interethnic contact or guarantee the quality of relations (R. L. Miller, 1989). A greater percentage of African American youths continue to be reared below the poverty level compared with any other ethnic group—47% (U.S. Bureau of the Census, 1991).

Asian American adolescents. Two representative examples of Asian American adolescents continue the discussion of the effects of SES on ethnic minority adolescents.

1. *Chinese American adolescents.* Peer group relationships among Chinese American adolescents are dependent entirely on the degree of acculturation of the family (Rice, 1993). Traditional Chinese parenting approaches use authoritarian methods, such as a strict interpretation of behavior, the limitation of social interaction, firm discipline involving physical punishment, little positive verbal communication, the expectation of obedience and conformity, and the absence of overt parental praise. Chinese children are taught that each has to work for the welfare of the family. Teenagers are responsible for supervising younger children, chores around the house, and contributing in the family business. Rebellion among adolescents is almost unknown. Respect for elders is so deeply ingrained that youths never question their parents' authority as it brings dishonor on their families.

Americanized Chinese parents, however, are more nurturant and more open. Acculturation has, however, yielded some negative consequences. For example, these Chinese American youths are more vocal than previous generations and more inclined to rebel. Many become involved in radical political protest or delinquent activities (Ho, 1992; Sih & Allen, 1976).

Ethnic and cultural prejudices remain important limiting factors in the lives of Chinese Americans (Rice, 1993). Many employers hire Chinese Americans because of their reputation of being hardworking and dependable, but often the jobs are low paying. Frequent reminders of their ethnicity makes some Chinese Americans feel that they are not fully accepted (Sih & Allen, 1976). As one Chinese American observed, "In the past we had the coolie who slaved. Today we have the high-tech coolie" (McLeod, 1986).

Segregated housing also represents discrimination against these people (Rice, 1993). Numerous Chinese Americans are forced to live in the "Chinatowns" of the metropolitan areas of the United States. Social conditions are appalling (e.g., rundown, overcrowded, cramped, and rat- and roach-infested). These tenements are usually owned by absentee landlords who charge high rents and do little repairs.

The complexities of acculturation have produced identity conflicts in Chinese American youths. Young women are rejecting the traditional image of Asian women as docile, submissive, and sexually exotic. Yet, many also resent being "too Americanized." In an effort to circumvent stereotypical gender roles, they may become active feminists and get involved to change these images.

2. *Southeast Asian adolescents.* Southeast Asian adolescents (e.g., from Vietnam, Cambodia, and Laos), new to the United States, are confronted with three major stresses: physiological and emotional upheavals, social and psychological adjustments as refugees, and intercultural conflicts caused by the immense value system variances between Asian and European American cultures (E. Lee, 1988). The greatest threat to a weak ethnic identity in refugee adolescents is not the feeling of belonging to two cultures but the feeling of belonging to neither (Tobin & Friedman, 1984).

Many refugee parents are preoccupied with their own survival, precluding physical and emotional access for their adolescent children. Many parents are burdened by depression and other forms of emotional distress and are unaware of adolescent identity struggles. In addition, low educational achievement and SES, poor English-speaking abilities, and lack of understanding of mainstream culture serve to transform Southeast Asian parents into inappropriate role models to their adolescent children (E. Lee, 1988; Rice, 1993). Intergenerational conflicts often force adolescents to feel an obligation to compensate for their parents' helplessness.

Native American Indian adolescents. A typical Native American Indian family no longer exists. Various family types exist among this group: traditional, transitional, bicultural, and assimilated (Herring, 1989, 1991, 1997). The adolescents reflect the value and belief structures of their family pattern.

The traditional Native American Indian family views children as assets to the extended family. Children are taught to be independent, unassuming, and patient. They are taught not to show emotions but to maintain a severe reserve. The ability to endure pain, hardship, hunger, and frustration is emphasized, as are bravery and courage. The transitional family is undergoing a move from traditional ways to those of mainstream society. The bicultural and assimilated families represent the qualities of the dominant European American society. As a result of these conflicting cultures, Native American Indian youths are faced with an identity crisis: whether to accommodate themselves to the European American world and learn to compete in it or to retain traditional customs and values and live apart from the European American world (Markstrom-Adams, 1990). As a consequence, most contemporary Native American Indian adolescents suffer psychological strain as they are caught between two cultures and immobilized from going in either direction easily (Rice, 1993).

Native American Indians have the highest birthrate, the highest death rate, and the shortest life expectancy of ethnic groups in this country (e.g., Backover, 1991; Snow & Harris, 1989). In addition, Native American Indians have one of the lowest standards of living of ethnic minority groups in the United States. Approximately 24% live below the poverty level, and reservational unemployment is as high as 90% (U.S. Bureau of the Census, 1991). Abuse and neglect among Native American Indian children are prevalent, as are effects of alcoholism, drug abuse, and other problems. As a result, 25% to 35% of Native American Indian children are removed from their families and placed in foster homes (McShane, 1988).

FROM CLIQUES TO CROWDS TO GANGS

A major concern in current school settings is the increasing violence in schools. Schools have tried suspensions, expulsions, locker searches, and metal detectors, but student violence is worse than it was 5 years ago. The leading causes of school violence, as seen by 700 school district officials, are the following: family breakdown (77%), TV and media violence (60%), alcohol and drug use (45%), access to weapons (43%), and poverty (40%; see Eskey, 1994). Some of these factors (families, alcohol, drugs, and poverty) have been alluded to previously and represent factors that have been present for years. Other factors (e.g., weapons and media violence) are relatively recently assessed factors in student violence. The relevance of student violence to the current topic of peer group relationships is evidenced in the increase in the number of adolescent gangs in this country. The immediate concern is the relationship between gangs and student violence. The evolution from normal adolescent developmental involvement in peer cliques to the unhealthy membership in adolescent gangs deserves some discussion.

Cliques.   Contrary to the popular myth, adolescents do not just spend their time in pairs of friends. Adolescent peer groups are organized around *cliques*, small groups with about five to seven members who are either close or good friends and, therefore, usually similar in age, ethnicity, and social class (Berk, 1993). During early adolescence, cliques are usually same-gender members, but mixed-gender groups become common during high school. Cliques within a typical educational setting can be identified by shared interests such as dress codes and other differentiating behaviors (e.g., the "jocks," the "brains," and the "druggies"; see Hartup, 1983).

Cliques play a central role in an adolescent's social life by providing a sense of belonging. In addition, clique membership supports identity development by providing a highly visible, temporary identity as adolescents begin to separate from the family (Berk, 1993). In the clique, they can experiment with different roles and receive feedback (Brown, Eicher, & Petrie, 1986). Cliques also offer a context in which adolescents can develop autonomous values and guidelines for behavior in the absence of adult monitoring. Adolescents tend to make decisions on the basis of their own principles when they are among their peers (Hill & Holmbeck, 1987).

Crowds. The structure of the clique changes as adolescents become more interested in issues of sexuality and gender. Several cliques combine to form a *crowd*. Crowds form and "hang out" together during the junior high years. They offer models for how to interact with the opposite sex without having to be intimate (Berk, 1993). By late adolescence, boys and girls feel comfortable enough about approaching each other directly that the crowd is no longer needed and disappears, resulting in the forming of couples (Padgham & Blyth, 1990).

Effects of peer pressure. The preceding discussion presumes a "normal" Eriksonian adolescence, however. A valuable ingredient is missing—the influence and effects of peer pressure. Peer conformity is greater during adolescence than at younger or older ages, and adolescents are most likely to surrender to peer pressure for antisocial behavior (Brown, Clasen, & Eicher, 1986). It is interesting to note that most adolescent peer pressures do not conflict with important adult values. Peers have greatest influence on short-term, day-to-day matters; adults have more impact on long-term values and educational plans (Sebald, 1986). Young people who feel worthwhile are less likely to succumb to peer pressure. In addition, authoritative child rearing, which fosters high self-esteem, social–moral maturity, and a positive view of parents, is related to greater resistance to unfavorable peer pressure (Baumrind, 1991).

Most teenagers become involved in some delinquent activity, but only a few are serious and repeat offenders. Young people under the age of 21 account for about 30% of police arrests in the United States (U.S. Department of Justice, 1991). However, this percentage does not reveal how many teenagers have committed crimes but have not been caught, how serious their crimes are, and whether many or a few are responsible for them (Henggeler, 1989). Most of these are boys (about three to seven times the number of girls) with a childhood history of antisocial behavior.

Factors related to chronic delinquency include low verbal intelligence, poor school performance, peer rejection in childhood, and membership in antisocial groups. Social class and ethnicity are also strong predictors of arrest records. However, these factors are mildly related to teenagers' self-reports of antisocial acts, probably a result of biases in the juvenile justice system: Specifically, low-income, ethnic minority youths tend to be arrested, charged, and punished more often compared with middle-class European American and Asian youths (Fagan, Slaughter, & Hartstone, 1987).

A consistent factor related to delinquency is a family environment low in warmth, high in conflict, and characterized by lax and inconsistent discipline (Snyder & Patterson, 1987). Such forms of child rearing promote antisocial behavior. Research indicates that the path to chronic delinquency unfolds through the following steps (Patterson, DeBaryshe, & Ramsey, 1989):

Step 1: Early childhood is characterized by a conflict-ridden home with lax and inconsistent disciplinary patterns, generally resulting in the child displaying conduct problems.

Step 2: Middle childhood is characterized by rejection by normal peers and academic failure. The child sees commitment to deviant peer groups as the only viable alternative.

Step 3: Adolescence is characterized by delinquency and violent gang membership. A pattern begins that may endure through adulthood without appropriate intervention.

As can be surmised, the substantive causes for adolescent gang membership are primarily found within the family. If emotional and social needs of adolescents are not met through interpersonal relationships in the family, they may turn to the gang to fulfill status needs that would otherwise go unfulfilled (Rice, 1993).

Nonfamilial or nonpeer factors also influence the adolescent's choice of antisocial gang membership and delinquency. Schools that fail to meet appropriate developmental needs have student populations that display higher rates of crime, even after other influences are controlled (Hawkins & Lam, 1987). Such schools are characterized by large classes, rigid rules, and poor-quality instruction. Poverty-stricken areas with high crime rates, fragmented community ties, and adult criminal subcultures also contribute to delinquency (Berk, 1993; Hawkins & Lam, 1987).

Prevention. Any effort to prevent delinquency and adolescent delinquent gang membership needs to emphasize prevention. Prevention includes identifying students who may be predisposed to getting in trouble. In addition, schools have to assist parents in learning more effective parenting skills (Rice, 1993).

Prevention must begin early and be incorporated at multiple levels: helping parents to use authoritative parenting, ensuring more effective education, and providing economic and social conditions necessary for healthy development.

When interventions are required or needed, they must address the multiple aspects that contribute to antisocial behavior or they are generally ineffective (Henggeler, 1989). The most appropriate interventions are lengthy and intensive and use problem-focused methods that teach cognitive and social skills needed to overcome family, peer, and school difficulties (Goldstein, 1990).

Educators must remember that positive behavior changes typically do not last once youths return to the settings that contributed to their difficulties (Quay, 1987). Consequently, prevention and treatment strategies need to revitalize community and governmental efforts to improve socioeconomic opportunities. For example, a feasible intervention could be placing antisocial youths into groups of prosocial peers (e.g., day camps) where their behavior is influenced positively.

The Role of the School Counselor

Several suggestions have been offered for school counselors working with ethnic minority youths. Additional comments and suggestions will conclude this discussion.

SOCIAL INTERACTIONS

School counselors can assist ethnic minority youths who are having social difficulties by arranging classroom or small-group situations that will help them improve their social skills. Peer interaction can be encouraged through ethnically and culturally integrated small groups, toys and materials involving more than one ethnic child, and activities such as puppets and sociodramatic play (e.g., Herring & Runion, 1994). In particular, use of cooperative learning and peer tutoring activities has been proven to increase peer acceptance and reduce rejections among ethnic minority students (Slavin, 1991, 1995). Also, ethnic minority students can be taught specific behaviors that will help them interact positively with peers (Slavin, 1995).

Gender factors associated with the counseling process pertain to potential advantages of same- versus opposite-sex pairings between the counselor and student (Nystul, 1993). Although research has been inconclusive, some evidence exists that female students prefer female counselors. For example, Jones et al. (1987) found that female counselors elicited less negative affect and fewer interpersonal difficulties in female clients than did male counselors.

Identification with members of outside groups appears to be blocked for ethnic minority students, and identification with their own ethnic group is filled with difficulties (Mendelberg, 1986). Cross-cultural studies support the observation that the submissiveness and adaptation of the ethnic minority group to the ethnic majority's needs seem to be perpetuated by the introjection of the inferior image into the ethnic minority student's identity (Erikson, 1950/1966).

FAMILIAL INFLUENCES

Career development literature has largely ignored the role that family dynamics play in career decisions by ethnic minority youths. Some ethnic minority adolescents are enmeshed and undifferentiated from their parent(s). They suffer from low self-esteem, external locus of control, anxiety, and poor career choice. Decisions are frequently emotionally based and reactive to the perceived wishes of parents (Kimmier, Brigman, & Noble, 1990). School counselors exert a major influence on the plans of students during senior high school. They need to use this influence to ensure appropriate and realistic career decisions by ethnic youths.

DROPOUT PREVENTION

A primary concern of school personnel is lowering the dropout rates of students. Ethnic minority students have a much higher dropout rate compared with European American students, especially in inner cities (Herr & Cramer, 1996; U.S. Bureau of the Census, 1991). Their value orientations and difficult socioeconomic and familial conditions are not conducive to continuing education (Rice, 1993).

Adolescents most at risk for dropping out need to be identified early in school so preventive measures can be taken (O'Sullivan, 1990) (see **Research Highlight 7.1**).

School counselors need to incorporate these factors, along with environmental and historical influences and the degree of acculturation, in their interventions with ethnic minority adolescents. Through synergetic methods, the school counselor can provide the most appropriate ethnic-specific counseling to their students.

Summary

This chapter has described important socioeconomic and political influences that affect ethnic minority students. Society in general can help alleviate the many causative factors of a limiting SES among ethnic minority families. By using political activities resources, society can reduce poverty, promote effective parenting, and ensure that educational philosophies and missions respect the ethnic and cultural heritages of ethnic minority youths. These

---

RESEARCH HIGHLIGHT 7.1

Indicators of Potential Dropouts

Signs of possible early school withdrawal have been identified. The best indicators are presented below, in no particular order.

1. Consistent failure to achieve
2. Grade level placement 2 or more years below average age for grade
3. Irregular attendance
4. Active antagonism to teachers/principals
5. Marked disinterest in school with feelings of not belonging
6. Low scholastic aptitude
7. Low reading ability
8. Frequent changes of schools
9. Nonacceptance by schoolmates
10. Nonacceptance by school staff
11. Serious physical or emotional handicap
12. A record of delinquency
13. Friends much younger or older
14. Unhappy family situation
15. Marked differences from schoolmates with regard to size
16. Inability to compete with/ashamed of siblings
17. Nonparticipation in extracurricular activities
18. Inability to afford the normal expenditures of schoolmates
19. Performance consistently lower than potential
20. Being a discipline case

SOURCE: Adapted from "Dropouts Speak Out: Qualitative Data in Early School Departures," by R. Tidwell, 1988, *Adolescence, 23*, pp. 939–954.

---

improvements in turn will facilitate the development of positive and multiple opportunities for career and work success. Adequate and equitable career opportunities will eventually provide the necessary socioeconomic foundation that will ensure that all youths in this nation have equal opportunities for advancement and success. The improvement in SES will result in improved socialization patterns, which in turn will result in less disillusioned youths. Dropout rates will decrease and delinquent adolescent gangs will become less popular. With a smaller pool of potential members, gangs themselves may become less and less influential and criminal.

Experiential Activities

1. The literature agrees that sexism and racism do exist in employment and career establishment. Evidence also exists that demonstrates that the internalization of attitudes associated with these biases has a negative effect on the career aspirations of young African American women.

The concomitant deterioration of self-esteem and self-confidence presents unique new challenges for the school counselor who works with young African American women. Unfortunately, benchmarks to guide the efforts to meet these challenges are yet to be developed. Brainstorm possible school counselor efforts to meet these challenges.

2. **Chart 7.1** listed the eight major reasons why ethnic minority families do not normally use mental health agencies. From a school counselor's perspective, how can these reasons be addressed? What strategies can be developed that incorporate natural support systems and traditional healing practices?

3. What ethnic-gender appropriate strategies could have prevented the following:

> Tomas, a Mexican American 10th-grader, daydreamed during classes, crumpled his notes into his pocket after class, and rarely did his homework. On test days, he twirled a rabbit's foot for good luck but left most of the questions blank. He would usually cut school at least once a week. Finally, he stopped coming to school altogether. Some days later the school counselor, a European American female, recognized him working as a bagger in a local supermarket. She asked him why he had quit school, and he responded with the following answer. "Come on, you oughta know. There wasn't nothin' for me there. Got to the point where I just couldn't go back. I'd go to those classes, and the minute I got there I'd wanna get out. My mind just turned off, I felt so ashamed and stupid."

References

Alden, L., & Safran, J. (1978). Irrational beliefs and nonassertive behavior. *Cognitive Therapy and Research, 2,* 357–364.

Arredondo, P. (1991). Counseling Latinas. In C. C. Lee & B. L. Richardson (Eds.), *Multicultural issues in counseling: New approaches to diversity* (pp. 143–157). Alexandria, VA: American Association for Counseling and Development.

Atkinson, D. R., & Hackett, G. (1995). *Counseling diverse populations.* Dubuque, IA: Brown & Benchmark.

Atkinson, D. R., Morten, G., & Sue, D. W. (1989). *Counseling American minorities: A cross-cultural perspective* (3rd ed.). Dubuque, IA: William C. Brown.

Bachhuber, T. (1992). 13 ways to pass along real information to students. *Journal of Career Counseling & Development, 52,* 67–69.

Backover, A. (1991). Native Americans: Alcoholism, FAS puts a race at risk. *Guidepost, 33,* 1–9.

Baruth, L. G., & Manning, M. L. (1991). *Multicultural counseling and psychotherapy: A lifespan perspective.* New York: MacMillan.

Baumrind, D. (1991). The influence of parenting styles on adolescent competence and substance use. *Journal of Early Adolescence, 11,* 56–95.

Bellah, R. (1985). *Habits of the heart: Industrialism and commitment in American life.* Berkeley: University of California Press.

Berk, L. E. (1993). *Infants, children, and adolescents.* Boston: Allyn & Bacon.

Berrigan, L. P., & Garfield, S. L. (1981). Relationships of missed psychotherapy appointments to premature termination and social class. *British Journal of Clinical Psychology, 20,* 239–242.

Berry, G. L., & Asamen, J. K. (1989). *Black students: Psychosocial issues and academic achievement.* Newbury Park, CA: Sage.

Billingsley, A. (1988). The impact of technology on Afro-American families. *Family Relations, 37,* 420–425.

Brown, B. B., Clasen, G., & Eicher, S. (1986). Perceptions of peer pressure, peer conformity dispositions, and self-reported behavior among adolescents. *Developmental Psychology, 22,* 521–530.

Brown, B. B., Eicher, S., & Petrie, S. (1986). The importance of peer group ("crowd") affiliation in adolescence. *Journal of Adolescence, 9,* 73–96.

Burris, B. (1983). *No room at the top: Underemployment and alienation in the corporation.* New York: Praeger.

Campbell, N. K., & Hadley, G. B. (1992). Creating options: A career development training program for minorities. *Journal of Counseling & Development, 70,* 645–647.

Carrasquillo, A. L. (1991). *Hispanic children and youths in the United States: A resource guide.* New York: Garland.

Cayleff, S. E. (1986). Ethical issues in counseling gender, race, and culturally distinct groups. *Journal of Counseling & Development, 64,* 345–347.

Choney, S. K., Berryhill-Paapke, E., & Robbins, R. R. (1996). The acculturation of American Indians: Developing frameworks for research and practice. In J. G. Ponterotto, J. M. Casas, L. A. Suzuki, & C. M. Alexander (Eds.), *Handbook of multicultural counseling* (pp. 73–92). Thousand Oaks, CA: Sage.

Codega, S. A., Pasley, B. K., & Kreutzer, J. (1990). Coping behaviors of adolescent mothers: An exploratory study and comparison of Mexican-Americans and Anglos. *Journal of Adolescent Research, 5,* 34–53.

Costantino, G., Malgady, R. G., & Rogler, L. H. (1988). Folk hero modeling therapy for Puerto Rican adolescents. *Journal of Adolescence, 11,* 155–165.

del Pinal, J. H., & DeNavas, C. (1990). *The Hispanic population in the United States: March 1989* (Series P-20, No. 444). Washington, DC: U.S. Department of Commerce.

Dorn, F. J. (1987). Dispelling career myths: A social influence approach. *The School Counselor, 34,* 263–267.

Drummond, R. J., & Hansford, S. G. (1992). *Career aspirations of pregnant teens. Journal of Adolescence Health: Vol. 1. Summary and policy options (1991).* Washington, DC: Congress of the United States, Office of Technology Assessment.

Dryden, W. (1979). RET and its contributions to careers. *British Journal of Guidance and Counseling, 7,* 181–187.

Duberman, L. (1975). *The reconstituted family: A study of remarried couples and their children.* Chicago: Nelson-Hall.

Erikson, E. (1966). The concept of identity in race relations. Notes and queries. *Daedalus, XCV,* 145–170. (Original work published 1950)

Eskey, K. (1994, January 6). Schools try countermeasures but report violence worse. *The Arkansas Democrat-Gazette*, p. 10-A.

Evans, K. M., & Herr, E. L. (1991). The influence of racism and sexism in the career development of African American women. *Journal of Multicultural Counseling and Development, 19,* 130–135.

Fagan, J., Slaughter, E., & Hartstone, E. (1987). Blind justice? The impact of race on the juvenile justice process. *Crime & Delinquency, 33,* 259–286.

Fields, C. (1988). The Hispanic pipeline: Narrow, leaking, and needing repair. *Change, 20*(3), 20–27.

Garfield, J. C., Weiss, S. I., & Pollack, E. A. (1973). Effects of the child's social class on school counselors' decision-making. *Journal of Counseling Psychology, 20,* 166–168.

Goldstein, A. P. (1990). *Delinquents on delinquency.* Champaign, IL: Research Press.

Gonzalez, G. M. (1991). Cuban Americans: Counseling and human development issues. In C. C. Lee & B. L. Richardson (Eds.), *Multicultural issues in counseling: New approaches to diversity* (pp. 157–171). Alexandria, VA: American Association for Counseling and Development.

Gunnings, B. B., & Gunnings, T. S. (1983). A bias review procedure for career counselors. *Journal of Non-White Concerns, 11,* 78–83.

Haase, R. F., Reed, C. F., Winer, J. L., & Bodden, J. L. (1979). Effect of positive, negative, and mixed occupational information on cognitive and affective complexity. *Journal of Vocational Behavior, 15,* 294–301.

Hartup, W. W. (1983). Peer relations. In E. M. Hetherington (Ed.), *Handbook of child psychology: Vol. 4. Socialization, personality, and social development* (4th ed., pp. 103–196). New York: Wiley.

Hawkins, D. J., & Lam, T. (1987). Teacher practices, social development, and delinquency. In J. D. Burchard & S. N. Burchard (Eds.), *Prevention of delinquent behavior* (pp. 241–274). Newbury Park, CA: Sage.

Henggeler, S. W. (1989). *Delinquency in adolescence.* Newbury Park, CA: Sage.

Herr, E. L., & Cramer, S. H. (1996). *Career guidance and counseling through the life span: Systematic approaches* (5th ed.). New York: HarperCollins.

Herring, R. D. (1989). The American Native family: Dissolution by coercion. *Journal of Multicultural Counseling and Development, 17,* 4–13.

Herring, R. D. (1990). Attacking career myths among Native Americans: Implications for counseling. *The School Counselor, 38,* 13–18.

Herring, R. D. (1991). Counseling Native American youth. In C. C. Lee & B. L. Richardson (Eds.), *Multicultural issues in counseling: New approaches to diversity* (pp. 37–47). Alexandria, VA: American Association for Counseling and Development.

Herring, R. D. (1997). *Counseling diverse ethnic youth: Strategies and interventions for school counselors.* Fort Worth, TX: Harcourt Brace.

Herring, R. D., & Runion, K. B. (1994). Counseling ethnic children and youth from an Adlerian perspective. *Journal of Multicultural Counseling and Development, 22,* 215–226.

Hetherington, C., & Orzek, A. (1989). Career counseling and life planning with lesbian women. *Journal of Counseling & Development, 68,* 52–57.

Hill, P. M., & Holmbeck, G. N. (1987). Family adaptation to biological change during adolescence. In R. M. Lerner & T. T. Foch (Eds.), *Biological–psychosocial interactions in early adolescence* (pp. 207–224). Hillsdale, NJ: Erlbaum.

Hispanic Research Center. (1991). *Background and demand for engineering training and need for professional engineers in South Texas*. San Antonio: University of Texas Press.

Ho, M. K. (1992). *Minority children and adolescents in therapy*. Newbury Park, CA: Sage.

Ivey, A. E., Ivey, M. B., & Simek-Morgan, L. (1993). *Counseling and psychotherapy: A multicultural perspective* (3rd ed.). Boston: Allyn & Bacon.

Jones, E. E., Krupnick, J. L., & Kerig, P. K. (1987). Some gender effects in a brief psychotherapy. *Psychotherapy, 24,* 337–352.

June, L. N., & Pringle, G. D. (1977). The concept of race in the career development theories of Roe, Super, and Holland. *Journal of Non-White Concerns, 6,* 17–24.

Kavanaugh, P. C., & Retish, P. M. (1991). The Mexican American ready for college. *Journal of Multicultural Counseling and Development, 19,* 136–144.

Kerr, G., & Colangelo, N. (1988). College plans of academically talented students. *Journal of Counseling & Development, 67,* 42–48.

Kimmier, R. T., Brigman, S. L., & Noble, F. C. (1990). Career indecision and family enmeshment. *Journal of Counseling & Development, 68 ,* 309–312.

Lafromboise, T. D., & Bigfoot, D. S. (1988). Cultural and cognitive considerations in the prevention of American Indian adolescent suicide. *Journal of Adolescence, 11,* 139–153.

Lee, C. C. (Ed.). (1995). *Counseling for diversity: A guide for school counselors and related professionals*. Boston: Allyn & Bacon.

Lee, E. (1988). Cultural factors in working with Southeast Asian refugee adolescents. *Journal of Adolescence, 11,* 167–179.

Lee, S. D. (1968). *Social class bias in the diagnosis of mental illness* (Doctoral dissertation, University of Oklahoma, 1968). (University Microfilms No. 68–6959).

Locke, D. C. (1992). *Increasing multicultural awareness: A comprehensive model*. Newbury Park, CA: Sage.

Locke, D. C. (1995). Counseling interventions with African American youth. In C. C. Lee (Ed.), *Counseling for diversity: A guide for school counselors and related professionals* (pp. 21–40). Boston: Allyn & Bacon.

Mahoney, F. E. (1992). Adjusting the interview to avoid cultural bias. *Journal of Career Planning and Employment, 52*(23), 41–43.

Manaster, G. J. (1977). *Adolescent development and life tasks*. Boston: Allyn & Bacon.

Manaster, G. J., Chan, J. C., & Safady, R. (1992). Mexican-American migrant students' academic success: Sociological and psychological acculturation. *Adolescence, 27*(105), 124–135.

Marin, G., & Marin, B. V. (1991). *Research with Hispanic populations*. Newbury Park, CA: Sage.

Markstrom-Adams, C. (1990). Coming of age among contemporary American Indians as portrayed in adolescent fiction. *Adolescence, 25,* 225–237.

Mayfield-Brown, L. (1989). Family status of low-income adolescent mothers. *Journal of Adolescent Research, 4,* 202–213.

Mboya, M. M. (1986). Black adolescents: A descriptive study of their self-concepts and academic achievement. *Adolescence, 21,* 689–696.

McLeod, B. (1986, August). The Oriental express. *Psychology Today, 20,* 48–52.
McLoyd, V. C. (1990). Minority children: Introduction to the special issue. *Child Development, 61,* 260–263.
McShane, D. (1988). An analysis of mental health research with American Indian youth. *Journal of Adolescence, 11,* 87–116.
Mendelberg, H. E. (1986). Identity conflict in Mexican-American adolescents. *Adolescence, 21*(81), 215–225.
Miller, M. J., Springer, T. P., & Wells, D. (1988). Which occupational environment do Blacks prefer? Extending Holland's typology. *The School Counselor, 36,* 103–106.
Miller, R. L. (1989). Desegregation experiences of minority students: Adolescent coping strategies in five Connecticut high schools. *Journal of Adolescent Research, 4,* 173–189.
Nystul, M. S. (1993). *The art and science of counseling and psychotherapy.* New York: MacMillan.
O'Sullivan, R. G. (1990). Validating a method to identify at-risk middle school students for participation in a dropout prevention program. *Journal of Early Adolescence, 10,* 209–220.
Padgham, J. J., & Blyth, D. A. (1990). Dating during adolescence. In R. M. Lerner, A. C. Petersen, & J. Brooks-Gunn (Eds.), *The encyclopedia of adolescence* (Vol. 1, pp. 196–198). New York: Garland.
Patterson, G. R., DeBaryshe, B. D., & Ramsey, E. (1989). A developmental perspective on antisocial behavior. *American Psychologist, 44,* 329–335.
Pete, J. M., & DeSantis, L. (1990). Sexual decision making in young Black female adolescents. *Adolescence, 25,* 145–154.
Ponterotto, J. G., & Casas, J. M. (1991). *Handbook of racial/ethnic minority counseling research.* Springfield, IL: Charles C Thomas.
Ponterotto, J. G., Casas, J. M., Suzuki, L. A., & Alexander, C. M. (Eds.). (1995). *Handbook of multicultural counseling.* Thousand Oaks, CA: Sage.
Quay, H. C. (1987). Institutional treatment. In H. C. Quay (Ed.), *Handbook of juvenile delinquency* (pp. 244–265). New York: Wiley.
Rice, F. P. (1993). *The adolescent: Development, relationships, and culture.* Boston: Allyn & Bacon.
Richmond, L. J., Johnson, J., Downs, M., & Ellinghaus, A. (1983). Needs of non-Caucasian students in vocational education: A special minority group. *Journal of Non-White Concerns, 12,* 13–18.
Rogler, L. H., & Procidano, M. E. (1989). Egalitarian spouse relations and wives' marital satisfaction in intergenerationally linked Puerto Rican families. *Journal of Marriage and the Family, 51,* 37–39.
Sebald, H. (1986). Adolescents' shifting orientation toward parents and peers: A curvilinear trend over recent decades. *Journal of Marriage and the Family, 48,* 5–13.
Sih, P. K. T., & Allen, L. B. (1976). *The Chinese in America.* New York: St. Johns University.
Slaney, R. B. (1983). Influence of career indecision on treatments exploring the vocational interests of college women. *Journal of Counseling Psychology, 30,* 55–63.
Slavin, R. E. (1991). *Educational psychology: Theory into practice* (3rd ed.). Englewood Cliffs, NJ: Prentice Hall.

Slavin, R. E. (1995). *Cooperative learning* (2nd ed.). Boston: Allyn & Bacon.

Snow, J. T., & Harris, M. B. (1989). Disordered eating in South-Western Pueblo Indians and Hispanics. *Journal of Adolescence, 12,* 329–336.

Snyder, J., & Patterson, G. R. (1987). Family interaction and delinquent behavior. In H. C. Quay (Ed.), *Handbook of juvenile delinquency* (pp. 216–243). New York: Wiley.

Svec, H. (1986). School discrimination and the high school dropout: A case for adolescent advocacy. *Adolescence, 21,* 449–452.

Thomas, M., & Hughes, M. (1986). The continuing significance of race: A study of race, class and equality of life in America, 1972–1985. *American Sociological Review, 51,* 830–841.

Tidwell, R. (1988). Dropouts speak out: Qualitative data in early school departures. *Adolescence, 23,* 939–954.

Tiedt, P. L., & Tiedt, I. M. (1995). *Multicultural teaching: A handbook of activities, information, and resources* (4th ed.). Boston: Allyn & Bacon.

Tobin, J. J., & Friedman, J. (1984). Intercultural and developmental stresses confronting Southeast Asian refugee adolescents. *Journal of Operational Psychiatry, 15,* 39–45.

U.S. Bureau of the Census. (1990). *Statistical abstracts of the United States: 1990* (110th ed.). Washington, DC: Government Printing Office.

U.S. Bureau of the Census. (1991). *Statistical abstracts of the United States: 1991* (111th ed.). Washington, DC: Government Printing Office.

U.S. Department of Justice. (1991). *Crime in the United States.* Washington, DC: Government Printing Office.

U.S. Office of Technology Assessment. (1990, January). *Indian adolescent mental health: OTA special report* (Report No. OTA-H-446). Washington, DC: Author. (ERIC Document Report Service No. ED 324 177 RC 017 777)

Vega, W. A. (1990). Hispanic families in the 1980s: A decade of research. *Journal of Marriage and the Family, 52,* 1015–1024.

Weighill, V. E., Hodge, J., & Peck, D. F. (1983). Keeping appointments with clinical psychologists. *British Journal of Clinical Psychology, 22,* 143–144.

Williams, J. H. (1979). Career counseling for the minority students: Should it be different? *Journal of Non-White Concerns, 7,* 176–182.

Wilson, L. L., & Stith, S. M. (1991). Culturally sensitive therapy with Black clients. *Journal of Multicultural Counseling and Development, 19,* 32–43.

Yee, A. H., Fairchild, H. H., Weizmann, F., & Wyatt, G. E. (1993). Addressing psychology's problems with race. *American Psychologist, 48,* 1132–1140.

Zambrana, R. E., & Silva-Palacios, V. (1989). Gender differences in stress among Mexican immigrant adolescents in Los Angeles, CA. *Journal of Adolescent Research, 4,* 426–442.

Zapata, J. T. (1995). Counseling Hispanic children and youth. In C. C. Lee (Ed.), *Counseling for diversity: A guide for school counselors and related professionals* (pp. 85–108). Boston: Allyn & Bacon.

8 | Psychoeducational Issues and Concerns in School Counseling

It is in part the very uniqueness of every individual that makes him [her],
not only a member of a family, race, nation or class, but a human being.
—HELEN MERREL LYND

A primary emphasis of this chapter concerns increasing the awareness of school counselors to psychoeducational aspects of diverse students. A secondary emphasis focuses on school counselors' role in ensuring an appropriate education for all students. However, appropriate education for all students is affected by many factors, within and outside school systems. Important influences include societal roles, school resources, quality of instruction, and parental involvement. These multiple factors become even more apparent when public educational practices are examined from a cross-cultural perspective.

In recent years, considerable attention has been directed on the comparative status of public education in the United States with education in other nations. A brief comparison between educational practices in the United States and two Asian nations will highlight the rationale for this attention.

International Education and Education in the United States

In international studies of math and science achievement, students in the United States score at the mean of participating countries, although they often score at the bottom (International Education

Association, 1988; McKnight et al., 1987). More important, these trends emerge early in cognitive development. A study by Stevenson and Lee (1990) compared elementary students in Japan, Taiwan, and the United States. Significant differences in math achievement were revealed in kindergarten and became greater with increasing grade level. Less significant differences were observed in reading, in which Taiwanese students scored highest, Japanese students lowest, and U.S. students in between. In addition, clear evidence attests that too many students in the United States graduate from high school with weak reading, writing, and mathematical skills (Mullis, Dossey, Foertsch, Jones, & Gentile, 1991; Mullis, Dossey, Owen, & Phillips, 1991).

WHY DO STUDENTS IN THE UNITED STATES LAG IN ACADEMIC ACHIEVEMENTS?

Research has studied closely the learning environments in top-performing Asian nations, in particular, Japan and Taiwan. Asian students do not achieve well because they are "smarter," as they do not score higher on intelligence tests than do students in the United States (Stevenson et al., 1985). Rather, a variety of social forces combine to foster a strong commitment to learning in Asian families.

The dominant cultural influences on Asian educational programs include the following:

Cultural valuing of academic achievement. Mastery of academic skills is of central importance to Asian countries, and ultimately Asian families, because these countries lack sufficient natural resources and depend on scientific and technological progress. Many parents in the United States, on the other hand, believe that it is more important to encourage their children to feel good about themselves and to explore various areas of knowledge than to perform well academically (Berk, 1993).

A strong emphasis on effort. Asian parents and teachers tend to believe that all students have the potential to master academic tasks if they work hard enough. In contrast, many parents and teachers in the United States regard natural ability as the key to academic success. In addition, Asian students spend more time reading and playing academic-related games than do students in the United States (Stevenson & Lee, 1990).

Involvement of parents in education. Overall, parents in the United States spend less time helping with homework, hold much lower standards for their children's academic performance, and are far less concerned about how well their children are doing in school compared with Asian parents (Chen & Stevenson, 1989; Stevenson & Lee, 1990).

High-quality education for all students. Japanese and Taiwanese teachers do not make early educational decisions on the basis of achievement. Separate ability groups or tracks do not exist in elementary schools. Students receive the same high-quality instruction. Mathematical topics are treated in greater depth, and less repetition of previous material is rendered (McKnight et al., 1987; Stevenson & Lee, 1990).

More time devoted to instruction. In Japan and Taiwan, the school year is 50 days longer than in the United States, and more school time is devoted to academic pursuits, especially mathematics (Berk, 1993).

Communication between teachers and parents. Japanese and Taiwanese teachers teach the same students for several years and make home visits. Teachers and parents communicate continuously with the aid of notebooks that students ferry and in which messages about assignments, academic performance, and behavior are written. No similar formalized system of frequent teacher–parent communication exists in the United States (Stevenson & Lee, 1990).

A viable concern of Japanese, Taiwanese, and other Asian educational philosophies is that students pay a tremendous price for the pressure placed on them to succeed. By high school, academic work often displaces other experiences important for healthy development, because Asian adolescents must pass a highly competitive entrance examination to gain college admission. Yet the approach in the United States appears to err in the other direction—by placing too little emphasis on diligence and excellence (Berk, 1993).

IMPLICATIONS OF ASIAN EDUCATIONAL POLICIES

Japanese and Taiwanese educational philosophies illustrate broad cultural environments for achievement. However, programs cannot simply be transplanted and be expected to solve all problems. The United States faces different challenges from those in Asian nations, for example, how to educate ethnically diverse students for successful participation in a common culture (Leetsma, August, George, & Peak, 1987). Nevertheless, members of these ethnic groups agree about one thing: the importance of education and the need to improve it (Stevenson & Lee, 1990).

Perhaps, awareness of the ingredients of Asian educational success will prompt educational policy makers in the United States to rethink current educational practices. The Japanese and Taiwanese examples underscore the need for families, schools, and the larger society to collaborate to upgrade education in the United States (Herring & White, 1995). Progress is already being made. Academic standards and teacher certification requirements are being strengthened. Increased parent involvement is evident in many schools. Parents who create stimulating learning environments at home, monitor their children's academic progress, and communicate often with teachers have children who consistently show superior academic progress (Bradley, Caldwell, & Rock, 1988; Dossey, Mullis, Lindquist, & Chambers, 1988; Stevenson & Baker, 1987).

In the following section, representative statistics and commentary will focus on the educational achievement among selected ethnic groups.

Educational Attainment and Achievement Among Ethnic Groups

Racism and discrimination continue to affect the lives of many ethnic adolescents. Continued inequities in the United States are manifested by the numbers of ethnic minority people who are poor, homeless, living in substandard housing, in prisons, unemployed, or dropouts (Committee for Economic Development, 1987; Kozol, 1996). Socioeconomic difficulties and incongruent value systems frequently result in ethnic minority students being labeled as unmotivated or lazy in schools (Bellah, 1985).

EDUCATIONAL STATISTICAL REALITIES

The demographic realities of the education of ethnic minority youths are worthy of review. The following two illustrations acknowledge the tragedy of education for ethnic minority students in this country. The reader is cautioned to consider these negatives concurrently with the positive educational achievements of these ethnic groups (see **Something to Consider 8.1**).

Native American Indians and Alaskan Natives.   The education of Native American Indians and Alaskan Natives (referred to as Natives in this discussion) has always been a source of controversy. Historical issues have revolved around the basic pressures of domination, values conflict, and self-

SOMETHING TO CONSIDER 8.1

High School Dropout Rates by Ethnic Group, 1989
(Percentage of 10th Graders in 1980 Who Later Dropped Out
of School)

Asians	8
European Americans	15
African Americans	22
Hispanics	28
Native American Indians and Native Alaskans	36

SOURCE: Adapted from *Dropout Rates in the U.S.: 1988*, by the National Center for Educational Statistics, 1989, p. 26.

determination (Axelson, 1993). In addressing these issues, the federal government has never developed a realistic policy for the education of Native students.

To a large extent, the type of school attended affects educational success. The majority of Native students attend public schools, whereas smaller numbers attend Bureau of Indian Affairs day or boarding schools. However, the type of school may be moot as predominantly non-Native teachers are employed. The schools' fundamental flaw (other than economics) rests in their negligence to incorporate appropriate learning-style characteristics within their curricula.

Native students have the highest dropout rate of any ethnic minority group. The National Center for Educational Statistics report a Native dropout rate of 35.5%, compared with 22.2% for African Americans and 27.9% for Hispanic Americans. More revealing is that Native students account for 3.1% of all dropouts although they constitute only 0.9% of all students (National Center for Educational Statistics, 1989). These statistics reflect the educational attainment level of Native students—the lowest of all ethnic minority groups.

The data appear to reflect, in large measure, the continual inappropriate education of Native peoples and misunderstanding of Native culture (Herring, 1991). In addition, poverty and unemployment are combined with substandard housing, malnutrition, inadequate health care, and shortened life expectancy to limit opportunities for educational attainment (LaFromboise, 1988). Suicide and suicidal ideation among Native adolescents continue to increase at an alarming rate. For example, suicidal ideation among Zuni adolescents are 2.8 times higher than for other youths (Howard-Pitney, LaFromboise, Basil, September, & Johnson 1992).

Hispanic American students. Alarming numbers of Hispanic American students "give up" on education during middle school. Of all Hispanic American dropouts, 25% who enter high school are older than the average age and 40% drop out before the 10th grade ("Closing the Gap," 1988). For every 100 Hispanic American students, only 63 graduate from high school and only 17 decide to pursue an education beyond high school (Fields, 1988, p. 25).

One particular Hispanic American group—Mexican Americans—may enhance the picture. Over 60% of Mexican American students are in schools that have more than 50% ethnic minority students (Kavanaugh & Retish, 1991). Because of their low educational levels, Mexican American parents have difficulty advocating for their children's educational needs. In addition, many Mexican American students come to school suffering from culture shock. Their difficulty with the English language places them at an immediate disadvantage, and many students who desperately need some degree of bilingual education are never referred (Santiago & Feinberg, 1981)

Life circumstances force many Mexican American students to start school at one grade level behind their European American peers. Many Mexican American students are also placed in vocational "tracks" in which they experience nonacademic curricula. A lack of bilingual education and biased standardized testing programs results in a much higher than normal percentage of Mexican American students being referred to special education classes (Whitworth, 1988).

Without the benefits of traditional academic programs, these students are not prepared for collegiate admission criteria. "The national high school dropout rate for Mexican American youths is about forty percent, and at least ten percent do not even enroll in high school" (Fields, 1988, p. 20). Chacon, Cohen, and Strover (1986) stated, "High rates of dropout from high school is simply the most important factor accounting for the underrepresentation of Mexican Americans in college" (p. 97).

INTELLECTUAL ABILITY AND MEASUREMENT

A cogent area of educational achievement, or lack thereof, exists in how traditional educational psychologists and school personnel use measures of intellectual and cognitive ability. Traditional indexes of these concepts typically yield small numbers of ethnic minority students among the highest scorers, with the exception of Asian American students. The ethnic minority groups commonly underrepresented in high intellectual and cognitive ability measurements reflect those minority groups most economically disadvantaged (e.g., African American, Native American Indian, and Mexican American students; Van Tassel-Baska, 1987). The following discussion discloses that ethnic-appropriate measures may need to be developed for accurate indications of the intellectual and cognitive abilities of ethnic minority youths. Or, at the least, those assessments currently being used need to be reexamined in relation to cultural and ethnical biases.

Piagetian implications. According to Piaget (1973), brain maturation, combined with experience in a rich and varied external world, should lead all children to reach the concrete operational stage. Piaget did not accept that operational thinking depended on particular kinds of experiences. Yet, recent evidence indicates that specific cultural practices have a great deal to do with mastery of Piagetian tasks (Rogoff, 1990) and is incongruent with the Piagetian assumption that mastery of concrete operational tasks emerges spontaneously in all children (Berk, 1993).

A large body of evidence reveals that conservation develops at quite different times in different cultures and is often delayed, especially in non-Western societies (Berk, 1993). For example, among the Hausa of Nigeria, who live in small agricultural settlements, even the most basic conservation tasks— number, length, and liquid—are not understood until age 11 or later (Fahrmeier, 1978).

In addition, a repeated finding of cross-cultural research is that individuals of non-Western cultures who have no formal schooling do not use or benefit from instruction in memory strategies (Rogoff, 1990). Western children get so much practice with memorizing techniques that they do not refine other techniques for remembering that rely on spatial location and arrangement of objects, cues that are readily available in everyday life. Australian aboriginal and Guatemalan Mayan children, for example, are considerably better at these type of memory skills than the average Western student (Rogoff, 1986)

Instrumental intelligence assessment. Many researchers argue that the assessment of intelligence is affected by specific information acquired as part of a middle-class upbringing. Even nonverbal test items (believed to be less culturally loaded) seem to depend on subtle learning opportunities. Ethnic minority children from low socioeconomic status (SES) families are often reared in homes that are more "people-oriented" than "object-oriented," which reduce their opportunities to use games and objects that promote certain intellectual skills (Sternberg, 1988).

Performance on intelligence tests is also affected by specific experiences. When same-age children who are in different grades are compared, those who have been in school longer score higher on intelligence tests (Ceci, 1990). Similarly, dropping out of school leads to a decrease in intelligence performance, and the earlier students leave school, the greater their decrease in intelligence scores. Together, these findings indicate that a more intelligent student may attend school with a greater ability to profit from instruction. However, teaching students the factual knowledge and cognitive styles valued in classrooms has a sizable impact on intelligence test performance (Ceci, 1990).

Achievement results. **Chart 8.1** depicts a distribution of eighth-grade students by the level of their math performance. Other than Asian American students, the largest percentage perform at the basic level. Hispanic American, African American, and Native American Indian and Alaskan Native students have the smallest percentage of advanced performance.

CHART 8.1

Distribution of Eighth-Grade Students (in Percentages) by Level of Performance in Mathematics

Performance Level	European American	Asian	Hispanic	African American	Native American/ Native Alaskan
Advanced	22.4	34.7	8.7	5.3	4.8
Intermediate	24.3	21.2	16.9	16.5	13.0
Basic	37.9	30.7	46.8	49.4	49.8
Below basic	15.5	13.4	27.6	28.9	32.3

SOURCE: Adapted from *Dropout Rates in the U.S.: 1988*, by the National Center for Educational Statistics, 1989, p. 26.

Another example exists in American College Test (ACT) scores (Van Tassel-Baska, 1987). Nine percent of students scoring at or above the 95th percentile (ACT composite score of >28) self-identify as ethnic minorities, which is underrepresentative of the 17% of ethnic minority students who take the test. Great variation is often evident, however, in test performance among ethnic minority students. Asian American students continue to be overrepresented (14%) among high scorers (Kerr & Colangelo, 1988). Ethnic minority students who suffer the highest poverty rate are also the most underrepresented high scorers: African Americans (0.8%), Native American Indians (0.3%), and Mexican Americans (0.7%). This trend makes sense in that, in the United States, the local community's SES also determines the quality of education.

Kerr and her associates (Kerr & Colangelo, 1988; Kerr, Colangelo, Maxey, & Christensen, 1992) have researched this issue extensively. Despite the close relationship between SES and ACT scores, these researchers found that a surprising number of very poor ethnic minority students do attain the 95th percentile on the ACT: African Americans (15%), Native American Indians (24%), Mexican Americans (17%), other Hispanic Americans (10%), and Asian Americans (8.7%). These students are present in families earning less than $18,000 a year. Another 23% of Mexican Americans, 19% of other Hispanic Americans, 25% of African Americans, 8.3% of Native American Indians, and 13.8% of Asian Americans have family incomes between $18,000 and $30,000. Remember that the current poverty level stands at $14,400 for a family of four.

The patterns of gender and achievement among ethnic minority groups are similar to those among European Americans. The majority of high-scoring students are boys. Only among African American students do girls approach the number of male high achievers (52%). Boys represent 63% of Native American Indian, 66% of Mexican American, 61% of Asian American, 63% of Hispanic American, and 61% of European American high scorers (Kerr et al., 1992). These statistics are encouraging as they demonstrate that ethnic minority students are achieving despite sociocultural barriers and SES constraints.

Previous research on the high school achievement of Mexican Americans has documented substantial underachievement. However, recent immigrants appear to be achieving at a somewhat higher level (Duran & Weffer, 1992). Familial values placed on education and length of residence in this country have an important effect on achievement when those values are translated into participation in enrichment programs (Duran & Weffer, 1992).

EXPLAINING INDIVIDUAL DIFFERENCES IN INTELLIGENCE

Certain ethnic groups are advantaged when individuals are compared in terms of academic achievement, years of education, and occupational status. In explaining these differences, researchers have examined the intelligence test performance of students from different ethnic and SES backgrounds. For example, many studies show that African American students score, on the average, 15 points below European American students (Brody, 1985). Social class differences are also found with a difference between middle-income and low-income students of about 9 points (Jensen & Figueroa, 1975). These figures are, of course, averages. Considerable variation exists within ethnicity and SES. Still, ethnic and SES class differences in intelligence test performance are large enough to not be ignored.

Nurture versus nature. The much debated question will not go away: Which is stronger, nurture or nature? Jensen (1969) queried, "How much can we boost IQ and scholastic achievement?" Jensen's answer to this question was "not much." He argued that heredity is largely responsible for individual, ethnic, and SES differences in intelligence (Jensen, 1980, 1985a). For example, high heritabilities obtained from kinship studies have suggested that differences in intelligence have a genetic basis (Jensen, 1969, 1985b, 1988). Jensen's research received widespread attention and evoked considerable response.

However, this line of rationale is regarded as unreliable and discriminatory. Heritabilities computed on mostly European American samples do not provide any evidence about what is responsible for intelligence test differences between ethnic groups (Berk, 1993). Data demonstrate that when African American and European American children are placed in similar socioeconomic home environments at an early age, they do not differ in intelligence (Scarr & Weinberg, 1983).

Perhaps the most serious criticism of heritability estimates and concordance rates focuses on their usefulness (Berk, 1993). They do not offer any precise information about how traits (e.g., intelligence and personality) develop or how children might respond when exposed to environments designed to help them develop as far as possible (see **Topics for Discussion 8-A**).

A widespread misconception exists that if a characteristic is heritable, then the environment can do little to affect it. A kinship study, involving adopted children and their biological and adoptive relatives, demonstrated that this assumption is unfounded (Berk, 1993). Adoption research also reveals the origins of the African American and European American intelligence test performance gap. African American children placed into well-to-do European American homes during the first year of life also score high on intelligence tests. In two such studies (Moore, 1986; Scarr & Weinberg, 1983), adopted African American children attained mean intelligence test performance scores of 110 and 117, well above average and 20 to 30 points higher than children growing up in low-SES African American families.

Another study by Kerr et al. (1992) of 3,545 ethnic minority students who scored in the top 5% on the ACT reinforced this point. These authors examined the relationship of specific ethnic minority group membership, gender,

TOPICS FOR DISCUSSION 8-A

Considerable research and discussion have debated the effects of heredity and environment on intelligence, especially among ethnic groups. The *heritability coefficient* indicates the extent to which variation in characteristics is related to genetic factors, or an index of variation rather than of absolute amount. Here are some examples of the research.

1. Intelligence test scores are increasingly similar with increasing genetic similarity. In a review of 99 different groups, the median correlation for unrelated people reared apart was nearly 0, indicating complete lack of relationship. Identical twins reared together yielded a median correlation of .90, indicating a very high relationship (Erlenmeyer-Kimling & Jarvik, 1963).

2. The intelligence test performances of monozygotic twins correlate far more highly than any other group, but they also show the effects of environment by the differences between the correlations of twins reared apart (.67) and together (.85). Thus, intelligence is the consequence of both genetics and environmental shaping (Bouchard & McGue, 1981).

3. Scarr, Pakstis, Katz, and Barker (1977) found no relationship between degree of African ancestry (as estimated by skin color and blood type) and intellectual ability.

4. A study of illegitimate children fathered by U.S. servicemen during the occupation of Germany after World War II found no overall difference in average intelligence test performance between children whose fathers were African American and those whose fathers were European American. Because these children were all reared by German mothers of similar social status and were matched with same-age children, the results provide strong support for viewing environment as the major determinant of racial differences in intelligence test performance (Eyferth, Brandt, & Wolfgang, 1960).

5. When African American or interracial children (those with one African American parent) are adopted before they are 1 year old and reared by European American families with above-average incomes and education, they score higher than underprivileged African American children reared by their biological families. The performance of the adopted children on school achievement tests is slightly above the national norms (Scarr & Weinberg, 1976).

6. The mean intelligence test performance in Japan has increased significantly during this century, as assessed by performance scales of the Wechsler Intelligence Scale for Children—Revised. During the period 1910–1945, the mean was 102–105; during 1946–1969, the mean was 108–115. This change could not be genetic over such a small number of years (Lynn, 1982).

7. Ethnic groups differ in average intelligence test performance at various times in various places, but all broad populations contain the full spectrum of cognitive ability as measured by intelligence tests. That the group averages may sometimes differ should make no difference in a society in which people are taken as individuals (Brown & Herrnstein, 1975, p. 523).

career interests, needs for services, postsecondary educational plans, desires for extracurricular activities, and satisfaction with educational experiences. They found that academically talented ethnic minority students are achieving despite the restrictions of societal stereotypes, racial barriers, and SES.

These research findings reveal that genetic factors cannot be responsible for lower intelligence test performances of African American or other ethnic minority children. Instead, the effect of poverty depresses intelligence test performance of large numbers of ethnic minority students. And in many cases, unique cultural values and customs do not prepare these children for the kinds of intellectual tasks that are sampled by intelligence tests and valued in school (e.g., Herring, in press).

The controversy has not been quieted. The publication of *The Bell Curve* (Herrnstein & Murray, 1994) has regenerated the debate. This book has been labeled as "the most incendiary piece of social science to appear in the last decade or more" (Fraser, 1995, p. 1). Fraser described the book as "confirming for some their secret belief in the innate inferiority of certain 'races' or ethnic groups, angering many who view the book as an ill-concealed racist manifesto, and worrying untold others who fear the further racial polarization of American society" (back cover notes). The turmoil spurned the publication of *The Bell Curve Wars* (Fraser, 1995), in which researchers dismantled Herrnstein and Murray's alleged scientific foundations and criticized their conclusions. In reality, research results "provide little or no conclusive evidence for genetic influences underlying racial differences in intelligence and achievement" (Waldman, Weinberg, & Scarr, 1994, p. 29). Sternberg (1995) suggested that one could interpret the book *The Bell Curve* as scapegoating, intentionally or unintentionally, people with low intelligence test performances.

Research estimates that the heritability of intelligence is about 50% (e.g., Loehlin, 1990). However, these figures risk overstating genetic influences and understating the importance of environment (Berk, 1993). Heritability research offers convincing evidence that genetic factors contribute to intelligence; however, much disagreement persists over just how large the role of heredity really is (Ceci, 1990). Most researchers have reached the reasoned conclusion that both heredity and environment play important, albeit different, roles in mental ability.

THE TASK OF EDUCATION

As Axelson (1993) concluded, "formal education in the United States is the assimilation into a cultural tradition and is nonvoluntary up to a certain age" (pp. 192–193). How will this inalienable social institution adapt to meet the needs of a rapidly increasing multicultural nation? This question is the fore-most issue and concern as this nation enters the next millennium.

Most school counselors are trained in traditional, mainstream, middle-class value systems. Incongruity often exists between what they are accustomed to and what may be the actual background of the students in a culturally diverse setting (Axelson, 1993). No one single person is at fault or can solve this dilemma. School counselors can be sensitive to this issue and assist in its solution.

The first step is accepting students for who they are and helping them to improve their existences. To achieve this, school counselors must be skillful and knowledgeable in implementing that knowledge. A second step is to review the instructional methods and materials to ensure their relevance to today's students.

For example, cooperative learning has been identified as a culturally sensitive pedagogical approach (Haynes & Gebreyesus, 1992; Slavin, 1995). Evidence suggests that ethnic minority students, especially traditional Native American Indian and Alaskan Native students, excel in cooperative learning situations (Herring, 1989, 1990, 1991, 1997; Herring & Meggert, 1994; Herring & Runion, 1994). This learning approach is consistent with the social learning values and reward structures of their environments. So, why not incorporate cooperative learning approaches to offset the preponderance of competitive learning tactics normally found in schools?

Adults have difficulty existing in two worlds, and children experience much more difficulty to do so. When the cultural world of the student is incongruent with the cultural world of the classroom, the student often is forced either to adapt to the alien culture of the school or to withdraw in disgust and frustration. Many ethnic minority youths adapt successfully, whereas many others fall through the cracks.

AN ALTERNATIVE THEORY OF INTELLIGENCE

Perhaps, educational psychologists and school officials need to revisit their conceptualizations of intellectual assessment. Alternative theories of intelligence are certainly available. For example, Herring (in press) identified more ethnic-appropriate assessment modalities for the identification of gifted and talented Native American Indian and Alaskan Native students. The theory of multiple intelligences also deserves consideration when planning, implementing, and assessing educational opportunities for ethnic minority students, regardless of their at-risk level (e.g., Blythe & Gardner, 1990). The concept of multiple intelligences contends that learners have various types of intelligence rather than a single intelligence. Its usage has several implications for ethnic minority students having considerable talent in some areas while experiencing difficulty in other areas (Manning & Baruth, 1995). First, human abilities and talents can be addressed rather than the commonly emphasized linguistic and logical-mathematical intelligences (Gardner, 1987). Second, shifts in instructional emphases may be necessary to accommodate varied learning styles. Third, multiple-intelligences theory challenges the variability of standardized, machine-scored, multiple-choice assessments, which do not allow each intelligence to be measured (Blythe & Gardner, 1990). These alternatives may offer definitions and interpretations that are more congruent with both innate intelligence and the development of innate intelligence.

Social and Personal Growth

School counselors and related professionals must recognize that being an ethnic or cultural minority youth is *not* synonymous with an at-risk youth. Ethnic and cultural diversity is not an at-risk condition in and of itself (Manning & Baruth, 1995). Attitudes of racism, discrimination, and prejudice amplify at-risk conditions such as substance abuse, low achievement, teenage pregnancy, and delinquency. School counselors and helping professionals must acknowledge these challenges facing diverse students, yet not allow stereotypes to distort their views. School counselors and other educators must carefully avoid considering "differences" to be "deficits" or "at-risk indicators" (Manning & Baruth, 1995).

However, ethnic minority youths are clearly having difficulties in completing high school. Problems of identity formation, education, substance abuse, sexuality, acculturation, antisocial behavior, suicide, and others are affecting disparately not only their mental health, but also their chances of a quality life. The social–personal growth experiences of these youths also differ from those of most European American youths. The development of positive self-concepts and self-esteems is inherent to the improvement of ethnic minority youths' educational and career opportunities as well as emotional health. A review of these issues will provide insight into the unique developmental processes of this student populaiton.

SELF-CONCEPT

The *self* may be defined as that part of personality of which one is aware. *Self-concept* may be defined as one's "self-hypothesized identity" (Wayment & Zetlin, 1989) or as one's "ego identity" (Erikson, 1968). Self-concept is one's personal identity, which is the sum total of one's self-definitions or self-images (Chassin & Young, 1981). The first step in the development of a self-concept is the recognition that one is a distinct, separate individual. Rice (1993) described an adolescent girl's first awareness as follows: "I was sitting in the taxi with my mother when I suddenly realized, it dawned on me, that I am I and she is she" (p. 246).

Self-concept is often described as comprising multiple self-conceptions, with concepts developed in relation to different roles (Griffin, Chassin, & Young, 1981). Different aspects of self may differ, which explains why behavior vacillates. The concept of multiple self-concepts is highlighted in **Something to Consider 8.2.**

Strang (1957) developed four basic dimensions of the self. First, the *overall, basic self-concept* is students' view of their personality and of their external roles and abilities. Second, students' *temporary* or *transitory self-concepts* are influenced by the mood of the moment or by a recent or continuing experience (e.g., a low grade), which may produce a temporary deflated self-worth.

Third, students' *social selves* represent the selves that they think others see, which influences how they see themselves. For example, if they perceive that others think they are socially unacceptable, they tend to think of themselves in that negative way. Carlyle (1970, p. 10) surmised, "Show me the man who is your friend and I will know what your ideal of manhood is—and what kind of man you wish to be."

SOMETHING TO CONSIDER 8.2

The Multiple and Transitive Self-Concept

An accurate self-concept is significant. As Rice (1993) concluded, all people are six different selves: the people they are, the people they think they are, the people others think they are, the people they think others think they are, the people they want to become, and the people they think others want them to become. These multiple selves may or may not reflect close approximations of reality, and they are always in the process of change, particularly during childhood. Allport (1950) emphasized that personality is less a finished product than a transitive process. Personalities incorporate some stable features, but concurrently, it is experiencing change. Allport coined the word *proprium*, which he defined as "all aspects of personality that make for inward unity" (p. 172). This is the self or ego that has a core of personal identity that is developing in time.

SOURCE: Adapted from *The Adolescent: Development, Relationships, and Culture*, by F. P. Rice, 1993, p. 246, and *Becoming: Basic Considerations for a Psychology of Personality*, by G. W. Allport, 1950, p. 172.

The fourth self is the *ideal self,* the person that students aspire to become. This self may become a two-edged sword as their expectations may be too low or too high. Realistic self-concepts are necessary for realistic goal accomplishment.

Preschool years. Children emerge from toddlerhood with a firm view of their differentness from others. During these years, new powers of representation permit them to reflect, and they begin to develop a set of beliefs about their own characteristics—a self-concept. Ask a 3- to 5-year-old to tell you about self, and something like this will be the response:

> I'm Nancy. See, I got this new red dress. I'm 5 years old. I can brush my teeth, and I can wash my hair all by myself. I have a new tea set, and I can make you some tea. Do you want me to?

The ability to distinguish self from others underlies more than children's disagreements. It also permits them to cooperate for the first time in resolving disputes over objects, playing games, and solving simple problems (Brownell & Carriger, 1990; Caplan, Vespo, Pedersen, & Hay, 1991).

Middle school years. During middle school years, children's self-concepts undergo two distinct changes (Berk, 1993): (a) a change from concrete, observable characteristics to an emphasis on general dispositions and (b) the ability to make social comparisons, for example, children judge their appearance, abilities, and behavior in relation to those of others. Children also look to more people for information about themselves as they enter a wider range of settings in school and community.

Adolescence. Perhaps no other aspects of adolescence has received more attention over the years than self-concept, self-esteem, and identity (Stefanko, 1984). By the end of middle childhood, children start to describe themselves in terms of personality traits. This change allows adolescents to establish links between their past, present, and future selves. But the self-statements of early adolescents are not interconnected, and sometimes they even include contradictory descriptions.

By middle to late adolescence, teenagers combine their various traits into an organized system. Older adolescents also add integrating principles, which make sense out of apparent contradictions. Compared to earlier ages, teenagers also place more emphasis on social virtues such as being friendly, considerate, and kind.

Erikson (1968) insisted that the primary psychosocial task of adolescents is the development of a self-identity. From a cross-cultural perspective, the

search for self-identity is incongruent with many ethnic societies, specifically those that stress the identity of the family, the clan, or the tribe over
individuality.

SELF-ESTEEM

Students make judgments about their own worth or goodness—their level of
self-esteem. Self-esteem is also defined as the evaluative side of self-concept.
As they perceive themselves, adolescents place a value on themselves, resulting in either self-acceptance and approval or feelings of self-worth. If they
experience self-acceptance, then they have the self-esteem to accept and live
with themselves. If they are to have self-esteem, a correspondence between
concepts of self and self-ideals must be present.

Rogers (1961) contended that the end of personality development reflects a
congruence between the phenomenal field and experience and the concept of
the self. The existence of this congruence results in freedom from internal
conflicts and anxiety. Psychological maladjustment occurs when an incongruence exists between their relational selves and their self-perceived selves.

Preschool years. Preschoolers' sense of self-esteem is not as well developed as that of adolescents. Young children distinguish between how well
others like them (social acceptance) and how "good" they are at doing things
(competence), but before age 7, they do not discriminate competence at
different activities. They also overrate their ability and underestimate the
difficulty of the task (Harter, 1990). Preschoolers' sense of self-esteem is
adaptive during a period in which new skills must be mastered, and it contributes greatly to their sense of initiative. Once preschoolers enter school,
they become more aware of how well they are doing at tasks in comparison
with their peers, which often results in a declining self-esteem.

Adolescence. Self-esteem is also modified during the teenage years. New
dimensions are added to the increasingly differentiating self-esteem, such as
close friendships, romantic appeal, and job competence (Harter, 1990).

Adolescents vary widely in self-esteem. Teenagers who are delayed in
pubertal development, who are heavy drug users, and who fail in school tend
to feel poorly about themselves. In addition, girls tend to score lower than
boys in overall sense of self-worth (Simmons & Blyth, 1987). Another factor
related to self-esteem is social class. Middle-class teenagers evaluate themselves more positively than do lower-class adolescents. Reasons for this higher
self-evaluation include increased experiences of authoritative parenting, re-

ceiving positive feedback from teachers, and performing well academically (Rosenberg, Schooler, & Schoenbach, 1989).

ETHNIC DIFFERENCES

Erikson (1968) noted the likelihood of ethnic minority youths to internalize the negative views of the dominant society, thereby developing negative self-identity and self-hatred. Such internalization would be detrimental to psychological health and has been the subject of much investigation (Rotheram-Borus, 1989). Factors that ethnic minority children uniquely encounter and that in turn affect their mental health include ethnic minority reality, impact of the external system on their cultures, biculturalism, language differences, social class differences, skin color differences, belief systems, and help-seeking behaviors. This section will primarily emphasize self-concept and self-esteem development, as well as ethnic differences within those processes.

Overview. Identity development has not historically concerned the majority of European American adolescents (Rotheram-Borus, 1989). Future demographics indicate this will change. However, ethnic minority adolescents currently battle difficult and sometimes overwhelming challenges. As they develop cognitively, they become more sensitive to the negative influences of discrimination and inequality. Ethnic minority youths often feel caught between the standards of the mainstream society and the traditions of their own culture. Some even respond by rejecting aspects of their ethnic background. In one study, Asian American 15- to 17-year-olds were more likely than African Americans and Hispanic Americans to express negative attitudes toward their cultural group (Phinney, 1989). Other ethnic minority teenagers react to years of shattered self-esteem, school failure, and barriers to success in the European American mainstream. Others dodge the task of forming an ethnic identity, probably because it is too painful or confusing. As many as 50% of ethnic minority high school students are diffused or foreclosed on ethnic identity issues (Phinney, 1989) (see **Something to Consider 8.3**).

Lack of concern by many European American youths with ethnic origins implies a view of society that is not in touch with the pluralistic nature of today's society and their increasing demise as the ethnic majority. The ethnic distinctions with which most are familiar (European Americans, African Americans, Hispanic Americans, Asian Americans, and Native American Indians) oversimplify the rich cultural diversity of the nation's population (Spencer & Dornbusch, 1990). School counselors need to incorporate interventions that increase the multicultural sensitivity of European American students to greater awareness of their own ethnic heritage. For example, European Amer-

---

SOMETHING TO CONSIDER 8.3

Ethnic Identity Development

Phinney (1989) studied the ethnic identity development of 91 U.S. born 10th graders in two high schools in metropolitan Los Angeles. The group included Asian Americans, African Americans, Hispanic Americans, and European Americans. Some interesting results were found.

1. Slightly over half the students were at the diffused or foreclosed stage, characterized by lack of exploration of ethnicity as an identity issue.
2. About 25% of the students showed evidence of involvement in ethnic identity search and were in the moratorium stage. There was an increasing awareness of the importance of this issue.
3. About 25% of the students revealed a confident sense of self as a minority group member, after a search that indicated an achieved ethnic identity.
4. About 20% of all the students expressed a desire to change their ethnicity if they could. The students with the most negative attitudes were mainly Asian Americans.
5. European American students, even though in the minority in these schools, did not show evidence of these stages and were frequently unaware of their own ethnicity apart from being American.

SOURCE: Adapted from "Stages of Ethnic Identity Development in Minority Group Adolescents," by J. S. Phinney, 1989, *Journal of Early Adolescence, 9*, pp. 34–49.

---

ican adolescents who are secure in their own ethnic identity are less likely to hold negative stereotypes of their ethnic-dissimilar peers (Rosenthal, 1987; Rotheram-Borus, 1993).

The influence of dissonance on self-esteem is also felt among ethnic minority groups. In general, African American youths evidence a lower self-esteem when attending predominantly European American schools than when attending predominantly African American schools (Rice, 1993). African American students in segregated schools have higher self-esteem than African American students in integrated schools. Some evidence exists that African American youths have higher self-esteem when not exposed to European American biases. Findings also suggest that with the increase of racial and ethnic pride generated by the civil rights and African American consciousness movements, self-esteem among African Americans has risen considerably (Richman, Clark, & Brown, 1985; Rust & McCraw, 1984).

Some efforts have been made to do cross-cultural studies of adolescents. Comparisons of adolescents from India, Australia, Ireland, and the United States indicate that U.S. adolescents have higher self-concept and self-esteem than do the others (Agrawal, 1978). When Irish, Israeli, and U.S. youths are compared, youths from the United States rank highest, with Irish and Israeli youths lower but similar to each other (Eilberg, 1984). However, an adequate self-image depends on a strong and stable sense of ethnic identity and the degree of social pride and support from one's cultural group (Rosenthal, Moore, & Taylor, 1983). Research needs to be conducted that differentiates between the effects of ethnic, cultural, religious, and other identities on the development of self-esteem and self-concept. The cited studies appear to have assessed these aspects from a national perspective.

Moral reasoning. Cross-cultural research indicates that youths living in industrial nations evolve through stages of moral reasoning more quickly and advance to higher levels than do individuals in less complex, nonindustrial societies, who rarely advance beyond the morality of interpersonal cooperation. In tribal and village cultures, moral cooperation is based on direct interactions between individuals, as laws and governmental institutions for regulation do not exist. Higher stages of moral reasoning require an understanding of the role of larger societal structures in resolving moral conflict (Walker, 1988).

In cultures in which the youths participate in the institutions of their society at early ages, moral development is advanced. For example, on *kibbutzim*, small but technologically advanced agricultural settlements in Israel, children get training in the governance of their community in middle childhood. By third grade, kibbutz children integrate more concerns about societal laws and rules when discussing moral conflicts than do Israeli city-reared children or children in the United States of similar ages (Fuchs, Eisenberg, Hertz-Lazarowitz, & Sharabany, 1986). During adolescence, a greater percentage of kibbutz children than children in the United States reach higher stages of moral reasoning (Snarey, Reimer, & Kohlberg, 1985).

Kohlberg's (1969) stages of moral reasoning (preconventional, conventional, and postconventional) emphasized the value of individualism that reflected his socialization in a Western culture. Whether his theory applies to cultures that prize the good of the group or of the family more highly than the good of the individual is not documented extensively. Kohlberg established that moral reasoning ability occurred in the same order and similar age in the United States, Mexico, Taiwan, and Turkey (Kohlberg, 1969). Cross-cultural validation of his theory has extended his conclusions even more globally (Edwards, 1981, 1986; Gielen, 1990; Hwang, 1986; Moon, 1986; Snarey, 1985; Vasudev & Hummel, 1987). Over 50 studies using the Moral Judgment Interview (MJI) and over 30 studies using the Defining Issues Test (DIT) in a variety of cultures outside the United States are available (Gielen, Miao, & Avellani, 1990; Moon, 1986) (see **Topics for Discussion 8-B**).

TOPICS FOR DISCUSSION 8-B

One of Kohlberg's (1969) most controversial claims concerns his contention that moral reasoning develops according to a universal sequence of stages that transcends culturally specific ethical value systems, religions, political ideologies, and conceptions of the cosmic order. Kohlberg's proposition is based on the following assumptions.

1. In all societies there exists a common set of moral problems, issues, and conflicts.
2. Social role taking is based on the recognition that self and others share universal human features regardless of more specific personal differences in all societies.
3. Moral conflicts can be conceptualized in a limited number of ways that reflect underlying sociomoral perspectives based on role taking.
4. A developmental hierarchy of increasingly differentiated, integrated, and universal conceptions will be found in all societies, unless powerful social pressures and fundamentalist ideologies prevail over this "natural hierarchy."
5. The hierarchies of increasingly differentiated conceptions will be universally found, regardless of more specific, culturally variable social roles, moral prescriptions, and choices.
6. The MJI can be easily adapted to specific circumstances and can be used successfully with persons from widely differing educational backgrounds. The DIT, however, as a written test, can be used only with selected groups, depending on their educational background.

SOURCE: Adapted from "Research on Moral Reasoning," by U. P. Gielen, 1991. In L. Kuhmerker (Ed.), *The Kohlberg Legacy for the Helping Professions* (pp. 39–60).

One limitation of Kohlberg's (1969) initial research was his disproportionately male participant population. Subsequent research involving moral development in female participants has found that male participants' moral development revolves primarily around issues of justice, whereas female participants are more concerned about caring and responsibility (Gilligan, 1985). Kohlberg later revised his theory on the basis of early criticisms (Levine, Kohlberg, & Hewer, 1985), and recent research supports the lack of gender differences on Kohlberg's theories (Kuhmerker, 1991; Lee & Snarey, 1988).

The more important cross-cultural research findings on Kohlberg's model are synthesized in the following questions (Gielen, 1991).

1. *Can the MJI and the DIT be successfully adapted to a wide variety of cultural situations?* Moral dilemmas indigenous to a culture can be readily developed, as evidenced by the studies of Haitian villages (White, 1986) and the Kipsigis of Kenya (Harkness, Edwards, & Super, 1981). The research evidence for the cross-cultural usefulness of the DIT is mixed, however. For example, whereas East Asian students from Hong Kong, Japan, South Korea, and Taiwan respond easily to the DIT (Gielen et al., 1990), Arabic students from Sudan and Kuwait have major difficulties (Ahmed, Gielen, & Avellani, 1987).

2. *Does moral reasoning develop according to a universal sequence of stages?* The strongest research evidence in answer to this question derives from longitudinal studies conducted in Israel, Taiwan, and Turkey (Lei, 1990; Nisan & Kohlberg, 1982; Snarey et al., 1985). Their results strongly indicate the existence, coherence, and sequentiality of moral stages in these societies (Gielen, 1991).

Moral judgment assessments are more strongly influenced by the complexity and institutional integration of societies, by educational levels, and by the influence of rigorous ethical systems such as Confucianism than by degree of Westernization. Traditional, face-to-face village societies can reach a satisfactory moral equilibrium based on role-oriented, interpersonal expectations (Edwards, 1986). Higher moral conceptions, however, are based on the system perspective found in large, diversified societies.

Postconventional thinking is reported only in studies conducted among well-educated, predominantly urban female and male individuals from a variety of Eastern and Western nations. Research evidence suggests that the following conditions must be met for the emergence of postconventional thinking (Gielen, 1991):

1. Residence in structurally complex societies.
2. Exposure to formal schooling at least through adolescence.
3. Exposure to competing, complex value systems and displays of ideological awareness.
4. Exposure to value systems that include abstract considerations (e.g., Hindu metaphysics, Confucian ethics, and socialist ideals of an egalitarian society).
5. Demonstration of a high level of formal or postformal cognitive operations.

6. Exposure to highly generalized and abstract role-taking opportunities through education, opportunities for reflective thinking, and responsible decision making.

In addition, individuals from a variety of cultural backgrounds may evaluate postconventional thinking positively although they themselves are unable to produce principled moral arguments (Moon, 1986).

3. *Can cross-cultural research contribute to the understanding of socio-moral experiences that support or hinder the development of moral reasoning?* Several areas of clarification can be addressed by additional research. Additional studies can determine the degree to which Kohlberg's (1969) conceptions of a highest level of moral thinking may be culture-bound or whether alternative postconventional thinking versions exist. For example, does the Hindu Indian's concept of *ahimsa* (nonviolence) equate with Kohlberg's concept of justice?

A global interpretation of Kohlberg's (1969) perspective suggests that it is compatible with a variety of worldviews. Most questions relating to the generalizability and applicability of Kohlberg's stages have been answered. The developmental sequence of preconventional, conventional, and postconventional levels of moral thinking may indeed be global, but the highest level of moral thinking (i.e., universal ethical principles orientation) may not be (Gielen, 1991).

However, criticisms of Kohlberg's (1969) model as being mostly cognitive, with little attention paid to affective aspects, will not fade away (Peters, 1977). The question is whether a student's moral reasoning is applied consistently in all situations. Lickona (1976) concluded that "variations in the situation produce variations in moral behavior" (p. 15). Lickona added, however, that evidence suggests that some students are more morally "integrated" or consistent than others.

The Council for Research in Values and Philosophy, a group of scholars concerned with the moral dimension of education, promotes an *integrative model* that combines cognition, affect, and behavior. The integrative model perceives moral development as occurring along vertical and horizonal dimensions. The *vertical* dimension involves the ability to coordinate the perspectives and needs of others, to discriminate values that advance the humanity from values that do not, to make principled decisions, and to be aware of one's moral weaknesses (Ryan & McLean, 1987). The *horizontal* dimension of moral growth involves the application of a student's moral reasoning affective capacity to an increasingly wider range of real-life siutations. Horizontal growth requires that students not only think and feel but also act in accordance with their cognitive and affective capacities.

An integrative model of moral education (sometimes called *character education*, emphasizing a concern with issues beyond moral reasoning) requires that attention be paid to vertical growth issues: reasoning, clarifying values, and pursuing moral principles. It means also that students should use their thinking in a wide variety of ways, that is, that they pay attention to horizonal development. Horizonal development could be used to explain the classic Hartshorne and May (1930) findings: Good intentions do not always mean moral actions.

In *Character Development in the Schools and Beyond* (Ryan & McLean, 1987), Lickona presented an integrative model of moral education. Lickona's model identifies four processes that need to operate in classrooms if teachers are to influence the developing character of their students: (a) building self-esteem and social community, (b) encouraging cooperative learning and helping relations, (c) eliciting moral reflection, and (d) effecting participatory decision making. The Lickona model has been applied in a variety of classrooms. However, its application requires a teacher who believes deeply in the value of moral education. School counselors can collaborate with classroom teachers to ensure positive moral education and development.

Psychosocial development. Although Erikson's (1959) psychosocial theory is not generalizable across all ethnic groups, his work does contain concepts that enable a school counselor to understand and assess ethnic minority youths. First, psychological development extends through the life span, with specific phases of conflictual patterns. The school counselor must be able to assess and understand the phase-specific developmental issues, conflicts, and anxieties. This knowledge is a key element in advancing the development of a student in a given age period.

Second, Erikson's (1959) emphasis on life span continuity included youths and adults as simultaneous participants, allowing school counselors to assess the status of youths and parents together. The goal is to determine the degree of attainment of age-appropriate individuation and the extent of freedom from development-arresting forces in the individual and in the environment (Ho, 1992). Assessment of a child's relationship with significant others is vitally important in the prevention, rehabilitation, and treatment of the child's problem.

A third precept concerned the interpretation of mental problems. Whereas the medical model views mental difficulties as indicative of disease, the developmentalist perceives them as disturbances that impair current functioning and impede further development. Counseling facilitates developmental processes that are not congruent with the phase or age status of the student and achieves this in an ethnically appropriate way (see **Chart 8.2**).

CHART 8.2

The "Normal" Interview Versus the "Navajo" Style Interview

"Normal" American Interview Typical Criteria	Interviewing Navajo Style Criteria
1. **Self-confidence:** strong handshake; good eye contact.	1. **Respect:** a tactful handshake and limited eye contact.
2. **Goal orientation:** able to express short- and long-term goals.	2. **Harmony:** at ease with self and the world; able to be comfortable with silence and be more intent on listening than talking.
3. **Enthusiasm:** an animated conversationalist with an easy smile.	3. **Cooperation:** a history of working with others for the good of the group; avoids making boastful statements about self.
4. **Leadership:** able to provide examples of specific individual achievements and strengths.	4. **Leadership:** true leadership is through quiet example, not words.

SOURCE: Adapted from "Adjusting the Interview to Avoid Cultural Bias," by F. E. Mahoney, 1992, *Journal of Career Planning and Employment, 52*(23), pp. 41–43.

Erikson's (1959) emphasis on environment as an important ingredient for students' development may lead one to assume that the self-concept of ethnic minority youths is negatively affected by the stigma of membership in a devalued ethnic group (Ho, 1992). However, studies (e.g., Powell, 1985) have indicated that this is not the case. The dual-cultural perspective explains the differences and, therefore, may be useful when counseling focus concerns the psychosocial development of ethnic students.

Dual-cultural perspective. The *dual-cultural perspective* is defined as a conscious and systematic process of simultaneously perceiving, understanding, and comparing the values, attitudes, and behaviors of the larger societal system with those of the child's immediate family and community system (Norton, 1978). This concept has also been studied as *developmental expectations,* or *timetables*—the components of belief systems (e.g., Edwards,

Gandini, & Giovaninni, 1996). Every ethnic child is embedded simultaneously in at least two systems: that of the immediate nurturing environment and that of the larger sustaining environment. Although the sustaining system houses the instrumental needs of a person (goods, services, and economic sources), the nurturing system can be compared with Erikson's (1959) "significant others," those closest and most important in the determination of a child's sense of identity (Ho, 1992).

The degree of incongruence between these two systems may be very diverse, which may cause value, attitudinal, and behavioral conflicts between the systems. The school counselor can evaluate the psychosocial development of an ethnic minority student by viewing presenting problems from perspectives and from within the subsystems of each of the major systems involved (Ho, 1992).

Cognitive development. The classical Piagetian position presumed the mind's fundamental conceptual structures to be both general and universal (Piaget, 1973). Neo-Piagetian theorists would state that what is seen as universal is the mind's potential for constructing central conceptual structures, once a specific developmental stage has been attained. This basic difference between these research foci is applicable to the cognitive development of ethnic minority groups as well. Whereas classical Piagetians use the term "apparent differences across cultures," neo-Piagetians conclude that these apparent differences across different cultures are indeed "real."

Fiati's (1991) research with primary-school-age children and adult Ewe from urban, town, and village (unschooled) locations in the Volta Region of West Africa illustrates this neo-Piagetian conclusion. Three results were identical to those that have been obtained with Western samples. The first result indicated that African children's mean scores on Counting Speed and Counting Span measures could be applied to the data produced by children from Western cultures (Kurland, 1981). The second finding revealed that the absolute score each group attained on the Counting Span test was close in magnitude to its score on the Balance Beam task. This result is not demanded by neo-Piagetian theory, as it requires previous experience and/or knowledge of the operation of a physical system (i.e., the balance beam). The third result was that no adult group—whether schooled or unschooled, strongly or minimally Westernized—failed to develop to the 6-year-old level on any of the structurally oriented measures.

Obviously, one cannot infer too strongly from the study of subcultural variation in one specific non-Western society. Yet, when this study is coupled with other researchers' work (e.g., Saxe, Guberman, & Gearhart, 1987),

Fiati (1991, p. 340) suggested the following hypothesis: Certain domains of development, such as number, are ones to which all human beings are innately sensitive.

Considering the apparent universality of a basic cognitive system and the parameters that constrain its development as demonstrated by the preceding discussion, the nonuniversality of the operations and structures that are acquired at higher cognitive developmental levels involves four variables: automaticity, working memory, terminal level of structural development, and line of structural development at higher structural levels (Fiati, 1991). Fiati concluded that children's level of conceptual development was not uniform across the three general conceptual domains of logico-mathematical thought, social and emotional thought, and spatial thought. The children's performance also varied according to their schooling and to their degree of Westernization.

Developing Healthy Self-Concept and Self-Esteem

The development of healthy self-concepts and self-esteems among ethnic minority students requires the interaction of parents and formal education. Although tremendous within-group differences exist, general guidance for school personnel can be gleaned from the literature (e.g., Herring, 1997; Locke, 1989, 1995; Zapata, 1995):

1. Be open and honest.
2. Be open to and genuinely respect and appreciate culturally different attitudes and behaviors.
3. Demonstrate value of ethnic cultures.
4. Participate in activities in ethnic communities.
5. Eliminate all behaviors that suggest prejudice or racism.
6. Expect ethnic minority students to succeed.
7. Develop programs based on a systemic perspective that takes into account the social, economic, and political context within which ethnic youths live and learn.
8. Develop systematic procedures for assessing the characteristics and needs of ethnic students.
9. Plan, develop, and evaluate programs responsive to those characteristics and needs.
10. Recognize within-group variances and degree of acculturation.

The influence of parenting style is also inalienable to positive self-concept and self-esteem development. Within the context of the family, this development follows a pattern similar to that of an internal locus of control (Heath,

1995). High levels of parental support and general control, specifically inductive methods of control, are all associated with greater self-esteem in children, and high levels of coercion are associated with lower self-esteem (Rollins & Thomas, 1979). Self-esteem growth in daughters appears to be associated with high levels of mothers' general support and fathers' physical affection (Barber & Thomas, 1986) and the general support and participation (time spent in activities) of both mothers and fathers (Gecas & Schwalbe, 1986). The self-esteem of sons is associated with mothers' companionship and fathers' sustained contact (Barber & Thomas, 1986) and parental, especially paternal, control (Gecas & Schwalbe, 1986).

In summary, school personnel need to demonstrate knowledge, respect, and understanding for ethnic minority students. They need to recognize the varied socialization processes that students experience and develop programs that reflect those experiences. The schools also need to establish evaluative procedures to ensure continual effectiveness.

Within the family, high levels of support, specifically physical affection, have demonstrated positive outcomes in every area except academic achievement for girls in middle-class families. Second, inductive methods of control are more often linked to positive outcomes in youths than are coercive methods. Third, perceptions by youths of parental power are associated with high levels of conformity and identification with parents.

Summary

This chapter attempted to increase the awareness of school counselors about the psychoeducational aspects of diverse students. Commentary reviewed the comparative status of public education in the United States. An effort was made to demonstrate why students in the United States lag in academic achievements when compared with students from other countries (e. g., Japan, Taiwan, Nigeria, India, Australia, Ireland, Mexico, Turkey, and West Africa).

In addition, the current educational attainment and achievement among selected ethnic minority groups received attention. The realities of educational statistics were acknowledged, and discussions on intellectual ability and measurement were presented. The chapter also addressed social–personal growth issues such as self-concept, self-esteem, as well as the concepts of moral reasoning, psychosocial development, and cognitive development. A dual-cultural perspective was offered as an alternative to traditional developmental paradigms.

Suggestions on how school counselors can ensure an appropriate psychoeducational development permeated the chapter. Important influences affecting psychoeducational development in ethnic minority students include societal roles, school resources, quality of instruction, parental encouragement, and the development of healthy self-concept and self-esteem.

Experiential Activities

1. Natasha, a low-income African American female third grader, was quiet and withdrawn while taking an intelligence test. Later she remarked to her mother, "I can't understand why that lady asked me all those questions, like what a ball and stove are for. She's a grown-up. She must know what a ball and stove are for!" Using Sternberg's (1988) triarchic theory, explain Natasha's reaction to the testing situation. Why is Natasha's score likely to underestimate her intelligence?

2. **Something to Consider 8.2** described the multiplicity and transitory nature of an individual's self-concept. Frequently, students have difficulty identifying their self-concepts. Attempt to identify your own perceptions of your six selves. What obstacles did you experience in this process? How accurately do you think your list reflects your true selves? How and why does your personality constantly change?

3. Discuss the commonalities and contrasts between Rice's (1993) six selves and Strang's (1957) four basic dimensions of the self. Are they the same concepts but with different terms, or are they distinctively different? Can they be integrated? What are the implications for ethnic minority youths?

4. Much discussion has arisen during the last 20 years about the applicability of traditional developmental theories to ethnic minority individuals. In what areas do these theories neglect to recognize ethnic considerations?

References

Agrawal, P. (1978, March). A cross-cultural study of self-image: Indian, American, Australian, and Irish adolescents. *Journal of Youth and Adolescence, 7,* 107–116.

Ahmed, R. A., Gielen, U. P., & Avellani, J. (1987). Perceptions of parental behavior and the development of moral reasoning in Sudanese students. In C. Kagitcibasi (Ed.), *Growth and progress in cross-cultural psychology* (pp. 187–219). Lisse, The Netherlands: Swets & Zeitlinger.

Allport, G. W. (1950). *Becoming: Basic considerations for a psychology of personality.* New Haven, CT: Yale University Press.

Axelson, J. A. (1993). *Counseling and development in a multicultural society* (2nd ed.). Pacific Grove, CA: Brooks/Cole.

Barber B. K., & Thomas, D. L. (1986). Dimensions of fathers' and mothers' supportive behavior: The case for physical affection. *Journal of Marriage and the Family, 48,* 783–794.

Bellah, R. (1985). *Habits of the heart: Industrialism and commitment in American life.* Berkeley: University of California Press.

Berk, L. E. (1993). *Infants, children, and adolescents.* Boston: Allyn & Bacon.

Blythe, T., & Gardner, H. (1990). A school for all intelligences. *Educational Leadership, 47*(7), 33–36.

Bouchard, T. J., & McGue, M. (1981). Familial studies of intelligence: A review. *Science, 212,* 1055–1059.

Bradley, R. H., Caldwell, B. M., & Rock, S. L. (1988). Home environment and school performance: A ten-year follow-up examination of three models of environmental action. *Child Development, 59,* 852–867.

Brody, N. (1985). The validity of tests of intelligence. In B. B. Wolman (Ed.), *Handbook of intelligence* (pp. 353–389). New York: Wiley.

Brown, R., & Herrnstein, R. J. (1975). *Psychology.* Boston: Little, Brown.

Brownell, C. A., & Carriger, M. S. (1990). Changes in cooperation and self–other differentiation during the second year. *Child Development, 61,* 1164–1174.

Caplan, M., Vespo, J., Pedersen, J., & Hay, D. F. (1991). Conflict and its resolution in small groups of one- and two-year-olds. *Child Development, 62,* 1513–1524.

Carlyle, W. (1970). *You're my friend so I brought you this book.* New York: Random House.

Ceci, S. J. (1990). *On intelligence . . . more or less.* Englewood Cliffs, NJ: Prentice Hall.

Chacon, M. A., Cohen, E. G., & Strover, S. (1986). Chicanas and Chicanos: Barriers to progress in higher education. In M. A. Olivas (Ed.), *Latino college students* (pp. 97–123). New York: Teachers College Press.

Chassin, L. C., & Young, R. D. (1981, Fall). Salient self-conceptions in normal and deviant adolescents. *Adolescence, 16,* 613–620.

Chen, C., & Stevenson, H. W. (1989). Homework: A cross-cultural examination. *Child Development, 60,* 551–561.

Closing the gap for U.S. Hispanic youths. (1988). Washington, DC: The Hispanic Policy Development Project.

Committee for Economic Development. (1987). *Children in need: Investment strategies for the educationally disadvantaged.* New York: Author.

Dossey, J. A., Mullis, I. V. S., Lindquist, M. M., & Chambers, D. L. (1988). *The mathematics report card: Are we measuring up?* Princeton, NJ: Educational Testing Service.

Duran, B. J., & Weffer, R. E. (1992). Immigrants' aspirations, high school process, and academic outcomes. *American Educational Research Journal, 29*(1), 163–181.

Edwards, C. P. (1981). The comparative study of the development of moral judgment and reasoning. In R. H. Munroe, R. L. Munroe, & B. B. Whiting (Eds.), *Handbook of cross-cultural human development* (pp. 55–79). New York: Garland.

Edwards, C. P. (1986). Cross-cultural research on Kohlberg's stages: The basis for consensus. In S. Mogdil & C. Mogdil (Eds.), *Lawrence Kohlberg: Consensus and controversy* (pp. 212–252). London: Falmer.

Edwards, C. P., Gandini, L., & Giovaninni, D. (1996). The contrasting developmental timetables of parents and preschool teachers in two cultural communities. In S. Harkness & C. M. Super (Eds.), *Parents' cultural belief systems: Their origins, expressions, and consequences* (pp. 270–288). New York: Guilford Press.

Eilberg, A. (1984). Views of human development in Jewish rituals: A comparison with Eriksonian theory. *Smith College Studies in Social Work, 55,* 1–23.

Erikson, E. (1959). Identity and the life cycle. *Psychological Issues, 1,* 1–10.

Erikson, E. (1968). *Identity: Youth and crisis.* New York: Norton.

Erlenmeyer-Kimling, L., & Jarvik, L. F. (1963). Genetics and intelligence: A review. *Science, 142,* 1477–1479.

Eyferth, K., Brandt, U., & Wolfgang, H. (1960). *Farbige Kinder in Deutschland* [Colored children in Germany]. Munich: Juventa.

Fahrmeier, E. D. (1978). The development of concrete operations among the Hausa. *Journal of Cross-Cultural Psychology, 9,* 23–44.

Fiati, T. A. (1991). Cross-cultural variation in the structure of children's thought. In R. Case (Ed.), *The mind's staircase: Exploring the conceptual underpinnings of children's thought and knowledge* (pp. 319–342). Hillsdale, NJ: Erlbaum.

Fields, C. (1988). The Hispanic pipeline—narrow, leaking, and needing repair. *Change, 20*(3), 20–27.

Fraser, S. (1995). *The bell curve wars: Race, intelligence, and the future of America.* New York: Basic Books.

Fuchs, I., Eisenberg, N., Hertz-Lazarowitz, R., & Sharabany, R. (1986). Kibbutz, Israeli city, and U.S. children's moral reasoning about prosocial moral conflicts. *Merrill-Palmer Quarterly, 32,* 37–50.

Gardner, H. (1987). Developing the spectrum of human intelligence. *Harvard Education Review, 57,* 187–193.

Gecas, V., & Schwalbe, M. L. (1986). Parental behavior and adolescent self-esteem. *Journal of Marriage and the Family, 48,* 37–46.

Gielen, U. P. (1990). Some recent work on moral values, reasoning and education in Chinese societies. *Moral Education Forum, 15*(1), 3–22.

Gielen, U. P. (1991). Research on moral reasoning. In L. Kuhmerker (Ed.), *The Kohlberg legacy for the helping professions* (pp. 39–60). Birmingham, AL: REP Books.

Gielen, U. P., Miao, E., & Avellani, J. (1990). Perceived parental behavior and the development of moral reasoning in students from Taiwan. In Chinese Culture University, *Proceedings of Chinese Culture University-International Chinese Programs International Conference: Moral values and moral reasoning in Chinese societies* (pp. 464–506). Taipei, Taiwan: Chinese Culture University.

Gilligan, C. (1985, August). *Remapping development.* Paper presented at the biennial meeting of the Society for Research in Child Development, Toronto, Ontario, Canada.

Griffin, N., Chassin, L., & Young, R. D. (1981, Spring). Measurement of global self-concept versus multiple role-specific self-concept in adolescents. *Adolescence, 16,* 49–56.

Harkness, S., Edwards, C. P., & Super, C. M. (1981). Social rules and moral reasoning: A case study in a rural African community. *Developmental Psychology, 17,* 595–603.

Harter, S. (1990). Issues in the assessment of the self-concept of children and adolescents. In A. LaGreca (Ed.), *Through the eyes of a child* (pp. 292–325). Boston: Allyn & Bacon.

Hartshorne, H., & May, M. A. (1930). *Studies in deceit.* New York: Macmillan.

Haynes, N. M., & Gebreyesus, S. (1992). Cooperative learning: A case for African-American students. *School Psychology Review, 21*, 577–585.

Heath, D. T. (1995). Parents' socialization of children. In B. B. Ingoldsby & S. Smith (Eds.), *Families in multicultural perspective* (pp. 161–186). New York: Guilford Press.

Herring, R. D. (1989). Counseling Native American children: Implications for elementary guidance. *Elementary School Guidance & Counseling: Special Issue on Cross-Cultural Counseling, 23*, 272–281.

Herring, R. D. (1990). Understanding Native American values: Process and content concerns. *Counseling and Values, 34*, 134–137.

Herring, R. D. (1991). Counseling Native American youth. In C. C. Lee & B. L. Richardson (Eds.), *Multicultual issues in counseling: New approaches to diversity* (pp. 37–47). Alexandria, VA: American Association for Counseling and Development.

Herring, R. D. (1997). *Counseling diverse ethnic youth: Strategies and interventions for school counselors.* Fort Worth, TX: Harcourt Brace.

Herring, R. D. (in press). The unrecognized gifted: Toward a more humanistic philosophical perspective for Native American Indian and Alaska Native students. *Journal of Humanistic Education and Development.*

Herring, R. D., & Meggert, S. (1994). Humor as a counseling intervention with Native American Indian youth. *Elementary School Guidance and Counseling, 29*, 67–76.

Herring, R. D., & Runion, K. R. (1994). Counseling ethnic minority children and youth from an Adlerian perspective. *Journal of Multicultural Counseling and Development, 22*, 215–226.

Herring, R. D., & White, L. (1995). School counselors, teachers, and the culturally compatible classroom: Partnerships in multicultural education. *Journal for the Professional Counselor, 34*, 52–64.

Herrnstein, R. J., & Murray, C. (1994). *The bell curve: Intelligence and class structure in American life.* New York: Free Press.

Ho, M. K. (1992). *Minority children and adolescents in therapy.* Newbury Park, CA: Sage.

Howard-Pitney, B., LaFromboise, T. D., Basil, M., September, B., & Johnson, M. (1992). Psychological and social indicators of suicide ideation and suicide attempts in Zuni adolescents. *Journal of Consulting and Clinical Psychology, 60*, 473–476.

Hwang, K. (1986). *A psychological perspective of Chinese interpersonal morality.* Unpublished manuscript. Taipei, Taiwan: National Taiwan University.

International Education Association. (1988). *Science achievement in seventeen countries: A preliminary report.* Oxford, England: Pergamon Press.

Jensen, A. R. (1969). How much can we boost IQ and scholastic achievement? *Harvard Educational Review, 39*, 1–123.

Jensen, A. R. (1980). *Bias in mental testing.* New York: Free Press.

Jensen, A. R. (1985a). Methodological and statistical techniques for the chronometric study of mental abilities. In C. R. Reynolds & V. L. Wilson (Eds.), *Methodological* and statistical advances in the study of individual difference (pp. 51–116). New York: Plenum.

Jensen, A. R. (1985b). The nature of the black–white difference on various psychometric tests: Spearman's hypothesis. *Behavioral Brain Sciences, 8,* 193–219.

Jensen, A. R. (1988). Speed of information processing and population differences. In S. H. Irvine & J. W. Berry (Eds.), *Human abilities in cultural context* (pp. 105–145). New York: Cambridge University Press.

Jensen, A. R., & Figueroa, R. A. (1975). Forward and backward digit-span interaction with race and IQ: Predictions from Jensen's theory. *Journal of Educational Psychology, 67,* 882–893.

Kavanaugh, P. C., & Retish, P. M. (1991). The Mexican American ready for college. *Journal of Multicultural Counseling and Development, 19,* 136–144.

Kerr, G., & Colangelo, N. (1988). College plans of academically talented students. *Journal of Counseling & Development, 67,* 42–48.

Kerr, B., Colangelo, N., Maxey, J., & Christensen, P. (1992). Characteristics of academically talented minority students. *Journal of Counseling & Development, 70,* 606–609.

Kohlberg, L. (1969). Stage and sequence: The cognitive–developmental approach to socialization. In D. Gosling (Ed.), *Handbook of socialization theory and research* (pp. 347–480). Chicago: Rand McNally.

Kozol, J. (1996). Amazing voices. *The Family Therapy Networker, 20*(1), 52–59.

Kuhmerker, L. (Ed.). (1991). *The Kohlberg legacy.* Birmingham, AL: REP Books.

Kurland, K. M. (1981). *The effect of massive practice on children's operational efficiency and short term memory.* Unpublished doctoral dissertation, University of Toronto, Ontario Institute for Studies in Education, Toronto, Ontario, Canada.

LaFromboise, T. D. (1988). American Indian mental health policy. *American Psychologist, 43,* 388–397.

Lee, L., & Snarey, J. (1988). The relationship between ego and moral development: A theoretical review and an empirical analysis. In D. Lapsley & C. Power (Eds.), *Self, ego and identity: Integrative approaches* (pp. 151–178). New York: Springer-Verlag.

Leetsma, R., August, R. L., George, B., & Peak, L. (1987). *Japanese education today: A report from the U.S. Study of Education in Japan.* Washington, DC: Government Printing Office.

Lei, T. (1990). A longitudinal study of Chinese character change, special reference to young adulthood. In Chinese Culture University, *Proceedings of Chinese Culture University-International Chinese Programs International Conference: Moral values and moral reasoning in Chinese societies* (pp. 250–276). Taipei, Taiwan: Chinese Culture University.

Levine, C., Kohlberg, L., & Hewer, A. (1985). The current formulation of Kohlberg's theory and a response to critics. *Human Development, 28,* 94–100.

Lickona, T. (Ed.). (1976). *Moral development and behavior: Theory, research and social issues.* New York: Holt, Rinehart & Winston.

Locke, D. C. (1989). Fostering the self-esteem of African-American children. *Elementary School Guidance & Counseling, 23,* 254–259.

Locke, D. C. (1995). Counseling interventions with African American youth. In C. C. Lee (Ed.), *Counseling for diversity: A guide for school counselors and related professionals* (pp. 21–40). Boston: Allyn & Bacon.

Loehlin, J. C. (1990). Partitioning environmental and genetic contributions to behavioral development. *American Psychologist, 44,* 768–778.

Lynn, R. (1982). IQ in Japan and the U.S. shows a disparity. *Nature, 297,* 222–223.

Mahoney, F. E. (1992). Adjusting the interview to avoid cultural bias. *Journal of Career Planning and Employment, 52*(23), 41–43.

Manning, M. L., & Baruth, L. G. (1995). *Students at risk.* Boston: Allyn & Bacon.

McKnight, C. C., Crosswhite, F. J., Dossey, J. A., Kifer, E., Swafford, J. O., Travers, K. J., & Cooney, T. J. (1987). *The underachieving curriculum: Assessing U.S. school mathematics from an international perspective.* Champaign, IL: Stipes.

Moon, Y. L. (1986). A review of cross-cultural studies on moral judgment development using the Defining Issues Test. *Behavior Science Research, 20*(1–4), 147–177.

Moore, E. G. J. (1986). Family socialization and the IQ test performance of traditionally and transracially adopted Black children. *Developmental Psychology, 22,* 317–326.

Mullis, I. V. S., Dossey, J. A., Foertsch, M. A., Jones, L. R., & Gentile, C. A. (1991). *Trends in academic progress.* Washington, DC: Government Printing Office.

Mullis, I. V. S., Dossey, J. A., Owen, E. H., & Phillips, G. W. (1991). *The state of mathematics achievement: Executive summary* (National Association for Elementary School Principals' 1990 assessment of the nation and the trial assessment of the states). Princeton, NJ: Educational Testing Service.

National Center for Educational Statistics. (1989). *Dropout rates in the U.S.: 1988.* Washington, DC: Author.

Nisan, M., & Kohlberg, L. (1982). Universality and cross-cultural variation in moral development: A longitudinal and cross-cultural study in Turkey. *Child Development, 53,* 865–876.

Norton, D. (1978). Black family life patterns: The development of self and cognitive development of Black children. In G. Powell, J. Yamamoto, A. Romero, & A. Morales (Eds.), *The psychosocial development of minority group children* (pp. 181–193). New York: Brunner/Mazel.

Peters, R. (1977, August). *The place of Kohlberg's theory in moral education.* Paper presented at the First International Conference on Moral Development and Moral Education, Leicester, England.

Phinney, J. S. (1989). Stages of ethnic identity development in minority group adolescents. *Journal of Early Adolescence, 9,* 34–49.

Piaget, J. (1973). *The child and reality.* New York: Viking.

Powell, G. (1985). Self-concepts among Afro-American students in racially isolated minority schools: Some regional differences. *Journal of the American Academy of Child Psychiatry, 24,* 142–149.

Rice, F. P. (1993). *The adolescent: Development, relationships, and culture.* Boston: Allyn & Bacon.

Richman, C. L., Clark, M. L., & Brown, K. P. (1985). General and specific self-esteem in late adolescent students: Race × Gender × SES effects. *Adolescence, 20,* 555–566.

Rogers, C. R. (1961). *On becoming a person: A therapist's view of psychotherapy.* Boston: Houghton Mifflin.

Rogoff, B. (1986). The development of strategic use of context in spatial memory. In M. Perlmutter (Ed.), *Perspectives on intellectual development* (pp. 107–123). Hillsdale, NJ: Erlbaum.

Rogoff, B. (1990). *Apprenticeship in thinking: Cognitive development in social context.* New York: Oxford University Press.

Rollins, B. C., & Thomas, D. L. (1979). Parental support, power, and control techniques in the socialization of children. In W. R. Burr, R. Hill, F. I. Nye, & I. L. Reiss (Eds.), *Contemporary theories about the family* (Vol. 1, pp. 317–364). New York: Free Press.

Rosenberg, R. N., Schooler, C., & Schoenbach, C. (1989). Self-esteem and adolescent problems: Modeling reciprocal effects. *American Sociological Review, 54,* 1004–1018.

Rosenthal, D. A. (1987). Ethnic identity development in adolescents. In J. S. Phinney & M. J. Rotheram (Eds.), *Children's ethnic socialization* (pp. 156–179). Newbury Park, CA: Sage.

Rosenthal, D. A., Moore, S. M., & Taylor, M. J. (1983, April). Ethnicity and adjustment: A study of the self-image of Anglo-, Greek-, and Italian-Australian working class adolescents. *Adolescence, 24,* 689–698.

Rotheram-Borus, M. J. (1989). Ethnic differences in adolescent's identity status and associated behavioral problems. *Journal of Adolescence, 12,* 361–374.

Rotheram-Borus, M. J. (1993). Bicultural reference group orientation and adjustment. In M. Bernal & G. Knight (Eds.), *Ethnic identity* (pp. 105–137). Albany: State University of New York Press.

Rust, J. O., & McCraw, A. (1984, Summer). Influence of masculinity–femininity on adolescent self-esteem and peer acceptance. *Adolescence, 19,* 357–366.

Ryan, K., & McLean, G. F. (Eds.). (1987). *Character development in schools and beyond.* New York: Praeger.

Santiago, R. L., & Feinberg, R. C. (1981). The status of education for Hispanics. *Educational Leadership, 38,* 292–297.

Saxe, G. B., Guberman, S. R., & Gearhart, M. (1987). Social processes in early number development. *Monographs of the Society for Research in Child Development, 52*(Serial No. 216).

Scarr, S., Pakstis, A. J., Katz, S. H., & Barker, W. B. (1977). The absence of a relationship between degree of White ancestry and intellectual skills within a Black population. *Human Genetics, 857,* 1–18.

Scarr, S., & Weinberg, R. A. (1976). IQ test performances of Black children adopted by White parents. *American Psychologist, 31,* 726–739.

Scarr, S., & Weinberg, R. A. (1983). The Minnesota Adoption Studies: Genetic differences and malleability. *Child Development, 54,* 260–267.

Simmons, R. G., & Blyth, D. A. (1987). *Moving into adolescence.* New York: Aldine De Gruyter.

Slavin, R. E. (1995). *Cooperative learning* (2nd ed.). Boston: Allyn & Bacon.

Snarey, J. R. (1985). Cross-cultural universality of socio-moral development: A critical review of Kohlbergian research. *Psychological Bulletin, 97,* 202–232.

Snarey, J. R., Reimer, J., & Kohlberg, L. (1985). The development of social–moral reasoning among kibbutz adolescents: A longitudinal cross-cultural study. *Developmental Psychology, 21,* 3–17.

Spencer, M. B., & Dornbusch, S. M. (1990). Challenges in studying minority youths. In S. Feldman & G. R. Elliott (Eds.), *At the threshold: The developing adolescent* (pp. 123–146). Cambridge, MA: Harvard University Press.

Stefanko, M. (1984, Spring). Trends in adolescent research: A review of articles published in adolescence, 1976–1981. *Adolescence, 19,* 1–14.

Sternberg, R. J. (1985). Beyond IQ: A triarchic theory of human intelligence. In B. B. Wolman (Ed.), *Handbook of intelligence* (pp. 59–118). New York: Wiley.

Sternberg, R. J. (1988). A triarchic view of intelligence in cross-cultural perspective. In M. H. Bornstein & M. E. Lamb (Eds.), *Developmental psychology: An advanced textbook* (2nd ed., pp. 261–295). Hillsdale, NJ: Erlbaum.

Sternberg, R. J. (1995). For whom the bell curve tolls: A review of *The Bell Curve. Psychological Science, 5,* 257–261.

Stevenson, H. W., & Baker, D. P. (1987). The family–school relation and the child's school performance. *Child Development, 58,* 1348–1357.

Stevenson, H. W., & Lee, S. Y. (1990). Contexts of achievement: A study of American, Chinese, and Japanese children. *Monographs of the Society for Research in Child Development, 55*(1–2, Serial No. 221).

Stevenson, H. W., Stigler, J. W., Lee, S. Y., Lucker, G. W., Litamura, S., & Hsu, C. (1985). Cognitive performance and academic achievement of Japanese, Chinese, and American children. *Child Development, 56,* 718–734.

Strang, R. (1957). *The adolescent views himself.* New York: McGraw-Hill.

Van Tassel-Baska, J. (1987). The disadvantaged gifted. In J. Feldhusen, J. Van Tassel-Baska, & K. Seeley (Eds.), *Excellence in educating the gifted* (pp. 321–365). Denver, CO: Love.

Vasudev, J., & Hummel, R. C. (1987). Moral stage sequence and principled reasoning in an Indian sample, *Human Development, 30,* 105–118.

Waldman, I. D., Weinberg, R. A., & Scarr, S. (1994). Racial group differences in IQ in the Minnesota Transracial Adoption Study: A reply to Levin and Lynn. *Intelligence, 1,* 29–44.

Walker, L. J. (1988). The development of moral reasoning. *Annals of Child Development, 5,* 33–78.

Wayment, H., & Zetlin, A. G. (1989). Theoretical and methodological considerations of self-concept measurement. *Adolescence, 24,* 339–349.

White, C. B. (1986). Moral reasoning in Bahamian and United States adults and children: A cross-cultural examination of Kohlberg's stages. *Behavior Science Research, 20*(1–4), 47–70.

Whitworth, R. H. (1988). Comparison of Anglo and Mexican-American male high school students classified as learning disabilities. *Hispanic Journal of Behavioral Sciences, 10*(2), 127–137.

Zapata, J. T. (1995). Counseling Hispanic children and youths. In C. C. Lee (Ed.), *Counseling for diversity: A guide for school counselors and related professionals* (pp. 85–108). Boston: Allyn & Bacon.

The School Counselor's Role in Multicultural Schools

III

The roles that school personnel, other than the school counselor, play are inalienable to the effectiveness of multiculturalism in schools. Part III emphasizes the influence that classroom teachers have on the healthy development of diverse students. School counselors certainly have a vital function in the multicultural environment of school settings. However, the classroom teachers are in daily contact with students and provide their immediate learning environment. They are the frontrunners in providing culturally and ethnically congruent learning environments for student population.

The development and maintenance of culturally compatible learning environments is prerequisite to a truly multicultural school environment. The formation of collaborations between multiculturally aware school counselors and multiculturally aware classroom teachers is regarded as an extremely worthwhile endeavor. Students are tremendously influenced by their school environments, especially if these environments are congruent with the multicultural mission of the school.

Part III describes the most compatible manner in which to truly achieve multicultural school environments. Suggestions are presented that are offered as inspiration for school counselors and classroom teachers to reach beyond the chapter's suggestions and to generate additional ways to ensure the compliance of educational settings to multiculturalism.

9 | School Counselors and Teachers:

Synergetic Partnerships in Multicultural Education

There is always one moment in childhood when the door opens and lets the future in.

—GRAHAM GREENE, *The Power and the Glory* (1940)

Collaboration and consultation are two of the many tasks required of school counselors. This chapter emphasizes the need for school counselors to activate their talents and become collaborative team members in the development of school counselor and teacher partnerships. This partnership can be of vital importance in the prevention or discontinuation of culturally incompatible learning environments. Synergetic perspectives can only enhance these efforts.

Multicultural education has become an enigmatic concept in current educational philosophy. Although this concept is not innovative to education, student diversity has heightened the urgency for instruction relevant to, and inclusive of, ethnic minority students (Goodwin, 1994). One response to this need exists in the development of partnerships between the multiculturally weak teacher and the multiculturally aware school counselor (Herring, 1995a; Herring & White, 1995a, 1995b).

School counselors are not necessarily more multiculturally aware than are teachers. However, they are trained in developmental issues that teachers do not generally receive. In addition, school counselors receive training in fulfilling the roles of being a resource and support professional. Thus, this chapter will briefly address the status of cultural pluralism in schools and suggest how teachers and school counselors can work collaboratively to reduce and eventually eradicate culturally incompatible learning environments. Through synergetic partnerships, this development can become a reality.

Cultural Pluralism in the Schools

The demographic shifts in age, ethnic composition, and social class membership of students projected for the next decade have been addressed in previous chapters. However, these meaningful changes do have relevance to the thrust of this chapter. For example, a glimpse of the high school graduating class of 2001 amplifies this importance.

The senior class of 2001, which entered school in 1988, reflects ethnic minority levels ranging from 70% to 90% in this nation's 15 largest school systems (Gordon, 1991). In the United States, 25% of this class currently live below the poverty level, and 15% are physically or mentally challenged. Twenty-five percent (or more) will not finish high school (Herring, 1995a; Herring & White, 1995a, 1995b; Kellogg, 1988). Educating these students will be even more complex because they are more diverse, less cared for, and less ready to profit from schools designed for middle-class European American students (Eggen & Kauchak, 1994).

Currently, educational philosophy is experiencing a paradigm shift from the historical focus of the middle-class, Protestant work ethic to an emphasis on multiculturalism (Herring, 1995a). To effectively make the shift, teachers and school counselors must vacate their comfort zones and recognize different educational issues (Herring & White, 1995a, 1995b). Teachers and school counselors must be prepared to meet this challenge. In addition, the responsibility of counselor and teacher preparation programs cannot be abdicated in this effort.

The School Counselor–Teacher Partnership

Teachers are a vital link in the integration of a comprehensive school guidance and counseling program. In reality, teachers are the most important participants in the delivery of counseling services to student populations. They are in daily contact with students and frequently observe the behavioral patterns of their students. School counselors, at all developmental and grade levels, must cultivate collaborative and varied relationships with their teaching colleagues.

The school counselor–teacher partnership, however, cannot be a mutual admiration society. The purpose of such collaborations is to foster a genuine respect for each other's purpose and role in the appropriate education of this nation's youths. This collaboration can become a relationship in which purposes are identified, goals established, strategies planned, and responsibilities appropriately designated (Herring & White, 1995a).

An extremely popular example of school counselor–teacher collaboration is one-on-one partnerships. A more efficient vehicle, however, may exist in teacher support groups. By relying on the expertise of teachers, school counselors can facilitate such groups in discussions while avoiding the role of "master advisor" (Schmidt, 1993). School counselors also have the opportunity to be more aware and appreciative of the difficult tasks of teachers. Reciprocally, teachers have a similar opportunity to observe firsthand the facilitative and communicative skills of the school counselor. The bottom line is that multicultural education is more effective when teachers and school counselors cooperate in action plans (Schmidt, 1993).

Culturally Compatible/Incompatible School Environments

School counselors are responsible for planning, implementing, and evaluating services for students and staff. They have the primary responsibility of developing comprehensive and developmental programs for students. This mission, however, cannot be fulfilled without the cooperation and collaboration of school teachers. The development of *culturally compatible* classrooms and school environments is a primary concern in the delivery of a multicultural educational environment, but the continual existence of *culturally incompatible* environments hinders the full implementation of this development (Herring, 1995a; Herring & White, 1995a, 1995b). Too often, students are housed in learning environments that restrict their exposure to a multicultural learning environment (see **Case Study 9.1**).

THE CULTURALLY INCOMPATIBLE CLASSROOM AND SCHOOL ENVIRONMENT

The culturally incompatible classroom and school environment reflect characteristics such as the following (see Clark, DeWolf, & Clark, 1992; Herring, 1995a; Herring & White, 1995b; Neugebauer, 1994):

- discussion of cultures only as they existed in the past
- an incorrect or stereotypical version of how those cultures live or lived
- emphasis on similarities to rather than differences from other groups

CASE STUDY 9.1

Turning the Tables

A non-Native American Indian student is enrolled in a predominantly Native American Indian school. When the non-Native American Indian student enters the class, the Native American Indian students are gathered around the teacher. The students begin to stare, giggle, and whisper. The teacher says, "You're the new student. You're not a Native American Indian, are you? We were just talking about your people." The non-Native American Indian student glimpsed the bulletin board title, "Christmas: A Non-Native American Indian Holiday," with a picture of a non-Native American Indian man in a Santa Claus outfit.

The teacher continues, "Now, class, it's very important to remember that our new student is not responsible for what his [her] ancestors did. They stole our land and destroyed our buffalo, but that was long ago. We're not going to discuss that today. Rather, who knows what kind of houses non-Native American Indians live in?"

SOURCE: Adapted from "Teaching Teachers to Avoid Having Culturally Assaultive Classrooms," by L. Clark, S. DeWolf, & C. Clark, 1992, *Young Children, 47*, pp. 4–9.

- use of songs, stories, and other devices that objectify the culture and emphasize group characteristics, ignoring individuality within the group
- token representations of the group in the classroom
- "holiday units" on ethnic minority groups instead of saturation of the year-round curriculum with cultural diversity

Culturally incompatible environments do not foster an appropriate multicultural educational opportunity. In fact, ethnic minority students often experience such educational situations as teacher expectations of low academic and social expectations, pregnancy, involvement in drugs, and becoming dropouts. Some educators continue to view schools as the place to "weed out" certain types of students or to separate the winners from the losers (Manning & Baruth, 1995). Other educators and educational practices frequently neglect the needs of exceptional and ethnically different students, sometimes placing them at risk.

Within incompatible classrooms, the classroom climate may be described as being tense, unpleasant, inflexible, repressive, and suppressive. Ethnic minority students often receive negative consequences for their misbehaviors while positive behaviors go unnoticed (Charles, 1992). In addition, little attempt is made to develop the positive self-concept of this population.

THE CULTURALLY COMPATIBLE CLASSROOM AND
SCHOOL ENVIRONMENT

Culturally compatible classrooms attempt to eliminate examples of racism, classism, sexism, and ethnic prejudice while still providing a multicultural learning opportunity. Tharp (1989) observed that "two decades of data on cultural issues in classroom interactions and school outcomes have accumulated. When schools are changed, children's experiences and achievement also change" (p. 349). Tharp outlined the following dimensions of classrooms that school counselor–teacher partnerships can adapt to fit the needs of students.

Social organization. "A central task of educational design is to make the organization of teaching, learning, and performance compatible with the social structures in which students are most productive, engaged, and likely to learn" (Tharp, 1989, p. 350). Social organization in an educational context describes how teachers and students interact to fulfill their appropriate goals. For example, the social organization of European American society depends heavily on competition, thus inferring competitive one-on-one learning strategies for European American students. However, when similar strategies are attempted with many traditional Native American Indian students, the result is ineffective. These students are socialized in cooperative environments wherein the group is more important than the group member and competition is deemphasized.

Learning styles. Psychological and educational researchers have documented ethnic differences in the learning styles of students. For example, many Hispanic American students prefer cooperative activities and dislike being forced to compete with fellow students (Garcia, 1992). Many African American students, on the other hand, prefer a focus on people and relationships rather than on routine step-by-step learning (Bennett, 1995). Native American Indian students appear to have a more global, visual style of learning and sometimes show strong preferences for learning privately, through trial and error, rather than having their mistakes made public (Tharp, 1989).

Research on learning styles, however, indicates three concerns to which teachers and school counselors need to be alerted (Woolfolk, 1995). First, the validity of some learning styles research is questionable. Second, identifying ethnic differences in learning preferences may represent a dangerous, racist, or sexist endeavor. Third, assuming that every individual in a group shares the same learning style is dangerous. A "typical" learning style of a particular ethnic or cultural group can become just one more basis for stereotyping (Gordon, 1991; O'Neil, 1990). School counselor–teacher partnerships can monitor the use of learning style differentiation activities to ensure their sensitivity to individual differences (Herring, 1995a; Herring & White, 1995a, 1995b).

Sociolinguistics. Sociolinguistics is the study of "the courtesies and conventions of conversation across cultures" (Tharp, 1989, p. 351). A knowledge of sociolinguistic patterns will help the teacher and school counselor understand why communication among faculty, staff, and administrators is sometimes not effective. For example, the sociolinguistic patterns of students may be incongruent with the expectations of teachers (Woolfolk, 1995). School counselor–teacher partnerships can ensure that students understand the communication rules of the classroom: when, where, and how to communicate (Herring, 1995a; Herring & White, 1995a, 1995b). If students are required to raise their hands to get the teacher's attention, the teacher should not respond to students who do not follow that rule.

Suggestions for Appropriate Strategies to Ensure Culturally Compatible Learning Environments

School counselors and teachers, through collaborative partnerships, can generate appropriate strategies to ensure culturally compatible classrooms and school environments. The following suggestions, as adapted from Tharp (1989) and Woolfolk (1995), represent viable examples for consideration:

1. Experiment with varied grouping arrangements to encourage social co-operation (e.g., "study buddies").
2. Provide multiple ways to teaching to accommodate diverse learning styles (e.g., verbal materials at different reading levels, visual and auditory materials, activities and projects).
3. Teach classroom procedures directly, even ways of doing things that you thought everyone would know (e.g., how to get the teacher's attention, how to interrupt the teacher).
4. Recognize the meaning of different behaviors for your students (e.g., how do they feel when they are corrected, especially in front of the other students).
5. Stress meaning in teaching (e.g., make sure students understand what they read; relate abstract concepts to everyday experiences).
6. Know the customs, beliefs, and values of your students (e.g., analyze different traditions for common themes; use holidays as a chance to discuss origins and meanings).

7. Help students identify stereotypes and racist or sexist messages (e.g., analyze curriculum materials for biases; make students report biased comments from the media).

In addition to these suggestions, additional strategies and interventions can be adapted to ensure a multicultural curriculum and multicultural classroom activities.

MULTICULTURAL CURRICULUM

Multicultural education requires a multicultural curriculum. School counselors and teachers can consider the following recommendations, as adapted from Sleeter and Grant (1988, pp. 153–155):

1. The curriculum should be reformed in such a way that it regularly presents diverse perspectives, experiences, and contributions. Similarly, concepts should be presented and taught that represent diverse cultural groups and both sexes.
2. The curriculum should include materials and visual displays that are free of race, gender, and other stereotypes, and which include members of all cultures in a positive manner.
3. The curriculum should provide as much emphasis on contemporary culture as on historical culture, and groups should be represented as active and dynamic (e.g., women's suffrage movement should be addressed, but more contemporary problems confronting women also should be addressed).
4. The curriculum should ensure the use of nonsexist language.
5. The curriculum and the teaching–learning methods should draw on children's experiential background, and curricular concepts should be based on children's daily life and experience.
6. The curriculum should allow equal access for all students (i.e., all students should be allowed to enroll in college preparatory courses or other special curricular areas).

MULTICULTURAL CLASSROOM ACTIVITIES

In addition to implementing a multicultural curriculum, school counselors and teacher partnerships can also monitor the infusion of multicultural activities in the classroom. Frequently, multicultural curricula exist on "paper" with little transfer to the actual learning in the classroom. Even in those educational environments that are authentically multicultural, monitoring the use of multicultural classroom activities provides reinforcement and variety to the learning situation. A list of such activities, as adapted from a Florida State Department of Education (1990) guide, is a start.

• Make newcomers feel welcome through a formal program.
• Be sure that assignments are not offensive or frustrating to students of cultural minorities (e.g., asking students to discuss or write about their Christmas experiences is inappropriate for non-Christian students). Let students discuss their similar holidays.
• Form a school committee to address the implementation of multicultural education.
• Let faculty who are knowledgeable about multicultural topics be guest teachers in your class.
• Take a cultural census of the class or school; let students be the ethnographers.
• Form a multicultural club.
• Select a theme to tie various multicultural activities together; hold school programs with art, music, and dramatic presentations; hold a multicultural fair or festival.
• Hold a school cross-cultural food festival.
• Have multicultural celebrations and teach-ins with schoolwide activities in all classes.
• Feature stories in the local newspaper on multicultural topics.
• Decorate classrooms, hallways, and the library media center with murals, bulletin boards, posters, artifacts, and other materials representative of the students in the class or school.
• Supplement textbooks with authentic material from different cultures.
• Use community resources: representatives of various cultures talking to classes; actors portraying characters or events; and musicians and dance groups.
• Make reminders during daily announcements about multicultural activities.
• Develop a radio or television program on multicultural themes.
• Study works in science, art, music, and literature of various cultures.
• Have students write short stories or essays on multicultural topics.
• Have student debates, speeches, or skits on multicultural topics.
• Discuss the relevance of the U.S. Constitution and government in dealing with today's problems relating to ethnic minorities and cultural diversity.
• Have children of other cultures or their parents share native songs with classmates.
• Take field trips to local multicultural sites.

- Establish pen pal or video exchange programs with students from other cultures.
- Discuss what it means to be a responsible citizen in this country and in others.
- Focus on everyday artifacts of cultures that differentiate the way people behave in different cultures (e.g., greeting, friendly exchanges, farewells, expressing respect, verbal taboos, body language, gender roles, folklore, childhood literature, discipline).

ASSESSING EFFECTIVENESS IN ACHIEVING MULTICULTURAL GOALS

A major component of a multicultural education is the evaluation of that program. The efforts are fruitless if evaluative assessments are not conducted. How can school counselors and teachers know if classrooms and school environments are fair and positive toward all ethnicities and cultures, conditions of disability, and issues of gender and sexuality? Baruth and Manning (1992, pp. 202–203) provided a self-evaluation guide, adapted as follows.

1. Have efforts been made to understand and respect cultural diversity among students, not as a problem to be reckoned with, but as a challenging opportunity and a rich gift?
2. Have efforts been made to provide a classroom in which students feel free to speak and express diverse opinions? Are students free to express opinions contrary to middle-class European American beliefs?
3. Have efforts been made to have the classroom reflect cultural diversity? Do the walls, bulletin boards, and artwork of the classroom demonstrate respect for cultural diversity?
4. Have efforts been made to provide organizational patterns that do not result in segregation of some students according to race, culture, ethnicity, or social class?
5. Have efforts been made to understand language differences and differing learning styles?
6. Have efforts been made to understand culturally different students' perspectives toward motivation, excelling among one's peers, competition, group welfare, and sharing?
7. Have efforts been made to understand culturally diverse parents and extended families?
8. Have efforts been made to treat each student with respect, to consider each student as equal to other students, and to treat each learner as a valued and worthwhile member of the class?

9. Have efforts been made to allow (and indeed encourage) all students to work in cross-cultural groups, to carry on meaningful dialogue, and to feel a valued member of the group?

10. Have efforts been made to instill multiculturalism as a genuine part of the teaching–learning process and overall school environment?

Through constant and persistent monitoring, school counselors can assist the classroom teacher in the development of, and the maintenance of, culturally and ethnically appropriate environments.

Suggestions for School Counselor Training Programs

School counselor training programs must address the topic of culturally incompatible learning environments. Training programs must address important aspects that influence the ability of school counselors to function within a multicultural environment. Three recent research efforts have relevance for school counselor training programs: (a) school counselor-led support groups for preservice and novice teachers, (b) assessing the a priori knowledge of preservice school counselors, and (c) authentic or performance assessment.

SCHOOL COUNSELOR-LED SUPPORT GROUPS

One alternative for school counselor education is reflected in the positive effects of counselor-led support groups for preservice and novice teachers (Reiman, Bostick, Lassiter, & Cooper, 1995). Reiman et al. found that innovative intervention programs coordinated by mentor counselors and mentor teachers assist in the amelioration of preservice and novice teacher concerns. Paisley (1990) also explored the effects of support groups on beginning teachers. School counselors, who were skilled as coleaders, addressed the concerns of beginning teachers, using the original framework of Fuller (1969). Paisley found positive trends in beginning teacher movement through the phases of concern (for self and for students).

Herring (1989) found similar trends in a concerns-based approach with counselor-led support groups for preservice teachers. With the use of a three-group design, findings indicated that one of the three groups shifted to the consequence phase (i.e., "How does my teaching affect the pupils"), whereas the other two groups reached the management phase (i.e., "How can I organize my teaching and materials to best control the class?").

These studies parallel the findings of Fuller (1969), who directed the original research on group work with novice teachers. However, they do not represent irrefutable evidence that counselor-led support groups will encourage novice or preservice teachers to shift more quickly to concerns for students rather than self. They do establish a positive trend (Reiman et al., 1995). In addition, although this research addressed concerns of preservice and novice teachers in relation to personal adaptation to new experiences, they can provide a model for understanding the multicultural concerns that student teachers experience during their preservice internships and initial years of teaching.

ASSESSING A PRIORI KNOWLEDGE

Previous discussion has drawn attention to the insufficient attention devoted by many school counselor and teacher training programs to preservice interns' a priori knowledge and ideas of multiculturalism (e.g., Goodwin, 1994; Herring, 1995b). C. M. Clark and Peterson (1986) confirmed that teachers' conceptions of the nature of teaching and learning are the basis and the parameters of the decisions they make in the classroom situation. Incongruence between personal beliefs and actual training program precepts, relative to multiculturalism, can contribute to in-service teachers' perpetuating culturally incompatible environments (Herring, 1995a; Herring & White, 1995a, 1995b).

Efforts by school counselor and teacher educators to prepare multicultural educators should begin with an understanding of how students view multicultural education (Goodwin, 1990, 1994; Grant & Secada, 1990; Herring, 1995b). Teacher education programs are included in this discussion because many states require applicants to have experience as teachers before certification as school counselors. Traditional pedagogical and experiential activities of preservice educators require improvement if multicultural education is to become a reality. Training programs need to reassess current training paradigms and consider alternative modalities if they are to prepare effective multicultural educators.

AUTHENTIC OR PERFORMANCE ASSESSMENT

The most efficacious method to assess student ability has traditionally been a debated issue. Parents demand assessments that accurately reflect the essential capabilities of their children prerequisite to becoming successful adults. Educators, on the other hand, mandate assessments that serve as an integrated component of the instructional process (i.e., assessment should model high-quality instruction and promote student learning).

Educational psychologists are concerned with ethnic-appropriate assessment and the concept of multiple intelligences. They have begun experimenting with assessment models that expand the simple measurement of learning. The most notable example of these new approaches concerns *authentic* or *performance assessment,* defined simply as "an evaluation of how well individuals can do something, as opposed to determining what they know about doing something" (Educational Testing Service, 1995, p. 6).

Supporters of this assessment approach view it as a major policy initiative for education reform. However, performance assessment faces some controversy. For example, performance assessment is reminiscent of the time-inefficient, subjective assessment techniques that were rejected long ago in favor of more objective, less expensive alternatives. Other detractors challenge the practical and psychometric problems of performance testing.

Regardless, training programs must, at the least, expose their students to the increasing support for authentic methods of assessment. The educational, policy, and assessment communities must unite to determine the appropriate balance of assessment tools that will facilitate their shared goal: improved learning for all students (Educational Testing Service, 1995). School counselor training programs must become active participants in this endeavor.

EMPOWERMENT WITH MULTICULTURALISM

School counselor training programs can generate a cycle of empowerment beginning with their advocacy of a pedagogy that results in professionals who are competent in representing the needs and aspirations of an increasingly diverse school population (Herring, 1995a; Herring & White, 1995a, 1995b). Much of this effort must occur during the training of preservice school counselors. The following suggestions are offered as a guide to inspire additional strategies for empowerment of multiculturalism (Martin, 1991; Sleeter, 1991).

1. Preservice educators must be given multicultural tools for empowerment, for example, knowledge of the historical and legislative context of multicultural education, and the understanding of the power governing the settings in which they will attempt to use those strategies.
2. Training programs should not only be concerned with the ways in which they train their students in the use of technical skills, but must also develop a clearer and more integrated understanding of the realities present in the learning environments.
3. The cooperating onsite supervisor has been acquainted with and consequently is willing to encourage the practice of multicultural strategies.
4. Preservice educators should enter the intern experience armed with multicultural strategies that they have authored in an original unit of instruction.

A three-step training process has been suggested to ensure the preparation of preservice teachers with multicultural competence (L. Clark et al.,

1992; Neugebauer, 1994). This model is adapted for school counselor training as well. The training necessitates student involvement in the following stages of development:

- Sensitization: School counselors experience and continue to experience the culturally assaultive classroom.
- Skill development: School counselors learn to critically evaluate the environment and plan culturally diverse curricula.
- Curriculum development: School counselors develop a saturated, culturally diverse curriculum.

Tran, Young, and DiLella's (1994) study presents another effort to provide an effective multicultural education. These authors investigated the effects of a multicultural education course on the forming of attitudes toward European Americans, Mexican Americans, and African Americans. The results indicated that such a course can be useful in changing attitudes in a positive direction. The study also revealed that courses requiring direct contact with ethnically diverse group activities are likely to have an emotional and intellectual effect on students.

McWhirter (1994) presented three implications necessary for multicultural empowerment for counselor training: (a) counselors and other mental health professionals must pay attention to the person of the counselor; (b) they must be aware of how counseling can be a vehicle of oppression; and (c) coursework in multicultural perspectives must be an integral component (pp. 227–231). Traditional theories of counseling are largely based on research conducted by European middle-class men using samples of European men—hence, the masculine perspective (Unger, 1983). Such research has yielded considerable information relative to the middle-class European American men to the detriment of women, ethnicities, and people of lower socioeconomic status (McWhirter, 1994). Integration of these perspectives into training programs is a prequisite to the true empowerment of multiculturalism.

Bringing It All Together

Three general principles are suggested to guide school counselors in their efforts to assist teachers in "bringing it all together." Effective teachers must be able to achieve these principles. School counselors represent a valuable resource.

KNOW THE STUDENTS

Reading, graduate courses, and in-service workshops can enhance multicultural knowledge. However, these resources are not sufficient for school counselors and teachers to understand the lives of their students. Some additional learning opportunities are offered to encourage school counselors and teachers to brainstorm and to be creative in efforts to obtain information (Herring, 1995a; Herring & White, 1995a, 1995b):

- Take other courses in college about other cultures, especially if you have not had one, or read about other cultures.
- Get to know the students' families and communities.
- Spend time with students and parents outside school hours, for example, eat lunch with them.
- Ask parents to help in class or to speak to students about their jobs and careers, their hobbies, or the history and heritage of their ethnic group.
- Do not wait until a student is in trouble to have the first meeting with a family member, especially in the elementary grades.
- Watch and listen to the ways that students interact in large and small groups.

RESPECT ALL STUDENTS

Knowledge should generate respect for students' learning strengths—for the struggles they face and the obstacles they overcome (Woolfolk, 1995). The development of self-esteem and pride among students requires their genuine acceptance by school personnel. The integration of culture into the school environment must reflect more than the "tokenism" of sampling ethnic foods or wearing ethnic costumes. Students should be exposed to the social and intellectual contributions of ethnic groups as well (Herring, 1995a; Herring & White, 1995a, 1995b).

Tiedt and Tiedt (1990) provided several ideas for multicultural education and culturally compatible environments:

- Ask students to draw a picture or bring in a photograph of themselves.
- Study in depth the various ethnic and cultural groups represented in the student population.
- Create learning centers that are based on particular ethnicities and cultures.
- Have students draw maps, calculate distances, convert money, and act out historical events.

TEACH ALL STUDENTS

Teaching students to read, write, speak, compute, think, and create represent the most important goals teachers need to develop and be able to accomplish.

School counselors can be valuable resources in assisting teachers in the development of such instructional activities (Herring & White, 1995a, 1995b). Knapp, Turnbill, and Shields (1990) offered these suggestions:

- Focus on meaning and understanding from beginning to end, for example, by orienting instruction toward comprehending reading passages.
- Balance routine skill learning with novel and complex tasks from the initial stages of learning.
- Provide context for skill learning that establishes clear reasons for needing to learn the skills.
- Influence attitudes and beliefs about the academic content areas as well as skills and knowledge.
- Eliminate unnecessary redundancy in the curriculum.

Finally, teachers can teach students about how to be students. In the early grades, students need to be taught directly the courtesies and conventions of the classroom. For example, students need to understand how to get recognized or how to get help in a small group. Students in the higher grades need to know how study skills differ in the various academic disciplines. Students may be socialized at home in ways that are incongruent to the school's expectations.

KNOW ONESELF

The personal background, experiences, culture, and values of school counselors and teachers prescribe and describe them. They must be aware of their own educational philosophies. The danger of becoming encapsulated must be controlled through self-awareness. Personal perspectives and worldviews must be considered in the context of other cultural value systems. For example, a novice upper-class, European American teacher listed one of her primary goals for her students as "learning to respond quickly" to questions asked of them. This multiculturally unaware teacher had failed to consider her Japanese American and Native American Indian students' culturally socialized preference for a period of silence before responding (see **Something to Consider 9.1**).

Summary

School counselors must be available to assist their teaching colleagues in creating learning environments that enhance the self-worth and mutual respect of each student. In developing collaborative partnerships with teachers, school counselors must demonstrate an appreciation and a valuing of diverse

---

SOMETHING TO CONSIDER 9.1

Indigenous Versus Traditional Learning

A group of Native American Indian Elders were asked how educators could provide Native American Indian students with an "understanding" of their Nativeness using traditional ways or teaching. The Elders all seemed to be concerned about the commonly accepted way of having the child learn what is being told to them and having to perform publicly. The emphasis on public achievement was considered by them to create an atmosphere of embarrassment. The traditional Native American Indian way encourages the younger child to observe, then allows peer and adult guidance or mentoring. Then, with guidance, the child is encouraged to be involved in performing or demonstrating his or her understanding.

SOURCE: Inspired by "Understanding Indian Children, Learning From Indian Elders," by J. T. Garrett, 1993–1994, *Children Today, 22*(4), pp. 18–21.

---

cultures, ethnicities, and ideologies. These collaborations can ensure the encouragement of self-esteem, the teaching of honor and respect of others, and the fostering of cooperative learning. School counselors can also successfully promote classroom accommodation of individual differences among students through these partnerships. However, whereas in-service professionals can avail themselves of accessible resources, the basic preparation for this mission lies within training programs.

Experiential Activities

1. Revisit **Case Study 9.1.** Put yourself in the place of the non-Native American Indian student. How would you respond to this situation? Do you get a flavor of incompatible learning environments?

2. How do you perceive the role of the school counselor as a collaborator with teachers in the effort to ensure multicultural learning environments?

3. This chapter has presented numerous suggestions relevant to the role of school counselors in the development and maintenance of culturally compatible classrooms. What ideas can you generate?

4. As a school counselor, how can you assist in the recognition of authentic or performance assessment? Or, do you disagree with this emerging trend?

5. How would you integrate indigenous learning styles in your interactions with ethnic and cultural minority students?

6. What are your concerns about being/becoming a multiculturally aware school counselor? Are they personal? Professional? Do they involve the curricula? Training? Prepare a list, in order of priority, of your concerns.

References

Baruth, L. G., & Manning, M. L. (1992). *Multicultural education of children and adolescents*. Needham Heights, MA: Allyn & Bacon.
Bennett, C. I. (1995). *Comprehensive multicultural education: Theory and practice* (3rd ed.). Boston: Allyn & Bacon.
Charles, C. M. (1992). *Building classroom discipline*. White Plains, NY: Longman.
Clark, C. M., & Peterson, P. L. (1986). Teachers' thought processes. In M. C. Wittrock (Ed.), *Handbook of research on teaching* (3rd ed., pp. 255–296). New York: Macmillan.
Clark, L., DeWolf, S., & Clark, C. (1992). Teaching teachers to avoid having culturally assaultive classrooms. *Young Children , 47*(5), 4–9.
Educational Testing Service. (1995). *Performance assessment: Difficult needs, difficult answers* (Trustees' colloquy) [Pamphlet]. Princeton, NJ: Author.
Eggen, P., & Kauchak, D. (1994). *Educational psychology* (2nd ed.). Columbus, OH: Charles E. Merrill.
Florida State Department of Education. (1990). *Multicultural teaching strategies* (Tech. Rep. No. 9). Tallahassee, FL: Author.
Fuller, F. (1969). Concerns of teachers: A developmental conceptualization. *American Educational Research Journal, 6,* 207–226.
Garcia, E. E. (1992). "Hispanic" children: Theoretical, empirical, and related policy issues. *Educational Psychology Review, 4,* 69–94.
Garrett, J. T. (1993–1994). Understanding Indian children, learning from Indian Elders. *Children Today, 22*(4), 18–21, 40.
Goodwin, A. L. (1990). *Fostering diversity in the teaching profession through multicultural field experiences*. Tampa, FL: American Association for Colleges of Teacher Education.
Goodwin, A. L. (1994). Making the transition from self to other: What do preservice teachers really think about multicultural education? *Journal of Teacher Education, 45,* 119–131.
Gordon, E. W. (1991). Human diversity and pluralism. *Educational Psychologist, 26,* 99–108.
Grant, C. A., & Secada, W. G. (1990). Preparing teachers for diversity. In W. R. Houston (Ed.), *Handbook of research on teacher education* (4th ed., pp. 403–422). New York: Macmillan.
Herring, R. D. (1989). *Psychological maturity and teacher education: A comparison of interactional models for preservice teachers*. Unpublished doctoral dissertation, North Carolina State University, Raleigh.
Herring, R. D. (1995a). Creating culturally compatible classrooms: Roles of the school counselor. *The North Dakota Journal of Counseling & Development, 1*(1), 28–33.

Herring, R. D. (1995b, November). *Reflecting on multicultural training in counselor education*. Paper presented at the annual conference of the Southern Association for Counselor Education and Supervision, Knoxville, TN.

Herring, R. D., & White, L. (1995a). School counselors and school teachers: Partners in multiculturalism. In J. Bowman & D. Fleniken (Eds.), *Reshaping the profession through partnerships: An Arkansas perspective* (pp. 93–117). Conway: Arkansas Association of Colleges for Teacher Education.

Herring, R. D., & White, L. M. (1995b). School counselors, teachers, and the culturally compatible classroom: Partnerships in multicultural education. *Journal of Humanistic Education and Development, 34*(2), 52–64.

Kellogg, J. (1988). Forces of change. *Phi Delta Kappan, 70*(3), 199–204.

Knapp, M., Turnbull, B. J., & Shields, P. M. (1990). New directions for educating children of poverty. *Educational Leadership, 48*(1), 4–9.

Manning, M. L., & Baruth, L. G. (1995). *Students at risk*. Boston: Allyn & Bacon.

Martin, R. J. (1991). The power to empower: Multicultural education for student school counselors. In C. E. Sleeter (Ed.), *Empowerment through multicultural education* (pp. 279–197). Albany: State University of New York Press.

McWhirter, E. H. (1994). *Counseling for empowerment*. Alexandria, VA: American Counseling Association.

Neugebauer, B. (1994). *Alike and different: Exploring our humanity with young children* (2nd ed.). Washington, DC: National Association for the Education of Young Children.

O'Neil, J. (1990). Link between style, culture proves divisive. *Educational Leadership, 48*(2), 8.

Paisley, P. (1990). Counselor involvement in promoting the developmental growth of beginning teachers. *Journal of Humanistic Education and Development, 29*, 20–31.

Reiman, A. J., Bostick, D., Lassiter, J., & Cooper, J. (1995). Counselor- and teacher-led support groups for beginning teachers: A cognitive–developmental perspective. *Elementary School Guidance & Counseling, 30*, 105–117.

Schmidt, J. J. (1993). *Counseling in schools: Essential services and comprehensive programs*. Boston: Allyn & Bacon.

Sleeter, C. E. (Ed.). (1991). *Empowerment through multicultural education*. Albany: State University of New York Press.

Sleeter, C. E., & Grant, C. A. (1988). *Making choices for multicultural education: Five approaches to race, class, and gender*. Columbus, OH: Charles E. Merrill.

Tharp, R. G. (1989). Psychocultural variables and constraints: Effects on teaching and learning in schools. *American Psychologist, 44*, 349–359.

Tiedt, P. L., & Tiedt, I. M. (1990). *Multicultural education: A handbook of activities, information, and resources*. Boston: Allyn & Bacon.

Tran, M. T., Young, R. L., & DiLella, J. D. (1994). Multicultural education courses and the student school counselor: Eliminating stereotypical attitudes in our ethnically diverse classroom. *Journal of Teacher Education, 45*, 183–189.

Unger, R. K. (1983). Through the looking glass: No wonderland yet! (The reciprocal relationship between the methodology and models of reality). *Psychology of Women Quarterly, 8*(1), 9–32.

Woolfolk, A. E. (1995). *Educational psychology* (6th ed.). Boston: Allyn & Bacon.

Multicultural School Counseling in the Twenty-First Century

IV

A multitude of critical and emerging multicultural topics are facing school counselors in the twenty-first century. These topics, without regard to prioritizing, include the following: the most efficacious manner of integrating indigenous models of traditional mental intervention into school counseling paradigms; the breakdown of authority and control of students' education, especially among male ethnic youths; the most appropriate multicultural means of personality and intelligence assessment; the counseling of diverse children and adolescents in educational environments; the incorporation of career development and counseling from multicultural perspectives; and the role of ethnic and cultural family counseling in school counseling endeavors. The implications for school counseling are tremendous, especially considering the other multitude of previously mentioned issues facing school counselors.

Part IV addresses some of these implications and offers some possible solutions to these issues. The bottom line can be found in the appropriate training of future school counselors, as well as continual educational efforts for in-service school counselors. Whether the students of tomorrow's schools will be equipped to enter the world of work and to enjoy wholesome daily lives is hinged on the successful interventions and preventive efforts of the school counselor. Suggestions are offered for consideration as to how these challenges might be answered.

10 | Implications for School Counselor Education for the Twenty-First Century

Before starting on a journey, we first develop some idea of the destination.
—BRILHART, 1974

Numerous implications for school counselor training programs have been suggested in the preceding chapters. This chapter will concentrate on issues and concerns not emphasized previously. School counselors face numerous challenges as the twenty-first century approaches. A synergetic focus will provide school counselor training programs with multiple options in the preparation of their students.

Rather than demand that ethnic minority students adapt to the school counselor's frame of reference, synergetic training encourages school counseling students to adjust to, and work within, the ethnic minority student's worldview (Atkinson, Morten, & Sue, 1989). Given the obvious need for school counseling trainees to acquire a multicultural perspective (Pedersen, 1988, 1994), school counselor training programs must prepare school counselors to become competent in various intercultural and intracultural counseling situations.

Dynamics Affecting Multicultural School Counselor Education

School counselor programs can be enhanced by incorporating synergetic principles and emphases in the following critical areas. These counseling qualities are not inclusive but offer an idea of what can be achieved by school counselor educators if they are willing to recognize and infuse synergetic components into their current programs, regardless of theoretical orientation of the program.

REDUCTION OF CULTURAL ENCAPSULATION

The issue of sensitivity is one with which school counselors must deal. If school counselors are not sensitive to the similarities and differences between themselves and the families with whom they work, they may make assumptions that are incorrect and unhelpful (Boynton, 1987). Such school counselors have been described as *culturally encapsulated* counselors (Wrenn, 1962). They tend to treat everyone the same and in so doing make mistakes. For example, school counselors must understand that every Native American Indian student differs in regard to his or her familial makeup and the strategies family members use to resolve problems. If school counselors are not sensitive to this fact, they may try the same methods with all Native American Indian students and get mixed results.

Richardson and Molinaro (1996) reviewed the literature regarding European American counselor self-awareness. This review is valuable as most school counselors are European American and are required to interact with dissimilar ethnic students. School counselors and counselors-in-training are advised to engage in culturally relevant self-analysis as an initial step in developing multicultural competence. By not confronting personal issues (e.g., worldview, ethnic identity, and cultural value system), a counselor risks conducting ineffective counseling and potentially, though unintentionally, harming a student (Ivey, Ivey, & Simek-Morgan, 1993). Research efforts need to address other issues (e.g., gender, religion, and socioeconomic status) that may also affect multicultural and cross-cultural counseling.

School counselors must guard against the possibility of becoming culturally encapsulated by the ethnic or cultural group with which they identify. When such encapsulation occurs, assumptions and beliefs may not be questioned, and students from dissimilar perspectives may not be treated effectively because of biases on the part of the professional (Capuzzi & Gross, 1995). Eliminating culturally encapsulated school counseling students will reduce inappropriate interviewing development.

School counseling students must internalize the fact that the same skills may have different effects on different students. For example, eye contact patterns vary across cultures. In mainstream society, direct questions may be appropriate, but in some ethnic groups (e.g., Alaskan Natives), indirect questions encourage responses.

RAISING THE CONSCIENTIOUSNESS LEVEL OF SCHOOL COUNSELOR EDUCATION

Most school counselor training programs will benefit as well by the increased conscientiousness level of school counseling students. The acquisition of cross-cultural communication skills, the increased awareness of personal attitudes toward ethnic minorities, and the increased knowledge about ethnic student populations will be reflected in the trainees. The adoption of diverse training formats will encourage trainees to develop a multicultural counseling identity by expanding and synthesizing their awareness, knowledge, and skills in this area.

Ensuring Development of Multicultural Counseling Standards

The Association for Multicultural Counseling and Development (AMCD) Executive Council approved a set of multicultural counseling competences in April 1995. The establishment of a set of multicultural counseling competencies is necessary for effective counseling efforts within the context of an increasingly diversified society. In developing these competences, AMCD made a distinction between the terms *multiculturalism* and *diversity* (Arredondo & D'Andrea, 1995). *Multiculturalism* emphasizes ethnicity, race, and culture. *Diversity* refers to other characteristics by which individuals may prefer to self-define. For example, such characteristics may include age, gender, sexual identity, religious/spiritual identification, social and economic class, and residential location (i.e., urban, rural).

In the process of gaining multicultural competency, counseling students will need to be able to differentiate between various dichotomous perspectives regarding multicultural and cross-cultural counseling. Examples of these are discussed briefly.

INCLUSION VERSUS EXCLUSION

Much debate is being generated among leaders in multicultural counseling relating to the scope of the definition of multiculturalism (Arredondo et al., 1992; Hughes & Brinks, 1992; Pope, 1995). The issue is basically whether multiculturalism should be inclusive or exclusive. The *inclusive* view recognizes that discrimination and unequal treatment for racial, ethnic, and sexual minorities are widespread and affect clients, counselors, and the counseling process in ways that should be studied. An *exclusive* perspective contends that the influences of racism will be ignored or diluted if other cultural differences such as gender, age, sexual orientation, or disability are also included (Jackson, 1995).

Counseling students and professionals will have to take a stand on this issue. According to Pedersen (1991a), "One advantage to the term 'multiculturalism' is that it implies a wide range of multiple groups without grading, comparing, or making them as better or worse than one another and without denying the very distinct and complementary perspectives that each group brings with it" (p. 4). Pedersen (1991b) also noted that "the broad definition of culture is particularly important in preparing counselors to deal with the complex differences among clients from or between every cultural group" (p. 7). Pope (1995) added that "the multicultural salad bowl is large enough for us all" (p. 303).

ETIC AND EMIC

The *etic* approach emphasizes the universal elements of counseling that all cultural groups are assumed to share (e.g., discrimination, identity development, validation and empowerment, communication, social class differences, acculturation, transference, and countertransference; Das, 1995; Lee, 1994). The *emic* approach emphasizes the indigenous or specific characteristics of each cultural group that may have an effect on the counseling process.

SIMILARITIES AND DIFFERENCES

Pedersen (1996) contended that three very serious errors can be made in multicultural counseling. One error is overemphasizing similarities, which trivializes cultural identity. Another error is overemphasizing differences, which leads to stereotyping. The third error is to assume that either must be emphasized.

Patterson (1996), in his proposal for universality in multicultural counseling, perceived five problems with a technique orientation to multicultural counseling. First, descriptions of ethnic and cultural groups become generalizations, describing the model individual. Second, the assumptions regarding the characteristics of ethnic and cultural groups result in the self-fulfilling prophecy. Third, the assumption that the counselor's knowledge of the culture of his or her client will lead to more appropriate and effective therapy has not been proven. Fourth, the greatest difficulty with accepting assumptions about the characteristics and needs of clients from differing cultures is that they will lead to failure. Fifth, client self-disclosure is more than desirable—it is necessary for client progress.

These may or may not represent legitimate problems. School counselors will have to decide which path they will walk: universality or diversity. However, school counselors will do well to heed Pedersen's (1996) rebuttal, "The controversy about whether multicultural counselors should impose a universal perspective irrespective of cultural differences or should allow each particular cultural group to define its own rules is a false dichotomy" (p. 236).

School counseling students need to become multiculturally competent. These competencies need to be stressed by counselor educators and incorporated into the training programs' academic and experiential components. The establishment of a clear definition of multicultural counseling is vital "so that it will become increasingly recognized and respected as a central force within the counseling profession" (Arredondo & D'Andrea, 1995, p. 28).

Continued Efforts at Counseling for Racial Understanding

Events in the 1990s substantiate that prejudice is not dead, nor is it localized or confined to a small group of extremists. Bryant (1994) concluded, "The reality is that few of us are proof against holding negative prejudices" (p. ix). For example, everyday speech continues to include words and references connoting negative prejudices: xenophobia, homophobia, anti-Semitism, anti-Black, anti-Irish, bigotry, intolerance, ethnocentrism, stereotype, racism, segregation, and discrimination. A primary goal of counselor education should be to educate students how to counsel those who act on their feelings of negative prejudice toward others.

School counselors often unintentionally use language and actions that serve to reinforce stereotypes of people with challenges, the elderly, women, and gay or lesbian individuals. School counselors can reduce discrimination against these groups and increase their credibility and effectiveness with these students by eliminating imprecise and demeaning language from their vocabulary, and by sensitively and knowledgeably using the terminology used by these groups (Atkinson & Hackett, 1995). Disability etiquette is not a typical component of many counselor training programs (Parette & Hourcade, 1995). The implications of these courtesies become especially significant in light of the Americans With Disabilities Act (1990). This legislation prohibits discrimination against persons with disabilities in (a) private sector employment, (b) all public services, and (c) public accommodations, transportation, and telecommunication. School counselors have a critical role in making all students welcome in the schools.

Atkinson and Hackett (1995) recommended three components necessary for counselor education programs to train school counselors to work with special populations: (a) a faculty sensitive to diversity and its inherent issues and concerns, (b) a curriculum that is designed to train school counselors to work with special populations, and (c) students who are receptive to training in the area. "All three are essential ingredients; the absence of any one of these components will seriously jeopardize the effectiveness of the training program" (p. 355).

Advocate and Change Agent Roles

A recurring theme in this text has been that many of the difficulties faced by ethnic students and special populations result from oppression experienced by them and their families, currently and historically. Counselors may have opportunities to aid these students in overcoming the effects of oppression. Thus, the need arises for school counselors to enhance their roles as advocates and social change agents.

In the advocacy role, the school counselor speaks on the students' behalf when students are unable to speak for themselves. For example, a student with a physical or mental challenge may be limited in the ability to communicate effectively. In the change agent role, the counselor attempts to change the oppressive environment by directly or indirectly promoting the empowerment of the oppressed group (Atkinson & Hackett, 1995). Change and advocacy can be accomplished through either individual efforts or collaborative endeavors.

The Increasing Dilemmas

The following discussions address the "increasing dilemmas" of current and future populations. Counselor education programs must be ready to prepare their students appropriately for these conditions.

DROPOUT PREVENTION

Counselor education programs must prepare school counselors to address the issue of student dropouts. Chodsinski (1994) stressed that school counselors need to be able to establish a network of professional and volunteer teams dedicated to the prevention of dropouts and who are qualified in multicultural counseling, human relations, culture and identity, and conflict resolution techniques. School counselors also need to be prepared to urge educators to view the dropout problem as a loss of valuable resources and talents and to be able to establish a drop-in environment instead of a dropout environment.

Blyth (1991) emphasized that no panaceas exist for eliminating dropping out, primarily because schools cannot directly control the two root causes: poverty and breakdown of positive family support. Nevertheless, Garrett (1995) reminded school counselors and other educators of the need to come to the educational setting with the willingness to learn. "If counselors and educators come first as students and second, as professionals, they might be surprised at how much growth would take place by members of both worlds" (p. 194).

THE SCOURGE OF AIDS

School counselors trained in the 1990s will be required to interact with AIDS-related issues. School counselors need to be prepared to do AIDS education and prevention work as adolescents are at high risk of contracting HIV. AIDS is a relatively new problem, and many counselors are not knowledgeable about its complexities. However, the literature suggests that counselors may not be receiving substantive training related to AIDS. In a survey of 243 counselor education programs (of which 77% or 189 offered school counseling specialization), AIDS was identified as a high priority for inclusion in curricula (House, Eicken, & Gary, 1995); however, nearly 40% of these programs did not include AIDS training in their curricula. Furthermore, 70% of all programs did not include either advocacy for people living with AIDS or sociopolitical issues in their curricula. It is alarming that only 63% thought these topics should be addressed.

School counselors need to be prepared to address AIDS-related issues in their professional roles and to do so comfortably and effectively (House et al., 1995). The implications of the decision in *Tarasoff v. Regents of University of California* (1976) may have potential influence on the school counselor's guarantee of confidentiality (Gehring, 1982). Counselor training programs must accept the reality of this scourge and their mission in its prevention.

COMPUTER TECHNOLOGY

The exact shape of future education is unclear; however, schools will be unable to resist the new technology (Mehlinger, 1996). Considerable evidence is building that the appropriate use of technology does contribute to student learning. When student access to computers has been sufficient, the results have been positive for learning (e.g., Dwyer, 1994; "Integrated," 1995; "Report," 1994).

A recent special edition on "Applications of Computer Technology" (Special Issue Editor: Edwin R. Gerler, Jr.) of the *Elementary School Guidance &*

Counseling Journal emphasized the rapidly increasing application of computer technology in school counseling and counselor education. This entire issue is recommended for examples of innovative ideas and activities available to school counselors. Gerler (1995) discussed the advantages of national and international communications to school counselors. In addition, multimedia is described as "the wave of the future for helping to prepare school counselors and for assisting in the delivery of school counseling services" (p. 12). Software tools (e.g., image processing, digital video capture, graphics production, and three-dimensional modeling) present multiple possibilities for the delivery of counseling and guidance programs to school populations.

Gerler (1995) suggested two ways school counselors can become computer literate and contribute to the enhancement of school counseling programs. First, counselor educators must get involved in and become familiar with the electronic network so they can communicate their creative ideas and programs over the network. Counselor educations can lead the profession by demonstrating the efficacy of computer technology. Second, school counselors themselves need to be innovative and challenge the limits of the network. Counselor educators and school counselors can vastly expand the delivery of counseling and guidance services through the use of computer technology

USE OF CULTURALLY BIASED INSTRUMENTS

Inaccuracies in the assessment and diagnosis of ethnic minority students can have three consequences: overdiagnosis, underdiagnosis, and misdiagnosis. Biases in testing are generally considered determinant factors in such inaccuracies. Many attempts have been made to eliminate or control biases in the assessment and diagnosis of cultural groups, including the translation of tests into the language of the group being tested and the development of culturally appropriate norms (e.g., Westermeyer, 1993). Despite these attempts, the overall sense among researchers and clinicians is that biases in cross-cultural testing still exist (e.g., Dana, 1993b).

Flaherty et al. (1988) emphasized that culture-free tests (i.e., a test that is not biased against specific culturally diverse groups) must fulfill five validity criteria.

1. Content equivalence: Are items relevant for the culture being tested?
2. Semantic equivalence: Is the meaning of each item the same in each culture?
3. Technical equivalence: Is the method of assessment comparable across cultures?

4. Criterion equivalence: Would the interpretation of variables remain the same when compared with the norm for each culture studied?
5. Conceptual equivalence: Is the test measuring the same theoretical construct across cultures?

Currently, researchers and clinicians lack a test or assessment of any kind that could fulfill these criteria (Escobar, 1993). Escobar's conclusion suggests that culture-free tests are not yet available in the assessment of the major ethnic minority groups (Paniagua, 1994). However, the literature suggests many guidelines that school counselors may use to minimize bias during the assessment and diagnosis of ethnic minority and cultural groups using current instruments. As an overall approach, school counselors may use Dana's (1993a, 1993b) assessment model in minimizing biases.

Promoting Professional Development

To be effective and culturally responsive, school counselor education must encourage school counselors to engage in professional development. Lee (1995) suggested the following activities that will promote professional development:

1. Continue to actively explore one's own culture.
2. Keep current in multicultural theory, research, and interventions.
3. Advocate for comprehensive in-service professional development programs conducted in work settings.
4. Attend professional meetings, conferences, and workshops that address multicultural issues.
5. Be actively involved in state, regional, and national professional associations and organizations that promote cultural diversity.
6. Expose themselves to forms of artistic expression of diverse groups.
7. Experience cultural diversity firsthand by being among students from diverse backgrounds and interacting with them in their environments.

Other Challenges

Additional areas exist in which much work must be done to improve multicultural school counselor preparation.

CULTURAL INTENTIONALITY

School counselor training programs that are successfully functioning are better able to build on students' cross-cultural counseling competencies by assisting them to develop a clear sense of multiculturalism and cultural intentionality (Ivey et al., 1993). *Cultural intentionality* is "acting with a sense of capability and deciding from among a range of alternative actions" (Ivey, 1994, p. 11). School counselors must integrate an understanding of individual multicultural differences so that they can use various counseling techniques or approaches to work more effectively with culturally diverse ethnic minority students (D'Andrea & Daniels, 1991). Thus, in acquiring a sense of cultural intentionality, school counseling students infuse a basic rule of synergetic counseling: If one technique is not effective, do not try to force it on the student, try something else.

Hamer (1995) concluded that the first priority for future counselor intentions research should be to clarify conceptual problems and investigate and resolve methodological and measurement problems. His critical review of the literature indicated specifically the following areas (p. 268):

1. The extent to which reporting of intentions is confounded by recall.
2. The extent to which session outcome affects the reporting of counselor intentions.
3. Determination of the most reliable and valid method for assessing intentions.

In addition to methodological issues, Hamer (1995) concluded that numerous interesting questions of practical concern deserve research attention. These questions include the following (p. 269):

1. From a process-outcome perspective, how do counselor intentions interact with client and contextual variables to affect the process and outcomes of counseling?
2. From a task-analytical perspective, what role do counselor intentions play in the process of resolution of in-session tasks?
3. What are the specific conditions under which intentions tend to occur? What kinds of clients in what kind of conditions tend to elicit specific intentions?
4. How do counselor intentions relate to overall process and treatment goals? How are process and treatment goals modified as counselors act on their intentions and receive feedback?

The reader is encouraged to review the entire text of this relevant literature review. It is hoped that school counselors-in-training will be inspired to consider counselor intentionality as a future inquiry into the nature and impact that counselor intentions have on the counseling process.

RACIAL AND ETHNIC IDENTITY THEORIES

An important trend in the 1990s is the effort on models and theories of racial and ethnic identity development. These efforts resulted from the realization that variables existed in the counseling dyad that were not being measured and that two of these variables were the racial or ethnic identity of the counselee and the counselor (Wehrly, 1995). Historically, identity development research concentrated on the identity development of ethnic minority individuals. Recent demographic projections, however, have inspired attention to theories related to European American (White) racial identity development (e.g., Hardiman, 1994). In addition, attention has also been directed to genetically mixed individuals (e.g., Herring, 1994; Miller & Rotheram-Borus, 1994).

MULTICULTURAL AND CROSS-CULTURAL SPECIALIZATION

The number of counselor education programs with specializations in cross-cultural or multicultural counseling remains limited. For example, given an 80% return rate, Hills and Strozier (1992) reported that 43 counseling psychology programs approved by the American Psychological Association (APA) included at least one multicultural course; 31 programs included multicultural units in other courses; 29 programs had a requirement for a multicultural course; and 22 programs could create a subspecialty in multicultural counseling. The availability of a subspecialty in multicultural counseling was reported in 45% of the programs and was "directly related to the research activity of full professors, and secondarily to the teaching activity of the adjunct faculty" (p. 48). The availability of multicultural and cross-cultural specialties deserves expansion.

ETHNIC MINORITY GRADUATE STUDENTS

The challenge to recruit ethnic minority students into graduate programs and to hire them as faculty in counselor education programs has not improved much since the 1980s (Atkinson, 1993; Ponterotto & Casas, 1991). Kohout, Wicherski, and Cooney's 1989–1990 survey of APA graduate departments of psychology (1992) reported that 92% of the full-time faculty in clinical, counseling, and school psychology programs were European American, 5% African American, 2% Hispanic American, 1% Asian American, and less than 1% Native American Indian. This survey's results were similar to those of Hills and Strozier (1992), who reported that 11% of the faculty members in the APA-approved counseling psychology programs were non-European American, with the percentage of non-European American faculty increasing as rank decreased.

In June 1993, the Association for Counselor Educators and Supervisors division of the American Counseling Association (ACA) revealed membership rates of African Americans (5.4%), Hispanic/Latinos (1.6%), Asian Americans (1.3%), Native American Indians (0.9%), other (2.5%), and European Americans (88.3%). The "other" classification may represent genetically mixed individuals who are beginning to self-identify in this category. Brinson and Kottler (1993) discussed the problems of recruiting and retaining ethnic minority faculty and suggested several guidelines to improve retention of ethnic minority faculty.

RACIAL AND ETHNIC MINORITY COUNSELING RESEARCH

Many problems still exist in racial and ethnic minority counseling research. Recent efforts have attempted to address these issues. For example, Ponterotto and Casas's (1991) *Handbook of Racial/Ethnic Minority Counseling Research* remains a definitive source on topics related to racial and ethnic minority counseling research. In addition, the Association for Assessment in Counseling (a division of the ACA) published a monograph, *Multicultural Assessment Standards: A Compilation for Counselors* (Prediger, 1993), as an effort to resolve some of the issues.

INDIGENOUS PRACTICES VERSUS WESTERN APPROACHES

Anthropologists and sociologists have historically had an interest in traditional and folk healing. Recently, psychologists and other behavioral scientists have begun to consider the importance of these practices to ethnic minority individuals. All ethnic groups have brought to the United States beliefs and practices connected to healing (Koss-Chioino, 1995). Symbols inherent to these practices represent concerns about ethnic identity, selfhood, worldview, expressions of family and community, religious and political goals, and reaffirmations of cultural cohesiveness and tradition.

The combination of indigenous and Western models really poses the question of interface or integration. The question of how to interface with traditional healing can be discussed at four levels: (a) counselor–counselee interaction, (b) consultation with or referrals to traditional healers, (c) institutional attempts to work with traditional healers, and (d) innovation of synthesized therapies combining Western and indigenous approaches. The integration of indigenous and traditional models has yielded very promising results. The reader is referred to Vargas and Koss-Chioino (1992) for a guide to the development of culturally responsive therapies (i.e., syntheses) and their evaluation.

Examples of effective syntheses can be found in the literature. For example, the Japanese therapies, Naikan and Morita, are considered quite successful with specific syndromes, such as social anxiety and attitudinal blocks to action (Ishiyama, 1987, 1990) and bulimia nervosa (Le Vine, 1991, 1993). Das (1987) incorporated traditions of Buddhism, Hinduism, and Islam to reduce stress in traditional societies of India, China, and Japan. Nwachuku and Ivey (1991) developed an Afrocentric model for use with the Igbo culture in Africa. The Native American Indian sweat lodge ritual appears to be effective with anxiety, depression, and stress-related disorders (Wilson, 1993). Gonzalez (1990) used Native American Indian practices (e.g., stories, metaphors) with perpetrators and adult victims of child abuse.

FAMILY COUNSELING AND EDUCATION

School counselors are discovering that family counseling and family education are effective components of their guidance and counseling programs (Hinkle, 1993). These services represent a distinctive alternative for resolving persistent problems in the schools (Amatea, 1989). Family interventions by school counselors can address a student's misbehavior, making special placements unnecessary (Peeks, 1990). Peeks (1991) has also suggested that after eliminating intraschool causes for presenting problems, school counselors should consider etiology that is found outside the school. School children and adolescents are members of a larger unit that includes the family, and they react to changes and distress within that unit (Peeks, 1990).

However, limited family counseling training is offered in school counseling programs, resulting in minimal family counseling experience among counselors in the schools (Hinkle, 1993). School counseling training programs must broaden the scope of their training to include family counseling, and school counselors must receive retraining opportunities and an avenue in which to develop confidence as family counselors and educators (Palmo, Lowry, Weldon, & Scioscia, 1988).

Encouragement of Synergetic Approaches

Section II-B-2 of the *Multicultural Counseling Competencies* approved by the Association for Multicultural Counseling and Development (1995; see Appendix C) states:

> Culturally skilled counselors understand how race, culture, ethnicity, and so forth may affect personality formation, vocational choices, manifestation of psychologi-

cal disorders, help-seeking behavior, and the appropriateness or inappropriateness of counseling approaches. (Arredondo et al., 1996, p. 64)

An accompanying explanatory statement establishes that a competent multicultural school counselor, well-grounded with literature about attitudes and beliefs, can describe and give examples of how a counseling approach based primarily on attitudes and beliefs may or may not be appropriate for a specific group of students. Counselor educators must understand that ignoring cultural differences in the presentation of theories of counseling is simply miseducation, as well as inappropriate and insensitive to diverse populations. In addition, imposing an ethnocentric definition of mental health and counseling reflects the counselor educator's own set of cultural, gender, and social class assumptions (Pedersen, 1988). Rather, training programs must be committed to implementing experiential and academic activities designed to nurture the acquisition of various counseling techniques (Corey, 1991). Through a synthesis of theoretical orientations, the school counselor can be prepared to use the most appropriate technique or strategy for an individual student with regards for historical and environmental influences.

Summary

This chapter has presented issues, trends, and concerns challenging school counselor training programs currently and that will continue in the twenty-first century. In relevant instances, multiple perspectives were offered to allow for comparative consideration. The intent was not to present an all-inclusive listing, but rather a sampling of those trends that appear to be the most threatening to school counselors and counselor education. Numerous important topics were omitted (e.g., learning style differentiation) because of time and space constraints.

If school counselors are to be prepared to meet the myriad of challenges facing diverse students, counselor education will need to address those issues. However, in many situations, counselor educators themselves are not willing or qualified to train students in many of the areas discussed in this chapter. Training programs must become introspective and challenge counselor educators to ensure their credibility in this endeavor. With dedication and commitment, counselor training programs will be ready—they must be ready.

Experiential Activities

1. As a student or in-service school counselor, where are you in relation to the issues of cultural encapsulation?

2. What are your thoughts about the debate over inclusion and exclusion in multiculturalism? Which is the most appropriate? Why?
3. In your current position/situation, what has been your educational and experiential background in the issues of AIDS? Have you been trained to address related issues of this problem? Why not?
4. What is the role of indigenous healing practices in traditional school counseling efforts? In your situation, are they a viable option for you?
5. Generate some examples of synergetic approaches that can be included in school counselor training programs. What does your particular training program offer that promotes synergetic counseling?

References

Amatea, E. S. (1989). *Brief strategic intervention for school behavior problems.* San Francisco: Jossey-Bass.

Americans With Disabilities Act of 1990, 42 U.S.C.A. § 12101 *et seq.*

Arredondo, P., & D'Andrea, M. (1995, September). AMCD approves multicultural counseling competency standards. *Counseling Today, 38*(3), 28–32.

Arredondo, P., Lee, C., Leong, F., Ponterotto, J., Redleaf, V., & Vontress, C. (1992, September). *Valuing pluralism.* A panel presented at the meeting of the Association for Counselor Education and Supervision, San Antonio, TX.

Arredondo, P., Toporek, R., Brown, S. P., Jones, J., Locke, D. C., Sanchez, J., & Stadler, H. (1996). Operationalization of the multicultural counseling competencies. *Journal of Multicultural Counseling and Development, 24*, 42–78.

Atkinson, D. R. (1993). Reaction. Who speaks for cross-cultural counseling research? *The Counseling Psychologist, 21*, 218–224.

Atkinson, D. R., & Hackett, G. (1995). *Counseling diverse populations.* Dubuque, IA: Brown & Benchmark.

Atkinson, D. R., Morten, G., & Sue, D. W. (1989). *Counseling American minorities: A cross-cultural perspective* (3rd ed.). Dubuque, IA: William C. Brown.

Blyth, J. R. (1991, January). *The Education Digest,* pp. 32–36

Boynton, G. (1987). Cross-cultural family therapy: The ESCAPE model. *American Journal of Family Therapy, 15*, 123–130.

Brilhart, J. K. (1974). *Effective group discussion.* Dubuque, IA: William C. Brown.

Brinson, J., & Kottler, J. (1993). Cross-cultural mentoring: A strategy for retaining minority faculty. *Counselor Education and Supervision, 32*, 241–253.

Bryant, B. K. (1994). *Counseling for racial understanding.* Alexandria, VA: American Counseling Association.

Capuzzi, D., & Gross, D. R. (1995). *Counseling and psychotherapy: Theories and interventions.* Englewood Cliffs, NJ: Merrill.

Chodsinski, R. T. (1994). Dropout intervention and prevention: Strategies for counselors. A multicultural perspective. In P. B. Pedersen & J. C. Carey (Eds.), *Multicultural counseling in schools: A practical handbook* (pp. 1–18). Boston: Allyn & Bacon.

Corey, G. (1991). *Theory and practice of counseling and psychotherapy* (4th ed.). Pacific Grove, CA: Brooks/Cole.

Dana, R. H. (1993a, November 5). Can *"corrections" for culture using moderator variables contribute to cultural competence in assessment?* Paper presented at the annual convention of the Texas Psychological Association, Austin, TX.

Dana, R. H. (1993b). *Multicultural assessment perspectives for professional psychology.* Boston: Allyn & Bacon.

D'Andrea, M., & Daniels, J. (1991). Exploring the different levels of multicultural counseling training in counselor education. *Journal of Counseling & Development, 70,* 78–85.

Das, A. K. (1987). Indigenous models of therapy in traditional Asian societies. *Journal of Multicultural Counseling and Development, 15,* 25–36.

Das, A. K. (1995). Rethinking multicultural counseling: Implications for counselor education. *Journal of Counseling and Development, 74,* 45–52.

Dwyer, D. (1994, April). Apple classrooms of tomorrow: What we've learned. *Educational Leadership,* 4–10.

Escobar, J. E. (1993). Psychiatric epidemiology. In A. C. Gaw (Ed.), *Culture, ethnicity, and mental illness* (pp. 43–73). Washington, DC: American Psychiatric Press.

Flaherty, J. H., Gaviria, F. M., Pathak, D., Michell, T., Wintrob, R., Richman, J. A., & Birz, S. (1988). Developing instruments for cross-cultural psychiatric research. *Journal of Nervous and Mental Disease, 176,* 257–263.

Garrett, M. W. (1995). Between two worlds: Cultural discontinuity in the dropout of Native American youths. *The School Counselor, 42,* 186–195.

Gehring, D. (1982). The counselor's duty to warn. *Personnel and Guidance Journal, 60,* 208–210.

Gerler, E. R., Jr. (1995). Advancing elementary and middle school counseling through computer technology. *Elementary School Guidance & Counseling* [Special Edition on Applications of Computer Technology], *30,* 8–15.

Gonzalez, M. C. (1990, April). *Treatment with dignity: A method for working with perpetrators and adult victims of child abuse.* Paper presented at the annual National American Indian Conference on Child Abuse and Neglect, Falls Church, VA.

Hamer, R. J. (1995). Counselor intentions: A critical review of the literature. *Journal of Counseling & Development, 73,* 259–270.

Hardiman, R. (1994). White identity development in the United States. In E. P. Salett & D. R. Koslow (Eds.), *Race, ethnicity, and self: Identity in multicultural perspective* (pp. 117–142). Washington, DC: National MultiCultural Institute.

Herring, R. D. (1994). Native American Indian identity: A people of many peoples. In E. P. Salett & D. R. Koslow (Eds.), *Race, ethnicity, and self: Identity in multicultural perspective* (pp. 170–197). Washington, DC: National MultiCultural Institute.

Hills, H. L., & Strozier, A. L. (1992). Multicultural training in APA-approved counseling psychology programs: A survey. *Professional Psychology, 23,* 43–51.

Hinkle, J. S. (1993). Training school counselors to do family counseling. *Elementary School Guidance & Counseling, 27,* 252–257.

House, R. M., Eicken, S., & Gray, L. A. (1995). A national survey of AIDS training in counselor education programs. *Journal of Counseling & Development, 74,* 5–11.

Hughes, M., & Brinks, D. (1992, September). *Looking forward through diversity.* Paper presented at the meeting of the Association for Counselor Education and Supervision, San Antonio, TX.

Integrated learning systems: What does the research say? (1995, February). *Computing Teacher, 1*(1), 7–10.

Ishiyama, F. I. (1987). Use of Morita therapy in shyness counseling in the West: Promoting clients' self-acceptance and action taking. *Journal of Counseling & Development, 65,* 547–551.

Ishiyama, F. I. (1990). A Japanese perspective on client inaction: Removing attitudinal blocks through Morita therapy. *Journal of Counseling & Development, 68,* 566–570.

Ivey, A. E. (1994). *Intentional interviewing and counseling: Facilitating client development in a multicultural society* (3rd ed.). Pacific Grove, CA: Brooks/Cole.

Ivey, A. E., Ivey, M. B., & Simek-Morgan, L. (1993). *Counseling and psychotherapy: A multicultural perspective* (3rd. ed.). Boston: Allyn & Bacon.

Jackson, M. L. (1995, August). The demise of multiculturalism in America and the counseling profession. *Counseling Today, 37*(10), 30–31.

Kohout, J., Wicherski, M., & Cooney, B. (1992). *Characteristics of graduate departments of psychology: 1989–1990.* Washington, DC: American Psychological Association.

Koss-Chioino, J. D. (1995). Traditional and folk approaches among ethnic minorities. In J. F. Aponte, R. Y. Rivers, & J. Wohl (Eds.), *Psychological interventions and cultural diversity* (pp. 145–163). Boston: Allyn & Bacon.

Lee, C. C. (1994). Pioneers of multicultural counseling: A conversation with Clemmont E. Vontress. *Journal of Multicultural Counseling and Development, 22,* 66–78.

Lee, C. C. (1995). Multicultural literacy: Imperatives for culturally responsive school counseling. In C. C. Lee (Ed.), *Counseling for diversity: A guide for school counselors and related professionals* (pp. 191–198). Boston: Allyn & Bacon.

Le Vine, P. (1991). Morita psychotherapy: A theoretical overview for Australian consideration. *Australian Psychologist, 26,* 103–106.

Le Vine, P. (1993). Morita-based therapy and its use across cultures in the treatment of bulimia nervosa. *Journal of Counseling & Development, 72,* 82–90.

Mehlinger, H. D. (1996). School reform in the information age. *Phi Delta Kappan, 77*(6), 400–407.

Miller, R. L., & Rotheram-Borus, M. J. (1994). Growing up biracial in the United States. In E. P. Salett & D. R. Koslow (Eds.), *Race, ethnicity, and self: Identity in multicultural perspective* (pp. 143–169). Washington, DC: National MultiCultural Institute.

Nwachuku, U. T., & Ivey, A. E. (1991). Culture-specific counseling: An alternative training model. *Journal of Counseling & Development, 70 ,* 106–111.

Palmo, A. J., Lowry, L. A., Weldon, D. P., & Scioscia, T. M. (1988). Schools and family: Future perspectives for school counselors. In W. M. Walsh & N. J. Giblin (Eds.), *Family counseling in school settings* (pp. 39–47). Springfield, IL: Charles C Thomas.

Paniagua, F. A. (1994). *Assessing and treating culturally diverse clients: A practical guide.* Thousand Oaks, CA: Sage.

Parette, H. P., Jr., & Hourcade, J. J. (1995). Disability etiquette and school counselors: A common sense approach toward compliance with the Americans With Disabilities Act. *The School Counselor, 42,* 224–232.

Patterson, C. H. (1996). Multicultural counseling: From diversity to universality. *Journal of Counseling & Development, 74,* 227–231.

Pedersen, P. B. (1988). *A handbook for developing multicultural awareness.* Alexandria, VA: American Association for Counseling and Development.

Pedersen, P. B. (1991a). Introduction to the special issue on multiculturalism as a fourth force in counseling. *Journal of Counseling & Development, 70,* 4.

Pedersen, P. B. (1991b). Multiculturalism as a generic approach to counseling. *Journal of Counseling & Development, 70,* 6–12.

Pedersen, P. B. (1994). *A handbook for developing multicultural awareness* (2nd ed.). Alexandria, VA: American Counseling Association.

Pedersen, P. B. (1996). The importance of both similarities and differences in multicultural counseling: Reaction to C. H. Patterson. *Journal of Counseling & Development, 74,* 236–237.

Peeks, B. (1990). A family approach for treating behaviorally impaired students in the schools. *Oregon Counseling Journal, 12,* 12–15.

Peeks, B. (1991). *Parent-student-school: The problem-solving triad.* Unpublished manuscript.

Ponterotto, J. G., & Casas, J. M. (1991). *Handbook of racial/ethnic minority counseling research.* Springfield, IL: Charles C Thomas.

Pope, M. (1995). The "salad bowl" is big enough for us all: An argument for the inclusion of lesbians and gay men in any definition of multiculturalism. *Journal of Counseling & Development, 73,* 301–304.

Prediger, D. J. (1993). *Multicultural assessment standards: A compilation for counselors.* Alexandria, VA: Association for Assessment in Counseling.

Report on the effectiveness of technology in schools, 1900–1994. (1994). Washington, DC: Software Publishers Association.

Richardson, T. Q., & Molinaro, K. L. (1996). White counselor self-awareness: A prerequisite for developing multicultural competence. *Journal of Counseling & Develoment, 74,* 238–242.

Tarasoff v. Regents of University of California, 551 P. 2d 334 (Cal. 1976).

Vargas, L. A., & Koss-Chioino, J. D. (1992). *Working with culture: Psychotherapeutic interventions with ethnic minority children and adolescents.* San Francisco: Jossey-Bass.

Wehrly, B. (1995). *Pathways to multicultural counseling competence: A developmental journey.* Pacific Grove, CA: Brooks/Cole.

Westermeyer, J. J. (1993). Cross-cultural psychiatric assessment. In A. C. Gaw (Ed.), *Culture, ethnicity, and mental illness* (pp. 125–144). Washington, DC: American Psychiatric Press.

Wilson, J. P. (1993). Culture and trauma: The sacred pipe revisited. In J. P. Wilson (Ed.), *Trauma, transformation, and healing: An integrative approach to theory, research, and post-traumatic therapy* (pp. 38–71). New York: Brunner/Mazel.

Wrenn, C. G. (1962). The culturally-encapsulated counselor. *Harvard Educational Review, 32,* 444–449.

11 | School Counseling: Future Trends and Issues

No bird soars too high if he [she] soars with his [her] own wings.
—WILLIAM BLAKE

P redicting the future is a complicated task, laden with potential errors. Yet, plans must be made, and they have to be based on indicators of future needs and trends. School counseling in the future will require counselors to be more involved not only in their counseling and guidance functions but also in the leadership of their schools, school districts, and communities. To accomplish this effort, counselors will need to collaborate with colleagues, parents, and community leaders to improve education for students.

The appropriate education of diverse student populations requires energetic and committed school counselors who are not afraid to take a stand that is in the best interest of their students. Ayers (1993) opined that "Education is bold, adventurous, creative, vivid, illuminating—in other words education is for self-activating explorers of life, for those who would challenge fate, for doers and activists, for citizens" (p. 138).

Students need to be aware of the trends and issues that will affect education well into the twenty-first century before entering the school counseling profession. Some of these future possibilities include national standards for public education, the length of the school day and school year, inclusion, home schooling, gender equity and single-sex high schools, the need for more women and minority school administrators, and technological advances (Farris, 1996).

School counseling as a specialty area emerged in the early 1990s and has continued to evolve as a result of sociopolitical, educational, and economic trends (Paisley & Borders, 1995). The divergent needs of school-age youths of the early 1990s required specialized interventions beyond those that had previously been provided by teachers (Schmidt, 1993). These needs have changed or intensified, and the corresponding trends within the larger society have contributed to discussions concerning the appropriate focus for school counseling (Paisley & Peace, 1995).

Discussions of the future of school counseling must recognize demographic and socioeconomic trends that will affect the profile of tomorrow's schools, the families, and the structure of schools (e.g., Commission on Precollege Guidance and Counseling, 1986; Hodgkinson, 1985). School counselors must be prepared to deal with increasing numbers of single-parent and low-socio-economic families, women in the workforce, students from cultural and ethnic minority groups (including European Americans), issues of sexuality and sexual harassment among student populations, frequent career changes, increasing numbers of homeless youths, students with disabling challenges, and increasing violence in schools, families, and communities (e.g., Daniels, 1992; Paisley & Borders, 1995; Parker, 1994; Robinson, 1994; Roscoe, Strouse, Goodwin, Taracks, & Henderson, 1994; Salend, 1994; Street, 1994). In addition, program evaluation and accountability will be emphasized (Borders & Drury, 1992a, 1992b). Counselor education will need to address these issues if school counselors are to be prepared. However, additional concerns speak directly to the school counselor as a practitioner rather than as a preservice student. Those issues receive most of this chapter's attention.

Control Over the Profession

One very important issue exists in the shift in the ways the tasks of the school counselor are perceived (Benjamin & Walz, 1988). Paisley and Borders (1995) concluded that "the most overriding issue for the school counseling specialty is the lack of control school counselors have over their day-to-day work activities and the development of their profession" (p. 151). The school counselor's role continues to be defined by school principals and system directors who may not be knowledgeable, or care to be, about the essentials of school counseling and guidance. In addition, school counselors are frequently requested (or unilaterally directed) to perform tasks that are incongruent with their missions (e.g., substitute teaching, clerical duties). School counselors also are affected by state and federal legislation about, and funding for, the provision of counseling services in schools (Paisley & Borders, 1995). For instance, movements to replace school counselors with bachelor-level personnel are increasing, especially in the areas of substance abuse and home visitation. Reform movements need to be generated to block the legislation of such certifications. Legislators need to be more informed about the unique status of school counselors. One example exists in the state of Arkansas, which enacted The Public School Student Services Act (908) in 1991 that requires school counselors to spend at least 75% of their time doing counseling and guidance activities. School counselors possess the expertise and skills to facilitate reforms such as this one (Perry & Schwallie-Giddis, 1993).

The School Counselor's Role

The lack of control over one's professional life contributes as well to a second basic issue: the ongoing confusion and controversy about the proper focus for school counselors, despite numerous task force reports and professional statements (Paisley & Borders, 1995). Administrators, teachers, parents, and lay leaders must be educated about the appropriate role(s) of the school counselor. School counselors are more than "lackeys" for administrators and play more important roles than those of master schedule planner, schedule changer, or test administrator.

School counselors exist for students who want to talk to someone and not be fearful that their concerns will be publicized. Students want to trust someone other than their parents and peers with those private and personal issues of which only they are aware. The school counselor serves as that person who will listen, give alternatives, and still allow the student to make the decision. These roles are inalienable to the function of school counselors, and they deserve to be recognized.

Welch and McCarroll (1993) provided an interesting description of the present and future school counselor. They envisioned that the old model of a school counselor "as a professional who deals with school personnel within the confines of the school is a function that has little place in the future" (p. 52). Rather, the school counselor of the future "may well be a community resource specialist who assesses needs within the school and community and who matches resources with needs as a counselor-teacher-administrator" (p. 52) (see **Something to Consider 11.1**).

In another interesting article, Hardesty and Dillard (1994) researched the role of elementary school counselors compared with middle and secondary school counselors. These authors found three major differences in the ranking of counselor activities by elementary school counselors compared with middle and secondary school counselors. First, elementary school counselors perform

---

SOMETHING TO CONSIDER 11.1

Past, Present, and Future Roles of the School Counselor

The Past and Present	The Future
1. The school counselor is a primary provider of direct services (supplier, furnisher, caterer, purveyor, provider).	The school counselor is a conduit between needs and resources (passage, passageway, channel).
2. The school counselor is in a closed system.	The school counselor is a community resource specialist.
3. The school counselor provides individual counseling.	The school counselor provides family and group counseling.
4. The school counselor is perceived as an "ex-teacher."	The school counselor is perceived as a teacher.
5. The school counselor is an administrator or teacher.	The school counselor is a teacher, counselor, and administrator.
6. The "line and staff" model prevails.	The "systems" model comes into play.
7. Power (perceived or real) is a political necessity.	Power (perceived or real) is an educational tool.
8. Self-development is assumed.	Self-development is planned.

SOURCE: Adapted from "The Future Role of School Counselors," by I. D. Welch and L. McCarroll, 1993, *The School Counselor, 41*, pp. 43–53.

---

more consultative and coordination activities. Second, elementary school counselors may perform less administrativelike activities (scheduling and paperwork). Third, elementary school counselors work systematically with student concerns, involving families, teachers, and community agencies. Secondary and middle school counselors tend to work with student concerns on an individualistic basis. Additional research is needed to assess whether these roles can be generalized.

Philosophical Questions

Additional philosophical questions pertain to the role of the school counselor as well. The implementation of the responses to these queries will considerably affect the role of school counselors within the larger context of general education.

DELIVERY OF A DEVELOPMENTAL PROGRAM

The education of students must be founded on a developmental perspective if that education is to be appropriate. However, developmentally focused programs are rarely implemented; rather, scope and sequence are confused with a theoretically based approach using what is known about development and how it occurs (Gerler, 1992; Paisley & Borders, 1995; Paisley & Hubbard, 1994; Paisley & Peace, 1995). One challenge for school counselors is to clearly articulate the need of, and advocate for, a developmental focus.

COUNSELING IN THE SCHOOLS

A frequent response to the question "What is counseling in the schools?" is "School counselors do not do therapy" (Paisley & Borders, 1995). These authors, and this author, contend that the distinction between counseling and therapy is often ambiguous, if not irrelevant. School counselors cannot divorce themselves from working with families, either through family counseling programs or through family education efforts.

Perhaps, the most visible discussion about what counseling is can be found in the tremendous literature proposing that school counselors provide family counseling and education (e.g., Hinkle, 1993; Nicoll, 1992; Peeks, 1993). A change is necessary in how educators think about students in relation to their extended social units (Peeks, 1993). Cetron (1985) predicted that schools of the future will become family centers, in which family health and employment services are offered for stress-laden families. Schools will need programs to protect children and adolescents against the influences of social disorganization and family collapse (London, 1987). The establishment of such programs will necessitate family involvement in the context of the school by school counselors who understand the powerful systemic connection between the student and family (Peeks, 1993).

Parent involvement in the school in almost any form appears to produce measurable gains in student achievement (A. Henderson, 1988). Working with families in some capacity will continue to be important as the nation becomes more ethnically and culturally diverse. The increasing numbers of single-parent homes, blended families, extended family patterns, and teenage parents will require the assistance of the school counselor.

GUIDANCE IN THE SCHOOLS

The "guidance counselor" has slowly become the "school counselor" over the years, and rightfully so. Guidance and counseling represent completely different functions for the school counselor. However, in the opinion of this author, the term *guidance* is rapidly disappearing conceptually, especially on secondary levels. In practice, guidance appears to be subsumed by the concept of *school counseling*. If this trend continues, school populations will be dealt a severe blow. Guidance activities represent a valuable tool in the prevention of inappropriate behaviors among children and adolescents. Without guidance intervention, school counselors will be overly burdened with the remedial focus of counseling. One hopes that the future will bring a resurgence in its recognition.

HOME SCHOOLING

The number of home-schooled students has increased dramatically in the last decade. The number of families that home school their children range from 200,000 to over 1 million (Knowles, Marlow, & Muchmore, 1992). Generally speaking, parents who believe in home schooling think that local public and private schools cannot devote as much individual attention to their children's education as they, themselves, can (Farris, 1996). State and federal laws have changed the requirement that only certified teachers be allowed to teach because many parents who home schooled their children thought that they, too, would be required to be certified to teach.

Typically, home-schooled children come from two-parent families with the father working outside of the home. Most home-schooled children have never been enrolled in a public school, but they enter secondary school when the content of the subject areas becomes more difficult. At this point, school counselors become involved. They must be prepared to facilitate the transition from home schooling to public or private school settings. These students will arrive with unique adjustment problems and probably differentiated skill levels.

INCLUSION

Inclusion means placing students who are emotionally, mentally, or physically challenged in regular classrooms. Often, the regular classroom teacher has had no special training in working with these students. In addition, teachers with large classes find it difficult to work individually with regular students without adding students with special needs. Shanker (1994) stated, "The movement in American education that is taking hold the fastest and is likely to have the profoundest—and most destructive—effect is not what you might think. It's the rush towards full inclusion of disabled children in regular classrooms" (p. E23). Proponents of full inclusion emphasize the similarities between inclusion and the separate but equal education provided to African Americans before desegregation (Farris, 1996). They believe that, through inclusion, students with challenges and their regular classroom counterparts are better socialized as a result.

School counselors will have a vital mission whether inclusion is implemented or not. As mandated members of the School Based Committee (according to the Education Act for All Handicapped Children of 1975 [Public Law 94-142]), they cannot neglect their delivery of services to students with challenges. Inclusion will bring additional functions, such as facilitating this movement and assisting the classroom teacher during the transition.

GENDER EQUITY AND SINGLE-SEX HIGH SCHOOLS

The 1980s and 1990s have witnessed a greater emphasis on gender equity issues in the schools, including the need for gender role models for ethnic and cultural minority students. One result has been interest in creating separate single-sex public high schools (e.g., Willis, 1994). For example, in Detroit, an all-male public high school was developed in the later 1980s with a preponderance of male African American teachers and aides to serve as role models. The concept yielded positive achievement and social results. The program was discontinued after a gender discrimination lawsuit was filed.

Gender equity issues will continue to be debated in education. Two thirds of illiterate adults in the world are women (Glazer, 1994). The majority of the teachers in higher education are men, whereas in early childhood and elementary education the majority are women (Farris, 1996). A more equitable dispersion of genders in school administration is needed to facilitate gender role socialization. School counselors, as student advocates, need to monitor the curriculum and extracurricular activities of schools to ensure the fulfillment of gender equity. All students must be afforded equal opportunities to an education, regardless of gender. For example, research has long pointed out that more boys than girls take advanced math and science courses, and some media news stories have focused on how girls benefit from single-sex math and science classes (Farris, 1996).

Many urban school districts are exploring projects that will encourage girls to take math and science as well as to provide positive ethnic role models for both sexes. If single-sex high schools become a reality, school counselors must adapt to the situation and provide appropriate services. Education is beginning to see more and more innovative school settings that are as effective, and more effective in some instances, as traditional models (see **Something to Consider 11.2**).

Supervision

Counselor supervision represents one area that needs vast improvement during the next century. Considerable evidence indicates that school counse-

---

SOMETHING TO CONSIDER 11.2

A High School in a Shopping Mall

Five school districts near Bloomington, Minnesota, have collaborated on a high school on the first level of the world's largest shopping mall, the Mall of America. The Leila Anderson's Learning Center enrolled 200 students for the 1994–1995 school year and may add a kindergarten through third-grade elementary school for children of mall workers. The soundproof classrooms have no extra frills, including no windows (Winerip, 1994).

Currently, only junior and senior students are enrolled. Each class has a business partner. For example, students in an Arts in the Marketplace class work with the Camp Snoop Amusement Park. Internships are offered to students who work on an individual basis (Association Press, 1994).

Complaints include how the setting distracts students and hinders their learning. Educators are also concerned that the tempting environment might have a negative effect on attendance. One reporter noted that one third of the class was absent on the day he was present (Winerip, 1994).

Other mall schools are operating as well. In 1993, the Oglethorp Mall in Savannah, Georgia, opened a high school, and its success inspired a second school in Savannah Mall. These students had done poorly in more traditional classes. The Lancaster County Academy is located in the Park City Mall in Pennsylvania, and a similar school is located in the Dufferin Mall in Toronto, Ontario, Canada.

---

lors are not receiving appropriate services from qualified counseling supervisors (e.g., Borders & Usher, 1992; Roberts & Borders, 1994). For example, the number of state department school counseling personnel has declined by 33% from 209 in 1974 to 139 in 1991 (Wantz, 1992). State departments of guidance and counseling appear to be experiencing mergers into other disciplines and reductions in personnel. School counselors need to be provided with qualified supervisors in order to be effective and responsible. In school systems without counselor supervisors or unqualified supervisors, school counselors need to be creative in obtaining counseling support (e.g., Benshoff & Paisley, 1995; P. Henderson & Lampe, 1992).

Certification and Licensure

The professional status of school counselors requires regulation by an external agency. *Certification* is a nonstatutory process by which a governmental agency officially grants permission for an individual to use a title adopted by a profession, provided the individual has met certain predetermined professional qualifications (Forrest & Stone, 1991, p. 13). *Licensure* grants individuals the legal right to practice a profession provided that individual has met the minimum qualifications established by the profession; that is, licensure prescribes who can and cannot practice a profession (Bradley, 1995; Shimberg, 1981).

CERTIFICATION

Certification of school counselors began in the 1940s and 1950s, when the certification of school counselors was enmeshed with teacher certification (Forrest & Stone, 1991). All states currently have guidelines for school counselor certification. The National Board for Certified Counselors (NBCC) was established in 1983 to provide national certification (Brooks & Gerstein, 1990) and currently provides specialty certification in career, addictions, mental health, gerontology, and school counseling. The percentage of school counselors with specialty certification remains extremely low. For example, 1994 membership of the American School Counselor Association was 12,508 with a meager 633 (5%) certified by the NBCC (T. Clawson, personal communication, cited in Bradley, 1995). The percentage may be influenced by state regulations to be certified by their agencies (Bradley, 1995).

LICENSURE

Counselor licensure began in the early 1970s as a reaction to the restrictions proposed in 1967 by the American Psychological Association. In 1973, the Southern Association for Counselor Education and Supervision established the first licensure committee, and in 1974, the Board of Directors of the American Counseling Association adopted a position statement (Sweeney, 1991). As of the date of this writing, licensure laws on counseling have been passed in 41 states and the District of Columbia. These licensure regulations pertain to persons who desire to become private practitioners.

CURRENT ISSUES

School counselors are generally required to be certified by state departments of education. In many instances, states have changed the term *certification* to *license*, especially in regard to teacher certification. Terminology becomes ambiguous as many counselors need teacher certification to obtain school counselor certification. Individuals who seek certification information frequently become confused and disillusioned. In addition, differences in requirements from state to state infer that arbitrary requirements may exist (Bradley, 1995).

The idea of national examination and certification/licensure appeals to those individuals who may move interstate and discover that they need additional coursework to be certified/licensed in their new state. Critics, however, argue that a national examination and certification/licensure program will dilute the standards that some states have already established for their school and private counselors, standards that are more rigorous than those proposed nationally (Farris, 1996). Others argue that a large number of counselors in their particular state would not be qualified under the proposed national standards.

The basic issue for school counselors is whether licensure for private practice is necessary and relevant. Such licensure is certainly not necessary for one to be a school counselor, unless a state uses that term rather than certification. Licensure can be relevant in that, in most instances, the school counselor will have to accrue additional academic preparation and supervised counseling experience. These additional requirements may result in increased content and process abilities for school counselors. Most school counselors seek licensure to augment their income or to enhance their professional stature. One ethical aspect exists in the potential for soliciting clients for private practice from school populations or their families. Another possibility may be the chance of dual relationship situations, especially if the school counselor practices privately within the school's attendance zone.

Goals 2000: Educate America Act

In 1983, the report "A Nation at Risk" (National Commission on Excellence in Education, 1983) sent alarming signals across this nation that the public schools were not adequately preparing the nation's youths for the changing times. A call was made for state and national reform in the educational standards for students. Thousands of students move from one state to another before they complete their schooling. Thus, many educators and politicians argue that national standards for students will improve the overall quality of education nationally. The passage of Goals 2000: Educate America Act (e.g., Kamii, Clark, & Dominick, 1994; Lewis, 1994) in 1994 represented one of the most significant pieces of education legislation ever approved at the federal level.

The principles underlying Goals 2000 recognize that there is no simple or cookie-cutter approach to improving education. Rather, it supports a variety of state and local approaches to increase academic achievement and to provide a safe, disciplined learning environment for all students (Farris, 1996). This act has drawn broad support from both major political parties, parents, and representatives of the business community, governors, teachers, labor, school administrators, state legislators, school boards, and state school superintendents.

Supporters of Goals 2000 claim that the act creates a framework for setting up national standards that are both clear and high. Students will be required to be competent in challenging subject matter and will face appropriate penalties for not attaining the set standards (Farris, 1996). Each state is required to develop minimum standards for students, whether they adopt the national standards or not (see **Something to Consider 11.3**).

SOMETHING TO CONSIDER 11.3

Goals 2000: Educate America Act

Goals 2000 addresses several educational issues, including the following:

1. the quality and availability to all students of curricula, instructional materials, and technologies, including distance learning;
2. the capability of teachers to provide high-quality instruction to meet the diverse learning needs of all students in the content area;
3. the extent to which teachers, principals, and administrators have ready and continuing access to professional development, including the best knowledge about teaching, learning, and school improvement;
4. the extent to which curriculum, instructional practices, and assessments are aligned with voluntary national content standards;
5. the extent to which school facilities provide a safe and secure environment for learning and instruction and provide the requisite libraries, laboratories, and other resources necessary to provide students an opportunity to learn; and
6. the extent to which schools use policies, curricula, and instructional practices that ensure nondiscrimination on the basis of gender.

SOURCE: Adapted from "Goals 2000 Is Not More of the Same," by A. C. Lewis, 1994, *Phi Delta Kappan, 76*(7), pp. 660–661.

Inherently, school counselors interface with the implementation of these standards. National standards affect the curriculum in every classroom in the nation. School counselors have the mission of monitoring the process and ensuring its efficacy for the needs of all students. Together, school counselors and Goals 2000 can help develop a new ethic of learning in this nation. Concurrently, a critical role will be played in helping children and adolescents reach challenging goals and standards. School counselors can help create better education and training opportunities to best support youths' success in school, in the workplace, and as responsible citizens in this nation.

Summary

The Carnegie Forum, the Edison Project, Goals 2000, The Holmes Group, National Board for Professional Teaching Standards, Project Zero, The Standards Project for the English Language Arts. These, in alphabetical order, are only seven of the current national initiatives for improving education in this nation. Some aim to "fix" schools; some, teachers; some, curriculum; some, all of these and more (Fishman, 1996).

These initiatives, combined with site-based programs, state and local school board plans, and individual efforts, present tremendous pressure for educational change. However, the Sandia Report (Carson, Huelskamp, & Woodall, 1993) concluded that coordinating the necessary leadership for educational improvement "at local, state, and national levels will be extremely difficult because education has so many stakeholders" (p. 309).

School counselors certainly represent a stakeholder in the improvement of education in this nation. Numerous issues and concerns must be examined by school counselors, in collaboration with teachers, school administrators, and concerned citizens. These collaborations must determine what students need in counseling and guidance services and to what degree. The outcome of this examination will affect all students well into the twenty-first century.

National initiatives are created to address issues such as those presented, or alluded to, in this chapter: the availability and quality of a comprehensive school counseling and guidance program, founded on developmental and multicultural precepts; home schooling, inclusion, and gender equity; the availability and quality of professional supervision; and the issues of certification and licensure. School counselors are on the cutting edge of these issues and trends. They must ensure that their educational stakehold remains firm and well grounded. They must be equal to the task. I believe school counselors are up to the task.

Experiential Activities

1. What do you value or not value about Goals 2000? Are the goals realistic? Are they political? What role or roles will school counselors have in their implementation?
2. Ask a high school counselor if students who have been home schooled are properly prepared for high school.

3. Does treating people equally mean treating everyone the same and not acknowledging individual differences? In a multicultural society, do we not want to acknowledge differences?
4. Think back to when you were in elementary school. Who were the best students in math and science? Were they the same ones in your junior high math and science classes? If you took geometry or calculus in high school, what percentage of the class was boys and what percentage was girls? Did the teachers do anything to favor one sex of students over the other? Which sex seemed to be called on most? Was it those students who raised their hands? As a school counselor, how would you ensure that girls have equal opportunity to take math and science classes? What is your role in gender equity?
5. What is your position on private licensure as a school counselor? What do you see as the advantages? Disadvantages?

References

Associated Press. (1994, May 12). Students working—and learning—at mall. *Bloomington (MN) Daily Herald*, p. 3A.

Ayers, W. (1993). *To teach, the journey of a teacher.* New York: Teachers College Press.

Benjamin, L., & Walz, G. R. (1988). *9 for the 90s: Counseling trends for tomorrow.* Ann Arbor, MI: ERIC Clearinghouse on Counseling and Personnel Services. (ERIC Document Reproduction Service No. ED 291 012)

Benshoff, J. M., & Paisley, P. O. (1995). A structured peer consultation model for school counselors. *Journal of Counseling & Development, 74,* 225–320.

Borders, L. D., & Drury, S. M. (1992a). Comprehensive school counseling programs: A review for policy makers and practitioners. *Journal of Counseling & Development, 70,* 487–498.

Borders, L. D., & Drury, S. M. (1992b). *Counseling programs: A guide to evaluation.* Newbury Park, CA: Corwin.

Borders, L. D., & Usher, C. H. (1992). Post-degree supervision: Existing and preferred practices. *Journal of Counseling & Development, 70,* 594–599.

Bradley, L. J. (1995). Certification and licensure issues. *Journal of Counseling & Development, 74,* 185–186.

Brooks, D. K., & Gerstein, L. H. (1990). Counselor credentialing and interprofessional collaboration. *Journal of Counseling & Development, 68,* 477–485.

Carson, C. C., Huelskamp, R. M., & Woodall, T. D. (1993, May/June). Perspectives on education in America: An annotated briefing. *Journal of Educational Research, 86*(5), 309.

Cetron, M. (1985). *Schools of the future.* New York: McGraw-Hill.

Commission on Precollege Guidance and Counseling. (1986). *Keeping the options open: Recommendations.* New York: College Entrance Examination Board.

Daniels, J. (1992). Empowering homeless children through school counseling. *Elementary School Guidance & Counseling, 27,* 104–112.

Farris, P. J. (1996). *Teaching, bearing the torch.* Dubuque, IA: Brown/Benchmark.

Fishman, A. R. (1996). Worlds together, worlds apart: The multiple realities of American schools. *Phi Delta Kappan, 77*(5), 366–373.

Forrest, D. V., & Stone, L. A. (1991). Counselor certification. In F. O. Bradley (Ed.), *Credentialing in counseling* (pp. 13–23). Alexandria, VA: American Association for Counseling and Development.

Gerler, E. (1992). What we know about school counseling: A reaction to Borders and Drury. *Journal of Counseling & Development, 70,* 499–501.

Glazer, S. M. (1994). Teachers and education: Are we somehow tied to a class system? *Reading Today, 11*(6), 3.

Hardesty, P. H., & Dillard, J. M. (1994). The role of elementary school counselors compared with their middle and secondary school counterparts. *Elementary School Guidance & Counseling, 29,* 83–91.

Henderson, A. (1988). Best friends. *Phi Delta Kappan, 70*(2), 149–153.

Henderson, P., & Lampe, R. E. (1992). Clinical supervision of school counselors. *The School Counselor, 39,* 151–157.

Hinkle, J. S. (1993). Training school counselors to do family counseling. *Elementary School Guidance & Counseling, 27,* 252–257.

Hodgkinson, H. (1985). *All one system: Demographics of education, kindergarten through graduate school.* Washington, DC: Institute for Educational Leadership.

Kamii, C., Clark, F. B., & Dominick, A. (1994). The six national goals: A road to disappointment. *Phi Delta Kappan, 76*(7), 672–677.

Knowles, J. G., Marlow, S. E., & Muchmore, J. A. (1992). From pedagogy to ideology: Origins and phases of home education in the United States, 1970–1990. *American Journal of Education, 100,* 195–235.

Lewis, A. C. (1994). Goals 2000 is not more of the same. *Phi Delta Kappan, 76*(7), 660–661.

London, P. (1987). Character education and clinical intervention: A paradigm shift for U.S. schools. *Phi Delta Kappan, 68*(10), 211–215.

National Commission on Excellence in Education. (1983). *A nation at risk: The imperative for educational reform.* Washington, DC: U.S. Department of Education.

Nicoll, W. G. (1992). A family counseling and consultation model for school counselors. *The School Counselor, 39,* 351–361.

Paisley, P. O., & Borders, L. D. (1995). School counseling: An evolving specialty. *Journal of Counseling & Development, 74,* 150–153.

Paisley, P. O., & Hubbard, G. T. (1994). *Developmental school counseling programs: From theory to practice.* Alexandria, VA: American Counseling Association.

Paisley, P. O., & Peace, S. D. (1995). Developmental principles: A framework for school counseling programs. *Elementary School Guidance & Counseling, 30,* 85–93.

Parker, R. J. (1994). Helping children cope with divorce: A workshop for parents. *Elementary School Guidance & Counseling, 29,* 137–148.

Peeks, B. (1993). Resolution in counseling and education: A systems perspective in the schools. *Elementary School Guidance & Counseling, 27,* 245–251.

Perry, N. S., & Schwallie-Giddis, P. (1993). The counselor and reform in tomorrow's schools. *Counseling and Human Development, 25*(7), 1–8.

Roberts, E. B., & Borders, L. D. (1994). Supervision of school counselors: Administrative, program, and counseling. *The School Counselor, 41,* 149–157.

Robinson, K. E. (1994). Addressing the needs of gay and lesbian students: The school counselor's role. *The School Counselor, 41,* 326–332.

Roscoe, B., Strouse, J. S., Goodwin, M. P., Taracks, L., & Henderson, D. (1994). Sexual harassment: An educational program for middle school students. *Elementary School Guidance & Counseling, 29,* 110–120.

Salend, S. J. (1994). Strategies for assessing attitudes toward individuals with disabilities. *The School Counselor, 41,* 338–342.

Schmidt, J. J. (1993). *Counseling in schools: Essential services and comprehensive programs.* Boston: Allyn & Bacon.

Shanker, A. (1994, February 6). Where we stand: Inclusion and ideology. *New York Times,* E23.

Shimberg, B. (1981). *Licensure: What vocational educators should know.* Columbus, OH: National Center for Research in Vocational Education.

Street, S. (1994). Adolescent male sexuality issues. *The School Counselor, 41,* 319–325.

Sweeney, T. J. (1991). Counselor credentialing: Purpose and origin. In F. O. Bradley (Ed.), *Credentialing in counseling* (pp. 1–12). Alexandria, VA: American Association for Counseling and Development.

Wantz, R. A. (1992). *Counseling and guidance staff: Program resource directory. State departments of education.* Columbus, OH: National Consortium of State Career Guidance Supervisors.

Welch, I. D., & McCarroll, L. (1993). The future role of school counselors. *The School Counselor, 41,* 48–53.

Willis, D. (Producer). (1994, July 12). *Educating our children.* Indianapolis, IN: WRTV.

Winerip, M. (1994, May 2). All under one roof: Shopping and education. *New York Times,* p. 23.

12 | Selected Case Vignettes for Study

For most children only two places exist where they can gain a successful identity and learn to follow the essential pathways. These places are the home and the school. . . . if the home is successful, the child may succeed despite the school, but that is too big an if to rely upon. We must ensure that the child's major experience in growing up, the most constant and important factor in his life, school, provides within it the two necessary pathways: a chance to give and receive love and a chance to become educated and therefore worthwhile.

—WILLIAM GLASSER, 1969

In this chapter, selected vignettes will allow the counseling student to observe how synergetic principles can be used effectively in the counseling of diverse ethnic youths. The reader is cautioned that the analyses presented do not represent the singular strategy that can be used. Many theoretical orientations may be applied to the case studies. The question remains, however, whether those theoretical modalities take into consideration influences of history and environment as well as ethnicity and culture.

Vignette One: Decision Making

Traditional Native American Indian students are frequently faced with decisions regarding their futures. The following case presents one such situation (adapted from Herring, 1997, in press; Sodowsky & Johnson, 1994).

A European American counselor works in an urban high school that has a small number of Native American Indian students whose parents have moved from their reservations to a large city for work opportunities. Michael Redhorse, an academically and artistically talented sophomore, informs the counselor that he is considering returning to the reservation to live with his grandparents. Michael thinks that his return to his reservation may, for all practical purposes, end his scholastic education, but, at the same time, he feels intense interest in being immersed in his tribal culture and artwork. How would the counselor conceptualize Michael's conflicts? What counseling interventions could the counselor use? What would be the counseling goals?

AREAS OF CONFLICT

This case reveals several psychosocial conflicts for Michael. Apparently, Michael has not developed an ethnic identity but has made a tentative decision to identify with the traditional Native American Indian ethnic group. His decision to leave mainstream culture indicates a dichotomous either/or problem-solving style. Michael also may be reacting to his acculturated parents who probably conform to mainstream middle-class society. He may be attempting to redefine his ethnic group by stressing ethnic consciousness and pride. In addition, Michael may be valuing his grandparents' preference for simplicity of life, as made possible by the reservation, of being oneself and of relating harmoniously with others and nature.

The ethnic-dissimilar counselor's efforts to intervene in Michael's dilemma omit additional questions that need to be answered. How do Michael's teachers and classmates respond to his interest in tribal art? How satisfied is he in the social environment of the school? What kind of support does he have in the family, in the local community, and in the urban Native American Indian community? How are his parents and significant others responding to his wish to return to his reservation? What will he miss if he leaves for the reservation?

Regarding returning to the reservation, consideration must be given to these questions. What are the appealing aspects of reservational life? What are the disadvantages? What if he may not like reservation life? How does he feel when he is on the reservation? What kind of life does he hope to find there? What expectations does he have about his role with his grandparents and in his tribe in the reservation? What kind of extended family and support system will he have?

INTERVENTIONS AND COUNSELING GOALS

Synergetic counseling precepts offer an efficacious model for addressing Michael's concerns. Establishment of rapport and mutual respect is extremely important. Recognizing different worldviews and creating a culturally compatible environment are necessary prerequisites for the ethnic-dissimilar counselor. The European American counselor will need to establish these qualities in the initial session if successful intervention is to be attained.

The counselor's personal values about the importance of formal schooling and diplomas may be a hindrance in developing rapport with Michael. The counselor may also be under pressure from administrators to "fix the problem" by keeping Michael in school. The counselor must create an openness of interaction, maintain an open mind, and take care not to prejudge anything Michael discloses. The counselor must not be seen as an ally to Michael's parents or the school system, but must acknowledge and support Michael's desire to increase his tribal identity and knowledge of tribal art. The counselor must assume the role of advice giver rather than decision maker. Most traditional Native American Indian youths expect a counselor to know the "problem," the reasons for it, and how to eliminate it. Yet, these youths prefer to make the ultimate decision.

The counselor reinforces Michael's wish for knowledge of tribal culture and art while at the same time maximizing his educational opportunities. The counselor's most concrete options are (a) to affirm Michael's talent as a natural resource within himself that promotes beauty, balance, and harmony within self and community and (b) to reinforce a hopeful attitude about the future of his talent in tribal art.

Guided imagery activities will allow Michael to gain greater insight into the options that are available to him. As Michael appears to be vacillating about his degree of acculturation, the counselor will be most effective by being nondirective as he or she guides Michael through his self-exploration. Values clarification exercises can be useful counseling strategies. In addition, the establishment of a link with the Native American Indian community will facilitate Michael's decision making. Perhaps, one of the indigenous healing practices (e.g., sweat lodge, vision quest) could be useful for Michael. Naturally, the European American counselor would need to consult and collaborate with tribal elders for this intervention.

Whatever Michael chooses to do, the counselor must plan developmental activities and interactions with people who can help Michael. Resources in the Native American Indian community can suggest how to alleviate Michael's stress and facilitate his acceptance in the social–academic milieu at school.

VARIATIONS TO CONSIDER

1. The school counselor in this vignette represented the European American ethnic group. That counselor had to cope with personal biases and potential encapsulation. If a Native American Indian counselor had been

available, the counseling interventions would have reflected a different focus. The most viable change would have been evidenced in the use of indigenous healing practices. From the information presented in this text, what would be some efficacious and indigenous strategies for this counselor to use? Why couldn't the European American counselor use these strategies?

2. What factors would have changed if Michael chose the other alternative—that of remaining in mainstream society and education? What areas of conflict would remain the same, and what areas would be different? How would the counseling goals and interventions change to match this scenario?

Vignette Two: Responsibility

The following vignette represents one revealed in a practicum class. The school counselor-in-training was very perplexed with the situation and wanted some direction.

> Susan Smith, a European American girl, is referred to the school counselor by both parents and the primary teacher. Susan is the youngest of three children in an upper-middle-class family. Her siblings are a 29-year-old sister and a 17-year-old brother. Susan is 7 years old.
>
> In class, Susan seldom, if ever, completes assignments. She is also prone to temper tantrums when things do not go her way. Her parents are very concerned about the lack of progress in school. They want to have Susan tested for learning disability (LD) and her teacher believes she may have attention deficit disorder (ADD).
>
> The family has a maid. When asked about responsibility at home, Susan has a blank look on her face. When she is observed individually or in a group, she is bright eyed, alert, and eager to respond. When questions are asked, she raises her hand and waits her turn to respond. Susan appears to fully understand all questions and directions and never interferes with others.

AREAS OF CONFLICT

One obvious concern is Susan's apparent lack of any responsibilities at home and at school. The 10-year span between Susan and her next oldest sibling indicates a psychological birth-order position akin to an "only child." The most general characteristic of this position is that of being a "pampered, spoiled" child.

In addition, the premature diagnoses of LD and ADD tend to distract from a lack of parental attention and ineffective teaching style. Her classroom behaviors and tendencies to "tantrums" more accurately indicate that she is used to "getting her own way."

INTERVENTIONS AND COUNSELING GOALS

The school counselor might complete a family constellation exercise to confirm the psychological birth-order position. The primary counseling goal would be for Susan to gain more responsibility in her life. The school counselor can suggest such interventions as the assignment of chores in the home. Should Susan not complete her assigned chores, logical consequences would result. The parents might be advised to implement an allowance for Susan, if she is not already getting one. She would be required to purchase some of her needs with her allowance.

In the home, she should not be called by a "baby" name such as Suzie. Adhere to her given name of Susan. In addition, the maid needs to be monitored so she does not do everything for "little Suzie." At school, the teacher should reinforce these strategies. Failure to complete assignments results in whatever consequences are in place in that setting. Temper tantrums can be ignored if possible, or perhaps, time-out strategies can be used. The classroom teacher also needs to assign appropriate tasks for which Susan is responsible. For example, Susan may be assigned the task of collecting books or materials necessary for classwork.

VARIATIONS TO CONSIDER

1. The intervention in the vignette of Susan emphasized principles from the Adlerian perspective. How might other orientations be applied in this situation?
2. If all other factors remain the same, how would the areas of conflict and goals of counseling change if Susan came from a low socioeconomic family? Would the theoretical orientation need to be changed?
3. Change the vignette from an upper-class European American female to an African American female from a single-parent, low socioeconomic situation. What possibilities arise for effective intervention?

Vignette Three: Ethnic Identity Development

The following vignettes represent composites from the author's practical and clinical experiences, or they may represent adaptations from the literature.

Example One: Rosa, a 16-year-old half-Chippewa Native American Indian, came to her school counselor for support during a time when she and her mother, age 40, were in extreme conflict. Rosa had been dating an older non-Native adolescent who had a reputation for drug abuse. Within the past 2 years, Rosa's brother, age 18, had been to peer counseling training for the area of chemical dependence prevention, and the entire family has participated in the associated family program. Rosa's mother was proud of her son's growth, but she was very anxious about her daughter's choice of friends.

Rosa lived with her family on a reservation ranch, and her family enjoyed a comfortable lifestyle. Her mother worked in town as a licensed practical nurse and her non-Native father operated the ranch. She and her brother attended integrated schools in a nearby town, and both had done well academically and socially.

AREAS OF CONFLICT

Even though Rosa resides on a reservation, she represents a Heritage-Inconsistent Native American Indian (Herring, 1994; Zitzow & Estes, 1981). Her predominant orientation reflects behaviors and values adapted from the dominant culture. Issues that Rosa may face include the following: (a) denial and lack of pride in being a Native American Indian, (b) pressure to adopt the majority cultural values, (c) guilt feelings over not knowing or participating in her culture, (d) negative views of Native American Indians, and (e) lack of a support and belief system.

These conflicts are multiplied by an apparent generational conflict, as well as being genetically mixed. Rosa must synthesize her earlier identifications into a consistent personal identity as well as a positive ethnic and cultural identity (Herring, 1994). The following situations illustrate identity conflicts commonly experienced by biracial youths and reframe the conflict in the form of a question (Gibbs, 1989; Herring, 1994, pp. 181–182):

1. Who am I? (conflicts about biracial identity)
2. Where do I fit? (conflicts about social marginality)
3. What is my sexual role? (conflicts about dating and sexuality)
4. Who controls my life? (conflicts about separation from parents)
5. Where am I heading? (conflicts about career aspirations)

Successful intervention with Rosa will involve dealing effectively with these related developmental tasks, all of which are problematic (Erikson, 1968)

INTERVENTIONS AND COUNSELING GOALS

The school counselor will need to recognize and understand the importance of Rosa's socioeconomic and political history when planning and implementing psychosocial and other developmental interventions. The school counselor with sufficient knowledge to match strategy and developmental levels can formulate appropriate short-term and long-term counseling goals (Young-Eisendrath, 1985).

The following are some general suggestions that can be used by school counselors:

1. Understand the problems, tasks, and challenges of each developmental period of Rosa's life rather than assuming a developmental homogeneity that may not actually exist (Baruth & Manning, 1991).
2. Assessing the level of acculturation held by Rosa and her familial structure is essential (Baruth & Manning, 1991).
3. Ethnic-dissimilar counselors will experience less success with Rosa unless they are extremely knowledgeable about Native American Indian cultures.

The school counselor will emphasize the apparent generational conflict between Rosa and her mother. This conflict results from the different degrees of acculturation represented by Rosa and her mother. Rosa needs to understand where the conflict derives and how to learn to compromise. She will have to decide which values to accept and which values do not represent her worldview.

The school counselor may want to investigate Rosa's relationship with her brother as well. She may be experimenting with drugs as a reaction to her parents' tendency to praise the brother and criticize her. The school counselor can use cognitive–behavior decision-making activities to assist Rosa in deciding who she is and what she wants to accomplish in life. Genograms and sociograms can be used to elicit the sources of Rosa's support systems. Cognitive–behavioral strategies and guided imagery may assist in issues of career development and sexuality.

The school counselor is also alerted to Rosa's need for an ethnic identity. Rosa will need to be "felt out" regarding her wishes concerning an ethnic identity. To be truly effective, this intervention needs to involve the entire family. The possible reaction to her sibling's choice of ethnic identity may be important.

VARIATIONS TO CONSIDER

1. The sibling in this case may play a more important role than is noted. Generate additional conflicts that might have resulted from the relationship among Rosa, her brother, and her parents.
2. What factors might be changed if Rosa was a single child? Counseling goals and interventions?
3. How would the scenario change if Rosa was Rosario, a male adolescent?

Example Two: Josie, a 17-year-old daughter of Native American Indian parents, was found wandering aimlessly around town. The examining physician concluded she was severely depressed, acutely undernourished, suffered from hallucinations, and was in desperate need of sleep and relaxation. Josie had not eaten much in the past week, had slept only a few hours per night, and had been absent from school the week before.

Josie was 12 when she learned that her biological parents had died in an accident when she was 4 years old. Her paternal Native American Indian grandparents, who were respected shamans, assumed parental roles. They, by most standards, were very traditional: They spoke the native language in the home and frequently in social settings, gathered and preserved native foods, hunted and fished and smoked their catches, and in general abided by ancient customs. They were active in Native American Indian religious and ceremonial activities. Josie was involved in everything.

Josie had also learned considerable information about sorcery and spiritual methods. On a few occasions, partially out of bitterness and dislike for certain tribal members, including her estranged boyfriend, she had made use of her knowledge to seek revenge and redress and her actions had not gone unnoticed.

AREAS OF CONFLICT

Josie's case reflects characteristics of a Heritage-Consistent Native American Indian (Zitzow & Estes, 1981). Such youths exhibit signs that may include the following: (a) growing up on or near a reservation, (b) having an extended family orientation, (c) being involved in tribal religious activities, (d) being educated on or near a reservation, (e) socializing primarily with other Native American Indians, (f) being knowledgeable about or willing to learn about the tribal ways, (g) placing low priority on materialistic goals, and (h) using shyness and silence as signs of respect.

Common treatment issues should be explored with all Native American Indians (Zitzow & Estes, 1981). These issues would include concerns with prejudice and discrimination, concerns with alcoholism, possible feelings of distrust toward school counselors (especial ethnically dissimilar individuals), possible lack of strong self-identity, fear of failure and ridicule, a lack of exposure to successful Native American Indian role models, feelings of frustration that others are responding to them in a stereotypic fashion rather than as an individual, and possible conflicts over commitment to long-term goals such as education, with feelings of alienation from tribal and extended family networks.

Specific issues that may arise in treatment with Josie include the following (Herring, 1994, pp. 189–190; Zitzow & Estes, 1981):

1. The sense of security for Josie may be limited to the reservation and the extended family.
2. Nonverbal communication may be important as Josie may have difficulty with English.
3. Josie's socialization may have involved only other Native American Indians, and she may feel uncomfortable communicating with a dissimilar person.
4. Josie's basic academic learning skills may be underdeveloped.
5. The value of education may not fit into Josie's belief system, and she may feel a conflict between motivation to learn and values on the reservation.
6. Josie might be concerned about failure and its effect on the extended family and the tribe.
7. Josie may have difficulty establishing long-term goals.
8. The holding back of emotions may be perceived as a positive characteristic by Josie.
9. Paternalism from government agencies may have diminished Josie's feelings of personal responsibility in decision making.
10. Josie may be unfamiliar with the expectations of the dominant culture.

INTERVENTIONS AND COUNSELING GOALS

The school counselor can use the following interventions with Josie, as adapted from Shweder (1991) and Hoare (1991):

1. Assist Josie to understand the societal cause of her sense of not fitting in.
2. Assist Josie to calibrate her identity to contemporary society.
3. Understand that Josie's experience of prejudice may lead to her alienation, first from the society of her experience and then from her self.
4. Convey the understanding that Josie must first have a firm sense of her self before she can move to an inclusive and relational identity.
5. Reassure Josie that all humans may possess the seeds of pseudospeciation—of prejudice against dissimilar groups and values.
6. Foster Josie's understanding that current society is an individualistic, egocentric one.
7. Assist Josie to focus on her idealistic tendency to create future utopias by extending abstractions rather than capitalizing on peer orientations, repudiation, and autonomy forays of her teen years.

8. Consider providing alternative mechanisms for identifying the common ground that can serve as a unifying basis for cross-contextual identification.

VARIATIONS TO CONSIDER

1. As a school counselor, would you feel comfortable working with Josie, or would you prefer to refer? Give your rationale for your decision.
2. What counseling process changes would ensue if Josie were Joe? Does gender have any effect on the counseling process in this example?
3. If Josie's parents were available and all other aspects are the same, how might counseling with Josie be different?
4. Does this example lend itself for the use of indigenous healers and healing? What would be the justification for or against indigenous procedures?

Example Three: Johnny War Eagle, a Hunkpapa Sioux and European American mixed blood, initially used the label "half-breed" as his self-designation. He had traveled and lived in various parts of the world by the time he was 6 years old. His initial experience of differentness as devaluation occurred when a neighbor yelled a racial slur at him in the United States.

Johnny War Eagle has experienced the questioning routine of others ever since he was a little kid. People would ask him his name, and he would tell them. Afterward they would say, "What kind of name is that?" He would say, "It's Native American Indian." More times than not, they'd say, "You don't look Native American Indian." Johnny would explain, "Well, I'm half." But they would persist and want to know more about his parents.

Johnny War Eagle lately responds to questions about his ethnicity by using a biracial label. He understands now that not all people are racist or intent on defining him negatively. Johnny can now be self-expressive rather than defensive and reactive.

AREAS OF CONFLICT

Johnny War Eagle's situation differs considerably from the cases of Rosa and Josie. Whereas their socializations reflected a tremendous connection with traditional Native American Indian culture, Johnny's experiences evolved within the dominant culture; his degree of acculturation into mainstream society represented almost total commitment to that culture. Johnny's international experiences also present a different case.

In addition, discriminatory slurs and images appear to make his socialization and development dissimilar to that of Rosa's and Josie's, at least as presented. His negative experiences in this country contrast with his international ones. Johnny may exhibit confusion and bitterness about these experiences.

INTERVENTIONS AND COUNSELING GOALS

Johnny War Eagle illustrates successful identity development, according to Kich's (1982, 1992) developmental model of ethnic identity. His vignette depicts his transition from a questionable, sometimes devalued sense of self to one in which a biracial self-conception is highly valued and secure. Cyclical reenactment of these stages emerged during later development, often with greater intensity and awareness.

Kich (1982, 1992) compressed the biracial identity development process into three developmental stages. The stages describe not only Johnny's growth through childhood, adolescence, and into adulthood, but also his transitions and passages throughout life. The three major stages in Johnny's development and continuing resolution of biracial identity are as follows (Kich, 1982):

1. *Childhood: awareness of differences and dissonance.* An initial awareness of differentness and dissonance between self-perceptions and others' perceptions of them (initially, 3 through 10 years of age).
2. *Adolescence: struggle for acceptance.* A struggle for acceptance from others (initially, age 8 through late adolescence and young adulthood).
3. *Adulthood: self-acceptance and assertion.* Acceptance of themselves as people with a biracial and bicultural identity (late adolescence throughout adulthood).

The developmental task for genetically mixed youths is to differentiate critically among others' interpretations of them, various pejorative and grandiose labels and mislabels, and their own experiences and conceptions of themselves (Kich, 1992). The school counselor can guide this differentiation to facilitate the addressing of an ethnic identity for genetically mixed Native American Indian youths.

Several biracial identity development models are available for the school counselor's consideration (e.g., Gibbs, 1989; Jacobs, 1977, 1992; Root, 1992a, 1992b). These models are not designed for any specific ethnic or racial group. Rather, their flexibility allows general application to any genetically mixed individual. The reader is advised to review available models to discern their applicability to a particular situation.

VARIATIONS TO CONSIDER

1. What if Johnny had not attained self-acceptance as a genetically mixed individual? What options would the counselor need to consider?
2. If Johnny had been born to African American and European American parents, would his experiences be similar? If so, in what way(s)?

Vignette Four: Interracial Families

A child whose mother is African American and whose father is European American is reared in a predominantly European American, upper-class neighborhood. The child has blond, wiry hair and blue eyes. Her classmates and teachers assume she is European American until her mother picks her up from school one day. Her best friend runs away from the car, yelling, "I played with a nigger."

A child whose mother is European American and whose father is Japanese is reared within a traditional Japanese family, secured in the feeling that he is loved and accepted. But from television, magazines, and pictures in books, he sees that all the most successful, powerful people are European American. Even Santa Claus, who gives out all the gifts, is European American. When asked whether he would prefer to be European American or Japanese, he says White.

A child with light skin and green eyes grows up in the Bahamas until age 12. He is considered European American on the basis of his skin color; his mother has very dark, black skin and is considered African American. His family moves to the United States. When among his friends from the Bahamas in his neighborhood, he is still considered European American. When he goes to school, however, he is considered African American. His racial identity shifts when he goes from neighborhood to school; he adopts different self-perceptions, attitudes, beliefs, and behaviors in each environment.

A newly married Vietnamese man and Hispanic woman are expecting their first child. The couple and their parents have lived in an integrated community for over two decades. The neighborhood has stayed stable as both the Vietnamese and the Hispanic worked side by side to build a good school, a community center, and a sports complex. Both families have embraced the news of the new child. The couple will teach the child the customs of both cultures and the language and religion of both parents. They want their child to see himself/herself as biracial.

This text would be incomplete if some attention were not given to the school counselor's role in working with interracial/interethnic/intercultural families. The preceding vignettes illustrate common occurrences in this nation. The Supreme Court of the United States ruled the unconstitutionality of antimiscegenation laws 30 years ago. Cultural diversity and interracial couplings and marriages are no longer hidden and confined to isolation and ostracism.

AREAS OF CONFLICT

What is the effect of biracial status on children and adolescents? How do definitions of race and the experience of growing up in a racist society affect identity development for youths from interracial homes? What does their race mean to each of these children? How do they see themselves and how do others see them in relation to their racial group membership? How will their understandings of their own and other groups change as they grow older, and as society itself changes? An important concern for professionals is to not allow biracial or multiethnic family members to become scapegoats for the family's problems.

School counselors working with youths from interracial families face multiple challenges. To fully understand how these youths formulate an ethnic identity, school counselors must consider such factors as economic relationships and population ratios (e.g., Miller, 1992). Interracial identity development must also be viewed within the context of social, cultural, and institutional racism (Root, 1992b).

The biracial youth may in fact be even more vulnerable to racism than a monoracial adult (Miller & Rotheram-Borus, 1994). This circumstance occurs "because the biracial youth represents an affront to the racial divide; biracial persons must often cope with reactions reflecting the internalized racism of society" (p. 148). For example, if a biracial child with one European American parent "passes" as "European American," this child may avoid racial insults and discriminatory practices and may have an easier path in specific circumstances. However, it is important to distinguish between passing throughout one's life as opposed to passing for the purpose of obtaining a specific goal. To the extent that passing represents an attempt to deny one's heritage, it should be viewed as a maladaptive coping mechanism (Miller & Rotheram-Borus, 1994).

INTERVENTIONS AND COUNSELING GOALS

McRoy and Freeman (1986) identified several environmental factors as crucial in the treatment of interracial families. School counselors will need to do the following:

1. Inform parents of the need to encourage their children to acknowledge and discuss their ethnic and cultural heritages with their parents and other significant individuals.
2. Work with parents to acknowledge that their children's racial or ethnic heritage may be dissimilar to each other and/or to the parents and recognize that as positive.
3. Encourage parents to give their children opportunities to develop relationships with peers from many different backgrounds (e.g., integrated schools and neighborhoods).
4. Encourage parents to allow their children to meet role models through participation in social activities held by support groups.

5. Alert parents to the understanding that when a child is unable to identify with both parents, the child develops feelings of disloyalty and guilt over rejection of one parent.

6. Assist parents in forming as a family an identity as an interracial unit.

In addition, school counselors need to be cognizant of the following, as adapted from Miller and Rotheram-Borus (1994, pp. 162–164):

1. Counselors often presume to know a child's race or ethnicity on the basis of the child's physical characteristics, without inquiring about self-identification of the child or the parents. Racial, ethnic, and cultural background, including generational and socioeconomic, are basic domains to be reviewed when conducting an evaluation.

2. Counselors' attitudes and values influence their conceptualization of children's problem behaviors. Although there is no one answer about how to cope with the challenges presented in assisting a biracial youth, it is critical, as with all intervention planning, that the counselor be familiar with the youth's background.

3. Sensitization and education to the norms of many cultures are critical when conducting cross-cultural counseling. The counselor may misinterpret a youth's cues.

4. The identity formation process will evolve, often in a complex manner. Choices made by biracial children at one stage of development are likely to be rethought and reevaluated at later developmental stages.

5. A counselor typically addresses problems of individuals and promotes choices that are likely to reduce the individual's stress and enhance individual coping skills. Counselors must be careful to assess when issues are a function of racial or ethnic identity versus other factors.

Parents from interracial families often need assistance with the unique problems they and their children face outside of the family. For example, decisions must be made regarding how to facilitate their children's ethnic and personal identity developments, whether to live in an integrated or segregated residential area, and how to help their children negotiate challenges presented by harassing peers. To appropriately make these decisions, parents must clarify their own values and goals. Where are they positioned in the development of a positive ethnic identity? The school counselor is able to assist parents with these decisions, but they must recognize their own heritage and values before they can help others resolve their differences in background.

A viable resource for school counselors and interracial families is the I-Pride (Interracial Pride) movement. This national movement advocates the elimination of monoracial biases, such as census categories and "check one only" forms. This movement also endeavors to assist parents transmit to their children the values, attitudes, and behavior patterns consistent with their dual or multiple heritage. I-Pride groups are increasingly common, especially in major urban areas.

Parents and family can substantially influence the racial and ethnic identity developmental process of their children. However, as children mature, society's sanctions are likely to have an increasing influence. Whether the transaction between developmental challenges and social forces has a positive or negative influence is not clear, but a substantial influence will be exerted on interracial and interethnic youths as they seek to adopt a racial or ethnic identity (Miller & Rotheram-Borus, 1994). School counselors can play a significant role in this process.

VARIATIONS TO CONSIDER

1. As a school counselor, what interventions would you select in this chapter's vignettes? Are there any common factors? What is unique to each?
2. As a school counselor, how much time do you schedule for family counseling of education activities? What influences from environmental and historical data play during the sessions?
3. The percentage of pure-blooded individuals on earth has become miniscule. Families are increasingly becoming more interracial, interethnic, and intercultural. With that premise, describe your heritage from one of those perspectives. How have you been influenced by those influences?

References

Baruth, L. G., & Manning M. L. (1991). *Multicultural counseling and psychotherapy: A lifespan perspective.* New York: Merrill.

Erikson, E. H. (1968). *Identity: Youth and crisis.* New York: Norton.

Gibbs, J. T. (1989). Biracial adolescents. In J. T. Gibbs & L. N. Huang (Eds.), *Children of color: Psychological interventions* (pp. 322–350). San Francisco: Jossey-Bass.

Glasser, W. (1969). *Schools without failure.* New York: Harper & Row.

Herring, R. D. (1994). Native American Indian identity: A people of many peoples. In E. P. Salett & D. R. Koslow (Eds.), *Race, ethnicity, and self: Identity in multicultural perspective* (pp. 170–197). Washington, DC: National MultiCultural Institute.

Herring, R. D. (1997). Counseling with Native American Indian and Alaskan Native youth. In C. C. Lee (Ed.), *Multicultural issues in counseling: New approaches to diversity* (2nd ed.). Alexandria, VA: American Counseling Association.

Herring, R. D. (in press). Synergetic counseling with Native American Indian students. *Journal of Counseling & Development.*

Hoare, C. H. (1991). Psychosocial identity development and cultural others. *Journal of Counseling & Development, 70,* 45–53.

Jacobs, J. H. (1977). Black/White interracial families: Marital process and identity development in young children (Doctoral dissertation, Wright Institute, 1977). *Dissertation Abstracts International, 38*(10-B), 5023.

Jacobs, J. H. (1992). Identity development in biracial children. In M. P. P. Root (Ed.), *Racially mixed people in America* (pp. 190–206). Newbury Park, CA: Sage.

Kich, G. K. (1982). *Eurasians: Ethnic/racial identity development of biracial Japanese/White adults.* Unpublished doctoral dissertation, Wright Institute Graduate School of Psychology.

Kich, G. K. (1992). The developmental process of asserting a biracial, bicultural identity. In M. P. P. Root (Ed.), *Racially mixed people in America* (pp. 304–317). Newbury Park, CA: Sage.

McRoy, R. G., & Freeman, E. (1986). Racial identity issues among mixed-race children. *Social Work in Education, 8,* 164–174.

Miller, R. L. (1992). The human ecology of multiracial identity. In M. P. P. Root (Ed.), *Racially mixed people in America* (pp. 24–36). Newbury Park, CA: Sage.

Miller, R. L., & Rotheram-Borus, M. J. (1994). Growing up biracial in the United States. In E. P. Salett & D. R. Koslow (Eds.), *Race, ethnicity, and self: Identity in multicultural perspective* (pp. 144–169). Washington, DC: National MultiCultural Institute.

Root, M. P. P. (Ed.). (1992a). *Racially mixed people in America.* Newbury Park, CA: Sage.

Root, M. P. P. (1992b). Within, between, and beyond race. In M. P. P. Root (Ed.), *Racially mixed people in America* (pp. 3–11). Newbury Park, CA: Sage.

Shweder, R. A. (1991). *Thinking through diversity.* Cambridge, MA: Harvard University Press.

Sodowsky, G. R., & Johnson, P. (1994). World views: Culturally learned assumptions and values. In P. Pedersen & J. C. Carey (Eds.), *Multicultural counseling in schools: A practical handbook* (pp. 59–80). Needham Heights, MA: Allyn & Bacon.

Young-Eisendrath, P. (1985). Making use of human development in counseling. *Counseling and Human Development, 17*(5), 1–12.

Zitzow, D., & Estes, G. (1981). *Heritage consistence as a consideration in counseling with Native Americans.* Aberdeen, SD. (ERIC Document Reproduction Service No. ED 209 035).

Selected Journals Recommended for Multicultural and Cross-Cultural Counselors

American Psychologist

Published monthly by the American Psychological Association (750 First Street, NE, Washington, DC 20002-4242), this journal focuses on all aspects of counseling and occasionally examines multicultural issues and concerns.

Child Development

Published six times per year by the Journals Division of the University of Chicago Press (57205 Woodland Avenue, Chicago, IL 60637), this journal focuses on the development of children of all cultures, periodically addressing development in multicultural children.

Counseling and Human Development

Published nine times per year by Love Publishing Company (1777 South Bellarie Street, Denver, CO 80222), this journal examines counseling issues in the context of human development. The journal usually includes a featured article, more extensive than the rest.

The Counseling Psychologist

Published quarterly by Sage (2455 Teller Road, Thousand Oaks, CA 91320), this journal is the official publication of the Division of Counseling Psychology of the American Psychological Association. Each issue focuses on a specific theme of importance to the theory, research, and practice of counseling psychology. Special issues on aging (Vol. 12, No. 2) and on cross-cultural counseling (Vol. 13, No. 4) should be of interest to multicultural counselors.

The Counselor

Published bimonthly by the National Association of Alcoholism and Drug Abuse Counselors (1911 North Fort Myer Drive, Arlington, VA 22209), this journal addresses issues and concerns of health care givers who work in the field of alcoholism and drug addiction. Topics include cultural and ethnic influences on the treatment and care of chemically dependent persons.

Counselor Education and Supervision

Published quarterly by the American Counseling Association (5999 Stevenson Avenue, Alexandria VA 22304), this journal is concerned with matters relevant to the preparation and supervision of counselors in agency or school settings. Multicultural counseling considerations are occasionally examined.

Daedalus

Published quarterly by the American Academy of Arts and Sciences (136 Irving Street, Cambridge, MA 02138), this journal includes scholarly articles on contemporary topics of interest. Counselors intervening along the life span with culturally diverse clients will be especially interested in the issues on gender, aging, and cultural diversity.

Elementary School Guidance and Counseling

Published four times per year by the American School Counselor Association Division of the American Counseling Association, this journal examines the role of elementary, middle school, and junior high school counselors. Multicultural issues related to children are frequently addressed.

The Family Therapy Networker

Published bimonthly by The Family Therapy Network (7705 13th Street, NW, Washington, DC 20012), this journal targets mental health professionals who address issues and concerns within the context of the family. Ethnic and cultural issues are frequently emphasized.

The Gerontologist

Published bimonthly by the Gerontological Society of America (Department 5018, Washington, DC 20001-5018), this journal addresses concerns of the elderly of all cultures and ethnic groups.

Harvard Education Review

Published quarterly (Gutman Library, Suite 349, 6 Appian Way, Cambridge, MA 02138-3752), this journal features research and opinion in the field of education. Occasionally, articles have relevance for multicultural counselors.

Journal of American Indian Education

Published three times per year by the Center for Indian Education (College of Education, Arizona State University, Tempe, AZ 85287-1311), this journal is devoted to topics related to Native American Indian education.

Journal of Black Studies

Published four times annually by Sage, this journal discusses and analyzes issues related to people of African descent. Although counseling and development are not usually addressed, this publication does provide a comprehensive examination of Black culture.

Journal of Clinical Psychology

Published bimonthly by Clinical Psychology Company (4 Conant Square, Brandon, VT 05733), this journal directs attention to issues relevant to the clinician.

Journal of Counseling & Development

Published six times per year by the American Counseling Association, this journal focuses on a broad range of topics for a readership composed of counselors, counseling psychologists, and student personnel specialists. Articles occasionally deal with multicultural issues.

Journal of Counseling Psychology

Published quarterly by the American Psychological Association, this journal publishes articles reporting empirical studies related to the various counseling areas.

Journal of Cross-Cultural Psychology

Published four times annually by Sage, this journal publishes cross-cultural research reports exclusively, emphasizing individual differences and variations within cultures.

Journal of Multicultural Counseling and Development

Published four times per year by the American Counseling Association, this journal focuses on research, theory, or program application pertinent to multicultural and ethnic minority issues in all areas of counseling and human development.

Phi Delta Kappan

Published in 10 issues by Phi Delta Kappa, Inc. (Eighth and Union, P.O. Box 789, Bloomington, IN 47402), this magazine covers a broad range of educational issues, including cultural diversity.

The School Counselor

Published five times per year, *The School Counselor* is another publication of the American Counseling Association. It focuses primarily on secondary school issues and is geared toward the fields of guidance and counseling.

Teachers College Record

Published quarterly (Columbia University, 522 West 120th Street, New York, NY 10027), this journal focuses primarily on topics pertaining to education.

Selected Resources

ABUSE AND ADDICTIONS

Local Resources
(Local Telephone Directory)

Adult Children of Alcoholics
Al-Anon
Al-Ateen
Alcoholics Anonymous
Gambler Anonymous
Narcotics Anonymous
Overeaters Anonymous
Sex Addicts Anonymous
Sex and Love Addicts Anonymous
Women for Sobriety

National Resources

Addiction Research Foundation Dept.
c/o Marketing Services
33 Russell St.
Toronto, Ontario, Canada M55 2S1

Adult Children of Alcoholics
P.O. Box 3216
Torrance, CA 90510
(213) 534-1815

Al-Anon/Al-Ateen Family Group
  Headquarters
P.O. Box 182
Madison Square Garden
New York, NY 10010

Alcoholics Anonymous World Services
P.O. Box 459
Grand Central Station
New York, NY 10163
(212) 686-1100

Drug Abuse Council
1828 L St., NW
Washington, DC 20036

Drug Enforcement Administration
1405 Eye St., NW
Washington, DC 20537

Nar-Anon Family Group Headquarters
P.O. Box 2562
Palos Verdes, CA 90274-0119
(213) 547-5800

Narcotics Anonymous
P.O. Box 9999
Van Nuys, CA 91409
(818) 780-3951

National Association for Children of
  Alcoholics
35182 Coast Hwy., Suite B
South Laguna, CA 92677
(714) 499-3889

National Center for Alcohol Education
1901 N. Moore St.
Arlington, VA 22209

National Clearinghouse for Alcohol and
Drug Information
P.O. Box 2345
Rockville, MD 20852
(301) 468-2600

National Coordinating Council of Drug
Education
1526 18th St., NW
Washington, DC 20036

National Council on Alcoholism
2 Park Ave.
New York, NY 10016

National Council on Alcoholism and Drug
Dependency, Inc.
12 W. 21st St.
New York, NY 10010
(800) NCA-CALL

National Institute of Drug Abuse
11400 Rockville Pl.
Rockville, MD 20852

Talking About Alcohol: A Program for
Parents of Preteens
P.O. Box 1799
Ridgely, MD 21681
(800) 732-4726

National Federation of Parents for Drug-
Free Youth
8730 Georgia Avenue, Suite 200
Silver Spring, MD 20910
(301) 585-KIDS (in Maryland)
(800) 554-KIDS (elsewhere)

Parents' Resource Institute for Drug
Education (PRIDE)
100 Edgewood Ave., Suite 1002
Atlanta, GA 30303
(800) 241-7946

National Institute on Alcohol Abuse and
Alcoholism
5600 Fishers Ln.
Rockville, MD 20857

Overeaters Anonymous
4025 Spencer St., Suite 20
Torrance, CA 90503
Mail Address: P.O. Box 92870
Los Angeles, CA 90009
(213) 618-8835

Rational Recovery
5540 Davie Rd.
Davie, FL 33314-6066
(800) 328-4402
(305) 791-0298

Rutgers Center of Alcohol Studies
P.O. Box 969
Pitscataway, NJ 08903

Innovative Alcohol Abuse Education
Drug Free School and Communities
U.S. Department of Education
400 Maryland Ave., SW
Washington, DC 20202-6439
Donna Marie Marlowe
(202) 401-1258

Parents Against Drugs (PAD)
70 Maxome Ave.
Willowdale, Ontario, Canada M2M 3K1
(416) 225-6604

CHILD ABUSE AND NEGLECT

National Resources

National Center for the Prevention and
Treatment of Child Abuse and Neglect
University of Colorado Medical Center
1205 Onedia St.
Denver, CO 80220

National Center on Child Abuse and
Neglect
P.O. Box 1182
Washington, DC 20213
National Child Abuse Hotline, Childhelp
USA; 800-4-CHILD

National Committee for Prevention of
Child Abuse
111 E. Wacker Dr., Suite 510
Chicago, IL 60601

Parents Anonymous
2810 Artesia Blvd.
Redondo Beach, CA 90278

CHILDREN WITH SPECIAL NEEDS

National Resources—Physical Challenges

Arthritis Foundation
115 E. 18th St.
New York, NY 10003

International Center for the Disabled
Rehabilitation and Research Center
340 E. 24th St.
New York, NY 10010

National Easter Seal Society for
Crippled Children and Adults
2023 W. Ogden Ave.
Chicago, IL 60612

United Cerebral Palsy Association, Inc.
66 E. 34th St.
New York, NY 10016

National Resources—Sensory Challenges

Alexander Graham Bell Association for
the Deaf
3417 Volta Pl., NW
Washington, DC 20007

American Foundation for the Blind
15 W. 16th St.
New York, NY 10011

Association for Education of the Visually
Handicapped
206 N. Washington St.
Alexandria, VA 22314

National Association for the Deaf
814 Thayer Ave.
Silver Spring, MD 20910

National Association for the Visually
Handicapped
305 E. 24th St.
New York, NY 10010

National Resources—Chronic Illness

American Cancer Society
1599 Clifton Rd., NE
Atlanta, GA 30379
(800) ACS-2345

American Diabetes Association
2 Park Ave.
New York, NY 10016

American Heart Association
1615 Stemmons Fwy.
Dallas, TX 75207

Epilepsy Foundation of America
4351 Garden City Dr., Suite 406
Landover, MD 20785

Leukemia Society of America
800 Second Ave.
New York, NY 10017

Make Today Count
1017 S. Union St.
Alexandria, VA 22314
(703) 548-9674

Muscular Dystrophy Association of
America
810 Seventh Ave.
New York, NY 10019

National Multiple Sclerosis Society
205 E. 42nd. St., 3rd Floor
New York, NY 10017

National Resources—Learning Disabilities

Association for Children With Learning
Disabilities
4156 Library Rd.
Pittsburgh, PA 15234

National Network of Learning Disabled
Adults
P.O. Box 3130
Richardson, TX 75080

National Resources—Emotional and Behavioral Disorders

National Institute of Mental Health
5600 Fishers Ln., Suite 15C17
Rockville, MD 20857

Research and Training Center to Improve Services for Seriously Emotionally Handicapped Children and Their Families
Regional Research Institute for Human Services
P.O. Box 751, Portland State University
Portland, OR 97207-0751

National Resources—Mental and Cognitive Challenges

American Association on Mental Deficiency
5101 Wisconsin Ave., NW, Suite 405
Washington, DC 20016

National Association for Retarded Citizens
2501 Ave. J
Arlington, TX 76011

National Society for Children and Adults With Autism
1234 Massachusetts Ave., NW, Suite 1017
Washington, DC 20005-4599

National Resources— Multicultural

Mexican-American Legal Defense Fund
28 Geary St.
San Francisco, CA 94108

Multicultural Resource Center
8443 Crenshaw Blvd.
Englewood, CA 90305

Native American Rights Fund
1506 Broadway
Boulder, CO 80302
(303) 447-8760

National Resources— Miscellaneous

American Association for Gifted Children
15 Gramercy Park
New York, NY 10003

Association for the Care of Children's Health
3615 Wisconsin Ave., NW
Washington, DC 20016

Children's Behavioral Services
6171 W. Charleston
Las Vegas, NV 89158

Closer Look
Parents' Campaign for Handicapped Children and Youth
P.O. Box 1492
Washington, DC 20013

Compassionate Friends
P.O. Box 3696
Oak Brook, IL 60522-3696
(708) 990-0010

Council for Exceptional Children
1920 Association Dr.
Reston, VA 22091

Divorce Anonymous
2600 Colorado Ave., Suite 270
Santa Monica, CA 90404
(213) 315-6538

Health Services and Mental Health Adm.
Maternal and Child Health Services
Parklawn Bldg., Suite 739
5600 Fishers Lane
Rockville, MD 20852

National Information Center for Children and Youth With Handicaps (NICHCY)
P.O. Box 1492
Washington, DC 20013
(800) 999-5599

Sibling Information Network
Connecticut's University Affiliated Program on Developmental Disabilities
991 Main St.
East Hartford, CT 06108
(203) 282-7050

THEOS (Loss of Spouse)
1301 Clark Bldg.
717 Liberty Ave.
Pittsburgh, PA 15222-3510

Tough Love
P.O. Box 1069
Doylestown, PA 18901
(800) 333-1069/(215) 348-7090

CRIME VICTIMS

National Resources

National Coalition Against Domestic
Violence
P.O. Box 34103
Washington, DC 20043
(202) 638-6388

National Organization for Victim
Assistance
1757 Park Rd., NW
Washington, DC 20010
(202) 232-6682

National Self-Help Clearinghouse
25 W. 43rd St., Rm 620
New York, NY 10036
(212) 642-2944

National Victim Center
307 W. Seventh St., Suite 1001
Fort Worth, TX 76102
(817) 877-3355

Victim Services
(212) 577-7777 (Hotline)
(212) 577-7700

SEXUAL ABUSE

Local Resources
(local telephone directory)

Incest Survivors Anonymous

Survivors of Incest Anonymous

National Resources

Incest/Sexual Abuse Coordinator
c/o Parents United
232 E. Gish Rd., 1st Floor
San Jose, CA 95112
(408) 453-7616

Incest Resources Women's Center
46 Pleasant St.
Cambridge, MA 02139
(617) 492-1818

Incest Survivors Anonymous
P.O. Box 5613
Long Beach, CA 90805-0613
(213) 428-5599

Life Skills Education
Pamphlets That Communicate
314 Washington St.
Northfield, MN 55057
(800) 783-6743

Looking Up
P.O. Box K
Augusta, ME 04330
(207) 626-3402

National Child Abuse Hotline
Childhelp USA
(800) 4-A-CHILD

SARAH, Inc.
P.O. Box 20353
Bradenton, FL 34203
(813) 746-9114

Survivors of Incest Anonymous
P.O. Box 21817
Baltimore, MD 21222
(301) 282-3400 or 433-2365

VOICES in Action, Inc.
P.O. Box 148309
Chicago, IL 60614
(312) 327-1500

FBI National Child Abuse Hotline
1-800-422-4453

ADOPTION OPTIONS

Edna Gladney Home: serves as resource for adoption of undesired infants; provides prenatal care, hospital services; matches infants with potential adoptive parents.
1-800-GLADNEY

RESOURCES: Missing and Exploited Children

National Center for Missing and Exploited Children
2101 Wilson Blvd., Suite 550
Arlington, VA 22201
(703) 235-3900

State Law Enforcement Division Missing Persons Information Center	1-800-322-4433
National Center for Missing and Exploited Children	1-800-843-5678
Runaway Hotline	1-800-231-6946
National Runaway Switchboard	1-800-621-4000
Covenant House (Runaways)	1-800-999-9999
Parents Anonymous Hotline	1-800-421-0353
FBI Hotline	1-800-327-8529

Association for Multicultural Counseling and Development: Multicultural Counseling Competencies

I. Counselor Awareness of Own Cultural Values and Biases

A. *Attitudes and Beliefs*

1. Culturally skilled counselors believe that cultural self-awareness and sensitivity to one's own cultural heritage is essential.

Explanatory Statements

- Can identify the culture(s) to which they belong and the significance of that membership including the relationship of individuals in that group with individuals from other groups institutionally, historically, educationally, and so forth (include A, B, and C Dimensions as do the other suggestions in this section).*
- Can identify the specific cultural group(s) from which counselor derives fundamental cultural heritage and the significant beliefs and attitudes held by those cultures that are assimilated into their own attitudes and beliefs.
- Can recognize the impact of those beliefs on their ability to respect others different from themselves.
- Can identify specific attitudes, beliefs, and values from their own heritage and cultural learning that support behaviors that demonstrate respect and valuing of differences and those that impede or hinder respect and valuing of differences.
- Actively engage in an ongoing process of challenging their own attitudes and beliefs that do not support respecting and valuing of differences.
- Appreciate and articulate positive aspects of their own heritage that provide them with strengths in understanding differences.

---

*The A Dimension is a listing of characteristics that serve as a profile of all people (e.g., age, culture, ethnicity, gender, language, and sexual orientation). The B Dimension may represent the "consequences" of the A and C Dimensions (e.g., educational background, geographic location, income, marital status, religion, work experience, citizenship status, military experience, and hobbies/recreational interests). The C Dimension encompasses universal phenomena. All individuals must be seen in a context and not in a vacuum (e.g., historical moments, eras).

- In addition to their cultural groups, can recognize the influence of other personal dimensions of identity (PDI) and their role in cultural self-awareness.

2. Culturally skilled counselors are aware of how their own cultural background and experiences have influenced attitudes, values, and biases about psychological processes.

Explanatory Statements

- Can identify the history of their culture in relation to educational opportunities and its impact on their current worldview (includes A and some B Dimensions).
- Can identify at least five personal, relevant cultural traits and can explain how each has influenced the cultural values of the counselor.
- Can identify social and cultural influences on their cognitive development and current information-processing styles and can contrast that with those of others (includes A, B, and C Dimensions).
- Can identify specific social and cultural factors and events in their history that influence their view and use of social belonging, interpretations of behavior, motivation, problem-solving and decision methods, thoughts and behaviors (including subconscious) in relation to authority and other institutions and can contrast these with the perspectives of others (A and B Dimensions).
- Can articulate the beliefs of their own cultural and religious groups as these relate to sexual orientation, able-bodiedness, and so forth, and the impact of these beliefs in a counseling relationship.

3. Culturally skilled counselors are able to recognize the limits of their multicultural competency and expertise.

Explanatory Statements

- Can recognize in a counseling or teaching relationship, when and how their attitudes, beliefs, and values are interfering with providing the best service to clients (primarily A and B Dimensions).
- Can identify preservice and in-service experiences which contribute to expertise and can identify current specific needs for professional development.
- Can recognize and use referral sources that demonstrate values, attitudes, and beliefs that will respect and support the client's developmental needs.
- Can give real examples of cultural situations in which they recognized their limitations and referred the client to more appropriate resources.

4. Culturally skilled counselors recognize their sources of discomfort with differences that exist between themselves and clients in terms of race, ethnicity, and culture.

Explanatory Statements

- Able to recognize their sources of comfort/discomfort with respect to differences in terms of race, ethnicity, and culture.
- Able to identify differences (along A and B Dimensions) and are nonjudgmental about those differences.
- Communicate acceptance of and respect for differences both verbally and nonverbally.

- Can identify at least five specific cultural differences, the needs of culturally different clients, and how these differences are handled in the counseling relationship.

B. *Knowledge*

1. Culturally skilled counselors have specific knowledge about their own racial and cultural heritage and how it personally and professionally affects their definitions of and biases about normality/abnormality and the process of counseling.

Explanatory Statements

- Have knowledge regarding their heritage. For example, A Dimensions in terms of ethnicity, language, and so forth, and C Dimensions in terms of knowledge regarding the context of the time period in which their ancestors entered the established United States or North American continent.
- Can recognize and discuss their family's and culture's perspectives of acceptable (normal) codes of conduct and what are unacceptable (abnormal) and how this may or may not vary from those of other cultures and families.
- Can identify at least five specific features of culture of origin and explain how those features affect the relationship with culturally different clients.

2. Culturally skilled counselors possess knowledge and understanding about how oppression, racism, discrimination, and stereotyping affect them personally and in their work. This allows individuals to acknowledge their own racist attitudes, beliefs, and feelings. Although this standard applies to all groups, for White counselors it may mean that they understand how they may have directly or indirectly benefited from individual, institutional, and cultural racism as outlined in White identity development models.

Explanatory Statements

- Can specifically identify, name, and discuss privileges that they personally receive in society due to their race, socioeconomic background, gender, physical abilities, sexual orientation, and so on.
- Specifically referring to White counselors, can discuss White identity development models and how they relate to one's personal experiences.
- Can provide a reasonably specific definition of racism, prejudice, discrimination, and stereotype. Can describe a situation in which they have been judged on something other than merit. Can describe a situation in which they have judged someone on something other than merit.
- Can discuss recent research addressing issues of racism, White identity development, antiracism, and so forth, and its relation to their personal development and professional development as counselors.

3. Culturally skilled counselors possess knowledge about their social impact on others. They are knowledgeable about communication style differences, how their style may clash with or foster the counseling process with persons of color or others different from themselves based on the A, B, and C Dimensions, and how to anticipate the impact it may have on others.

Explanatory Statements

- Can describe the A and B Dimensions of Identity with which they most strongly identify.
- Can behaviorally define their communication style and describe both their verbal and nonverbal behaviors, interpretations of others' behaviors, and expectations.
- Recognize the cultural bases (A Dimension) of their communication style, and the differences between their style and the styles of those different from themselves.
- Can describe the behavioral impact and reaction of their communication style on clients different from themselves. For example, the reaction of older (1960s) Vietnamese male recent immigrant to continuous eye contact from the young, female counselor.
- Can give examples of an incident in which communication broke down with a client of color and can hypothesize about the causes.
- Can give three to five concrete examples of situations in which they modified their communication style to compliment that of a culturally different client, how they decided on the modification, and the result of that modification.

C. *Skills*

1. Culturally skilled counselors seek out educational, consultative, and training experiences to improve their understanding and effectiveness in working with culturally different populations. Being able to recognize the limits of their competencies, they (a) seek consultation, (b) seek further training or education, (c) refer to more qualified individuals or resources, or (d) engage in a combination of these.

Explanatory Statements

- Can recognize and identify characteristics or situations in which the counselor's limitations in cultural, personal, or religious beliefs or issues of identity development require referral.
- Can describe objectives of at least two multicultural-related professional development activities attended over the past 5 years and can identify at least two adaptations to their counseling practices as a result of these professional development activities.
- Have developed professional relationships with counselors from backgrounds different from their own and have maintained a dialogue regarding multicultural differences and preferences.
- Maintain an active referral list and continuously seek new referrals relevant to different needs of clients along A and B Dimensions.
- Understand and communicate to the client that the referral is being made because of the counselor's limitations rather than communicating that it is caused by the client.
- On recognizing these limitations, the counselor actively pursues and engages in professional and personal growth activities to address their limitations.
- Actively consult regularly with other professionals regarding issues of culture to receive feedback about issues and situations and whether or where referral may be necessary.

2. Culturally skilled counselors are constantly seeking to understand themselves as racial and cultural beings and are actively seeking a nonracist identity.

Explanatory Statements

- Actively seek out and participate in reading and in activities designed to develop cultural self-awareness, and work toward eliminating racism and prejudice.
- Maintain relationships (personal and professional) with individuals different from themselves and actively engage in discussions allowing for feedback regarding the counselor's behavior (personal and professional) concerning racial issues. (For example, a White counselor maintains a personal/professional relationship with a Latina counselor that is intimate enough to request and receive honest feedback regarding behaviors and attitudes and their impact on others: "I seem to have difficulty retaining Latina students in my class; given how I run my class, can you help me find ways that I may make it a more appropriate environment for Latina students?" or "When I said ___, how do you think others perceived that comment?") This requires the commitment to develop and contribute to a relationship that allows for adequate trust and honesty in very difficult situations.
- When receiving feedback, the counselor demonstrates a receptivity and willingness to learn.

(See Subsection A for strategies to achieve the competences and objectives for Area I.)

II. Counselor Awareness of Client's Worldview

A. *Attitudes and Beliefs*

1. Culturally skilled counselors are aware of their negative and positive emotional reactions toward other racial and ethnic groups that may prove detrimental to the counseling relationship. They are willing to contrast their own beliefs and attitudes with those of their culturally different clients in a nonjudgmental fashion.

Explanatory Statements

- Identify their common emotional reactions about individuals and groups different from themselves and observe their own reactions in encounters. For example, do they feel fear when approaching a group of three young African American men? Do they assume that the Asian American clients for whom they provide career counseling will be interested in a technical career?
- Can articulate how their personal reactions and assumptions are different from those who identify with that group (e.g., if the reaction on approaching three young African American men is fear, what is the reaction of a young African American man or woman in the same situation? What might be the reaction of an African American woman approaching a group of White young men?).

- Identify how general emotional reactions observed in oneself could influence effectiveness in a counseling relationship. (Reactions may be regarding cultural differences as well as along A and B Dimensions.)
- Can describe at least two distinct examples of cultural conflict between self and culturally different clients, including how these conflicts were used as "content" for counseling. For example, if a Chicana agrees to live at home rather than board at a 4-year college to support her mother, can a counselor be nonjudgmental?

2. Culturally skilled counselors are aware of their stereotypes and preconceived notions that they may hold toward other racial and ethnic minority groups.

Explanatory Statements

- Recognize their stereotyped reactions to people different from themselves (e.g., silently articulating their awareness of a negative stereotypical reaction, "I noticed that I locked my car doors when that African American teenager walked by").
- Consciously attend to examples that contradict stereotypes.
- Can give specific examples of how their stereotypes (including "positive" ones) referring to the A and B Dimensions can affect the counselor–client relationship.
- Recognize assumptions of those in a similar cultural group but who may differ based on A and B Dimension.

B. *Knowledge*

1. Culturally skilled counselors possess specific knowledge and information about the particular group with which they are working. They are aware of the life experiences, cultural heritage, and historical background of their culturally different clients. This particular competency is strongly linked to the minority identity development models available in the literature.

Explanatory Statements

- Can articulate (objectively) differences in nonverbal and verbal behavior of the five major cultural groups most frequently seen in their experience of counseling.
- Can describe at least two different models of minority identity development and their implications for counseling with persons of color or others who experience oppression or marginalization.
- Understand and can explain the historical point of contact with dominant society for various ethnic groups and the impact of the type of contact (enslaved, refugee, seeking economic opportunities, conquest, and so forth) on current issues in society.
- Can identify within-group differences and assess various aspects of individual clients to determine individual differences as well as cultural differences. For example, the counselor is aware of differences within Asian Americans (Japanese Americans, Vietnamese Americans, and so forth); differences between first generation refugees versus second or third generation; differences between Vietnamese refugees coming in the "first wave" in 1975 versus Vietnamese refugees coming to the United States in 1990.

- Can discuss viewpoints of other cultural groups regarding issues such as sexual orientation, physical ability or disability, gender, and aging.

2. Culturally skilled counselors understand how race, culture, ethnicity, and so forth may affect personality formation, vocational choices, manifestation of psychological disorders, help-seeking behavior, and the appropriateness or inappropriateness of counseling approaches.

Explanatory Statements

- Can distinguish cultural differences and expectations regarding role and responsibility in family, participation of family in career decision making, appropriate family members to be involved when seeking help, culturally acceptable means of expressing emotion and anxiety, and so forth (primarily along A Dimensions and portions of B Dimension).
- Based on literature about A Dimensions, can describe and give examples of how a counseling approach may or may not be appropriate for a specific group of people based primarily on an A Dimension.
- Understand and can explain the historical point of contact with dominant society for various ethnic groups and the impact of the type of contact (e.g., enslaved, refugee, seeking economic opportunities, conquest) on potential relationships and trust when seeking help from dominant cultural institutions.
- Can describe one system of personality development, the population(s) on which the theory was developed, and how this system relates or does not relate to at least two culturally different populations.
- Can identify the role of gender, socioeconomic status, and physical disability as they interact with personality formation across cultural groups.

3. Culturally skilled counselors understand and have knowledge about sociopolitical influences that impinge on the life of racial and ethnic minorities. Immigration issues, poverty, racism, stereotyping, and powerlessness may affect self-esteem and self-concept in the counseling process.

Explanatory Statements

- Can identify implications of concepts such as internalized oppression, institutional racism, privilege, and the historical and current political climate regarding immigration, poverty, and welfare (public assistance).
- Can explain the relationship between culture and power. Can explain dynamics of at least two cultures and how factors such as poverty and powerlessness have influenced the current conditions of individuals of those cultures.
- Understand the economic benefits and contributions gained by the work of various groups, including migrant farm workers, to the daily life of the counselor and the country at large.
- Can communicate an understanding of the unique position, constraints, and needs of those clients who experience oppression based on an A and B Dimension alone (and families of clients) who share this history.
- Can identify current issues that affect groups of people (A and B Dimensions) in legislation, social climate, and so forth, and how that affects individuals and families to whom the counselor may be providing services.

• Are aware of legal legislation issues that affect various communities and populations (e.g., in California it is essential for a counselor to understand the ramifications of the recent passage of Proposition 187 and how that will affect not only undocumented individuals, but also families and anyone who has Chicano features, a Mexican American accent, and speaks Spanish. In addition, the counselor must be aware of how this will affect health issues, help-seeking behaviors, participation in education, and so forth).

• Counselors are aware of how documents such as the book *The Bell Curve* and affirmative action legislation affect society's perception of different cultural groups.

C. Skills

1. Culturally skilled counselors should familiarize themselves with relevant research and the latest findings regarding mental health and mental disorders that affect various ethnic and racial groups. They should actively seek out educational experiences that enrich their knowledge, understanding, and cross-cultural skills for more effective counseling behavior.

Explanatory Statements

• Can discuss recent research regarding such topics as mental health, career decision making, education, and learning that focuses on issues related to different cultural populations and as represented in A and B Dimensions.

• Complete (at least 15 hours per year) workshops, conferences, classes, and in-service training regarding multicultural counseling skills and knowledge. These should span a variety of topics and cultures and should include discussions of wellness rather than focusing only on negative issues (medical model) related to these cultures.

• Can identify at least five multicultural experiences in which counselor has participated within the past 3 years.

• Can identify professional growth activities and information that are presented by professionals respected and seen as credible by members of the communities being studied (e.g., the book *The Bell Curve* may not represent accurate and helpful information regarding individuals from non-White cultures).

• Can describe in concrete terms how they have applied varied information gained through current research in mental health, education, career choices, and so forth, based on differences noted in A Dimension.

2. Culturally skilled counselors become actively involved with minority individuals outside the counseling setting (e.g., community events, social and political functions, celebrations, friendships, neighborhood groups) so that their perspective of minorities is more than an academic or helping exercise.

Explanatory Statements

• Can identify at least five multicultural experiences in which the counselor has participated within the past 3 years. These include various celebrations, political events, or community activities involving individuals and groups from racial and cultural backgrounds different from

their own, such as political fund-raisers, Tet (Vietnamese New Year) celebrations, and neighborhood marches against violence.
- Actively plan experiences and activities that will contradict negative stereotypes and preconceived notions they may hold.

(See Subsection B for strategies to achieve the competencies and objectives for Area II.)

III. Culturally Appropriate Intervention Strategies

A. *Beliefs and Attitudes*

1. Culturally skilled counselors respect clients' religious and spiritual beliefs and values, including attributions and taboos, because these affect worldview, psychosocial functioning, and expressions of distress.

Explanatory Statements
- Can identify the positive aspects of spirituality (in general) in terms of wellness and healing aspects.
- Can identify in a variety of religious and spiritual communities the recognized form of leadership and guidance and their client's relationship (if existent) with that organization and entity.

2. Culturally skilled counselors respect indigenous helping practices and respect help-giving networks among communities of color.
- Can describe concrete examples of how they may integrate and cooperate with indigenous helpers when appropriate.
- Can describe concrete examples of how they may use intrinsic help-giving networks from a variety of client communities.

3. Culturally skilled counselors value bilingualism and do not view another language as an impediment to counseling ("monolingualism" may be the culprit).

Explanatory Statements
- Can articulate the historical, cultural, and racial context in which traditional theories and interventions have been developed.
- Can identify, within various theories, the cultural values, beliefs, and assumptions made about individuals and contrast these with values, beliefs, and assumptions of different racial and cultural groups.
- Recognize the predominant theories being used within counselor's organization and educate colleagues regarding the aspects of those theories and interventions that may clash with the cultural values of various cultural and racial minority groups.
- Can identify and describe primary indigenous helping practices in terms of positive and effective role in at least five A or B Dimensions, relevant to counselor's client population.

4. Culturally skilled counselors are aware of institutional barriers that prevent minorities from using mental health services.

Explanatory Statements

- Can describe concrete examples of institutional barriers within their organizations that prevent minorities from using mental health services and share those examples with colleagues and decision-making bodies within the institution.
- Recognize and draw attention to patterns of usage (or nonusage) of mental health services in relation to specific populations.
- Can identify and communicate possible alternatives that would reduce or eliminate existing barriers within their institutions and within local, state, and national decision-making bodies.

5. Culturally skilled counselors have knowledge of the potential bias in assessment instruments and use procedures and interpret findings in a way that recognizes the cultural and linguistic characteristics of the clients.

Explanatory Statements

- Demonstrate ability to interpret assessment results including implications of dominant cultural values affecting assessment/interpretation, interaction of cultures for those who are bicultural, and the impact of historical institutional oppression.
- Can discuss information regarding cultural, racial, and gender profile of normative group used for validity and reliability on any assessment used by counselor.
- Understand the limitations of translating assessment instruments as well as the importance of using language that includes culturally relevant connotations and idioms.
- Use assessment instruments appropriately with clients having limited English language skills.
- Can give examples, for each assessment instrument used, of the limitations of the instrument regarding various groups represented in A and B Dimensions.
- Recognize possible historical and current sociopolitical biases in *DSM* (*Diagnostic and Statistical Manual of Mental Disorders*) system of diagnosis based on racial, cultural, sexual orientation, and gender issues.

6. Culturally skilled counselors have knowledge of family structures, hierarchies, values, and beliefs from various cultural perspectives. They are knowledgeable about the community where a particular cultural group may reside and the resources in the community.

Explanatory Statements

- Are familiar with and use organizations that provide support and services in different cultural communities.
- Can discuss the traditional ways of helping in different cultures and continue to learn the resources in communities relevant to those cultures.
- Adequately understand the client's religious and spiritual beliefs to know when and what topics are or are not appropriate to discuss regarding those beliefs.
- Understand and respect cultural and family influences and participation in decision making.

7. Culturally skilled counselors should be aware of relevant discriminatory practices at the social and the community level that may be affecting the psychological welfare of the population being served.

Explanatory Statements

- Are aware of legal issues that affect various communities and populations (e.g., in California's Proposition 187 described earlier).

C. *Skills*

1. Culturally skilled counselors are able to engage in a variety of verbal and nonverbal helping responses. They are able to send and receive both verbal and nonverbal messages accurately and appropriately. They are not tied down to only one method or approach to helping, but recognize that helping styles and approaches may be culture bound. When they sense that their helping style is limited and potentially inappropriate, they can anticipate and modify it.

Explanatory Statements

- Can articulate what, when, why, and how they apply different verbal and nonverbal helping responses based on A and B Dimensions.
- Can give examples of how they may modify a technique or intervention or what alternative intervention they may use to more effectively meet the needs of a client.
- Can identify and describe techniques in which they have expertise for providing service that may require minimal English language skills (e.g., expressive therapy).
- Can communicate verbally and nonverbally to the client the validity of the client's religious and spiritual beliefs.
- Can discuss with the client (when appropriate) aspects of their religious or spiritual beliefs that have been helpful to the client in the past.

2. Culturally skilled counselors are able to exercise institutional intervention skills on behalf of their clients. They can help clients determine whether a "problem" stems from racism or bias in others (the concept of healthy paranoia) so that clients do not inappropriately personalize problems.

Explanatory Statments

- Can recognize and discuss examples in which racism or bias may actually be imbedded in an institutional system or in society.
- Can discuss a variety of coping and survival behaviors used by a variety of individuals from their A and B Dimensions to cope effectively with bias or racism.
- Communicate to clients an understanding of the necessary coping skills and behaviors viewed by dominant society as dysfunctional that they may need to keep intact.
- Can describe concrete examples of situations in which it is appropriate and possibly necessary for a counselor to exercise institutional intervention skills on behalf of a client.

3. Culturally skilled counselors are not averse to seeking consultation with traditional healers or religious and spiritual leaders and practitioners in the treatment of culturally different clients when appropriate.

Explanatory Statements

- Participate or gather adequate information regarding indigenous or community helping resources to make appropriate referrals (e.g., be familiar with the American Indian community enough to recognize when, how, and to whom it may be appropriate to refer a client for indigenous healers).

4. Culturally skilled counselors take responsibility for interacting in the language requested by the client and, if not feasible, make appropriate referrals. A serious problem arises when the linguistic skills of the counselor do not match the language of the client. This being the case, counselors should (a) seek a translator with cultural knowledge and appropriate professional background or (b) refer to a knowledgeable and competent bilingual counselor.

Explanatory Statement

- Are familiar with resources that provide services in languages appropriate to clients.
- Will seek out, whenever necessary, services or translators to ensure that language needs are met.
- If working within an organization, actively advocate for the hiring of bilingual counselors relevant to client population.

5. Culturally skilled counselors have training and expertise in the use of traditional assessment and testing instruments. They not only understand the technical aspects of the instruments but are also aware of the cultural limitations. This allows them to use test instruments for the welfare of culturally different clients.

Explanatory Statements

- Demonstrate ability to interpret assessment results including implications of dominant cultural values affecting assessment and interpretation, interaction of cultures for those who are bicultural, and the impact of historical institutional oppression.
- Can discuss information regarding cultural, racial, and gender profile of norm group used for validity and reliability on any assessment used by counselor.
- Understand that although an assessment instrument may be translated into another language, the translation may be literal without an accurate contextual translation including culturally relevant connotations and idioms.

6. Culturally skilled counselors should attend to, as well as work to eliminate, biases, prejudices, and discriminatory contexts in conducting evaluations and providing interventions, and should develop sensitivity to issues of oppression, sexism, heterosexism, elitism, and racism.

Explanatory Statements

- Recognize incidents in which clients, students, and others are being treated unfairly based on such characteristics as race, ethnicity, and physical ableness and take action by directly addressing incident or perpetrator, filing informal complaint, filing formal complaint, and so forth.

- Work at an organizational level to address, change, and eliminate policies that discriminate, create barriers, and so forth.
- If an organization's policy created barriers for advocacy, the counselor works toward changing institutional policies to promote advocacy against racism, sexism, and so forth.

7. Culturally skilled counselors take responsibility for educating their clients to the processes of psychological intervention, such as goals, expectations, legal rights, and the counselor's orientation.

Explanatory Statements

- Assess the client's understanding of and familiarity with counseling and mental health services and provide accurate information regarding the process, limitations, and function of the services into which the client is entering.
- Ensure that the client understands client rights, issues, and definitions of confidentiality, and the expectations placed on that client. In this educational process, counselors adapt information to ensure that all concepts are clearly understood by the client. This may include defining and discussing these concepts.

(See Subsection C for strategies to achieve competencies and objectives in Area III. See Subsection D for the strategies to achieve competencies and objectives in all three areas.)

Adapted from "Multicultural Counseling Competencies and Standards: A Call to the Profession" (Sue, Arredondo, & McDavis, 1992).

REFERENCES

Sue, D. W., Arredondo, P., & McDavis, R. J. (1992). Multicultural counseling competencies and standards: A call to the profession. *Journal of Counseling & Development, 70,* 477–483.

Subsection A—Strategies to Achieve the Competencies and Objectives (I)

- Read materials regarding identity development. For example, a European American counselor may read materials on White or Majority Identity Development or an African American may read materials on Black Identity Development to gain an understanding of their own development. Additionally, reading about others' identity development processes is essential. The following are some resources specifically for European American or White counselors:

Carter, R. T. (1990). The relationship between racism and racial identity among White Americans: An exploratory investigation. *Journal of Counseling & Development, 69,* 46–50.

Corvin, S., & Wiggins, F. (1989). An antiracism training model for White professionals. *Journal of Multicultural Counseling and Development, 17,* 105–114.

Helms, J. (1990). *White identity development.* New York: Greenwood Press.

Pedersen, P. B. (1988). *A handbook for development of multicultural awareness.* Alexandria, VA: American Association for Counseling and Development.

Pope-Davis, D. B., & Ottavi, T. M. (1992). The influence of White racial identity attitudes on racism among faculty members: A preliminary examination. *Journal of College Student Development, 33,* 389–394.

Sabnani, H. B., Ponterotto, J. G., & Borodovsky, L. G. (1991). White racial identity development and cross-cultural training. *The Counseling Psychologist, 19,* 76–102.

Wrenn, C. G. (1962). The culturally encapsulated counselor. *Harvard Educational Review, 32,* 444–449.

Other Professional Activities

- Attend annual conferences and workshops such as:
  - Annual Conference on Race and Ethnicity in Higher Education sponsored by the Center for Southwest Studies Oklahoma (1995, Santa Fe)
  - Third World Counselor's Association Annual Conference (Palm Springs, 1995)
  - AMCD Annual Western Summit
- Engage a mentor from your own culture who you identify as someone who has been working toward becoming cross-culturally competent and who has made significant strides in ways you have not.
- Engage a mentor or two from cultures different from your own who are willing to provide honest feedback regarding your behavior, attitudes, and beliefs. Be willing to listen and work toward change!
- Film: *The Color of Fear* by Lee Muh Wah
- Film: *A Class Divided* produced by PBS for "Frontline"
- Film: *"True Colors"*—"20/20" Special
- Video: *The Trial Model* by Paul Pederson

Subsection B—Strategies to Achieve the Competencies and Objectives (II)

- The following reading list may be helpful for counselors to broaden their understanding of different worldviews (some of these materials would also be helpful in developing culturally appropriate intervention strategies):

  Atkinson, D., Morten, G., & Sue, D. W. (1989). *Counseling American minorities: A cross-cultural perspective.* Dubuque, IA: Brown.

  Collins, P. (1990). *Black feminist thought: Knowledge, consciousness and the politics of empowerment.* Boston: Unwin Hyman.

  Sue, D. W., & Sue, D. (1990). *Counseling the culturally different: Theory and practice* (2nd ed.). New York: Wiley.

- Attend annual conferences and workshops such as:
  - Annual Conference on Race and Ethnicity in Higher Education sponsored by the Center for Southwest Studies Oklahoma (1995, Santa Fe)
  - Third World Counselor's Association Annual Conference (Palm Springs, 1995)
  - AMCD Annual Western Summit
- Enroll in ethnic studies courses at local community colleges or universities that focus on cultures different from your own (if none are offered, communicate to that school your expectation that they will offer them in the future).
- Spend time in communities different from your own (e.g., shopping in grocery stores, attending churches, walking in marches).
- Read newspapers and other periodicals targeting specific populations different from your own (i.e., Spanish language newspapers, *Buffalo Soldier, Lakota Times*).
- Engage in activities and celebrations within communities different from your own (e.g., Juneteenth, Tet, Cinco de Mayo).
- Engage a mentor or two from cultures different from your own who are also working toward cross-cultural competency (be sure to discuss with them your contribution to the relationship).
- Accept that it is your responsibility to learn about other cultures and implications in counseling and do not expect or rely on individuals from those cultures to teach you.

- Learn a second or third language relevant to clients to begin to understand the significance of that language in the transmission of culture.
- Seek out and engage in consultation from professionals from cultures relevant to your client population.
- Spend time in civil service offices observing service orientation toward individuals of color (Chicano/Latino, African America, Asian American, Native American) and contrast that with service orientation toward White individuals. Also observe any differences in service orientation that may be based on class issues (e.g., someone alone and well dressed versus a woman with children wearing older clothing, somewhat disheveled).
- Film: *The Color of Fear* by Lee Mun Wah
- Film: *El Norte*
- Film: *Stand and Deliver*
- Film: *Roots*
- Film: *Lakota Woman*
- Film: *Daughters of the Dust*

Subsection C—Strategies to Achieve the Competencies and Objectives (III)

- The following reading list may be helpful for building a foundation to develop and apply culturally appropriate interventions:

Atkinson, D., Morten, G., & Sue, D. W. (1989). *Counseling American minorities: A cross-cultural perspective*. Dubuque, IA: Brown.

Ibrahim, F. A., & Arredondo, P. M. (1990). Ethical issues in multicultural counseling. In B. Herlihy & L. Golden (Eds.), *Ethical standards casebook* (pp. 137–145). Alexandria, VA: American Association for Counseling and Development.

Katz, J. (1978). *White awareness: Handbook for anti-racism training*. Norman, OK: Oklahoma University Press.

LaFromboise, T. D., & Foster, S. L. (1989). Ethics in multicultural counseling. In P. B. Pederson, W. J. Lonner, & J. E. Trimble (Eds.), *Counseling across cultures* (3rd ed., pp. 115–136). Honolulu: University of Hawaii Press.

LaFromboise, T. D., & Foster, S. L. (1990). Cross-cultural training: Scientist–practitioner model and methods. *The Counseling Psychologist, 20*, 472–489.

- Meet the leaders and heads of organizations that specifically focus on providing service to individuals of certain cultural groups (for example, in San Jose, CA, the AACI or Asian Americans for Community Involvement) to discuss how you may work cooperatively together and what support you may provide the organization.
- Conduct informal research of your clientele, your organization's clientele, to determine if there are patterns of use or nonuse along cultural and/or racial lines.

Subsection D—Overall Strategies for Achieving Competencies and Objectives in All Three Areas

- Assess self in terms of cross-cultural counseling competencies either by reviewing the competencies and giving examples in each area and/or using any of the following resources regarding assessment instruments:

Ho, M. K. (1992). *Minority children and adolescents in therapy*. Newbury Park, CA: Sage.

LaFromboise, T. D., Coleman, H. L. K., & Hernandez, A. (1991). Development and factor structure of the Cross Cultural Counseling Inventory—Revised. *Professional Psychology: Research and Practice, 22*, 380–388.

Ponterotto, J. G., Rieger, B. P., Barrett, A., & Sparks, R. (1994). Assessing multicultural counseling competence: A review of instrumentation. *Journal of Counseling & Development, 72*, 316–322.

- Learn a second or third language relevant to clients.
- Communicate to conference organizers and workshop providers that you will attend only if the activity addresses cross-cultural aspects of the topic.
- Actively communicate in your organization the need for training in cross-cultural training relevant to that organization.
- Speak up in your organization when you observe that clients, students, or others are being treated unfairly based on such characteristics as race, ethnicity, or physical ableness.
- Become a member of AMCD, Division 45/APA, or state and local organizations that provide cross-cultural exchanges.

American School Counselor Association: Ethical Standards for School Counselors

Preamble

The American School Counselor Association (ASCA) is a professional organization whose members have a unique and distinctive preparation, grounded in the behavioral sciences, with training in counseling skills adapted to the school setting. The school counselor assists in the growth and development of each individual and uses his/her specialized skills to ensure that the rights of the counselee are properly protected within the structure of the school program. School counselors subscribe to the following basic tenets of the counseling process from which professional responsibilities are derived:

1. Each person has the right to respect and dignity as a unique human being and to counseling services without prejudice as to person, character, belief, or practice.
2. Each person has the right to self-direction and self-development.
3. Each person has the right of choice and the responsibility for decisions reached.
4. Each person has the right to privacy and thereby the right to expect the counselor–client relationship to comply with all laws, policies, and ethical standards pertaining to confidentiality.

In this document, the American School Counselor Association has specified the principles of ethical behavior necessary to maintain and regulate the high standards of integrity and leadership among its members. The Association recognizes the basic commitment of its members to the *Ethical Standards* of its parent organization, the American Association for Counseling and Development (AACD, now the American Counseling Association), and nothing in this document shall be construed to supplant that code. The *Ethical Standards for School Counselors* was developed to complement the AACD standards by clarifying the nature of ethical responsibilities for present and future counselors in the school setting. The purposes of this document are to:

1. Serve as a guide for the ethical practices of all professional school counselors regardless of level, area, population served, or membership in this Association.
2. Provide benchmarks for both self-appraisal and peer evaluations regarding counselor responsibilities to students, parents, colleagues and professional associates, school and community, self, and the counseling profession.
3. Inform those served by the school counselor of acceptable counselor practices and expected professional deportment.

A. Responsibilities to Students

The School Counselor:

1. Has a primary obligation and loyalty to the student, who is to be treated with respect as a unique indiviudal, whether assisted individually or in a group setting.
2. Is concerned with the total needs of the student (educational, vocational, personal, and social) and encourages the maximum growth and development of each counselee.
3. Informs the counselee of the purposes, goals, techniques, and rules of procedure under which she/he may receive counseling assistance at or before the time when the counseling relationship is entered. Prior notice includes confidentiality issues such as the possible necessity for consulting with other professionals, privileged communication, and legal or authoritative restraints. The meaning and limits of confidentiality are clearly defined to counselees.
4. Refrains from consciously encouraging the counselee's acceptance of values, lifestyles, plans, decisions, and beliefs that represent only the counselor's personal orientation.
5. Is responsible for keeping abreast of laws relating to students and strives to ensure that the rights of students are adequately provided for and protected.
6. Avoids dual relationships which might impair his/her objectivity and/or increase the risk of harm to the client (e.g., counseling one's family members, close friends, or associates). If a dual relationship is unavoidable, the counselor is responsible for taking action to eliminate or reduce the potential for harm. Such safeguards might include informed consent, consultation, supervision, and documentation.
7. Makes appropriate referrals when professional assistance can no longer be adequately provided to the counselee. Appropriate referral requires knowledge of available resources.
8. Protects the confidentiality of student records and releases personal data only according to prescribed laws and school policies. Student information maintained through electronic data storage methods is treated with the same care as traditional student records.
9. Protects the confidentiality of information received in the counseling relationship as specified by law and ethical standards. Such information is only to be revealed to others with the informed consent of the counselee and consistent with the obligations of the counselor as a professional person.

   In a group setting, the counselor sets a norm of confidentiality and stresses its importance, yet clearly states that confidentiality in group counseling cannot be guaranteed.
10. Informs the appropriate authorities when the counselee's condition indicates a clear and imminent danger to the counselee or others. This is to be done after careful deliberation and, where possible, after consultation with other professionals. The counselor informs the counselee of actions to be taken so as to minimize confusion and clarify expectations.
11. Screens prospective group members and maintains an awareness of participants' compatibility throughout the life of the group, especially when the group emphasis is on self-disclosure and self-understanding. The counselor takes reasonable precautions to protect members from physical and/or psychological harm resulting from interaction within the group.
12. Provides explanations of the nature, purposes, and results of tests in language that is understandable to the client(s).

13. Adheres to relevant standards regarding selection, administration, and interpretation of assessment techniques. The counselor recognizes that computer-based testing programs require specific training in administration, scoring, and interpretation which may differ from that required in more traditional assessments.
14. Promotes the benefits of appropriate computer applications and clarifies the limitations of computer technology. The counselor ensures that (1) computer applications are appropriate for the individual needs of the counselee, (2) the counselee understands how to use the applications, and (3) follow-up counseling assistance is provided. Members of underrepresented groups are assured of equal access to computer technologies and the absence of discriminatory information and values within computer applications.
15. Has unique ethical responsibilities in working with peer programs. In general, the school counselor is responsible for the welfare of students participating in peer programs under her/his direction. School counselors who function in training and supervisory capacities are referred to the preparation and supervision standards of professional counselor associations.

B. Responsibilities to Parents

The School Counselor:

1. Respects the inherent rights and responsibilities of parents for their children and endeavors to establish a cooperative relationship with parents to facilitate the maximum development of the counselee.
2. Informs parents of the counselor's role, with emphasis on the confidential nature of the counseling relationship between the counselor and counselee.
3. Provides parents with accurate, comprehensive, and relevant information in an objective and caring manner, as appropriate and consistent with ethical responsibilities to the counselee.
4. Treats information received from parents in a confidential and appropriate manner.
5. Shares information about a counselee only with those persons properly authorized to receive such inforamtion.
6. Adheres to laws and local guidelines when assisting parents experiencing family difficulties which interfere with the counselee's effectiveness and welfare.
7. Is sensitive to changes in the family and recognizes that all parents, custodial and noncustodial, are vested with certain rights and responsibilities for the welfare of their children by virtue of their position and according to law.

C. Responsibilities to Colleagues and Professional Associates

The School Counselor:

1. Establishes and maintains a cooperative relationship with faculty, staff, and administration to facilitate the provision of optimal guidance and counseling programs and services.
2. Promotes awareness and adherence to appropriate guidelines regarding confidentiality, the distinction between public and private information, and staff consultation.
3. Treats colleagues with respect, courtesy, fairness, and good faith. The qualifications, views, and findings of colleagues are represented accurately and fairly to enhance the image of competent professionals.
4. Provides professional personnel with accurate, objective, concise, and meaningful data necessary to adequately evaluate counsel and assist the counselee.

5. Is aware of and fully utilizes related professions and organizations to whom the counselee may be referred.

D. Responsibility to the School and Community

The School Counselor:

1. Supports and protects the educational program against any infringement not in the best interest of students.
2. Informs appropriate officials of conditions that may be potentially disruptive or damaging to the school's mission, personnel, and property.
3. Delineates and promotes the counselor's role and function in meeting the needs of those served. The counselor will notify appropriate school officials of conditions which may limit or curtail their effectiveness in providing programs and services.
4. Assists in the development of: (1) curricular and environmental conditions appropriate for the school and community, (2) educational procedures and programs to meet student needs, and (3) a systematic evaluation process for guidance and counseling programs, services, and personnel. The counselor is guided by findings of the evaluation data in planning programs and services.
5. Actively cooperates and collaborates with agencies, organizations, and individuals in the school and community in the best interest of counselees and without regard to personal regard or remuneration.

E. Responsibilities to Self

The School Counselor:

1. Functions within the boundaries of individual professional competence and accepts responsibility for the consequences of her/his actions.
2. Is aware of the potential effects of her/his own personal characteristics on services to clients.
3. Monitors personal functioning and effectiveness and refrains from any activity likely to lead to inadequate professional services or harm to a client.
4. Recognizes that differences in clients relating to age, gender, race, religion, sexual orientation, socioeconomic, and ethnic backgrounds may require specific training to ensure competent services.
5. Strives through personal initiative to maintain professional competence and keeps abreast of innovations and trends in the profession. Professional and personal growth is continuous and ongoing throughout the counselor's career.

F. Responsibilities to the Profession

The School Counselor:

1. Conducts herself/himself in such a manner as to bring credit to self and the profession.
2. Conducts appropriate research and reports findings in a manner consistent with acceptable educational and psychological research practices. When using client data for research, statistical, or program planning purposes, the counselor ensures protections of the identity of the individual client(s).
3. Actively participates in local, state, and national associations which foster the development and improvement of school counseling.

4. Adheres to ethical standards of the profession, other official policy statements pertaining to counseling, and relevant statutes established by federal, state, and local governments.
5. Clearly distinguishes between statements and actions made as a private individual and as a representative of the school counseling profession.
6. Contributes to the development of the profession through the sharing of skills, ideas, and expertise with colleagues.

G. Maintenance of Standards

Ethical behavior among professional school counselors, association members, and nonmembers is expected at all times. When there exists serious doubt as to the ethical behavior of colleagues, or if counselors are forced to work in situations or abide by policies which do not reflect the standards as outlined in these *Ethical Standards for School Counselors* or the AACD *Ethical Standards*, the counselor is obligated to take appropriate action to rectify the condition. The following procedure may serve as a guide:

1. If feasible, the counselor should consult with a professional colleague to confidentially discuss the nature of the complaint to see if she/he views the situation as an ethical violation.
2. Whenever possible, the counselor should directly approach the colleague whose behavior is in question to discuss the complaint and seek resolution.
3. If resolution is not forthcoming at the personal level, the counselor shall utilize the channels established within the school and/or school district. This may include both informal and formal procedures.
4. If the matter still remains unresolved, referrals for review and appropriate action should be made to the Ethics Committees in the following sequence:

   • local counselor association
   • state counselor association
   • national counselor association

5. The ASCA Ethics Committee functions in an educative and consultative capacity and does not adjudicate complaints of ethical misconduct. Therefore, at the national level, complaints should be submitted in writing to the AACD Ethics Committee for review and appropriate action. The procedure for submitting complaints may be obtained by writing the AACD Ethics Committee, c/o The Executive Director, American Association for Counseling and Development, 5999 Stevenson Avenue, Alexandria, VA 22304.

H. Resources

School counselors are responsible for being aware of, and acting in accord with, the standards and positions of the counseling profession as represented in official documents such as those listed below.

Code of Ethics. (1989). National Board for Certified Counselors, Alexandria, VA.
Code of Ethics for Peer Helping Professionals. (1989). National Peer Helpers Association, Glendale, CA.
Ethical Guidelines for Group Counselors. (1989). Association for Specialists in Group Work, Alexandria, VA.

Ethical Standards. (1988). American Association for Counseling and Development, Alexandria, VA.

Position Statement: The School Counselor and Confidentiality. (1986). American School Counselor Association, Alexandria, VA.

Position Statement: The School Counselor and Student Rights. (1982). American School Counselor Association, Alexandria, VA.

Ethical Standards for School Counselors was adopted by the ASCA Delegate Assembly, March 19, 1984. This revision was approved by the ASCA Delegate Assembly, March 27, 1992.

Index